The Shrimp that Became a Tiger

Emerging Markets Studies

Edited by Joachim Ahrens, Alexander Ebner, Herman W. Hoen, Bernhard Seliger and Ralph Michael Wrobel

Vol. 3

Bernhard Seliger

The Shrimp that Became a Tiger

Transformation Theory and Korea's Rise After the Asian Crisis

Bibliographic Information published by the Deutsche Nationalbibliothek
The Deutsche Nationalbibliothek lists this publication in the Deutsche Nationalbibliografie; detailed bibliographic data is available in the internet at http://dnb.d-nb.de.

Cover Design:
© Olaf Gloeckler, Atelier Platen, Friedberg

Library of Congress Cataloging-in-Publication Data

Seliger, Bernhard, 1970-
The shrimp that became a tiger : transformation theory and Korea's rise after the Asian crisis / Bernhard Seliger.
pages cm. — (Emerging markets studies, 2190-099X ; vol. 3)
ISBN 978-3-631-60738-1
1. Korea (South)—Economic policy—1988- 2. Korea (South)—Economic conditions—1988- 3. Economic development—Korea (South)—History—21st century. 4. Financial crises—Asia—History. I. Title.
HC467.96.S45 2013
338.95195—dc23

2013020341

ISSN 2190-099X
ISBN 978-3-631-60738-1

PL Academic Research is an Imprint of Peter Lang GmbH.

Peter Lang – Frankfurt am Main · Bern · Bruxelles · New York · Oxford · Warszawa · Wien

www.peterlang.de

Dedicated to Ji-Hyun, Johann and Joseph

Preface

South Korea underwent dramatic change in the last one and a half decades, from being considered a "tiger in trouble" (Jomo 1998) in the wake of the Asian crisis to a showcase of economic development. The judgment of 1998 was itself a complete reversal of previous enthusiastic reviews of world record-high growth for several decades, from the 1960s to the 1990s. Korea, once considered a shrimp between two mighty whales, Japan and China, as neighbours, veritably made a jump to become a tiger. And, after the steep decline of 1998, this tiger again showed its claws, a miraculous transformation, as the following comparison ofKorea 1998 and 2011 shows.

In 1998, South Korea suffered from a severe recession, triggered by the currency crisis it experienced a year before. After two years of growing macroeconomic imbalances, in particular growing current account deficits, as well as a contagion from the spreading currency crisis in Southeast Asia since the summer of 1997, by the end of the year Korea had a record low of usable foreign reserves of barely more than 7 billion USD. The South Korean won had to be floated and drastically depreciated, and South Korea's sovereign rating was lowered, which made repaying debt more costly and caused the stock market to crash.

In 2011 the South Korean economy marked for the first time a trade volume of more than 1 trillion USD. The expected nominal per capita GDP will be, according to the IMF World Economic Outlook, a record 24,000 USD. South Korea's economy, though hurt by the subsequent financial crisis in 2008 and the lingering woes over the world economy, grew throughout this period. In July 2011, the free trade agreement between South Korea and the European Union took effect, and in late 2011 the FTA with the United States was approved in a tumultuous session of the Korean Parliament. From 2012, South Korea will enjoy free trade with an area representing two thirds of the world's GDP. Also, South Korea's national success becomes increasingly a benchmark for other countries as South Korea transforms into a leading world economy. From being a receiver of development aid it has become a major donor, hosting an OECD Development Assistance Committee (representing the most important donors of development aid) forum in November 2011 in Busan. It also took a leading role in the G20 during the financial crisis of 2008 and 2009, hosted a G20 summit in 2010 and is leading efforts to implement a new vision of green growth at the regional and international level.

What triggered this remarkable resurgence of South Korea? While international aid under the umbrella of the IMF, a steep depreciation of the Korean won and improving macroeconomic factors certainly helped to overcome the immediate crisis, it does not explain Korea's post-crisis development. Other countries working under the same external environment had much less success. To understand Korea's outperformance, one needs to look at institutional change after the crisis. While the popular explanation of the Korean crisis made it a macroeconomic crisis, and even an "IMF crisis", blaming international forces for the downfall, nevertheless the Korean government and companies understood that unresolved structural issues where at the heart of the crisis and started to embrace change, beginning with the unprecedented election of an opposition candidate and peaceful democratic power transfer in 1997 and 1998, and then implementing change in the public sector, the labour market, the private sector, monetary and financial policy, the foreign direct investment regime, trade relations and other areas.

This book, which looks at institutional change and economic performance (to borrow the title of a famous book by Douglass C. North) in Korea after the crisis, is the outcome of ten years of research on the Korean economy during my stay at Hankuk University of Foreign Studies and later at the Hanns-Seidel-Foundation, Korea Office. For this research, the German Habilitation has been awarded to me by the Faculty of Economics of the University of Witten/Herdecke. Compiling the research has been made possible by a grant from the Academy of Korean Studies (AKS). Research would not have been possible without the generous support of my family, to whom I dedicate this book.

Seoul, December 2011
Dr. Bernhard Seliger

Acknowledgements

This work was supported by a grant from the Academy of Korean Studies, which is funded by the Korean Government (MOEHRD, Basic Research Promotion Fund).

AKS-2007-CB-2002

This work benefitted from a vast number of conferences, meetings, talks, interviews, as well as various projects with students at Hankuk University of Foreign Studies (1998 to 2004) and University of Witten/Herdecke (since 1999). It is not possible to mention all those who contributed to the development of this book, but a few should be mentioned: Prof. Dr. Carsten Herrmann-Pillath (Frankfurt School of Finance and Management), Prof. Dr. Werner Pascha (Universität Duisburg/Essen), Dr. Sigrun Caspary (University of Witten/Herdecke), and many others introduced me to important aspects of institutional economics and the analysis of East Asian economies. Prof. Dr. Won-Soon Kwon (Hankuk University of Foreign Studies), Prof. Dr. Jong-Won Lee (Suwon University), Prof. Dr. Sung-Jo Park (Free University Berlin), Prof. Dr. Dalgon Lee (Former Minister of Public Administration and Security/Seoul National University) and many others helped me to deepen my understanding of the Korean economy. Special thanks go also to Sarah Kohls for managing the Academy of Korean Studies grant. Breda Lund did a great job to edit this book. Anna Benzin, Wing Cheng, Jaewhan Kim, Sang-Ah Kim and Noa Sharabi helped with the manuscript. All remaining errors and all judgments are solely mine.

Table of Contents

List of Figures

List of Tables

Abbreviations and Acronyms

ACU	Asian Currency Unit
ADB	Asian Development Bank
AMF	Asian Monetary Fund
AMS	Asian Monetary System
AMU	Asian Monetary Union
APEC	Asia-Pacific Economic Cooperation
ASEAN	Association of Southeast Asian Nations
BEPA	Bilateral Economic Partnership Agreement
BOK	Bank of Korea
CBI	Central Bank Independence
CEE	Central and Eastern Europe
CIS	Commonwealth of Independent States
CVLM	Cambodia, Vietnam, Laos and Myanmar
DDA	Doha Development Agenda
EBRD	European Bank for Reconstruction and Development
EC	European Community
EMS	European Monetary System
EPZ	Export Processing Zones
FDI	Foreign direct investment
FSC	Financial Supervisory Commission
FTA	Free trade agreement
FTC	Fair Trade Commission
G20	Group of 20
G8	Group of 8
GATT	General Agreement on Tariffs and Trade
GDP	Gross domestic product
GDR	German Democratic Republic (Germany)
GNP	Gross national product
HCI	Heavy and chemical industry
IAP	Individual Action Plan
IMD	International Institute for Management Development
IMF	International Monetary Fund
JKFTA	Japan-Korea Free Trade Agreement
KDI	Korea Development Institute (Korea)
KFCA	Korea Foreign Company Association
KOSPI	Korea Composite Stock Price Index
MDP	Millennium Democratic Party

MITI	Ministry of International Trade and Industry (Japan)
MNC	Multinational corporation
MOFE	Ministry of Finance and the Economy (Korea)
NGO	Non-governmental organization
NIC	Newly industrialized country
NIE	New institutional economics
OCA	Optimum currency area
OCR	Overnight call rate
OECD	Organization for Economic Cooperation and Development
PPP	Purchasing power parity
RTA	Regional trade agreement
SARS	Severe acute respiratory syndrome
SEZ	Special economic zone
UMNO	United Malays National Organisation (Malaysia)
WTO	World Trade Organization

Chapter 1: The Economic Crisis in South Korea as a Transformation Crisis of its Political and Economic Culture

1.1 Competing explanations for the economic crisis and the role of transformation theory

The reasons for the economic and financial crisis in East Asia in general and South Korea in particular are subject of intense debate. This is all the more true because economists completely failed to predict the crisis. No consensus was reached on the ultimate reasons for the economic meltdown, and often reasons and symptoms of the event were not clearly distinguished. For instance, the financial upheaval was described as a crisis of trust in the economic viability of the East Asian economies, which is clearly a symptom rather than an underlying cause. Observers have offered two broad competing groups of explanations for the crisis, namely the fundamental explanations and the financial architecture explanations.

The fundamental explanations focus generally on 'bad governance' in East Asian countries and South Korea, based on factors such as: an unsustainable currency peg; growing trade deficits; 'crony capitalism' (corruption and lack of transparency); credit decisions driven by politics rather than economics; a lack of competition in domestic markets; orientation of *chaebol* toward market share instead of profit; and generally the impossibility of maintaining the government-led, interventionist developmental models in the more global economy (The Economist, March 7, 1998; Seliger, 1999a). Financial architecture explanations focus on the growing instability of global capital markets, the moral hazard due to implicit bailout expectations, herding behavior, and financial contagion. Many authors also favor an explanation made up of a combination of these theories, putting more or less stress on the elements they think to be most plausible. The policy implications of the two explanations are quite different. According to the fundamental explanation, the economic systems of East Asian countries are mainly culpable and should be the main target for reform. According to the financial architecture explanation, international capital markets have to be reformed. Both factions favor either a more interventionist approach, including capital controls or Tobin taxes to fight market failure, or an approach favoring the dissolution of international financial institutions hampering the functioning of the market.[1]

---

1 A Tobin tax (named after the economic Nobel laureate James Tobin, who first proposed the tax) is a tax on currency trade to discourage short-term capital movements.

While both explanations of the crisis have their merits, from the point of view of economic theory they remain incomplete. Fundamental explanations raise two objections: First of all, the fundamentals as they were described in pre-crisis times, namely growth rates, inflation rates, investment and savings rates, budget deficits, but also other figures like investment in education, had been extraordinarily healthy and always been seen as conducive to the 'East Asian miracle' (World Bank, 1993). Second, those fundamental weaknesses blamed for the crisis – like crony capitalism, the unhealthy expansion of business or the lack of competition in domestic markets – have existed for years. Especially in the case of collusion of big business and government, the weaknesses have even been previously understood as part of a successful East Asian economic development model. Why did they suddenly become liabilities instead of assets?

Financial architecture explanations of the crisis also face skepticism: If fundamentals did not play an important role in the crisis, why was Taiwan – the one country not exhibiting the fundamental weaknesses of its neighbors – the country least affected by the crisis by far? More importantly, why did the post-crisis paths of the countries of East Asia diverge so markedly, from a market-oriented reform in Korea, to a temporary retreat from openness in Malaysia, to a grave political crisis in Indonesia? If the crisis was contagious and the underlying cause international, not national, then one would also expect the recovery from the crisis to be more uniform. The divergent paths seem to imply that fundamentals cannot be neglected when explaining the crisis.

1.2 Outline of the book

This book deals not with the causes of the crisis in retrospect, but rather with the implications for the development of a new economic model in the case of South Korea. It argues that the crisis and the following changes in South Korea can best be understood by applying the theory of economic transformation. The first part looks into the challenges the transformation in Central and Eastern Europe, as well as the later East Asian crisis, neither event foreseen by almost all economists, pose to economic theory. In Chapter 2 problems are discussed which cannot be solved with mainstream transformation theory. A reformulation of transformation theory is proposed, using the discussion of the *Ordnungsproblem* by German ordoliberals, the Austrian tradition, especially the evolutionary competition process for institutionals, new institutional economics (NIE), and public choice as the main ingredients. Such a theory could also be applied to transformation processes apart from those in CEE, making it a general theory of transformation. In the economic transformation in Korea after the Asian crisis external choices loomed large; today many Koreans understand the crisis as an "IMF crisis" rather than a domestic crisis. Chapter 3 discusses the role of external initial conditions, institutional arrangements and policy choices in transformation in CEE. Based on a brief outline of the theory of institutional competition the strategies of institutional transfer in the former German Democratic Republic, institutional imitation in countries aiming at EU membership, and institutional innovation are discussed. While closing the 'window of opportunity' in transformation, institutional transfer or imitation can considerably reduce uncertainties surrounding transformation for business and state. One of the problems of mainstream economics in understanding economic crises in CEE and East Asia was the lack of area-specific analysis in neoclassical formal models. Area studies and social sciences for some time now have lived in an 'uneasy coexistence,' as reviewed in Chapter 4. The debate between area specialists and social scientists is especially difficult in times of tight science and university budgets, but it has deeper, methodological roots. Area specialists accuse economists of economic imperialism, using mathematical tools in a 'one size fits all' way, and thereby loosing important information about the characteristics of a region and disregarding the cultural and environmental background of regional development. Social scientists blame area specialists for using a non-scientific approach, and point to important failures of area specialists to predict and interpret regional development. This chapter looks into the possibility of reconciling area studies with social sciences, in particular economics. NIE can be regarded as a 'missing link' between area and social science studies. This paper develops a research agenda for area studies applying NIE.

The second part of the book looks into the Korean financial and economic crisis of 1997 and 1998. As Chapter 5 explores, while there has been an intense debate on the causes and implications of the East Asian economic crisis, it would add to the analysis to understand the crisis and its aftermath in South Korea, the five years dubbed as "DJnomics", as a transformation process. This transformation process changed the institutional structure of the Korean economic system, until a new expectation-equilibrium was reached. The intended and especially the unintended consequences of transformation changed the traditional economic system of Korea. This chapter deals less with the causes of the South Korean economic and financial crisis in retrospect, and more so with the implications for the development of a new economic model in the case of South Korea. Korea's economic transformation did, however, not take place in isolation, but as part of the larger East Asian economic system. Chapter 6 looks into the changes in the economic systems of Malaysia, Indonesia and Korea, in particular focusing on the interdependence of economic orders; the interdependence of the economic order with the political, social and cultural order; the interdependence of external and internal institutions; and finally the interdependence of the national and international order. The debate about "Asian values" back in the early 90s suggested that that any desired mix of elements could exist. Authoritarian states (like Singapore, Malaysia and Indonesia) in varying degrees restricted the political freedom of their citizens. At the same time their generally open economies were in a varying degree mixed with more or less strong elements of central planning (like investment plans for selected export industries). The crisis, insofar it was not only a financial crisis, but also a structural crisis of East Asian economic orders, brought the interdependence of order back to light. One of the outstanding features of the Korean economy, in particular during the Korean crisis, is the role of large conglomerates (*chaebol*), which is reviewed in Chapter 7. *Chaebol* played a major role in the economic rise of South Korea since the 1950s and 1960s. Their intimate relationship with the government made them ideal tools for developmental policies of the state. However, this relationship was far from smooth already, and in the 1980s, when the economy was liberalized and the *chaebol* grew, their guidance by the state became less and less feasible. The growth- (not profit-) oriented businesses and their overinvestment in new business fields became more and more a liability for the Korean economic model. The East Asian financial and economic crisis of 1997 and 1998 was a turning point for the *chaebol*. A number of large companies (among them Hanbo Iron & Steel, Kia Motors, and later Daewoo) failed and others (like Hyundai Group) barely escaped bankruptcy. The new policies, beginning with the conditions of the IMF credits and elaborated by the "four plus one" policy of the Kim Dae-Jung government, put certain restrictions on the *chaebol*. However, decades-old business practices lived on and were difficult to erase in a couple of years. Therefore, old patterns of quantitative growth were reproduced (e.g., in the credit card market). This chapter analyzes the changing role of *chaebol* and the changing relationship between *chaebol* with the government in the years after the East Asian crisis. The Korean crisis proper ended in 1998. By 1999, Korea made a spectacular V-shaped rebound. However, transformation issues lingered over Korea throughout the last decade. In Chapter 8, an overview of economic development and economic policy debates in the post-crisis decade is given.

The interplay of external and internal institutions becomes visible, for example, in the formulation of Korean monetary policy after the Asian crisis, which is discussed in Part 3 of the book. Chapter 9 reviews monetary policy before and after the Asian crisis. Monetary policy was one of the most contested fields of economic policy during the financial and economic crisis of 1997 and 1998 in South Korea. After the plunge of the Southeast Asian currencies, beginning in Thailand in July 1997, the South Korean won came under pressure in the autumn of that year, leading to an IMF-led bailout in December 1997. The cooperation with the IMF led to a policy of temporarily high interest rates, which was heavily criticized as the cause of the deep recession of 1998. However, the goal of this policy, namely the restoration of trust in the South Korean currency, was achieved. Besides this change in monetary policy during the crisis and cooperation with the IMF, the institutional framework for monetary policy was thoroughly revised as well. Specifically the central banking law, the Bank of Korea Act, was revised. In the end of December 1997, the BOK became an independent central bank. Chapter 10 looks into the development of monetary policy within the new framework. While East Asian central banks before the crisis earned a reputation as "gatekeepers of growth" (Maxfield 1997), the change in the Bank of Korea Act prescribed price stability, not growth, as the main target of monetary policy. In this chapter, the problem of the interaction of political and economic decisions embedded in a specific cultural context, resulting in decision-making in the 'market for institutions' not conforming to the rational decision-making processes usually modelled is discussed. Therefore, concepts (like central bank independence) developed in the context of Western market economies cannot simply be transferred to East Asian economies. In South Korea, the conflicts between the Ministry of Finance and the Economy and the BOK show *de facto* central bank independence had to be earned as a reputation, rather than decreed by government.

Part 4 of the book looks into cognitive models and changing perceptions of the economic model of Korea after the crisis, looking in particular at the changing perception and role of foreign direct investment (FDI). To understand the background of these changes, Chapter 11 reviews the self-perception of Koreans stemming from ancient and recent history. In the self-perception of Koreans, three widely prevalent stereotypes can be found which are important to the political and economic development and interaction with other nations: Korea as victim of foreign aggression, Korea as nation with a 'pure,' unique culture which resists foreign influences ("Hermit Kingdom"), as well as Korea as the nation of the East Asian economic miracle ("tiger economy"). The role of Korea as victim of foreign aggression is historically rooted in relations with China and especially Japan, but also in the later development of Korea as pawn in the hands of foreign powers, as a Japanese colony and finally as a country divided during the Cold War. Certainly, the biggest collective trauma developed through the colonization and Japanization of Korea from 1910 to 1945 as a Japanese colony. The role as a "Hermit Kingdom" (originally a term for the Chosŏn Dynasty in the 19th century, which refused all contact with foreign powers), refers to Korea's long history as a homogenous kingdom. The preservation of this (racially and culturally founded) unity is an important paradigm in its economy, politics and cultural politics. The role as a prototype of a "tiger economy" refers to the experience of having the highest economic growth rate worldwide since the 1960s, which was expressed metaphorically as the East Asian economic miracle or the "miracle on the Han River" (which passes through Seoul). This stereotype leads to a special, positive view of the role of the economy and to opposing trends with regards to the "Hermit Kingdom" view, because in this case globalization is perceived quite positively as Koreanization, for example through exports and Korean investments in other countries, as well as the success of Korean culture abroad (*hallyu* or the Korean Wave). Chapter 12 looks into Korea's changes in FDI policy after the Asian crisis. The strong increase in FDI was one of the most obvious results of the Korean economic development after the economic and financial crisis of 1997 and 1998, and the policy to attract FDI was widely discussed. However, already in the time before the crisis there were changes in FDI policy, in particular during the Kim Young-Sam presidency (1993-1998) and his *segewha* (globalization) policy. In the Korean market for institutions, 1997 was a turning point regarding FDI, since now explicit opening for FDI and wooing of investors became an institutional innovation. It was part of the answer to formerly disregarded structural problems exhibited by the crisis, like the lack of competition in domestic markets, the lack of modern forms of corporate governance, and the inflow of short-term capital used for long-term investment projects. Second, in 1997 external influences in institutional competition were most obvious, as in the imitation of foreign policies regarding FDI as partly in liberalization conditions of external actors, namely the IMF. Thirdly, the new policy also can be seen as a change of perception based on cognitive schemata with regard to foreign capital no longer matching reality. To understand the resulting changes, an institutional economics viewpoint can be more fruitful than traditional theories of FDI like models of optimal regulation of FDI by host countries. South Korea has been a prototype of the developmental state in East Asia: long led by an authoritarian government, with close business-government relations, an export-oriented growth strategy and a selective import liberalization policy. In the last two decades, South Korea underwent not only a process of democratisation, but also a profound change of its economic paradigm, triggered by the East Asian economic crisis. South Korea entered the WTO and the OECD, opened its markets and formed in 2004 its first free trade agreement with Chile. Economic nationalism seems to be receding. The cultural sphere and cultural businesses have been to some extent the core of economic nationalism in Korea, since the justification for protection of Korean markets have been cultural rather than economic. The experience of Japanese colonization (1910-1945), as well as the contested identity of the "true" Korea through the division and Korean War, are equally responsible for this as the neo-Confucian heritage of the "Hermit Kingdom", when Korea (Chosŏn) was the last country in East Asia to open up to Western influences. Therefore, it is no wonder that the cultural markets have been especially highly protected, as well against the dominant Japanese market as against the U.S.-dominated Western influences. In the decade after the Korean economic and financial crisis, however, this has been fundamentally changed. While in the beginning of this new era, opening was still the result of outside pressure, more and more Korea became confident of the attractiveness of its cultural content industries and now enjoys the status of an important exporter of culture to other countries in the region and worldwide. The change from protectionism to opening is reviewed in Chapter 13 of the book.

The fifth part of the book looks into the interaction between Korea and the world economy after the Asian crisis. As in the fields of monetary policy and FDI policy, here again important changes took place. Here, in particular international institutional competition plays an important role in explaining the changes. In Chapter 14, trajectories of economic integration that were discussed during and immediately after the Asian crisis are analyzed. When in November 2001, the leaders of the Southeast Asian and Northeast Asian states met for the ASEAN Plus Three (China, Japan and Korea), President Kim Dae-Jung of South Korea proposed the exploration of an East Asian Free Trade Area and thereby opened a new chapter in East Asian integration. The special Northeast Asian perspective on regional cooperation became clear from the simultaneous decision to hold annual meetings of finance and trade ministers of China, Japan and Korea. At the same time, bilateral agreements like an FTA between Japan and Singapore, the tentative large FTA between ASEAN and China, and the beginning of work on a Japan-Korea FTA showed a new-found interest in regional trade agreements, which was diametrically opposed to the pre-crisis policy. The chapter reviews what triggered these changes and which factors shape economic integration in the region. As Chapter 15 shows, regional economic integration has been widely discussed in Korea and its neighboring states after the Asian crisis, but progress has been most pronounced elsewhere, namely in bilateral trade integration, and here not with neighbors, but rather with distant but important trading partners. This result could not have been expected after the crisis. Not all FTA negotiations were successful, but in 2011 Korea successfully entered a high-profile FTA with the European Union and finally ratified, after a four-year stalemate, the FTA with the U.S., thereby achieving free trade with an area representing 60 percent of world GDP. In this chapter, the unsuccessful attempt to negotiate an FTA with Japan is juxtaposed with the successful conclusion of an FTA with the European Union. The change in the external economic environment after the crisis resulted not only in a run to form FTAs by Korea and its neighbors and more cautious discussions of comprehensive regional integration, but also in more marketing efforts to position Korea in a pivotal role in Northeast Asia. Already since 2002 the administration of Kim Dae-Jung propagated the aim of making Korea the “hub of East Asia”, which seemed quite ambitious given the still low (though increasing) level of FDI and the rather low rankings in various measures of locational competition in the region. Under the Roh Moo-Hyun administration, the goal was even more pronounced, namely by introducing Korea as a “balancer in Northeast Asia”. While this idea understandably found no echo among the larger neighbors, the implemented reforms, in the sectors of logistics, finance and services, among others, had a positive impact on the Korean economy. Comprehensive economic integration in East Asia gained new momentum with the summit meeting in Kuala Lumpur in December 2005, when the ASEAN Plus Three states met, together with India, New Zealand and Australia, and decided to form a new economic integration area. However, the size of the new integration area has been a source of dispute: The number of states participating is of concern, as well as the regional implications of certain participants, due to the danger of overstretching, as in the case of APEC. At the same time, bilateral integration through FTAs flourishes in the region, but due to their frequent exceptions these FTA are barely able to be combined into a larger integration area (a “spaghetti bowl effect”). For the region, but in particular for South Korea, the question remains how economic integration can strike a balance between the large and small states. This question is reconsidered in Chapter 17. Given an appropriate integration area, South Korea can fully exert its role as a catalyst of integration. In this case, even Korea’s goal of national unification can benefit from international economic integration.

The last chapter, Chapter 18, again takes up the main theme of the preceding analysis: An understanding of economic crises from the point of view of institutional economics can enhance the understanding of these crises and thereby help to analyze policies, in the areas of the interplay between external and internal institutions, the role of cognitive models of the economy, as well as institutional competition.

PART 1
THE INSTITUTIONAL CHALLENGE AND THE TRANSFORMATION OF TRANSITION THEORY

Chapter 2: Toward a More General Theory of Transformation

2.1 Introduction

The scientific interest in studying problems of transformation of economic systems posed a major challenge for economic science after the revolutionary events of 1989 and 1990. As transition in CEE began, economic science (especially the neoclassical mainstream) was accused of having neglected systemic changes in favour of more and more exact mathematical formulations of equilibrium model economies. Afterwards, the study of changes of economic systems became central to new research programmes, journals and even institutes.[2] To give a complete bibliography of "transition studies" and "transformation studies" is no longer possible.[3] The problems studied are not confined to the concrete transitional phase from a centrally planned to a market economy, since "when stabilization, liberalization and privatization is mastered, transition is over. But transforming the system, as EU countries know only too well, is a never-ending process."[4] Nevertheless, the main focus of transition studies were the former centrally planned economies in CEE and Asia (Schulders, 1998).

In spite of this obvious interest in transition, the development of a scientific discussion on economic transition was often met with uneasiness (Horne, 1995: 25; Angresano, 1996: 474-477; Shleifer, 1997; Herrmann-Pillath, 1998a; Hermann-Pillath, 1999a; Polterovich, 1999). The uneasiness starts with the lack of clarity in defining transition and transformation, especially as separate from evolution of economic systems. Also, there is no consensus on whether transformation is an organized or a spontaneous process, how far cultural factors account for transformation, or how formal and informal institutions interact during transition.

Economics cannot rely on experiments like natural sciences. Therefore transformation on a large scale cannot be overestimated in its value to economic science (Herrmann-Pillath, 1991: 28). The large scale transformation in CEE represents

2 Examples are the Centre for Economic Reform and Transformation (CERT) of Heriot-Watt University, the Institute for Economies in Transition of the Bank of Finland (BOFIT) and the Frankfurt Institute for Transition studies (FIT) at the University Viadrina in Frankfurt/Oder.

3 Important references from the economic mainstream are Gros/Steinherr (1995), Kornai (1990), Lavigne (1995), Lipton/Sachs (1992), World Bank (1996), Gregory/Stuart (1998). For an overview of institutional approaches see Seliger (2007).

4 Csaba (1997: 15). It should be noted that other authors do not draw any distinction between both notions. In this article, interested in the broader aspects of systemic change, always the notion transformation is used.

an important source for the questions raised above. But are these experiences only applicable toward CEE (and the formerly centrally planned economies in other parts of the world)? Or is it possible to come to a more general theory of transformation phenomena? To give an example, the Asian crisis and the related changes in economic systems in several East-Asian states are another large-scale transformation process. In CEE, the change from a centrally planned economy and one-party system toward a democratic market economy was the common theme of all national transformation processes.[5] Similarly, the countries affected by the Asian flu have common themes (which in a very simplified way can be described not only as overcoming the financial crisis, but as redirecting the traditional way of development).[6]

The possibility of institutional learning in CEE from the successful development of East Asian countries has already been discussed extensively. Can there be, in the scientific sphere, learning from the transformation process in CEE when analyzing the transformation processes in East Asia? To discuss this question, the second section gives an overview of the development of transformation studies. Afterward, the integration of different approaches to overcome the shortcomings of transformation economics is proposed in Section 3. Section 4 gives an outline of a transformation theory founded on the proposed reformulation of theory in Section 3 and some examples for the application of such an integrated approach toward transformation, followed by an outlook of a new research agenda (Section 5).

2.2 The development of transition studies – an overview

> *"It is a poor makeshift to call any age an age of transition. In the living world there is always change. Every age is an age of transition."*
>
> *Ludwig von Mises* (1963: 860)

Economics from its very beginnings was a science of systemic dynamics and change. Adam Smith compared advantages of mercantilist versus free-trade oriented systems, a discussion later formalized by classical and neoclassical economics. The German historical school tried to identify characteristics of systemic change by collecting and analyzing vast amounts of historically available data.[7] Never-

5 This is not to deny the differences in the preconditions, speed, direction and goals of the transition, but might be called a common denominator.

6 Here again, heterogeneity must be stressed, even more than in the case of CEE, since a hegemonic power like the Soviet Union, unifying economic systems, is not given in East Asia.

7 See the overview from Schumpeter (1954) and Schmölders (1984). While ironically the opposition of the German historical school to the more and more abstract model theory of marginalists

theless, addressing economic change did not lead to a unified system of notions concerning evolution, development, systemic change, transformation. So transformation economics has to begin with a definition and a distinction from related notions, specifically from the notion of evolution.[8] The problem of that is twofold: First, transformation has to be defined as historically "short" period of time against long-term evolution of economic systems.[9] Second, especially neoclassical theories of transformation were accused of a certain blindness to the long-term evolution of economic systems. According to Herrmann-Pillath, transformation is a state-directed change of institutional regimes *(Ordnungen)* in a historically short period of time (Herrmann-Pillath, 1999a: 10). Transformation is the outcome of political changes, but not necessarily the outcome planned by those who initiated the change (Kloten, 1989: 100). In fact, the unplanned and even undesired results of change are often more obvious than the planned results; therefore transformation economics is a case for Hayekian analysis of the results of human action, but not of human design (Hayek, 1969). Long-term evolution of systemic change is part of this, insofar as the change resulting from transformation is interdependent with it.

The scientific study of transformation has to define *criteria distinctionis* as phenotypical characteristics of transformation phases and to analyze if these are repetitive phenomena (Kloten, 1989: 100). These phenomena have to be separated from those resulting from the unique historical situation of the transformation country, including its cultural, economic and political development. As for the already cited distinction between transition and transformation, the first can be seen as a closed process from a known starting point A to a known ending point B. In this transition process only the instruments of well-defined change are to be chosen. Transformation then describes the open (according to systems theory non-trivial) process of change (Baecker, 1998: 39-69). German economic systems theory, led by the Freiburg school of ordo-liberalism and especially the influential textbook of Eucken (1952), tried to identify Weberian "ideal types" of economic systems (according to their decision-making systems and their property rights structure). This led to a reduction of transformation to transition. The same problem was enhanced in the Anglo-Saxon economic science by neoclassical

today gains a certain new actuality, its deterministic development theories are very problematic. See also the discussion of Starbatty (1996: 42-43).

8 Some authors do not draw a distinction, like Gern (1995: 22), defining the "neolithic transition" of nomads becoming settlers as well as a transformation like the process of industrialization. For evolutionary theories of economic development see the overview of Witt (1995), Seliger (1999a: 59-97).

9 The discussion of long version short period of time is not confined to economic science, but well-known to historical science, where the discussion of the "longue durée" by Braudel (1977/1958) still provides valuable insights.

stress on equilibria, which implied the juxtaposition of economic systems in equilibrium. The problems of the mechanic juxtaposition of market economies and centrally planned economies are most obvious in the socialist calculation debate.[10]

The use of comparative statics in the analysis of economic systems is widespread in early economic systems analysis. This is as well true for the Marxian theory of development, one of the important early deterministic development models. In his analysis, the transformation toward socialism is practically neglected apart from a few allusions to affluence. Only the socialist calculation debate focussed on possible problems of transformation. Especially the analysis of successive intervention by Ludwig von Mises and the later extension of the theory of economic policy in the age of experiments by Eucken are important: Both deal with the "interdependence of order" as important characteristics inherent to any change (Mises, 1926/1981; Eucken, 1952).

Experiences with mixed economies later led to a debate on the convergence of economic systems. The convergence debate discusses the problem of the convergence of economic systems, more specifically centrally planned versus market economies, due to technological forces. Interestingly, two exactly opposite directions were assumed as inevitable due to these forces: one hand the convergence of socialist toward market economies (as Rostow saw it), and on the other hand the "march into socialism", which Schumpeter (1942) found inevitable. Tinbergen (1966) and Galbraith (1968) again saw a convergence from both pure forms of economic system (Windhoff, 1971; Bohnet, 1989). Convergence theories are relevant to studying the transformation problem, not only because they focus on unintended consequences of change (namely technological forces, which imply certain organizational forms), but also because they show the evident problem of multidimensional change and the problem of deterministic thinking in transformation studies.

Nevertheless, the aforementioned discussions barely influenced mainstream thinking or the evolutionary approaches to economics. The lack of theoretical formulation made them unsuitable to integration into the mainstream, the deterministic formulation (or, in the case of German *Ordnungspolitik*, the reduction to ideal types as a misinterpretation of Eucken's approach) excluded them from the evolutionary discourse. Therefore, in the beginning of the transformation processes in CEE, there was a dominance of neoclassical policy advice, ignoring any discussion of transformation problems.

---

10 Theoretically, centrally planned economies in these models (of the Lange-Lerner type) were not only stable, but even – given the complete internalization of external effects – superior to market economies characterized by market failure.

Neoclassical advisers like Jeffrey Sachs did not ignore possible long-term problems with transforming socialist enterprises into capitalist ones. But they thought of the problem as a problem of transition, where the transition of institutions could – given the political will – be solved in a fairly short time (Lipton/Sachs, 1990). "Getting the prices right" was the *Leitmotiv* of policy advice, which determines concrete steps of transformation. The transformation of the political system was almost ignored.[11] This overshadows the logic of neoclassical models taking functioning institutions as assumptions for their models rather than outcomes of competitive processes.

There the transformation debate in its first phase was characterized by the following elements.[12] The content of transformation was widely undisputed and can roughly be equalized with the Washington consensus, including fiscal austerity, tax reform, liberalization of trade and finance, unified exchange rate regimes, attracting foreign direct investment, privatization and deregulation.[13] The debate then focussed on timing and sequencing, in the political discourse described as "gradualism" and "shock therapy" (Dhanji, 1991; Jens, 1993; Falk/Funke, 1993). Overall, the Washington consensus represents a model of trivial, closed transformation with given and well-defined starting and ending points. Developed for the countries of Latin America, it could nevertheless be applied cum *grano salis* to CEE. Since the consensus is derived from a model postulating universal applicability, namely the neoclassical model, it also represents a universal theory of transformation. Even given different starting points in Latin America and CEE, the ending points were identical. Therefore reform programmes only had to be slightly different, for instance in trade liberalization speed or privatization methods, but not fundamentally.

Unfortunately, the Washington consensus that dominated the debate early had to consider problems arising from the reduction of price theoretical models: The expected J-curve of economic growth did not occur, and institutional reforms were either lagging, did not produce results, or did not produce the expected results. The economic systems of CEE developed quite differently from

11 Sinn/Sinn (1994: 141), conclude: "Political transformation will seem almost a child's play compared with economic transformation."

12 Admittedly, this is an extremely simplified version of it. The already cited articles of the ORDO journal are a reference to a distinct stream of discussion. However, especially policy advice in CEE was characterized by the described reductionist view of neoclassical economics.

13 Cf. Williamson (1990). In an extended version of the consensus, the creation of property rights also appears as a goal (cf. Williamson, 1997: 60-61), or even the inclusion of aspects of institutional economics (cf. Burki/Perry, 1998). Later, Kolodko (1999) postulated the need to define a "post-Washington consensus." However, this cannot overcome the inherent shortcoming of the consensus as a model of closed, trivial transition.

Western European ones. Specifically, identical reforms in different countries led to different results. This "paradox of transformation" clearly shows the limits of neoclassical models of economic transformation (Rosenbaum, 1999: 1-3.). The debate about shock therapy or gradualism turned out to be important for transformation policies, but less important for transformation theory, since the definition of starting points and ending points had to be renewed and transformation therefore no longer could be defined as closed process.[14]

The explanative deficits of the neoclassical theory are not only (but especially) important for transformation theory. With the proceeding refining of the mainstream since Marshall, heterodox approaches or extensions of the mainstream also came into existence, trying to reduce the alleged shortcomings. For a general theory of transformation, the integration of these approaches is important. Without extensively dealing with the existing critique of neoclassical equilibrium models, the formulation of such an integrated theory of transformation will be the goal of the next section.[15]

2.3 The role of heterodox approaches to transformation theory

While non-neoclassical theorists were aware of the shortcomings of neoclassical models in explaining transformation in CEE, they were sceptical about the possibility of integrating these approaches into transformation theory. Kloten, for instance, lamented the fact that the different approaches to transformation he discussed (like new institutional economics, constitutional economics or German *Ordnungstheorie*) show the heterogeneity of explications of systemic change mainly focusing on isolated elements of systems, not connected to each other, without any tendency toward integration into a consistent, general theory of transformation (Kloten, 1989: 108).

German *Ordnungstheorie*, as founded by the Freiburg school of economics and ordo-liberalism as the more general intellectual current, as previously mentioned used the juxtaposition of ideal types of economic systems to derive conclusions and was subsequently reduced to the comparative statics of such systems.[16] Since *Ord-*

14 Nevertheless, the debate about shock therapy and gradualism had its theoretical merits, insofar as it illuminated some relations between economic policy and political economy, as in the models of Dewatripont and Roland (1992).

15 For a critique of the mainstream see Arndt (1979), Streissler (1980) and Koch (1996).

16 This, however, ignores Eucken's preoccupation with the explanation of changes in economic systems in parts of his 1952 foundations, where he deals with questions like the degeneration of systems through successive intervention or the circulation of elites.

nungstheorie deals primarily with the definition and classification of economic systems, it is a valuable starting point for tackling the problem of transformation. Some questions which were discussed by that school since its beginnings, for instance the question of property rights and the privatization process necessary in transformation economies, are able to fill a gap left by mainstream economics. While the mainstream takes private property rights as given (abstracting from mixed forms of property rights often occurring in transformation economies) and assume that they can be changed by state directives, it does not take into account the problem of these changes itself. Ordo-liberalism systematically addresses these questions, e.g. the strategies of privatization.[17] Also, decision-making systems and the question of generation and integration of knowledge into economic processes have since its beginnings been part of *Ordnungstheorie* and useful for a theory of economic transformation.

Even more important is the aforementioned "interdependence of order", first formulated by Eucken (1952). This important part of transformation theory – namely the question of how elements of systems like political or judicial arrangements, which are often in different states of transformation themselves, interact with the economic system – was banned to the realm of assumptions by the mainstream. This was a constant source of critique from ordo-liberal economists (Starbatty, 1996). The lack of a model of the interdependence of political and economic systems, including cultural influences, is the most important barrier to a general theory of transformation. Nevertheless, postulating the "interdependence of order" does not show how to integrate the factors into a model of transformation, illustrating the limit of the approach of traditional *Ordnungstheorie*. In its search for ideal types of economic systems, *Ordnungstheorie* acknowledged the importance of integrating the various (political, cultural and economic) factors, but was not actually preoccupied with doing it.

A second important research approach to be integrated in transformation economics is public choice. Since the 1950s, public choice developed its critique of mainstream models of the state as a benevolent, general-welfare-maximising "black box". The analysis of the market of politics consisting of supply and demand side actors on an imperfectly competitive market became widely accepted. Nevertheless, mainstream transformation theory and policy advice again was not immune to the fallacy of heroic modelling of the state. So those parts of the Washington consensus aiming at introducing a more efficient tax system and thereby restricting privileges of former state firms neglected totally politico-economic relations. In the context of state transformation with the erosion of state

17 Cf. Leipold (1992), Thieme (1993) and for a classification into the history of thought on privatization Siegmund (1997: 15-19).

power, this is even more in danger to reach "nirvana conclusions" (in the sense of Demsetz 1969) than in the context of relatively stable institutional environments of developed market economies. The identification of actors of economic and political change and the modelling of their interests is a further indispensable precondition for a new transformation theory.[18] One problem concerning public choice is its context of development for democratic market economies and its form of maximisation models (vote maximisation of politicians, budget-maximisation of bureaucracies, and rent seeking of interest groups), which limits its application to problems of transformation states.[19] The theory of institutional competition introduced below tries to overcome these limitations.

A third approach important for transformation economics is new institutional economics (NIEs) (Eggertson, 1990; Feldmann, 1995). The neglect of the role of institutions (especially in its normative implications, in which institutions yield advantageous economic results) is a main fallacy of mainstream economics. This again is more important in transforming countries, where institutional change is omnipresent. Property rights theory focussed for a long time on the importance of property rights structure and the resulting problems for incentives (e.g. innovation) in centrally planned economies. The design of incentive structure is also a main theme of principal agent approaches and can be applied to changes in corporate governance in transformation countries. Transaction cost economics focus on transaction costs related to the change of institutional regimes.[20]

The most fruitful part of NIE is the analysis of the role of institutions for long term economic change as discussed by North (1990). The distinction between formal and informal institutions and their role in the functioning of an economic system is especially important for economic transformation. The dynamics of institutional change makes the choice of optimal institutions impossible. This again is an important limitation of NIE, if it is a mere extension of the maximisation problem of economic institutions. The same problem faces constitutional

18 Again, the critique of the lack of public choice analysis does not imply that it never was applied to problems of transition, but rather that this approach is not taken into account sufficiently. For a public choice analysis of transformation see Apolte (1992), Lohmann (1997: 185-209), with a model of transformation as distribution problem, and Seliger (2000a) for the modelling of the political market for the Eastern enlargement of the EU.

19 So one could argue that distributional coalitions as analyzed by Olson are a limited problem for states where those interest groups undergo a deep change. This, however, does not mean that (old and new) interest groups play no role in transformation, only that their role is different from that illustrated by traditional public choice.

20 However, transaction costs cannot really give a causal model of institutional change due to transaction costs. As Hermmann-Pillath (1991: 34-35), pointed out, transaction costs can only be measured relative to existing institutions, but are not yet known for new institutional arrangements.

economics as an integration of NIE and public choice (Buchanan, 1990). However, this limitation can be overcome if these approaches are integrated into the research programme of evolutionary economics. While the brief discussion above gives a caricature of these approaches, it should be noted that to a considerable extent some of the theories (for instance, public choice or principal agent theories) are linked to neoclassical economics. On the other hand, the most important public choice theorist is in his later works closely linked to evolutionary approaches. Also, *Ordnungstheorie* has a lot of common roots with the Austrian school, which can be called the basis for modern evolutionary economics (Streit/Wohlgemuth, 1997). Even neoclassical economists sometimes stressed the importance of evolutionary extension of theory.[21] The distinction in this text is drawn to clarify in a stylized form the differences among the approaches to simplify the following discussion.

The specific value added of evolutionary transformation can be the integration of institutional analysis, analysis of the market for politics and research, and the *Wirtschaftsordnung* into a model of competitive institutional development.[22] The basis of such a model can be found in the Austrian school with its stress on the role of competition and entrepreneurial activity of the "*homo agens*", the development of institutions and spontaneous order, and the relation of economic activity with the political and cultural sphere. Austrian economists always were aware of the problems of political power in economic decision making and the cultural embeddedness of economic activity. This extends to transformation economics, as it must integrate the results of sociological and psychological research, for instance the importance of cognitive models in economic decisions. What are the elements of such a model of transformation economics?

2.4 A reformulation of transformation theory

Institutions compete indirectly through the decisions in markets for goods and services and in the political market (Seliger, 1999b; Gerken, 1995). Choices in these markets are a Hayekian discovery procedure for new institutions and a control procedure for producers in both kinds of markets. Transformation can be seen as

---

21 Marshall in 1948 reportedly said, "The Mecca of economics lies in economic biology rather than economic mechanics." Cf. Nelson/Winter (1982: 44).

22 Here, only those evolutionary models are discussed which are based on the Austrian tradition. Those models, which according to Nelson's and Winter's analysis are an extension of neoclassical analysis, e.g. the model of institutional competition of Siebert (1996), are neglected here. They cannot solve the problems of transformation theory as discussed above. See for the roots of Austrian evolutionary models the analysis of Geue (1997).

a large-scale discovery procedure, extending the 'gene pool' for institutional development, since radical institutional change is quantitative, in terms of the number of emerging institutions, as well as qualitative, in terms of the robustness of institutional arrangements, differing from long term institutional change (Hutter, 1994: 16). However, institutional competition is characterized by incompleteness, which makes an extension of models developed in neoclassical economics, especially the model of perfect competition, impossible. The nonexistence of a competition system, the incompleteness of political competition, ex ante unknown institutional development, path dependence of institutional development, and ignorance of the identity and interdependence of often not even observable institutions in complex social systems are characteristics of institutional competition.

A reformulated transformation theory based on a model of institutional competition can overcome the puzzles and paradoxes that transformation theory and practice faces today. The neglect of institutions and cognitive models lead to the previously mentioned paradox of different outcomes for identical transformation steps. The role of institutions was already the centre of NIE approaches to transformation (Hermann-Pillath, 1994; Riker/Weimer, 1995; Liechtenstein, 1996; Mummert/Streit, 1996; Kozul-Wright/Rayment, 1996). Subsequent studies analyze the interrelation of formal and informal institutions in transformation (Mummert, 1995/1998). However, the analysis of institutional regimes and their role in human actions lead to the question of whether and how these institutions are seen by the actors of transformation themselves. Institutions, especially informal institutions, often are not accessible by observation. People form ideas about institutions and about acting in institutions in their minds. These cognitive models were already discussed by North (1990). However, their role in transformation theory was only lately analyzed (Hermann-Pillath, 1998b; Hermann-Pillath, 1999b; Rosenbaum, 1999; Stahl, 1999). The way that people see institutions and their possible actions under institutional regimes are important for a more realistic model of the possible role of the state and of cultural factors in transformation.

The role of the state has to be readjusted in transformation theory in two ways: To start, the modelling of the state as a "black box" must be revised according to public choice models. The modelling of the market for politics should not stop with the analysis of certain groups maximising votes or budgets, but should lead to as coherent a picture as possible of the forces in this market. That means especially extending to include external relations and constraints on transformation countries. The shaping of institutional development by external influences due to international organizations – in the case of CEE the European Union – is an example of this. External influences are a result of the international (or in the case of the EU, European) political market. Viewed as such, policy advice and accession treaties of the EU would be evaluated differently than through traditional welfare analysis. Also, the mixture of new and old interest groups in transformation states has to be modelled.

This also leads to a second change in the evaluation of the role of the state in transformation: The interdependence and simultaneity of political and economic transformation makes traditional assumptions of state possible actions seem unrealistic. This not only concerns heroic assumptions (like the benevolent, welfare-maximising state), but also standard assumptions of the state as owner of the legal power monopoly, and especially about the enforcement possibility of state rules (Hermann-Pillath, 1998a). Since the transformation of the state happens simultaneously with economic transformation, the "strong state" often seen as a remedy to failures in transformation is an irrelevant, nirvana alternative. This not only concerns the possibility of carrying out efficient industrial policy as a strategy borrowed from East Asian NICs. Also the traditional functions of the state, the creation and enforcement of efficient institutions (e.g. in the privatization process, in the tax chaos, in the labour market) cannot be taken for granted as an assumption. The analysis of "lack of efficient regulation" is a nirvana approach, if it is meant as an external problem to an otherwise optimal transformation strategy (Csaba, 1997: 14).

The endogeneity of institutional change as a result of political and economic transformation will change the evaluation of successful outcomes of transformation. Not optimal institutions seen from the viewpoint of existing successful market economies can be seen as the benchmark for transformational success. The creation of new institutions is costly, especially radical institutional change (Polterovich, 1998). Instead, transformation as a process of self-organization seems to be successful, if it leads to long-term viability of a society in institutional competition with other models of organization. Competitiveness in institutional competition or viability again has to be defined differently from (or as an extension of) traditional numerical measurements of economic success like growth rates.[23] The use of growth rates as an insufficient and misleading benchmark has already been experienced in the discussion of Soviet economic growth in the 1950s.[24]

---

23 Cf. Hermann-Pillath (1998a), and for the concept of viability Boulding (1968) and Prosi (1997). Competitiveness in institutional competition is not only an outcome of formal institutions and therefore cannot only be measured by comparing them. Specifically, viability should not be confounded with competitiveness of firms; see Straubhaar (1994) and Küchler (1996). The approach of the European Union to evaluate the convergence of CEE or of the World Competitiveness Forum are problematic in this respect.

24 More than a problem of statistical comparability – which definitely existed – this was a problem of insufficient information contained in growth rates; see Gardner (1998: 15-47), with further

A transformation theory analyzing the viability of institutional regimes will also re-evaluate the relation between transformation and regional and international economic integration. While transformation in CEE was explained as the outcome of systemic competition, nevertheless the analysis of transformation often concentrated on national institutions and institutional change. However, increased competition through integration does not only affect markets for goods and services, but also institutional regimes. Regional integration can lead to a restriction of possibilities in institutional competition, if integration requires the adaptation of institutions, like most notably in the case of the *acquis communautaire* of the EU (Seliger, 1998b).

The discussion of the interrelation of culture and economics has long been established by economic sociology. But the incorporation of insights – like those of Max Weber – into economic models seems impossible to date. Most economists agree that culture affects economic decisions in important ways, but how can this be related to transformation research? Therefore, culture must not be confined too narrowly to business culture, but rather seen as a phenomenon related to all those phenomena which are not yet fully explained by traditional analysis (Herrmann-Pillath, 1999a: 15). While the study of business culture is different from the meaning of culture as the human-made environment, in which economic decisions are embedded, it can be very useful as a starting point, since it developed methods – or more often borrowed them from other social sciences – to classify and analyze culture.[25] The problem of diverging development paths in spite of identical development strategies has emerged as a core problem of mainstream economics (Mankiw, 1995: 275). Therefore, the integration of research into cultural aspects into transformation economics has recently been demanded (Boettke, 1999).

The difficulties begin if one wants to define cultural factors of economic development.[26] The virtual omnipresence of cultural phenomena can lead to the fallacy of modelling it as a residual factor similar to the modelling of technical progress in early growth theories. Culture must be specified in its concrete mean-

---

references. The gross components analysis can give additional information on the viability of growth regimes: see for the Soviet Union Gregory/Stuart (1998: 221-242); for the NICs of East Asia Krugman (1994) and Crafts (1999;) and for transformation economies in CEE Stephan (1998).

25 This is especially true for intercultural studies on management in the tradition of Hofstede (1980) and marketing; for an overview see Hodgetts/Luthans (1997: 95-182) and Onkvisit/Shaw (1997: 203-247).

26 These difficulties are experienced by all social sciences interested in cultural phenomena; see Williamson (1958 and 1981).

ing using the research already done by other social sciences.[27] One well-known, and for economists somewhat embarrassing, example of culture as a residual are the different explanations of the influence of Confucian ethics on the development of East Asian economics: According to the actual fate of the analyzed country (China, Japan, Korea and Vietnam) Confucian ethics (or to be exact neo-Confucian ethics) was seen as major force behind or major stumbling block toward economic development.[28] While therefore the specification of culture seems required, the actual task of narrowing down the idea of culture is difficult.[29] The definition of a cultural "core" of constitutive characteristics, established by historical, anthropological, sociological and socio-psychological research, might be a way to overcome definitional difficulties (Herrmann-Pillath, 1999b: 6-19). This cultural core is shared by all members of a particular society, but they are not always aware of it.[30] An important caveat to be made is not to apply culture deterministically. People can belong to different cultures, for the term is not used here in the sense of Herder as in different national cultures, but as different cultures according to social position, religious affiliation, ethnic background, etc. While the classification of behaviour in post-socialist countries as "*homo sovieticus*" can be enlightening, it would be dangerous to ignore the numerous different cultures (for example, *nomenklatura*, dissidents, ethnic minorities, industrial working class or service industry) in which people in transformation countries are identified. Furthermore, these affiliations are not clear-cut, and membership in several of these cultural subgroups is possible.

Transformation processes explained by a model of institutional competition can integrate the cultural factors discussed above. Patterns of behaviour analyzed by socio-psychology can explain the formation of institutions. Cultural embeddedness can explain the viability of institutions and the way these institutions shape the behaviour of people. Those institutions again are relevant to the effect on the political market and the markets for goods and services. Such integration requires the extension of research on transformation into interdisciplinary research. Interdisciplinary research on a large scale has been done as part of "area studies" research programmes. However, those programmes, mostly located in the United States,

27 Herrmann-Pillath (1999a:. 2-10), discusses pitfalls in the integration of culture into economic models.

28 For a recent study of the relationship between religion and economic development worldwide, see Couplet/Heuchenne (1998).

29 Cf. Aleksandrowicz (1998). Aleksandorwicz therefore proposes to confine the notion culture to intuitive knowledge about the classes of objects belonging to it.

30 As Selma Lagerlöf once put it, culture is "what remains when that which has been learned is entirely forgotten." So while culture itself is a learned behaviour, it remains active even if an individual acquires new or different new knowledge.

developed a lot of practical difficulties (Samuels/Weiner, 1992). These problems result, to name a few, from the influence of the culture of the observer, from the accessibility of factual evidence, but most importantly from the difficulty in achieving interdisciplinary research results. It seems difficult for the researcher to attain as well the relevant regional and social science knowledge in diverse disciplines. Relevant research networks could help to overcome this difficulty.

A reformulation of transformation economics as outlined above seems to be in a paradoxical situation: Transformation had been defined as the state-directed change of institutional regimes *(Ordnungen)* in historically short periods of time. As we looked into the possibility of finding a general theory of transformation phenomena, problems to such a general theory specific to the transformation process arose: Transformation can only be analyzed in a specific political, social and cultural context. So a general theory of transformation cannot be formulated as a set of identical or similar transformation steps. The achievement of a "post-Washington consensus" seems futile. Instead, a general theory of transformation can identify problems relevant to every transformation process (namely, the role of the state, the cultural embeddedness and the role of institutions). But these problems can only be understood by understanding the specific context of a transformation country.

2.5 Toward a new research agenda for transformation theory

The new transformation theory outlined here is not a complete innovation, but rather the integration of different research approaches partially already applied to transformation problems but until now not interconnected. The discussion of the *Ordnungsproblem* by the German Ordo-liberals, the Austrian tradition, especially the evolutionary competition process for institutionals, NIE, and public choice are the main ingredients of such a theory. Objections may be raised on the compatibility of these diverse research directions, and so public choice maximisation models establishing equilibria on the political market sometimes face the same critique when compared with neoclassical equilibrium models. However, if this theory is adapted to the framework of evolutionary institutional development, thereby representing a model of highly incomplete political competition, these possible internal contradictions may be overcome. The resulting hypotheses on transformation processes will definitely be weaker than those of Washington consensus-type policy advice. Certainly hypotheses about the design and the ability to design transformation will be more sceptical. However, this attitude is not an acceptance of chaos. Rather it points out the weaknesses of former approaches to the transformation problem which will allow the development of new strategies.

For transformation economics new perspectives can be opened by such an extended agenda. Not only can transformation in CEE can be re-evaluated, though this is necessary, as the transformation paradoxes show. But in addition, transformation processes other than those from centrally planned to a market economies can be analyzed. As mentioned in the beginning, large scale transformation in CEE provided the economist with a valuable mass of experiences otherwise not attainable in social sciences. It is now the time to apply this experience to other transformation processes. By this, two goals can be achieved: First, this provides economists with the ability to classify repetitive and idiosyncratic phenomena of transformation processes. Thereby, the model derived from transformation processes in CEE can be corroborated and refined. Second, understanding of patterns of transformation elsewhere can be obtained by comparing transformation processes. That is, what we learned about simultaneous political and economic transformation in the case of CEE can, *mutatis mutandis*, also be applied to transformation processes which at the first glance have little in common with those in CEE. The countries affected by the Asian crisis and now undergoing transformation are a good place to apply what was learned in the CEE.

Chapter 3: Institutional Competition and External Constraints to Transformation

3.1 Introduction

The more years passed after the revolutionary changes in Central and Eastern Europe (CEE) 1989 to 1990, the more the direction of scientific interest in economic transformation theory changed.[31] While the initial debates about transformation strategies called 'shock therapy' or 'gradualism' lost much of their significance, now the literature focusing on reasoning about long-term successful and less successful transformation strategies is growing (for an overview see Seliger 2002a). This is not only of academic interest from an *ex post* perspective, but it also holds important implications for ongoing transformation policies as well as for transformation processes in other world regions. Especially the relation between macroeconomic performance, initial conditions in transforming countries, the institutional environment and transformation policies remains interesting. Take for example the diverging paths of transformation countries after 1989: After ten years, there were clear differences in economic performance.[32] At the same time, ten years after transformation in most countries (Poland and Slovenia being notable exceptions) economic performance was worse than in the beginning of transformation. This made the European transformation states look much worse than East Asian transformation states, where transformation often started with a take-off of growth rates.

31 In this study the term 'transition' is used for a change from a well-defined state A to a well-defined state B, while 'transformation' (the process we actually experience in formerly centrally planned economies) is used for the change from an ill-defined ('fuzzy') state A to an unknown state $B_{1...n}$.

32 See Havrylyshyn/Van Rooden (2000: 26), for a (rescaled) synopsis of institutional transformation indicators by Heritage Foundation, Freedom House, EBRD, World Bank and Euromoney. On a scale from zero (least successful) to one (completed transition), countries rank from only 0.26 (in the case of Turkmenistan) to 0.85 (the Czech Republic).

Table 1: A Comparison of GDP Levels in Transformation States in 1989 and 1998

Country	Level of Real GDP in 1998 (1989 = 100)	GNP Per Capita in USD/ GDP in USD in PPP	GDP Per Capita as % of Austrian GNP/GDP in 1998
Albania	89	810/1,490	3/6.5
Bulgaria	66	1,220/4,100	4.5/18.1
Croatia	78	4,620/5,100	17.2/22.5
Czech Republic	95	5,150/11,300	19.2/49.8
Estonia	77	3,360/5,500	12.5/24.2
FYR Macedonia	72	1,290/1,050	4.8/4.6
Hungary	95	4,510/7,400	16.8/32.6
Latvia	59	2,420/4,100	9/18.1
Lithuania	65	2,540/4,900	9.5/21.6
Poland	117	3,910/6,800	14.5/29.9
Romania	78	1,360/4,050	5/17.8
Slovak Republic	99	3,700/8,300	13.8/36.5
Slovenia	104	9,780/10,300	36.4/45.4
Russia	55	2,260/4,000	8.4/17.6

Sources: Column 1: EBRD, Annual report 1999; Column 2a (GNP): World Bank, World Development Report 2000; Column 2b (GDP/PPP): CIA World Fact Book; Column 3: own calculations; for information: Austrian GNP/capita in 1998: 26,830 USD; Austrian GDP/capita (PPP) in 1998: 22,700 USD.

The explanation of these differences focused initially only on the success of the introduction of a relatively well-defined set of transformation policies. Later, when these policies proved to be insufficient as guidelines of transformation, the roles of sound institutions and of good governance were explored.[33] However, institutional transformation was hindered by an internal and an external constraint. Internally, path dependency and the misfit between formal and informal institutions frustrated many attempts to introduce the sound institutions desired for the new market economies.[34]

33 See Mummert/Streit (1996); Herrmann-Pillath (1998). Institutions are all arrangements reducing uncertainty in society, i.e. formal institutions (like written law) and informal institutions (like customs and values). As North (1990) pointed out they are decisive for economic performance.

34 Transformation policies target (with other goals like macroeconomic stabilization) the change of formal institutions. However, the new formal institutions can clash with the old informal institutions (Mummert 1998). The transformation of informal institutions and their cumbersome transformation became a special study field; see Mummert (1998), Rosenbaum (1999), Herrmann-Pillath (1999a), and for the case of the former GDR, Seliger (1999b). A special problem was the simultaneous transformation of state and economy (see Shleifer 1997, Herrmann-Pillath 1999b). Public choice theory could explain why good governance generally could not be expected in CEE; see Apolte (1992) and Klein (1995).

Externally, institutional choice in transformation countries was constrained to various degrees. The German unification process and acceptance of West German institutions by the former German Democratic Republic (GDR), the Copenhagen criteria for membership in the European Union for CEE countries, and the conditionality of IMF loans are examples of such constraints. Generally all transformation policies are constrained by institutional competition, the exit of factors of production and the voice of voters and pressure groups, potential investors and workers. The attraction of foreign direct investment (FDI), migratory flows of capital and labour, and the influence of regulation on trade and investment are all determined by the interplay of internal conditions and restrictions of transformation and external conditions and restrictions. So policy choices in transformation countries are policy choices in a competitive environment, shaped by internal and external constraints. The nature and the positive and negative effects of external constraints will be discussed in the following section.

Models of institutional competition have existed for more than a decade, especially those analyzing locational competition and the federal design of states (Gerken, 1995; Seliger, 1998/1999a). They are also appropriate models to apply to the institutional choices of countries in transformation. The next section gives a brief overview of institutional competition.

3.2 The theory of institutional competition – a brief overview

The theory of institutional competition postulates that the model of competition developed for markets for goods has *mutatis mutandis* also explanatory power for the development of institutional systems. Public choice theory since the 1950s tried to model a market for politics with a supply side and a demand side.[35] However, not only parties and politicians are competing for power and office. The choice of voters for policies, the choice of investors between different investment possibilities and locations, and the voice of organized groups like labour also lead to competition among institutions. Different social security systems, tax systems, regulatory systems and even models of societal organization are evaluated in this competition process and eventually considered to be in need

35 For an overview see Mueller (1989). On the supply side of the market for politics, politicians and bureaucracy offer policies, for the supply of public (and publicly produced) goods, for redistribution and regulation. On the demand side voters decide between different election platforms. Lobbyists provide information to the supply side, information which is often asymmetric, i.e. only available for lobbyists.

of reform or abandonment. For example, attracting FDI as a major goal of economic policy (namely the extension of production possibilities beyond domestic investment) is a form of competition of immobile factors of production (a certain region with more or less immobile labour living in this region) for mobile factors of production (investment capital).[36] What are the effects of mobility? Firms can decide to change location to escape institutional rigidities like strict environmental regulation. In border regions, cross-border competition for consumers is fierce. Regions and nations try to attract FDI by changing tax codes, providing infrastructure and simplifying bureaucratic procedures (like the one-stop shop system for investors). Since there are choices for investors, consumers and tax payers, they can exploit 'institutional arbitrage,' e.g. shift capital to low-tax countries or import goods from countries with regulations favorable for production and therefore cheaper (Mussler/Wohlgemuth, 1994: 6-7). In cases where migration costs are lower than the benefits expected from migration, 'exit' is a possible strategy for citizens (or labour).[37] On a large scale, this leads to 'systemic conflict', where different political and social systems (as in the case of the Cold War) compete (Kaltefleiter, 1982: 21).

Three possible answers exist to institutional arbitrage: First of all, new institutions can be introduced (institutional innovation). Second, institutions from foreign countries (or other regions) can be transferred, either through a joint offer of the institution or through a transfer of the underlying regulation or law. Third, successful institutions can be imitated, without completely transferring them. Reviewing these three reactions, one can see more clearly the similarity between competition in markets for goods and services and in institutional markets: First, institutional competition provides an incentive for innovation and works as a Hayekian "discovery procedure". Second, institutional competition controls the power of the supply side, i.e. the generally monopolistic offer of institutions. In democracies, offices are contestable and therefore officeholders are forced to react to institutional competition. Institutional learning (the transfer or imitation of institutions and rejection of institutions which in other countries or regions have failed) is an important argument for the desirability of institutional competition.

36 Cf. Siebert/Koop (1993). The distinction between mobile and immobile factors of production is not easy: While capital in the form of financial capital is highly mobile, real capital has different degrees of immobility. The labour factor is technically mobile. However, social security systems (reducing the incentive for migration in the case of unemployment), social and cultural costs of migration (like learning a new language or abandoning family and friends), legal barriers to migration, and immobile wealth (like real estate in countries, where the real estate market is not very liquid) reduce mobility. Therefore, only highly skilled labour is also highly mobile, while middle and working classes often are immobile.

37 The classical model analyzing this process described as "voting with the feet" is Tiebout (1956). For the processes of exit and voice see Hirschmann (1970).

The falsification of 'economic models' or systems (like the centrally planned economy) in other countries or in history provides arguments for decision making and makes it less expensive (Prosi, 1991: 130). It should be noted that this view of institutional competition does not necessarily result in 'evolutionary optimism', i.e. the expectation of always better adapted institutions. First, states can – again in analogy to competition in markets for goods and services – try to obstruct competition, for example through barriers to trade or cartelization (Gerken 1995). Second, institutional innovations can lead to a dead end, when the environment changes.[38]

The emergence and change of institutions is not unconstrained.[39] Internally, path dependency ('history matters') constrains institutional development. Externally, the process of globalization and the membership in global or regional organizations like the WTO or the EU represent major constraints for innovations.[40] Institutional integration like the forming of a free trade agreement or application for membership in a customs union or common market are important restrictions to institutional development.[41] International or regional organizations might work as a competition system for institutional competition in that they guarantee the free circulation of goods, services, and in the case of a common market also factors of production. Therefore, institutional competition is increased by membership. They might also harmonize economic policies (e.g. social or regulatory policies), thereby reducing the degree of institutional competition.[42]

38 For example, it can be argued that the 'developmental state', which resulted in superior economic results before the 1990s, became in a more globalized world inferior to other institutional arrangements.

39 This is a major difference to neoclassical economic and institutional models, which assume a free choice of optimal institutions.

40 Recently, Rodrik argues that despite the discussion about globalization national borders still represent important obstacles, referring to the Feldstein-Horioka paradox and the home bias in investment decisions; see Rodrik (2000: 178-179). However, while absolutely the degree of global integration might be still small, also marginal movements (like capital outflows or migratory movements) might present enough of political pressure to lead to changes in institutional supply. The intense discussion about economic models and economic policy prescriptions in the 1980s (after the Reagan-Thatcher reforms) and the 1990s (after the globalization hype) seems to justify such an evaluation.

41 While it cannot be discussed here, it should be noted that the external impact is important for economic and also for political institutions; for the latter see the analysis of CEE and the EU in Vachudovva (2001).

42 In the European integration process, since the 1950s there was a debate of integration as removing of barriers (favored by Ludwig Erhard, then German economic minister) or the introduction of common policies (favored for example by Etienne Hirsch, then planning commissioner in France). This debate is still today virulent in the discussion of subsidiarity and centralization in Europe; see Gordon/Seliger (1999).

The impact of external constraints on institutional change is Janus-headed: The positive aspect is that institutions generally are aiming at reducing uncertainty and that rapid and frequent institutional change leads to a higher degree of uncertainty. For example, in transformation countries information about institutional development is weak, and therefore long term investment is rather avoided.[43] The negative aspect of institutional rigidity is the restriction of choices and the low degree of adaptability of institutions. However, in the case of transformation, an entire economic-political system might change rapidly. In the next section, the effects of such a change and its relation to institutional competition are discussed.

3.3 Transformation and institutional competition after 1989

Prima facie the transformation of an economic system seems to be a clear case of institutional imitation: the change from an unsuccessful economic system, coming under pressure from low growth and innovation rates, exit (mass migration) and voice (protestations in 1989), to a more successful model, or the change from centrally planned to a market economy. In a narrow sense of transition it was interpreted as the change of (relatively few) formal institutions of the economy. After the reform a market economy would spontaneously develop.[44] This view, very influential in the beginning of transformation, was developed at the Washington-based international institutions and accordingly named the Washington consensus model. First developed for the transition of Latin American economies in the 1980s, it was due to the universal neoclassical model upon which it was based also applicable to transformation in Central and Eastern Europe.[45] The starting and ending points of transformation are well-defined, as Table 1 shows. Only the timing and sequencing,

43 Walter Eucken in his *Foundations of Economic Policy* names the "steadiness of economic policy" as one of the founding principles of a market economy, since without steadiness rational economic decision making is not possible; see Eucken (1952: 285-289). The uncertainty in transformation countries can also be seen in socio-cultural adjustments, for example a sharp decline in marriage and birth rates.

44 In this study the notion of transition, characterizing a more restricted task, is therefore avoided, and the more encompassing term transformation is used.

45 Cf. Williamson (1990). In an extended version of the consensus, the creation of property rights also appears as a goal (cf. Williamson, 1997: 60-61) and even the inclusion of aspects of institutional economics (cf. Burki/Perry, 1998). Recently, Kolodko (1999) postulated the need to define a "post-Washington consensus". However, this cannot overcome the inherent shortcoming of the consensus, representing a model of closed, trivial transition.

in political discourse reduced to the alternatives of "gradualism" and "shock therapy", are disputed (Dhanji, 1991; Jens, 1993; Falk/Funke, 1993).

Table 1: Task of Transformations – Two Diverging Views

Establishing a Market Economy – Two Alternative Views

The establishment of a market economy is often represented as the change of relatively few formal institutions, which were typically identified as institutions of centrally planned economies, toward being institutions of market economies.

The Washington consensus includes the following institutional changes (Williamson 1990, 1997):
* Fiscal laxity → fiscal austerity
* Incoherent tax code → tax reform
* Closed markets → liberalization of trade and finance
* Official and black market exchange rates → unified exchange rate systems
* Closeness of economy to foreign capital → attraction of FDI
* Collectively owned firms → privatization
* High degree of regulation, especially price regulation → deregulation

In the extended version: the creation of property rights

Kornai (2000), in what he himself admits to be a minimalist characterization, points out the following changes:
* Undivided power of Marxist-Leninist party → political power friendly to private property and the market
* Dominant position of state and quasi-state ownership → dominant position of private property
* Preponderance of bureaucratic coordination → preponderance of market coordination
* Soft budget constraints/weak responsiveness to prices → hard budget constraint/strong responsiveness to prices
* Chronic shortage economy/seller's market/labour shortage → no chronic shortage/buyer's market/chronic unemployment

Source: The author after Williamson (1990, 1997) and Kornai (2000).

A transformation so defined, largely the imitation of Western capitalism by transformation states, is incomplete for two different reasons. The first reason is the neglect of institutional preconditions (including cultural and historical factors, informal institutions and cognitive models of the actors of transformation, and public choice considerations) for change; as a policy recommendation, the Washington consensus was a 'nirvana approach,' i.e. practically impossible to be implemented. This criticism is dealt with elsewhere. The second reason is the need for a transformation country to choose not an unspecified 'capitalist' or 'market economic' system (as a Weberian ideal type), but rather to implement one of the numerous possible forms of market institutions that which (either due to the ease of implementing the institutions or in terms of welfare economics) is best adapted for the transformation country.

A closer look at the actual transformation processes reveals important differences among different countries and groups of countries in this respect. In the first few years of transformation, countries did experiment with numerous reforms, ranging from Anglo-Saxon models of capitalism to more continental European one, due to geographic and historical proximity often the German model.[46] It should be remembered that some countries – notably Hungary and the former Yugoslavia – had a long history of internal reforms, which also led to quite different starting conditions for institutional changes toward a market economy (Adam, 1993). The early blueprints of transformation (like the Gaidar plan in Russia or the Balcerowicz plan in Poland) however, became obsolete due to political pressure and frequent government changes. Also, the laissez-faire approach chosen by the Czech Klaus government was often compromised in the same way. In the time between 1989 and 1991, the former GDR, with its complete transfer of external institutions from West Germany, was the only country which could finish the task of establishing the external institutions of a market economy. And, more and more, institutional transformation was constrained by external policy conditions, as is most clear in the case of East Germany.

East Germany followed a unique transformation path, which was initiated only half a year after the coming into force of the economic, monetary and social union in mid-1990 and reunification in October 1990.[47] This was virtually a complete transfer of West German formal institutions (laws, political institutions and economic institutions). Subsequently, the economic structure of East Germany became similar to West German structure.[48] Investment by foreigners was small as a part of West German investment in the former GDR. Initial problems with the enforcement of institutions were soon solved through a large transfer of West German specialists. This concerned not only civil service, especially the judicial sector, but all sectors of society, for example universities and other educational institutions.[49] Through this massive and unique transfer, the problems facing CEE countries due to the incompatibility of new formal institutions and weak enforcement mechanisms in relation to old informal institutions, could partly be avoided.

---

46 There is no room to present these models here. Regular updates on transformation strategies of specific countries can be found in the transition report of the EBRD. See also World Bank (1996).

47 For an overview, see Sinn/Sinn (1994), and for a discussion Seliger (2001a) and Yoder (2001), who speaks of "accelerated transition".

48 This does not mean a complete convergence, given that East Germany was characterized by 40 years of socialist allocation and the effects of the elevated exchange rate. However, in many sectors (like the banking sector) the West German industry structure is close to the East German.

49 Especially in the social sciences and in the management of universities and schools, an almost complete exchange of personnel took place.

But German reunification also shows the problems of institutional transfers: In addition to transferring West German market institutions, the rule of law, and appropriate enforcement mechanisms, the West also transferred its density and level of regulation in all fields to the East. Together with an exchange rate increasing the value of East German money by several times for political reasons, this led to grave consequences, especially for the labour market. East German business had not only to adapt to a new, competitive environment and to face the loss of old, secured markets in Eastern Europe, but also to adjust to a completely new and complicated set of regulations. Over night large parts of the former GDR's industries became obsolete, less for technical reasons (they could have combined low productivity with low production costs) than a combination of high regulation and costs and low productivity.[50] Subsequently, deindustrialisation led to high rates of unemployment.[51] This along with generous transfers of social security systems and the desire to overcome infrastructure deficits in a short time led to the high levels of monetary transfers, which since unification amounted to more than 1.2 trillion euros in 2010.Those monetary transfers alone are a problem, given the negative incentive effects linked to generous benefit levels, e.g. for the unemployed. But they are not the cause, rather only the effect of a policy of transferring institutions to East Germany without distinguishing those institutions which enhance competitiveness (like the reduction of uncertainty through introduction of the rule of law) from those which in West Germany were introduced only after, and probably because, high levels of income were achieved.

From the point of view of institutional competition, this is an example of cartelisation in the integration process: Neither West German firms and managers, nor Treuhand managers responsible for privatisation (which either came from the West or expected to be sacked anyway after some time, if they belonged to the old socialist ruling class), nor trade unions (also directed by their West German counterparts) had interest in a low-cost, low-regulation competitor in East Germany. All easily agreed therefore on inappropriate regulatory and wage levels, neglecting the productivity problem in East Germany.

In CEE, the Europe agreements of 1991 and the EU summit in Copenhagen in 1993 changed the prospects of institutional transformation dramatically (Dabrowski/Rostowski, 2001; Piazolo, 2001; Salvatore, 2001). Those countries focusing on

---

50 According to official figures, the productivity gap between East and West for the whole economy is more than 20 percent and is since 1994 only slowly decreasing; see Bundesministerium für Wirtschaft (1998: 89).

51 For a discussion see Siebert (1995: Ch. 6). Unemployment in 1995 was 14 percent on average in the former GDR (compared with 8.3 percent in West Germany), 15.7 percent (9.1 percent) in 1996, and 18.1 percent (9.8 percent) in 1997; see Bundesministerium für Wirtschaft (1998:148). Not included are those *de facto* unemployed in public work ("ABM") or qualification projects.

application for EU membership suddenly had a relatively clear goal, including technical advice on how to achieve it. EU membership was seen as a fast track toward political stability and economic prosperity, in which institutional imitation should be complemented by institutional integration.[52] Those countries not sure of membership or even where membership was clearly out of reach, as in Russia and most of the Commonwealth of Independent States (CIS), still were free in their choices in transformation.

Already at the beginning of transformation in CEE, the EU concluded trade and cooperation treaties with Hungary (1988), Poland (1989) and Czechoslovakia (1990) on the basis of Article 113 of the European Community Treaty. In December 1991, the first association treaties (or Europe agreements) were concluded (with the same three states), leading a step-by-step approach to free trade (with the exception of so-called sensible sectors like agriculture and factor markets) and convergence with EU law and institutions.[53] From 1993 on other CEE countries interested in EU membership also concluded those treaties, which included in their preamble a long-term perspective for EU membership.

In 1992 the EU Commission developed criteria for EU membership of CEE countries, which were formally endorsed at the summit in Copenhagen in 1993 (Commission fo the EC 1992:11). Those criteria were partly political, partly economic. The political criteria stated that "membership requires that the candidate country has achieved stability of institutions guaranteeing democracy, the rule of law, human rights and the respect for and protection of minorities." The protection of minorities was especially important, since most CEE countries had considerable minorities: Hungarian minorities in Central Europe, German minorities in Poland, and Russian minorities in the Baltic states. The economic criteria concerned the introduction of a functioning market economy and the capacity to cope with competitive pressure and market forces within the common market. Additionally, candidate countries would have to accept the *acquis communautaire*, i.e. the rules of the EU (including all treaties and all secondary laws of the European Court of Justice). This also includes the acceptance of the goals of political union and economic and monetary union, i.e. the candidate countries have no possibility of opting out of those policies, as the United Kingdom and Denmark did.

---

52 Welfens (2001) speaks of a "transfer of security".

53 The share of "sensible products" among all products was in the beginning of transformation considerable, between one-third (in the former CSSR) and more than 60 percent (in Bulgaria and Rumania); see Achten (1996: 5). The EU's attitude towards the liberalization of these products was typically characterized by a primary concern for protection of domestic industries. However, later the EU liberalized these exceptions and it turned out to be to the benefit of the EU, like in the agricultural sector, where the EU profited more from liberalization than CEE.

While it can be said that the existence of a functioning market economy is a *conditio sine qua non* of EU membership, it is difficult to measure the success in introducing it. When is a market economy functioning? When do economies cope with competitive pressure? Is a measurement on a macro-level possible and rational? Should the competitiveness of single firms be the benchmark? Is regional specialization according to comparative advantage, e.g. the use of lower labour costs, enough for coping with competitive pressure, or do CEE countries have to develop intra-industry trade?[54] All of these questions have to be answered, if the criteria are to be taken seriously. Given the differences in per capita income, it would be difficult to wait until CEE caught up with the rest of Europe. "Economic wealth" is less important for successful transition than "economic health", i.e. sound economic structures. The EU measures the existence of a functioning market economy by factors like the free interplay of market forces, price and trade liberalization, the absence of significant barriers to market entry and exit, a legal system preserving property rights, macroeconomic stability, a broad consensus about the essentials of economic policy, and a sufficiently developed financial sector (cf. European Commission 1998).

The capacity to withstand competitive pressure and market forces within the EU is assessed on the basis of criteria like the existence of a functioning market economy, a sufficient amount of human and physical capital, trade integration, competitiveness, and the proportion of small and medium enterprises (European Commission 1998). While the criteria used at the first glance seem to be well-defined, formulations such as "sufficient, appropriate, adequate" and the fact that no benchmarks are given, indicate that there is a broad room for discretionary evaluation of these criteria. Therefore, the decisions on EU accession have to be seen as political decisions, based partly on objective data, but partly also on subjective, political criteria.[55]

The Copenhagen summit not only defined criteria for candidate countries, but also decided that the Community itself must be able to absorb new member states before they can achieve membership.[56] This means that there is no automatic membership, rather only if they criteria are fulfilled. Not only was the monetary

54 In an empirical study of Hungary, Slovakia, the Czech Republic and Poland, Gabrisch and Segnana (1999) conclude that the trade structure is characterized by specialization according to comparative advantage, i.e. CEE countries specialized in lower quality production compared with Western Europe. They discuss the problem of a low catching up potential represented by such a trade structure. However, as a remedy to it they recommend a policy actively pursuing EU membership.

55 Csaba (2001) even speaks of "double talk", indicating different standards according to political expediency. Public choice theory is appropriate to study this problem as a political-economic problem; see Silarszky/Levinsky (2001).

56 The reform proposals of the European Commission were first published as "Agenda 2000"; see European Commission (1997).

union project seen as more important than immediate enlargement, but also reforms of the financial structure of the EU were important to make the EU fit for the absorption of new member states.

In 1994 the Essen summit decided to establish the "structured dialogue", i.e. regular consultations at various levels of government facilitating accession. In 1995 a white paper listed areas of priority for the approximation of legislation for accession to the common market (European Commission, 1995). In 1994, Hungary and Poland officially applied for membership in the EU, in June 1995 Rumania and the Slovak Republic followed, in autumn 1995 the Baltic states, and in January 1996 the Czech Republic. The EU first concluded its Intergovernmental Conference on the future of the EU in 1996 and 1997, before deciding how to handle the applications. Half a year after the treaty of Amsterdam was signed in 1997, the EU began membership negotiations with five states, namely Poland, the Czech Republic, Hungary, Estonia and Slovenia, but soon membership negotiations were extended to all applicant states.[57]

The decision for accession to the EU totally changed the policy options of CEE countries. While support of the EU for transformation is one side of the process, on the other hand the possibilities for carrying out independent policy change are radically reduced. More than 20,000 different laws of the EU, in their entirety the so-called *acquis communautaire,* must be adopted. EU law distinguishes regulations, which according to the EC Treaty are "general applications" and "binding in [their] entirety and directly applicable in all Member States", from directives, which are binding but leave 'to the national authorities the choice of form and methods", i.e. directives have to be transposed into national law, usually by a deadline, and decisions, which are directly binding upon those to who they are addressed. While in the case of regulations and decisions the applicant countries have no choice, in the case of directives they have some chances to adapt EU law according to their national institutional preferences. It should also be noted that, especially where the EU itself fears competition from transformation states (as in the case of low-skilled worker migration or participation in the Common Agricultural Policy), potentially long transitional periods might delay full participation in all EU policies.[58]

57 A somewhat different analysis applies to the two Mediterranean states of Cyprus and Malta and to Turkey, which is not dealt with here.

58 Recently, as the EU opened negotiations about migration, a request for delay of full freedom of migration from the side of the EU was negatively answered by transformation countries. Long transitional periods were for example negotiated in the two Southern enlargements of the EC in 1981 (Greece) and 1986 (Spain and Portugal). See for a discussion of the enlargement processes Tsoulakis (1981).

3.4 EU policies as constraints for EU accession of CEE

From the point of view of institutional competition, the policies of the EU which the transformation countries have to accept can be divided in three groups. The first group of policies consists of those in which imitation of the EU can increase institutional stability in transformation countries. In particular, this concerns trade liberalization, the implementation of the rule of law and the commitment to the four freedoms (of trade in goods and services, capital mobility and migration). Here the imitation of EU rules and commitment to their implementation will increase investor confidence, reduce risk premiums, and thereby improve the outlook for long-term stability of countries applying for EU membership. This can lead to a virtuous circle, since increased confidence leads to increased foreign investment, which again changes the informal institutions of a transformation economy. For instance, the problem of improving corporate governance has been identified as one of the main obstacles on the way toward a market economy. Foreign investment and attached transfer of management practices can help to solve this problem. This again means better conformity of the formal and informal institutions of society, which again leads to more confidence and investment, and so forth.[59]

In addition to trade and FDI, the accession countries show a superior performance compared with other transformation countries (Brenton et al., 2002; Kaminski, 2001). FDI inflows per capita were four times as high during 1989-1999 in CEE including the Baltic states (574 USD) as in the CIS (142 USD).[60] Within the accession candidates the three best performers were Hungary, the Czech Republic and Estonia. No direct link can be established with institutional performance, but among the factors determining FDI inflows, institutions are known to be important.[61] So the imitation of EU rules, including rules guaranteeing profit repatriation, seem to have had a positive influence on FDI and may lead to a virtuous cycle.

A second aspect concerning liberalization is the importance of increased competition in transformation countries with often monopolized or small domestic

---

59 For the impact of FDI on corporate governance see Meyer (1998), who stresses the importance of networking resulting from FDI in transformation countries.

60 Cf. EBRD (1999:16). Given that the EBRD includes Albania, Croatia and the FYR Macedonia in the CEE countries, which are not yet applicant countries for EU membership and two of which (with the exception of Croatia, with relatively high FDI/capita of 605 USD) had the lowest inflow of FDI/capita, the picture is even more positive for EU accession candidates. It should be noted that FDI is only a part of capital flows to CEE. For an overview over all capital flows see Claessens et al. (1998).

61 For empirical results in the Romanian case see Radulescu (1996).

markets. Problematic are the commitment to the economic and monetary union and the eventual entry into the European Monetary System II, as long as exchange rates as shock absorbers cannot be substituted by sufficiently flexible factor markets, and as long as the probability of asymmetric shocks remains high due to a relatively low degree of intra-industry trade in transformation countries.[62] However, this commitment can also work as an incentive for appropriate policy changes to prevent such problems. Here again (as with the Maastricht criteria of sound monetary and financial policies, which in the long run also apply to applicant countries) the EU can provide a benchmark for national policies.

The second group of policies concerns the regulatory policies of the EU, for example environmental and social regulation, labour market policy, and consumer policy. In these areas, the impact of institutional imitation is more dubious. For EU countries fearing competition from lowly regulated transformation countries, the application of EU standards works as a strategy of raising competitors' costs. The transformation countries, which today have relatively low labour costs but also low productivity, could loose their advantage without being able to compensate for it sufficiently with increased productivity.[63] Even for longtime members of the EU, which did not suffer from the allocative distortion of socialist system productivity, differences are enormous.[64] Therefore, a convergence of CEE to European standards of labour costs or regulatory levels will need a long adjustment period, and it is not clear if convergence can be achieved at all. Extended regulations, e.g. environmental standards, can generally be described as superior goods with income elasticity greater than one. For low-income countries in CEE, the acceptance of these policies means a loss of competitiveness and possibly a less favourable growth path in the long run. Nevertheless, citing the possibility of social or environmental 'dumping', an immediate adjustment to the EU levels is demanded (see for the environment Homeyer et al. 2001).

CEE countries can only accept this institutional cartel. An example is the need for Estonia to raise tariffs on agricultural products due to EU regulations (Wrobel 2000: 240-241). In the external relations of CEE countries, this can lead

62 The entry in EMS II will mean the pegging of the country's currency with a central parity to the euro, probably with a wide fluctuation band of +/- 15 percent. However, as the Asian crisis showed, pegging in countries with differences in fundamentals (especially inflation rates) to the peg country can lead to speculative attack.

63 For the impact of EU rules on labour markets in CEE see Belke/Hebler (2001).

64 See Siebert (1998) for a European comparison. In 1991 the gap in hourly wage costs between the richest and poorest EC members was 1:4 and was almost the same as the gap in productivity; see European Commission (1994: 134). Peneder similarly analyzed the wage and productivity gap between Poland, Hungary, the CSSR and Austria for 1993, which was 1:10; see Peneder (1993: 52-53).

to trade diversion. In the domestic policies, it requires acceptance of less flexible, more rigid EU regulations and regulations not in accordance with the preferences of citizens in low-income countries. The monolithic form of integration of the EU not allowing for any exceptions (like opt outs) can be harmful for CEE. Also, the commitment to those policies will not necessarily enhance the credibility of transformation and investor confidence. On the contrary, investors interested in long-term cost advantages might rather avoid those locations which in the medium and long term will converge with high-regulation EU countries.

The third group of EU policies affecting transformation countries is the redistributive policies, especially agricultural and regional policy.[65] CEE countries can expect to benefit considerably from those policies, given their elevated share of agriculture and their low level of income.[66] Therefore, participation in those policies can reduce the social costs of transformation and structural adjustment and can lead to higher investment (like the Cohesion Fund's investment in infrastructure and environmental projects in Southern European countries) and so presents a major incentive to join the EU and adapt to its rules. But this incentive is not unambiguous: The distorting effects of agricultural policy in the EU are well-known, and the effects of regional policies on the convergence process are at best mixed. From a point of view of institutional competition, redistributive policies reduce the incentive to implement institutional change. The case of Greece is often cited as an example, where generous EU aid led to a delay of structural adjustment rather than to its enforcement (Schäfers, 1993).

While the influence of institutional imitation according to the three groups discussed above is mixed for transformation countries, a second important aspect concerns the implementation of policies. Here, institutional imitation seems to provide three advantages: One is the previously cited commitment to already successful policies. Countries preparing to enter the EU will have fewer credibility problems in a number of policies, e.g. macroeconomic stabilization, where confidence and expectations are important. The second aspect is the domestic impact of EU membership application: Those transformation policies which are politically costly, like the hardening of the budget constraint and implementation of bankruptcy law with the following increase in unemployment, can be justified by

65 For the impact of regional funds see Szemler (2001); for the CAP see Jensen/Frandsen (2001).

66 See Baldwin (1995), Achten (1996: 151-189) and Pautola (1997). According to some estimates, the annual transfers for the first group of accession countries (for example Poland, Hungary, the Czech Republic and the Slovak Republic) might be as much as 60 billion euros. Given the annual difficulty in compromising on the EU budget even now, such a transfer seems to be highly unlikely. 'Re-nationalisation' is one of the possible and often cited solutions to this problem; see Rabinowicz (2002).

necessity of EU application.[67] The perspective and reality of market opening and increased competition is also an incentive to speed up corporate restructuring. This can be compared with those countries not applying for membership, where an alternative to corporate restructuring is lobbying for extended soft budget constraint (subsidies) and protective legislation.

The third aspect is more technical, but nevertheless important. Applicant countries – through the structured dialogue, transformation partnerships, and the negotiation process with the EU, including regular monitoring – constantly improve their administrative capabilities. One bottleneck in transformation countries is the lack of sufficiently skilled administration to implement transformation steps. The enlargement process can widen the bottleneck. Again, this is complemented by changes in the private sector, where FDI has a similar role (i.e. the private sector also must be skilled in applying the new regulatory framework, which is easier with the management transfer linked to FDI).

To summarise, in CEE countries applying for EU membership and in East Germany, similar problems arose: Institutional imitation (or transfer) was beneficial or problematic according to the policy area in which it was applied. The only difference was the immediate effect in the case of German reunification, while in the case of CEE there was a longer time delay and therefore maybe the desire for cartelisation was less pronounced from the point of view of the previous EU member states, which could prepare for accession.[68] Institutional competition, while closing the 'window of opportunity' opened by whole-scale transformation, also stabilized expectations of market participants and political deciders. The *acquis communautaire* comprised institutions obviously inappropriate for transformation countries, but as a whole it worked as a stabilizer for transformation countries.

The countries in the CIS and some of the other transformation countries were not applying for membership in the EU. However, also they are not completely free in their transformation path. Restrictions arise especially from the conditionality of IMF programmes, which almost all transformation countries concluded. Fund arrangements include so-called structural benchmarks concerning structural adjustment and long-term macroeconomic viability as well as performance crite-

---

67 In the early debate about political-economic aspects of transformation, the problem of the social costs of macroeconomic stabilization and corporate restructuring were often discussed as major obstacle for governments; see for example Dewatripont/Roland (1992). While governments indeed frequently changed, all (regardless of being post-communist or liberal) did not reverse reforms. Commitments to EU membership may have helped. In at least one country not applying for membership, Belarus, a reversal took place, and in others corporate restructuring was halted.

68 Also, the longer the period of negotiations and before accession, the higher the probability that productivity and income convergence makes institutional competition with unrestricted flows of factors less intense.

ria, i.e. numerical floors or ceilings placed on various macroeconomic policy instruments or outcomes (Mercer-Blackman/Unigovskaya, 2000). While these were restrictions, the character is quite different from those imposed by application for EU membership. The reason for IMF programmes was mostly financial assistance. Once initial financial assistance was granted or an immediate financial crisis is avoided, there is a certain incentive to 'free ride' and abandon conditionality.[69] In EU application this incentive is absent, since membership means permanent obligations and commitments.[70] Therefore, countries not applying for EU membership are free in institutional choice. While it allows for innovation, it is linked to the problem of an absence of benchmarks and guidelines that leaves countries without orientation in their transformation path.[71]

3.5 Outlook – some results and an agenda for future research

The comparison of institutional transformation in the former GDR with applicant countries to the EU and other transformation countries is difficult, since the institutional performance as such was not directly measurable. Also, the causality of results was not always clear: Was a superior growth performance linked to initial preconditions, to sound policies or to institutional imitation or innovation? Were countries applying for EU membership since they already achieved considerable systemic change, or was systemic change dependent on policies implemented for accession to the EU?[72] The same problem of causality arose in comparing single performance indicators. For instance, is a deep but early transformational recession crisis a sign of fast institutional change (requiring old, unprofitable industries to disappear) and a mild recession a sign of delayed adjustment? Or did those countries

69 For example, Belarus, Bulgaria, Kazakhstan, the Kyrgyz Republic, Romania, Ukraine and Uzbekistan had IMF programs going 'off track'.

70 This does not mean that countries with an application for membership always honored their commitments and proceeded in transformation. It only means that this could not be a successful strategy, since there is no such "free lunch" to gain, as in the case of IMF assistance.

71 See for the case of Russia vs. CEE Sutela (2000). Sutela maintains that missing commitment to reform is the main explanatory factor in the lagging performance of Russia compared with countries applying for EU membership.

72 Empirically, both can be observed: In some cases like Albania or some successor states of Yugoslavia, political turmoil and economic backwardness obviously makes an early application seem futile. On the other hand, countries committed early to reform could also use EU application for internal reforms and steps sometimes far beyond those of their neighbours, as in the case of Slovenia.

avoiding a deep initial slump do a better job in implementing institutional change appropriate for their conditions?

Nevertheless, by now it seems to be more and more clear that countries applying for EU membership have reached a far more favorable position than those outside of the EU accession track. Comparing the experience of East Germany, the only transformation country already inside the EU and experiencing complete institutional transfer, the following preliminary conclusions can be drawn: Clearly, reunification and the massive transfers following it meant that the social costs of transformation experienced in CEE could be avoided to some extent. And due to massive investments in infrastructure, some of the bottlenecks in transformation countries could also be avoided. This is evidenced also in the elevated GDP per capita.[73] However, the convergence process of East and West German income considerably slowed down in 1995, pointing to long-term problems of institutional transfer, namely the acceptance of institutional cartels working to obstruct more favorable arrangements in transformation countries to reduce possible competitive pressure. The challenge for East Germany involves the resumption of the convergence process through a breakup of those rigidities hindering it.[74]

Transformation countries cannot pick only those regulations that seem to be favorable for them, but have to accept the whole *acquis communautaire.* In the first years of transformation this might give them the advantage of a clear goal, a clear commitment and sufficient technical assistance to achieve superior results over transformation countries without such a goal. However, in the long run there might be the problem of a possible slowing of convergence due to these arrangements. Those countries not applying for EU membership suffered from the lack of credibility of their transformation programs. For them, shadowing the EU institutions aimed at establishing a market economy and announcing such a policy publicly was a possible strategy to import some of the EU's stability while avoiding those policies reducing the flexibility of markets.

---

73 The net wages in East Germany were in 1997 around 85 percent of the Western wages. The GDP per capita in purchasing power was estimated at around 22,700 USD in 1998 for Germany (East and West). In 1997 the GDP per capita in the East was reported to be 54.3 percent of the West German GDP.

74 The massive exit of East German employers from the employers association bargaining for wages far too high for the low level of productivity that occurred in the former GDR is an example of a spontaneous reaction to such rigidities.

Chapter 4: Area Studies and the Theory of Economic Transformation – from Uneasy Coexistence to Integration?

4.1 Area studies and social sciences – an uneasy coexistence

The debate between area specialists and social scientists is in times of tight science and university budgets especially hard, but has deeper, methodological roots. Area specialists for example accuse economists of economic imperialism, using mathematical tools in a "one size fits all" way, and thereby loosing important information about the characteristics of a region and disregarding the cultural and environmental background of regional development. Social scientists blame area studies for using a non-scientific approach and point out important failures of area specialists to predict and interpret regional development. However, on a closer inspection both area studies and social sciences failed to anticipate major economic, social and political changes like transformation in Central and Eastern Europe (CEE) and the breakup of the Soviet Union. The same is true for other major changes in politics and economics in other world regions, like the Asian financial crisis in 1997 or the radicalisation of Islamic groups since the late 1980s.

So both area studies and social sciences need a new approach which helps them to integrate the strengths of both fields. As an economist, in this discussion I will look back mainly at the relation between area studies and economics, since this is the area of my expertise. But I am sure that for the relation between area studies and other social sciences, the analysis would follow a similar pattern. In economics, heterodox approaches, which came to the fore in the development of transition economics over the last two decades, can be a useful starting point of an attempted integration, as we shall see later. This chapter proposes an integration of these theories to overcome ultimately the gap between social sciences and area studies. In the second section, there is a short overview of the debate between area studies and social sciences. The third section discusses heterodox approaches in economic science, useful for a more comprehensive view of the problem of the economic analysis of regions. Section four outlines the integration of these approaches.

4.2 The 'area studies debate' revisited

According to a standard reference, "[t]he basic concept of area studies is that the people of a definable geographical sector, acting in their society and their environment, offer an appropriate unit for scholarly attention" (Wood 1968, p. 401). Given the large number of area studies programmes and research centres, this might seem obvious. However, area studies are a relatively new development compared with social sciences. The rise of area studies began with the integration of language programmes *cum* social science specializations in the United States in and after World War II. The programmes, often in close collaboration with the Office of Strategic Services, the forerunner of the CIA, were the answer to the necessity of educating specialists for regional developments in war zones, occupied zones, and, during the Cold War, more and more in regions which were considered potential zones of conflict as well as actual adversaries.[75] The institutionalization of area studies programmes and research centres after the war was the beginning of academic competition as well as cooperation of area studies and social sciences. While the conflict was, especially in times of tight university budgets, about departmental organization and research funds, it also had deeper methodological roots. Area studies tried to formulate a programme of studying an area, for example the Soviet Union, by integrating economic and political aspects, which were the traditional focus of social science disciplines, with a deeper understanding of the area, understood as a cultural and geographic concept. Practically, this led to a number of problems and criticisms of area studies (see Samuels/Weiner 1992).

One important problem was the influence of the culture of the area specialist, the observer, on the formulation of the problems and theories of a region with a distinctly different culture. The so-called reflexive turn in sociological and anthropological research stresses this problem and, in its most radical version, completely denies the possibility of doing cross-cultural research at all. A second problem is the exclusive definition of the culture of an area, which tries to find and analyze a "pure" culture of the area, negating the influences of overlapping, sometimes contradictory, cultures in the same area, and even the same individual. To make the concept of culture operational, a certain form of distinction between cultures is necessary. In anthropology, Clark Wissler, Halford Mackin-

---

75 The collaboration of area studies with the intelligence community in the Cold War led to criticisms of intellectually compromising ideological activity; see Cumings (1998) for an interesting overview of the development of area studies programmes in and after World War II. However, his distinction between honorable, pure collaboration in World War II and dirty collaboration afterward seems itself to be ideologically determined.

der and Paul Vidal de la Blache introduced the concept of "cultural area", and in ethnology Fritz Graebner, Wilhelm Schmidt, Wilhelm Koppers and Erland Nordenskiold the concept of "*Kulturkreis*." Both concepts can easily lead to a mono-cultural approach, which might be compared with a closed economy approach in economics, not allowing for exchange with other cultural areas.[76]

The problem of such mono-cultural theorizing can be seen in the different waves of Confucianism explanations either for the inability or ability of East Asian countries to develop economically. In studying economic transformation in formerly socialist countries, culture can for example relate to a certain ethnic background (and the related historical experiences as well as cultural-linguistic framework of thinking), an ideological background (like the upbringing in a Communist environment and the related *homo sovieticus* attitudes), a religious background, an organizational background (for example, working for an 'oligarch' or a regional leader), etc., all in the same individual! So, the concept of culture, while being central to an area studies approach, needs to be applied in a way which is not easily operational.

Another problem is the limited access to data and the research region itself (for political reasons, because of language barriers, for geographic reasons and due to time restrictions), reducing the possibility of gaining intimate knowledge of the research region. The necessity of using the official data and documents of the research region had been a major problem of Soviet studies, which still today has major implications not only in terms of studying historical developments of the region, but also in terms of taking stock of current developments of the region. This implies a tendency of defending the *status quo* in a region as well as a predominance of official points of view, a form of collusion with those in power in the area of research.[77] While intimate knowledge of region a might be achievable through concentrating on its culture and language, this automatically will reduce the time available to disciplinary specialization like economics or political science. Area specialists without sufficient disciplinary specialization will have enormous difficulties putting their topic of research into the context of existing research as well as applying the tools and language necessary not only to analyze the topic, but also to publish their work.

The inherent tension between disciplinary (social science) specialization and regional (language, culture and geography) knowledge led to a dispute comparable

76 The problem also was virulent in marketing and management. For a clustering of countries according to cultural characteristics see Ronen/Shenkar (1985).

77 The problem is most acute in non-democratic countries, where certain research projects might even lead to the negation of visa status.

to the *Methodenstreit* in the 19th century.[78] The critique of area studies mainly focuses on the alleged dominance of description instead of explanation, the lack of analytical methods, the lack of interest in generalization, and the dominance of detail questions (Tessler et al., 1999: viii). The controversy of discipline and region, virulent after the expansion of area studies after World War II, was pronounced by the dominance of the "rational choice" paradigm in social sciences since the 1980s, and the increasing use of mathematical models in economics, in particular.[79] On this basis, a fruitful cooperation between area specialists and disciplinary social scientists was less and less possible.

While the disciplinary critiques of area studies, resulting from the difficulties in finding the operational concept of an area and its underlying culture, definitely had some important points to make, neither the process of formulation of their own social science theories, nor their own record of results in terms of applicability of their theories to area-related problems, were particularly impressive. Also, the universal theories of disciplines, for example in economics, are based on a regional context and are, as area specialists retorted, not much more than "parochial studies of an area limited to Western Europe and the United States, masquerading under a universal rubric".[80]

Both area studies and social sciences were twice put to the test in the early 1990s. First, the CEE states began to transform their economies, and in the course of transformation the degree of decline in their economic systems became obvious, a trend about which area specialists as well as social scientists had been unaware. The breakup of the Soviet Union posed problems equally unforeseen by social sciences as well as area studies. And early transformation theories, mainly devised by social sciences when the area specialists still had to recover from the shock of the rapid dismantling of their whole reference system, led to the failure of a universally applicable set of prescriptions, the Washington consensus. The second great test was the East Asian financial and economic crisis, which also radically dismantled a system of belief by area specialists in a certain

78 The *Methodenstreit* (dispute about methods) denotes the debate between the German historical school of economics, esp. Gustav von Schmoller (1838-1917), and the marginal school, esp. Carl Menger (1840-1921), about the correct method to study economics – as a historical science, including the cultural background of economic activities similar to modern area studies, or modeled after natural sciences, applying universally applicable concepts. Cf. the articles on *Methodenstreit* in Eatwell et al. (1987: 454-455), and Kirzner (1960: 14-17). Finally, the marginalists were clearly victorious in this dispute, when the historical school became more and more unable to process or rationally use the large amount of data it collected.

79 For an overview of the "rational choice" controversy between area studies and social sciences see Pye (1975), Johnson/Keehn (1994), Bates et al. (1997).

80 Wood (1968: 401) Tessler et al. (1999: xiv), calls the social scientists adhering to universal theories just "American area specialists".

definition of their topic, the "East Asian developmental model." And, as in the case of transformation of formerly socialist countries, the universal prescriptions by international financial institutions where rewarded with quite mixed results; obviously, they did not fit universally.[81]

One result of these failures was the rising prominence of 'heterodox approaches' in social sciences, which always had existed alongside the mainstream research and which looked, in the case of economics, at exactly some of those areas, where the mainstream had a lack of results: the understanding of economic development not as a universally applied maximisation problem, but through the institutional arrangements shaping the actions of privately maximising agents. These heterodox approaches have already been discussed in Section 2.3. They are the basis for the following reformulated theory of institutional change.

4.3 A reformulated theory of institutional change as a framework for area-related economic analysis

A reformulated theory of economic development and transformation based on a model of institutional competition as outlined above can overcome the puzzles and paradoxes that transformation theory and practice today face. The neglect of institutions and cognitive models lead to the paradox of different outcomes for identical transformation steps. The role of institutions was already the centre of the new institutional economics approach to transformation.[82] Newer studies analyze the relation between formal and informal institutions in transformation (Mummert, 1995/1998). However, the analysis of institutional regimes and their role in human action lead to the question of whether and how these institutions are seen by the actors of transformation itself. Institutions, especially informal institutions, often are not accessible by observation. People form ideas about institutions and about acting in institutions in their minds. These cognitive models were already discussed by North (1990). However, their role in transformation theory was only recently analyzed (Hermann-Pillath, 1998b; Hermann-Pillath, 1999b; Rosenbaum, 1999; Stahl, 1999). The way people see institutions and their choice of actions under institutional regimes are important for a more realistic modelling of the possible role of the state and the role of cultural factors in transformation.

81 While these two tests were mainly in the area of economics, a third test in the area of politics was the rise of radical Islam in the Middle East. Also regarding this phenomenon, area specialists as well as social scientists had difficulties to come up with *ex post* explanations, after being caught unaware *ex ante*.

82 For the role of institutions in transformation see Hermann-Pillath (1994), Riker/Weimer (1995), Liechtenstein (1996), Mummert/Streit (1996), Kozul-Wright/Rayment (1996).

The role of the state has to be readjusted in two ways: First, the modelling of the state as a 'black box' must be revised according to public choice models. The modelling of a market for politics should not stop with the analysis of certain groups maximising votes or budgets, but should lead to a picture as coherent as possible of the forces in this market. That means especially including external relations and constraints on transformation countries. The shaping of institutional development by external influences due to international organizations in an example of this. External influences again are a result of the international political market. Also, the mixture of new and old interest groups in transformation states must be modelled.

This also leads to the second change in the evaluation of the role of the state: The interdependence and simultaneity of political and economic development makes the traditional assumptions about state possibilities for action seem unrealistic. This not only concerns heroic assumptions (like the benevolent welfare-maximising state), but also standard assumptions of the state as owner of the legal power monopoly, and especially the enforcement possibility of state rules (Hermann-Pillath, 1998a). Since the transformation of the state happens simultaneously with economic transformation, the "strong state" often seen as remedy to failures in transformation is an irrelevant, nirvana alternative. This not only concerns the possibility of carrying out efficient industrial policy as a strategy borrowed from East Asian NICs. In addition, the traditional functions of the state, the creation and enforcement of efficient institutions – e.g. in the privatization process, in tax policy and in the labour market – cannot be taken for granted as an assumption. The analysis of "lack of efficient regulation" is a nirvana approach, if it is meant as an external problem in an otherwise optimal transformation strategy (Csaba, 1997: 14).

The endogeneity of institutional change as a result of political and economic development will change the evaluation of successful outcomes of development. Not optimal institutions seen from the viewpoint of existing successful market economies can be seen as the benchmark for transformational success. The creation of new institutions is costly, especially radical institutional change (Polterovich, 1998). Instead, transformation as a process of self-organization seems to be successful, if it leads to long-term viability of a society in institutional competition with other models of organization. Competitiveness in institutional competition or viability again has to be defined differently from (or as an extension of) traditional numerical measurements of economic success like growth rates.[83]

83 Cf. Hermann-Pillath (1998a), and for the concept of viability Boulding (1968) and Prosi (1997). Competitiveness in institutional competition is not only an outcome of formal institutions, and therefore cannot only be measured by comparing them. Specifically, viability should not be confounded with the competitiveness of firms; see Straubhaar (1994) and Küchler (1996). The approach of the European Union in evaluating the convergence of CEE or of the World Competitiveness Forum are problematic in this respect.

A transformation theory analyzing the viability of institutional regimes will also re-evaluate the relation between transformation and regional and international economic integration. While transformation in formerly socialist countries was explained as the outcome of systemic competition, nevertheless the analysis of transformation often concentrated on national institutions and institutional change. However, increased competition through integration does not only affect markets for goods and services, but also institutional regimes. Regional integration can lead to a restriction of possibilities in institutional competition, if integration requires the adaptation of institutions, as is most notably the case with the *acquis communautaire* of the EU (Seliger, 1998).

The discussion of the interrelations between culture and economics has long been established by economic sociology. But the incorporation of sociological and cultural insights – like those of Max Weber – into economic models seems impossible to date. Most economists agree that culture affects economic decisions in important ways, but how can this be related to transformation research? Therefore, culture must not be confined too narrowly to business culture, but rather seen as a phenomenon related to all those phenomena which are not yet fully explained by traditional analysis (Herrmann-Pillath, 1999a: 15). While the study of business culture is different from the meaning of culture here as the human-made environment, in which economic decisions are embedded, it can be very useful as a starting point, since it developed methods – or more often borrowed them from other social sciences – to classify and analyse culture.[84] The problem of explaining diverging development paths despite identical development strategies has emerged as a core problem of mainstream economics (Mankiw, 1995: 275). Therefore, the integration of research into cultural aspects of transformation economics has recently been demanded (Boettke, 1999).

The difficulties begin if one wants to define the cultural factors of economic development.[85] The virtual omnipresence of cultural phenomena can lead to the fallacy of modelling it as a residual factor similar to the modelling of technical progress in early growth theories. Culture must be specified in its concrete meaning using the research already done by other social sciences.[86] While therefore the specification of culture seems required, the actual task of narrowing down the

84 This is especially true for intercultural studies on management in the tradition of Hofstede (1980) and marketing; for an overview see Hodgetts/Luthans (1997: 95-182) and Onkvisit/Shaw (1997: 203-247).

85 These difficulties are experienced by all social sciences interested in cultural phenomena; see Williamson (1958 and 1981).

86 Herrmann-Pillath (1999a: 2-10), discusses pitfalls in the integration of culture into economic models.

notion culture is difficult.[87] The definition of a cultural "core" of constitutive characteristics, established by historical, anthropological, sociological and socio-psychological research, might be a way to overcome definitorial difficulties (Herrmann-Pillath, 1999b: 6-19). This cultural core is shared by all members of a particular society, but is not always known to them.[88] An important caveat to be made is not to apply culture deterministically. People can belong to different cultures, here not used in the sense of Herder as different national cultures, but to different cultures according to their social position, religious affiliation, ethnic background, etc. While the classification of behaviour in post-socialist countries as "*homo sovieticus*" can be enlightening, it would be dangerous to ignore the numerous different cultures (for example, *nomenklatura*, dissidents, ethnic minorities, industrial working class or service industry) in which people are embedded. Furthermore, these affiliations are not clear-cut, and the affiliation with several of these cultural subgroups is possible.

Among the most important elements of an economic system necessary to be analyzed are the formal and informal institutions.[89] Formal institutions are determined on the "market of institutions" of a country, which is a metaphor for the interaction of the markets for politics workers and investors, which choose by voice in democracies (elections, demonstrations and political debate), as well as by exit options (like migration and capital flight). The exit option relates the market for politics with the markets for goods and services. Interest groups take a mediating position between the supply and demand side, being characterized by asymmetrical information vis-à-vis both groups. Institutional alternatives become clear through exit and voice, i.e. institutional competition. The intensity of institutional competition depends on international as well as national regimes, for example trade. Globalization increased the intensity dramatically.

Informal institutions together with the formal institutions determine the economic system. They are central to understanding the performance of formal institutions. They are not static, but their change is piecemeal and slow. This is an important reason for the different results of the same formal institutions in different regions. The effectiveness of informal institutions, which are not enforced by the state monopoly for power, is dependent on the perception of market actors

87 Cf. Aleksandrowicz (1998). Aleksandorwicz therefore proposes to confine the notion culture to intuitive knowledge about the classes of objects belonging to it.

88 As Selma Lagerlöf once put it, culture is "what remains when that which has been learned is entirely forgotten." So while culture itself is a learned behaviour, it remains active even if an individual acquires new or different new knowledge.

89 While the definition of both is not universal, mostly they are distinguished by their enforcement mechanism (state monopoly in the case of formal, and private, decentralized enforcement by social norms, customs or other arrangements in the case of informal institutions).

about their legitimacy. Therefore, another factor for economic change and stability of an economic system becomes important, namely the perceptions the actors have about its functioning. Since market actors (as well as external observers) have no complete information, they formulate hypotheses about the functioning of the economic system, which determine their choice of goals and instruments. These hypotheses are again depending on cognitive schemata, which help the actors to reduce uncertainty in the face of incomplete information. When hypotheses are permanently frustrated, new hypotheses will be built. This does not automatically lead to a different action: As long as the enforcement mechanism for informal institutions works, opportunistic behaviour can prevail. However, this also means that relatively small changes in the perception of institutions can have large effects, if a critical mass for institutional change is reached, like during the transformation processes in formerly socialist states.

To understand the change of economic systems, first the relevant market for formal institutions has to be analyzed. This market is on the one side embedded in the context of international institutional competition, on the other side related to informal institutions in a functional relation. An equilibrium of expectations in an economy can be defined as the state, when *grosso modo* the expectations of actors about the functioning of institutions are not frustrated. These expectations again are dependent on cognitive schemata of actors about these institutions. These schemata, which are dependent on self-perception and the perceptions of others, are until now barely analyzed.

The equilibrium of expectations should not be confounded with a normatively optimal state of the economy. Stable expectations also can exist in face of dictatorship and economic decline, but permanent macroeconomic imbalances or crises will one day also lead to a crisis of the economic model.[90] The crisis of the model leads to transformation, which has again two aspects: namely the intended consequences initiated for example by the state to transform the economic system, and the often more important unintended consequences.[91] The unintended consequences are for example depending on the relation of formal and informal institutions or on the perception of human actors of the changed institutions. Looking at the change of economic systems from such a point of view also allows one to draw normative conclusions concerning the adaptive efficiency of an economic system. The following figure includes the different aspects discussed above in a framework for the analysis of economic change.

90 Economic model not understood in the sense of a Weberian ideal type, but as the model the actors have of an economy.

91 Cf. Hayek (1969). The analysis of unintended consequences of human actions is for Hayek the foremost aim of social science, cf. Hayek (1979: 41).

Figure 1: The Basic Market of Institutions Model

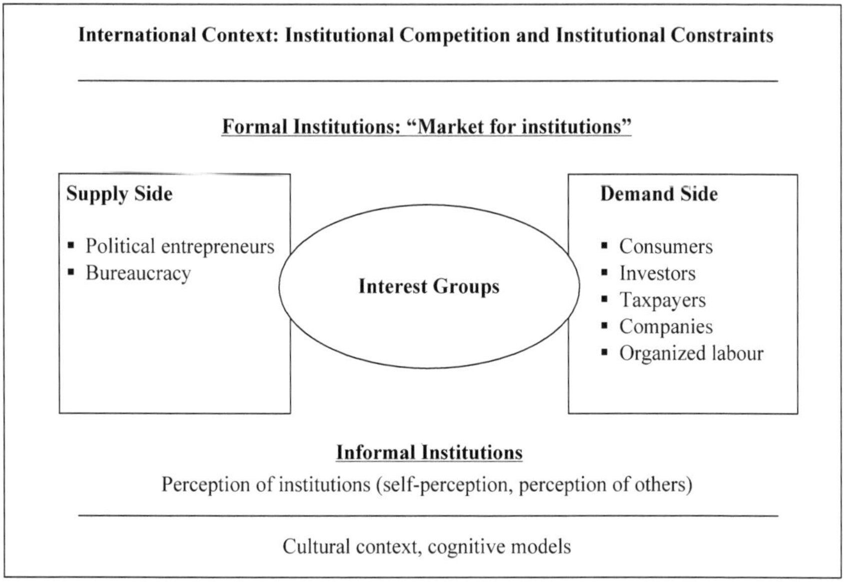

Source: The author.

4.4 Conclusion: Toward the integration of area studies and social sciences research

This chapter tried to outline a new research approach that integrates area studies and social sciences, which now live in a form of uneasy coexistence. A comprehensive analysis faces many difficulties. Ideally, it should be carried out by an interdisciplinary and cross-cultural team. It would require resources and time, and an enormous amount of learning, given a greater variety of theoretical approaches, the difficulty of integrating these approaches without committing the fallacy of opportunistic eclecticism (i.e. taking always those bits of a theory fitting nicely into a research purpose, while disregarding others), and also learning across disciplinary boundaries. All of this seems to be an unreachable ideal. But the fact that a comprehensive view of the problem is difficult to achieve does not mean that it is meaningless. It can give important new directions for further research and the improvement of existing research.

Part 2
The Korean Financial and Economic Crisis – a Short Review

Chapter 5: A Review of Five Years of DJnomics: Understanding the Economic Crisis in South Korea as a Transformation Crisis of its Political and Economic Culture

5.1 The Korean economic crisis and reform process – an overview

The economic development of Korea was long characterized by isolation. For the past 3,000 years, Korea has been ethnically and culturally homogenous, and the current North Korean-Chinese border has remained unchanged for centuries. Exchange with the outside world was rare and only happened through the nominal suzerain China and limited interaction with Japan. Only in the last quarter of the nineteenth century did Western pressure finally open the country. After a period of increasing Japanese involvement, Korea became a Japanese colony in 1910 and did not regain independence until 1945. Economically, Korea was deeply transformed by its period as a Japanese resource colony (especially for rice from South Korea and mining products from North Korea). To further enhance their exploitation, the Japanese modernized the economic structure in Korea. Korean general trading companies (*chaebol*) followed the Japanese *keiretsu* model, and, after liberalization, became the backbone of Korean industry.

After World War II and the division of Korea into two occupation zones, followed by the Korean War which caused extensive destruction to large parts of the country, North and South Korea took divergent economic paths. North Korea built a Stalinist economic system characterized by central planning, shortage and – after the breakup of the Soviet Union – famine. Ideologically, it was built upon the *juche* idea of extreme isolation and autarky. In the South, the political situation was unstable, with a succession of dictatorships and only slow progress toward democracy until the 1980s. In spite of its political instability, the burgeoning South Korean economy since the 1960s became the "miracle on the Han river." In the 1950s, after the Korean War, Korea tried to substitute imported goods with domestically produced goods. Together with a corrupt and weak leadership, the economic results of this policy were disappointing. However, under the Park Chung Hee dictatorship and its five-year plans, the interest shifted toward export orientation and selective liberalization. From 1963 to 1971, manufacturing was promoted, followed by the encouragement of heavy industry, chemical production, and shipbuilding later in the 1970s. As earnings from exports rose in the 1980s, the issue of macroeconomic stability in a fast-growing economy became important. The democratization since 1987 brought further liberalization of the economy. While the export orientation meant the production of goods competitive in price and quality on world markets, Korea's import policy had only been selectively liberalized (for intermediate goods and raw materials important for Korean industry).

The share of trade in GDP increased from one-third in 1970 to two-thirds in 1985. Korea's integration in the world economy and membership in international economic organizations like GATT (now the WTO) and the OECD since 1997 made further opening of the market inevitable. However, even then, many markets in Korea remain relatively closed. The market for automotives was a good example, with a foreign share in domestic sales of far less than 1 percent. Economic development since the 1960s has been characterized by great success. The average growth rate during the period was more than 8 percent annually. In 1995, GDP per capita was more than 10,000 USD, almost double the Malaysian GDP and more than ten times the Indonesian GDP. Inflation and unemployment were low, and this even brought problems, because since 1977 labour shortages had been routine. The state budget was mostly balanced. For manufactured goods, Korea was one of the most important exporters in the 1990s; for instance, Korean was the largest producer of semiconductors, the second largest shipbuilder and fifth largest car producer. The workforce gradually transformed from unskilled, low-wage labour to highly skilled labour, engaged in more capital-intensive production. It is therefore not surprising when the World Bank's 1993 report on the "East Asian miracle" spoke of the impressive macroeconomic situation in Korea.

While overall economic development was very successful, several problems appeared over time. State intervention was much less successful than Western and Korean observers sometimes believed. The Economic Planning Board, with a functional role similar to the famous Japanese Ministry of International Trade and Industry, made some severe mistakes. Its strategy to promote heavy and chemical industry led to overcapacities and a severe recession in 1981 in the midst of a global oil price shock. More importantly, Korean companies, encouraged by the government, followed a strategy of growth at all costs. Growth rather than profitability was the primary goal of these companies. Financing growth requires high rates of investment, and although Korea maintained a domestic savings rate much higher than that of other developed countries, domestic capital was insufficient. Credit hunger led to increased financing via the international capital market. Thus, Korean companies became more dependent on the trust of foreign investors. At the beginning of the crisis in 1997, Korean foreign debt totaled 120 billion USD. Although the "Asian hype" in the early 1990s brought massive capital inflows, they were mainly short-term investments. Long-term investments in the form of foreign direct investment (FDI) was inhibited by restrictive laws and the mistrust and animosity of Korean consumers and government, due to a mixture of economic nationalism – especially concerning the fear of Japanese domination – and the desire to guard protected national markets. To circumvent these obstacles, Korean companies used short-term debts to finance long-term investment, which caused sharp increases in their debt-to-equity levels. For example, Kia Motors had a debt-to-equity level of 520 percent in 1997, and the 30 largest *chaebol* had an average level of 330 percent.

The costs of servicing these debts greatly reduced the profitability of many projects. According to estimates of the Hyundai Economic Research Institute, the 12 Korean companies ranking among the world's 500 largest companies had some of the lowest profitability indicators among the 500 companies. *Chaebol* had the biggest share in Korean economic growth, and the 30 largest ones produced approximately 80 percent of Korean GDP. In addition to low profitability, many *chaebol* diversified without following a coherent strategy. For example, the fur maker Jindo – which went bankrupt in 1998 – had container, automotive parts, construction, waste management and retail subsidiaries. The five biggest *chaebol* in 1997 (Hyundai Group, Daewoo, Samsung Group, SK Corporation and LG CORPORATION) each had more than 100 subsidiaries, but only 10 to 20 percent of them were profitable. Internal cross-subsidization of a conglomerate's subsidiaries was the norm. This allowed also unprofitable business to stay in the market and reduced the allocative efficiency of the Korean economy. The lack of transparency in their business organization, caused by ties among families, financial institutions and areas of the media, led to allegations of 'crony capitalism'. State-mandated mergers created additional problems. Since the 1960s, the state arranged for healthy companies to merge with weak or bankrupt companies to minimize social problems like unemployment. For example, when the Gukje group, the 9th biggest *chaebol*, went bankrupt in 1985, it was taken over by Hanil group, the 17th biggest *chaebol*, but the state set up a fund for Hanil to cope with the merger.[92] This furthered the irrational growth of companies and the subsidization of unprofitable subsidiaries. The banking sector furthered this unhealthy growth. State banks (and after privatization, the banks with strong ties to the state)

92 It should be noted that bankruptcy did not happen often, since the state intervened before bankruptcy. Gukje is one of the few cases, which like Yulsan went bankrupt in 1978 when the government allowed for bankruptcy, due to political reasons. Gukje did not spend enough money on the ruling party, and Yulsan was said to be supporting opposition groups. But the restructuring of weak industries through mergers also occurred, for example during the crisis at the end of the 1970s, in the machine building, steel, chemical, electronics, shipbuilding and automobile industries.

granted credit based on political rather economic criteria. Eventually, dozens of banks, inundated with souring loans during the Asian crisis, faced bankruptcy.

The economic crisis in East Asia began as a crisis of trust among investors. In mid-1997, the highly speculative real estate market in Thailand crashed, and afterward stock exchanges and currencies in Southeast Asia tumbled one after another like dominoes. The currencies pegged to the dollar were highly overvalued and experienced depreciation of up to 60 percent. Korea had initially avoided the 'Asian flu'. In July 1997, however, several Korean companies like Kia Motors, Hanbo Iron & Steel and Jindo became insolvent. Partly due to 'contagion' from Thailand, Malaysia and Indonesia, and partly due to domestic factors such as the worsening situation in domestic capital and financial markets, the credit rating of South Korea was downgraded by major rating agencies such as Moody's and Standard & Poor's. Finally, in November 1997, Korea caught the flu, and the won dived.

November 21 saw South Korea follow the path of Thailand and Indonesia by asking the IMF for help. On December 3, Korea received the largest financial aid package ever drawn up by the IMF, worth 57 billion USD. The conditions for the package were severe: comprehensive structural reform of the economy and financial sector; state austerity policies; transparency; and opening to foreign investment. In 1998, Korea, like the other Asian crisis countries, suffered a severe recession. The GDP growth rate plummeted from more than 5 percent in 1997 to minus 6 percent in 1998, a post-war negative record in Korea. GDP per capita sank from 10,000 to 6,500 USD. Most importantly, unemployment stood at 8 percent, up from 2.7 percent in the preceding year, and the social safety net was practically nonexistent.

Everywhere in East Asia the causes of the crisis were hotly debated. As early as mid-1997, Malaysian President Mahathir spoke of "rogue capital" as being responsible for the crisis. He restricted capital movements and demanded an end to international currency speculation. In Korea, too, international investors and organizations were seen as scapegoats. Accordingly the crisis was dubbed the "IMF crisis". The financial crisis of 1997 and the following economic recession also had political consequences. In February 1998, Kim Dae Jung and his National Congress for New Politics (later called the Millennium Democratic Party) succeeded the former President Kim Young Sam and the Grand National Party. Kim Young Sam, linked to Kim Dae Jung through their common status as fighters for democracy, was the first civilian president in decades who tried to liberalize and modernize the economy beginning in 1993. However, his attempts failed due to the strong resistance from the bureaucracy and the *chaebol*. In 1994, the Kim Young Sam administration issued an industrial specialization plan to tackle the problem of growing overcapacity, for example, in steel production. The failure of this plan showed the paradoxical dilemma of relations between the state and business. On the one hand, the old model of the state governing the *chaebol* was no longer possible due to the size of the conglomerates. But on the other hand, the *chaebol* were still dependent on the state, and the state was unable to deny assistance, since *chaebol* were for political reasons 'too big to fail'.

During the crisis, the Kim Young Sam government made some mistakes. The government tried to maintain the unrealistic exchange rate of the won against the dollar, thereby aggravating speculation in the currency, which lead to its eventual fall. Eager to avoid bad press, the government did not correctly inform the public about the steady depletion of foreign exchange reserves. Consequently, the government's request for IMF assistance came as a shock and humiliation to many Koreans. A few months after he took over office, Kim Dae Jung and his government developed a reform program, which was publicized by the Ministry of Finance and the Economy as "DJnomics", named after the initials of President Kim Dae Jung.[93] Based on strict adherence to IMF conditions (which were relaxed several times due to Korea's worsening economic situation), the core of the reforms is the "four plus one" policy. This policy involved the simultaneous reform of the labour market, the financial sector, the public sector and the private sector, together with the opening of Korea's markets to foreign competition.

The first project of "four plus one" was the reform of the labour market, which was formerly characterized by strong antagonism between activist trade unions and powerful employers. In the late 1980s and early 1990s, following their legalization, trade unions frequently resorted to long and sometimes violent strikes to gain wage raises far above productivity levels. Negotiations between employers and trade unions lacked a legal framework and institutional routine. Under the reform program, tripartite (government-business-labour) negotiations were institutionalized, which allowed for more consensus-oriented negotiations. While strike threats are frequent and the tripartite negotiations often break down in some sectors, the labour negotiations after the crisis improved dramatically overall, especially in 1999 and 2000, as measured by the much lower number of strikes in these years. The *de facto* guarantee of lifelong employment, which existed before the crisis in the *chaebol*, has ceased. However, this brought new problems, including the need to increase the scope of the social welfare net. In previous times of crisis, families were still strong enough to act as a natural welfare net, but today, especially in Seoul and other major cities where traditional family structures are disappearing, provisions like extended unemployment benefit schemes and health care schemes are necessary. These measures have to be balanced against the financial strain they impose on state or company coffers.

93 The MOFE, which absorbed the influential former Economic Planning Board, was the main government body formulating economic policies in Korea.

With the worsening economic outlook in 2001 and 2002, the climate in the labour market changed again. The gradual introduction of a five-day work week, which will have an impact not only on the economy, but also on Korean society, is a highly contested issue, while unemployment remains low. While the strength of trade unions is low in terms of the overall economy, they remain a frequently cited obstacle for foreign investors.[94]

The second part of the reforms concerns the financial sector, which showed its weaknesses in the crisis when numerous banks and financial institutions went bankrupt. Banks, insurance companies and investment trust funds were all riddled with bad loans. As part of the IMF conditions, partial interests in Seoul Bank and Korea First Bank were sold to foreign investors to guarantee a freer market and increased competition. However, negotiations with foreign investors were slow and problematic, since the foreign buyers wanted government guarantees on bad debts, while the government wanted to prevent the Korean public from having the impression it was selling off Korean assets cheap, as well as employment guarantees. Ultimately, only massive state subsidies made the deals possible. Overall, the financial reform is the weakest part of the reform program. The subsequent bankruptcy of Daewoo and near-bankruptcy of Hyundai led to massive new debt problems. While the state funded the financial industry with huge sums (40 billion USD until 1999), Japan prolonged the crisis when its financial bubble burst in the early 1990s, showing that a banking crisis without the will for restructuring can last well over a decade. The 'too big to fail' mentality for companies like Daehan Investment Trust means that the state has to stabilize companies in order to prevent a breakdown of the whole financial market. This mentality leads to a moral hazard problem, when the assurance of government aid in case of need coupled with lax supervision by investors reduces the incentives for companies to independently engage in restructuring.

The third group of reforms was of the public sector, which was characterized by a strong bureaucracy in the Confucian tradition that acted closely with the *chaebol.* While the meritocratic bureaucracy in Korea's history was held in high esteem, the problems of corruption and favouritism as a result of its dominant position were well-known. The two last military rulers, Chun Do Hwan and Roh Tae U, have been convicted of corruption involving several hundred million dollars. Also, after democratization corruption flourished, as shown by the 1997 bribes-for-loans scandal at Hanbo Iron & Steel Company, one of the events directly preceding the Korean financial crisis. In 1999, the Berlin-based NGO Transparency International ranked Korea 50th out of the 99 nations analyzed,

94 This is the result of an empirical study recently carried out among European companies investing in Korea under my supervision; see Kang (2002).

compared with rank 32 for Malaysia, 28th for Taiwan and 7th for Singapore.[95] Even theoretically, one would expect a negative correlation of income and corruption (the richer a nation becomes, the less corruption there is), Korea has a high level of corruption given the nation's relatively high level of wealth. The government has tried to resolve this problem from two angles. First, deregulation and privatization make corruption pay off less: In private companies free from state involvement, only profits count. Second, an anticorruption commission was formed to erase corruption in office. This second part, however, has been inhibited by the frequent cases of corruption in the government itself, most visibly in the indictment of two sons and other relatives of President Kim Dae Jung. Another aspect of public sector reform is increased transparency and the reduction of red tape. Here again, DJnomics has been successful, reducing the number of business regulations by half and thereby reducing the necessity and scope for corruption.

The last reform is the reform of the private sector, especially of the debt-ridden, secretive *chaebol* and their system of maintaining unprofitable businesses by cross-subsidization. Here again, results of the reform were mixed. While cross subsidies almost disappeared and debt-equity ratios have fallen due to the improved economic situation in 1999, many *chaebol* have only superficially reformed, as the Daewoo and Hyundai cases show. In Hyundai's case in particular, it became clear that even after formal reorganization, the firm's strong old family ties did not disappear.

Together with the four major reform programs, the process of opening the market to foreign competitors began. In some sectors, state regulations that acted as obstacles to trade were abolished. In the tourism industry, for instance, foreign firms previously were not allowed to invest in Seoul area, and in the alcohol trade, discriminatory taxes against foreign brands were eliminated. In other sectors, such as the wholesale and retail systems, the *de facto* oligopolistic Korean market structure made market opening necessary.[96]

FDI is the field where the reform policy has brought major successful changes. For a long time, Korea had been hostile to foreign investment.[97] While the Kim Young San administration gradually lowered barriers to investment, the Kim Dae Jung administration more boldly opened markets and aggressively wooed FDI. Not only does FDI mean an inflow of capital, it also involves injections of management expertise, or technological capability. This was not only

95 Transparency International ranks countries according to a Corruption Perception Index, in terms of the degree to which countries are perceived to be the home of bribe-taking governments; for more information see www.transparency.de.

96 Non-tariff barriers include for example long delays in granting permits to build supermarkets for non-Korean chainstores like Wal-Mart or Tesco.

97 For a discussion see Kim H.-K. (1999).

seen as instrumental in overcoming the currency and financial crisis, but also in furthering Korean efforts to restructure its ailing corporate and financial sectors. Besides FDI, portfolio investment in Korea has also increased.[98] Portfolio investment does not aim at exerting influence on management. Nevertheless, companies desiring to attract and maintain foreign investment will give greater attention to the shareholder value and therefore also try to upgrade their management system. Overall, the opening of the Korean market for FDI has been a success, even if numerous problems with regulations, like ambiguity of the tax code, cumbersome customs and import procedures, and widely differing interpretations of regulations by different authorities, remained obstacles (Kim J.-D., 1999).

Generally, the economic policy of the Kim Dae Jung administration was successful compared with the policies of other Asian nations during and after the crisis. Thailand, the country first hit by the crisis, was still in a prolonged slump. Indonesia had been on the brink of civil war and slowly disintegrating politically, with the respective negative economic consequences. Malaysia, while being more stable than some of its neighbours, had poorer economic results than Korea and its restrictive economic policy made capital investors turn their back on the once attractive country. The success of the Korean economy can not only be shown by the return of confidence of consumers and investors, but also by the rise of various market indices and the return of growth. One even more important factor is the successful drive for FDI, a new policy of the Kim Dae Jung era. The record levels of FDI were a positive factor changing the Korean economy in the long run, through technology transfer, changes in business culture and competitive pressure in the domestic Korean market. This was also the ultimate reason behind the new policy of transforming Korea into a "hub of East Asia".[99]

Notwithstanding the success of the overall reform policy, important problems remained unsolved. The success of South Korea's reforms hinged upon their completion, but forces behind continued reforms are waning. In part, the economic recovery described above has cancelled out the immediacy and pressure for change. Paradoxically, because South Korea successfully overcame the crisis, it lost interest in more far-reaching reforms with their attendant hardships, especially in the private sector. Unfortunately, two years of reform have been not enough to affect the deep changes required to cure the problems of important sectors such as investment trust companies, in which reforms were superficial. The danger also lied in the government's unwillingness to take the political risk of pushing through unpopular but necessary reforms shortly before elections. Since the general elections in April

98 As of the end of August 2000, foreign investment in the stock market amounted to 75.2 trillion won, the equivalent of 30.1 percent of the total market capitalization; see Yu (2000).

99 While the success of this policy is questionable, it is definitely an important argument for domestic reforms; see Seliger (2002a).

2000, Korea has lost the reform momentum. A revival of this drive was unlikely given that the next presidential election is already looming. Maybe the government can carry out a policy based mainly on low interest rates and large public infusions to indebted companies for some time. In the long run, however, this reluctance to pursue the reforms to their final conclusion may provoke another crisis, causing even greater losses to the Korean national economy.

Another important problem that remains unresolved is the never-ending reform story of the *chaebol,* with their issues of corporate governance and debt workouts. So-called "big-deals", forced mergers of firms, are not necessarily the best way to reduce overcapacity (Seliger, 1999d). The government lacks the information to determine which companies are fittest to lead the merger, nor can the government determine the optimal number of companies in a specific sector. Both are types of information only available through the competitive process. However, the government chose political criteria to decide these questions.

The often cumbersome process of reforming the financial sector is only one indicator of danger of reforms. While Korea tried to overcome the "IMF crisis" by a low-interest rate policy in a deflationary environment, this policy later – with rising oil prices being only one danger for the price level – was more risky. Recently the Korean central bank warned that due to stabilization bonds worth 89.4 trillion won, sound monetary policy is barely possible. State debt increasingly restricts government policies, given the burden of servicing and repaying these debts. In this environment, government even has a hidden interest in inflation, since it works as an 'inflation tax' which lightens the public debt burden, but which raises risk for business and hurts consumers. The massive public injection of funds exacerbates this problem, since most of these funds are not recoverable. The experiences of European states since the 1970s and of Japan in the 1990s demonstrate the low likelihood of overcoming structural crisis without structural reform.

5.2 Transformation, the market for institutions and the viability of economic systems

The theory of economic transformation became a growing branch of economics with the transformation processes of former centrally planned economies to market economies in Central and Eastern Europe and the former Soviet Union.[100]

100 Today, a multitude of institutes exists focusing on "transition studies" or "transformation studies". The first term mainly describes the concrete transition from one known state of the economy (such as central planning) to another one (such as a market economy). Transformation studies rather focus on the transformation of the formerly centrally planned economies to new economic systems, where the exact characteristics of these systems are not yet well-known.

These transformation processes share many similarities with the countries experiencing a major crisis in East Asia. First, in both cases the process of rapid institutional change caught the experts – both regional experts and social scientists – totally unaware. The breakdown of centrally planned economies was as unforeseen as the outbreak of the East Asian crisis. Second, in both cases there existed a long-term discussion of fundamental problems of the economic system, in the case of centrally planned economies since the "socialist calculation debate" of the 1920s.[101] However, the transformation of the economic system was neither expected nor theoretically analyzed.

Third, just as economic conversion from a centrally planned economy creates a transformation paradox, so too does policy making after the East Asian crisis (Rosenbaum, 1999: 1-3). Similar policies, lauded by international institutions, led to markedly divergent results in the countries in crisis. In the transformation from centrally planned economies, it was a set of policies (known as the "Washington consensus") together with a debate about timing and sequencing of these reform steps.[102] In the East Asian crisis, it was the much-criticized conditions of IMF rescue packages.[103] However, soon it became clear that the analysis of these reform steps did not help in understanding the transformation of the economic systems after the crisis. Transformation can be defined as the "directed, government-initiated change of economic institutional regimes in a historically short period" (Herrmann-Pillath, 1999, p.10). This definition makes a crucial point in the explanation of the change of economic system, namely the institutional dimension. Reform policy blueprints and the implementation of policies are important and are dependent on the functioning of institutions. This is all the more true when the state as the main actor of the economic change is itself undergoing far-reaching alterations, sometimes even dissolution. Therefore, institutions as the "missing ingredient" (de Soto, 1993) become the central explanatory variable in transformation.

In the East Asian countries institutional peculiarities, described as the 'East Asian model', have long been known and sometimes been seen as central to the

---

101 In the socialist calculation debate, economists like Abba Lerner and Oskar Lange tried to show that central planning is compatible with optimal market outcomes as defined by neoclassical economic theory. However, they were contested by the Austrian economists Ludwig von Mises and Friedrich A. von Hayek on the grounds that the model itself, assuming optimal information, is wrong. Hayek stressed the role of market prices for collecting the information of millions of individuals, which no economic planning board can fulfil.

102 These reform steps were fiscal austerity, liberalization of trade and the financial sector, unified exchange rates, attraction of foreign direct investment, privatisation and deregulation. See Williamson (1990 and 1996).

103 These reform steps were fiscal austerity, market opening for FDI and foreign competition, increased transparency of the corporate and financial sector, deregulation and the enforcement of bankruptcy laws.

success of the respective economic miracles, for example in South Korea. The crises of these special forms of capitalism have not been expected. This is important, since there have been other crises, like in Korea around 1979 to1982 or in Japan since the late 1980s, which did not induce a fundamental questioning of the special form of capitalism in these countries. This leads to the question of when an economic crisis becomes a crisis of the economic system – in other words, when the viability of an economic system is endangered. Viability here means that the actors of an economy *grosso modo* find congruence between their expectations about the outcome of the economic system and the functioning of economic institutions, and therefore are neither expecting nor promoting a change of this system.[104] The viability of an economic system is not equal with a theoretical welfare optimum, but it is a necessary condition for institutional adaptive efficiency in the sense of North (1990).[105]

Among the characteristics of economic systems, their formal and informal institutions are most important.[106] Metaphorically speaking, formal institutions are formed on a country's 'market for institutions'. This is a metaphor for the interaction of the market for politics and the markets for goods and services of a country. The market for politics consists on the supply side of political entrepreneurs and the bureaucracy, offering various policies and packages of publicly produced goods.[107] The demand side consists of consumers, taxpayers, workers and investors, who decide among the various offers using their democratic voice. Interest groups are part of both the supply and the demand side of politics, since they take part in policy making by offering asymmetric information to the former while they are bundling their members' demand for politics and fuelling the

104 This notion of viability was first used by Boulding (1968) in the context of security policy and later translated to the position of countries in institutional competition by Prosi (1998). Here it is used analogous to the latter definition.

105 Without the congruence between expectations and outcomes economic systems cannot work, because plans will fail. However, viability is not a sufficient condition for adaptive efficiency, since economic systems like centrally planned economies for a long time showed viability without adapting institutions for a better use of resources.

106 Formal and informal institutions can be distinguished by their enforcement mechanism (the state monopoly of coercive power, i.e. central for formal institutions, private enforcement, by *internalisation*, i.e. decentralized for informal institutions). Sometimes they are also distinguished according to the way they are established, as written rules (formal) or as unwritten rules, customs, mores (informal). An example for formal institutions are laws enforced by the state. An informal institutions can be the establishment of a private arbitration court between business partners or the reliance on personal relations instead of written contracts in the Korean economy.

107 Until now, the supply by politicians is modelled by public choice theory mainly as a theory of individual entrepreneurs. However, in Western party democracies it should rather be modelled after the theory of the firm.

latter. The exit option, including the import of goods as an exit of national goods markets, or capital flight, links the market for politics with the markets for goods and services.[108] Institutional alternatives in other countries or forwarded by opposition parties, which are perceived to be more advantageous, will be preferred. Capital or persons can exit an economy (e.g. by capital flight or migration) and they can voice their protest, for example through demonstrations or the voting process. The intensity of institutional competition is dependent on the international regimes, for example trade and flows of factors of production, labour and capital. When trade is free, people can choose products produced under different institutional regimes, for example using different technical standards or produced under more or less severe environmental and social standards. When the movement of labour and capital is free, the decision about investment and the supply of labour is influenced by institutional regimes constraining their use. In the last decades it has considerably increased (cf. Seliger, 1999b).

The functioning of formal institutions is often only understandable by its interdependence with informal institutions. However, since informal institutions are observed and quantified only with great difficulty, they are often neglected in the discussion of economic systems or only applied to explain otherwise unexplainable residuals.[109] In transformation theory they were only lately reintroduced, after the models entirely neglecting institutions or only focusing on formal institutions have failed to explain various transformation paradoxes. Informal institutions are not static, with change occurring in a piecemeal, long-term fashion. This is a possible explanation for the fact that the same formal institutions render different results in different economies: They interact with different informal institutions, and their efficiency is dependent on this interaction.

The functioning of both formal and informal institutions requires that market actors have stable expectations of them. For formal institutions to be legitimate, the enforcement mechanism by state action requires that market actors expect a sufficient degree of enforcement taking place. For example, payments in arrears grew after the Asian crisis in some countries and state enforcement of debts was so weak that firms resorted to barter, thereby reducing the efficiency of the exchange. The functioning of informal institutions requires that they are sufficiently internalized by the market actors, for instance through education. When external as well as internal institutions result in the behaviour and results anticipated by all economic actors, an expectation-equilibrium is reached and the economic system can be said to be stable.

108 For the concepts of exit and voice see Hirschmann (1970).

109 An early exception was economic sociology and the research of the German so-called historical school.

Since market actors and external observers such as scientists do not have complete information, they build hypotheses about the functioning of the system, which are important for their goal setting and choice of instruments. For example, in a centrally planned economy, actors adapt to the constant problem of shortage by trying to underestimate their own capacity of production in the process of plan formulation to achieve 'weak plans' that are easy to fulfil and by producing outside the plan goods for barter with other firms experiencing shortages. In Korea, *chaebol* formed hypotheses about their relations with the government, especially the implicit guarantee of survival by the government. The hypotheses about the economy again are shaped by the cognitive schemata of actors operating in an uncertain environment. If they are permanently frustrated, new hypotheses are formed. However, this does not necessarily immediately translate into changed behaviour. As long as the enforcement mechanisms for institutions work, even the frustration of hypotheses might temporarily be accepted, since a deviation of behaviour can still effectively be sanctioned. But then, even small additional changes in perception might create the critical mass for a massive shift in behaviour by the actors: Transformation of the economic system occurs. For example, with the East Asian crisis, a reform of *chaebol* became politically feasible, even if the reasons for reform existed for a long time before.

The analysis of transformation processes therefore must begin with an analysis of the relevant market for formal institutions. This market is shaped by national political formal institutions, by their interaction in international institutional competition, and by their interaction with informal institutions. An expectation from equilibrium is the situation where all in all the expectations of actors about the functioning of institutions are matched. These expectations again are dependent on the cognitive models the actors developed about the institutions. Economic theory until now mostly neglected the importance of these models. They are formed by actors according to their own perceptions, interacting with the perception of other actors: For example, the "Asian model of development" or the "miracle on the Han river" were labels for the rapid and successful development process in Asia and Korea, originally created by external observers, but readily accepted by the actors in Korea itself.

The expectation equilibrium is not the same as a normative, theoretical welfare optimum.[110] Stable expectations exist also in dictatorships and in economies

110 The normative welfare optimum is the best economic situation achievable in a static environment under the constraints of scarcity of goods and resources by utility maximisation of all economic actors. While it is an important tool to discuss the general desirability of economic arrangements, the assumptions necessary to establish it theoretically make it impossible, to apply it to the more complex real economic systems.

achieving only weak economic results. Only if the results of economic activity deviate constantly from the anticipations of actors, a crisis of the economy, for example macroeconomic disequilibria, can translate into a crisis of the economic model actors have. This was the case in Korea after the financial crisis of 1997. The term "model" is here not used as a Weberian "ideal type", but as that model the actors formed of their economy. The crisis of the model led to a transformation process, which again has two characteristics. The first is that the political actors initiate formal institutional change: "DJnomics", the reform program of the government of Kim Dae Jung, was such a change. It consisted of the "four plus one" policy, the reform of the four sectors (private sector, public sector, labour market and financial market) and the opening of the Korean economy. As important as the initiated and intended institutional change are the changes unintended by the state actors, the side effects of transformation[111]. Unintended consequences, for example, occur through the interaction of changed formal institutions with old, unchanged informal institutions. The perceptions of the institutions are again very important for this: Do Koreans realize that the changed formal institutions require an adjustment of informal institutions? For instance, do Korean *chaebol* realize that historical ways of deciding about investment now might collide with a new state policy toward them? In the following section, the Korean transformation process since the economic crisis is sketched, followed by an analysis employing the outline of transformation theory used above.

5.3 The Korean crisis as a transformation of the economic and political system

The financial crisis of 1997, with the subsequent recession and the resulting changes in economic policies in Korea and other East Asian countries, has been intensely discussed. It is odd, however, that this discussion did not take place within the framework of economic transformation theory, since the puzzle of the East Asian crisis occurred only a few years after the failure of economic science to explain the former socialist states' transformation. Therefore, additional insight might be derived from an analysis of the Korean crisis employing the theory of institutional transformation described in the last section. At the same time a transformation of the economic system and of the political system takes place and it is important to understand these processes as simultaneous and interdependent, to

111 Cf. Hayek (1969). The analysis of unintended consequences of man's action, of the results of human interaction, but not human design is for Hayek the most important goal of social science; see Hayek (1979: 41).

understand the difficulty in the search for a new equilibrium of expectations for the economic actors in Korea. The application concentrates on the role of the state, of institutions and of culture on the economic system.

The role of the state in the East Asian countries has always been central to explanations of economic successes, due to the state-led development model emphasizing industrial policy and forced export orientation (World Bank, 1993; Smith, 1995; Weder, 1998). In the United States, the so-called revisionists claimed the superiority of these developmental models compared with Western market economies, predicting the dominance of the Japanese and East Asian economies for the future (Johnson, 1982; Johnson, 1995; Prestowitz, 1993; Lindsey/Lukas, 1998). In the tiger states of East Asia, the role of the state was seen as a "developmental dictatorship", securing the development of market economies, especially their competitiveness in world markets, through political authoritarianism and an interventionist approach to industrial policy.[112] After 1997, this hypothesis lost much of its appeal. While revisionists continued to assert that a special role of the state existed, two objections can be raised to their explanations. First, the role of industrial policy for economic success was sometimes greatly exaggerated. Second, the role of the state and the efficiency of state intervention changed considerably over time. In Korea, the growth of the *chaebol* made their control by the government more and more difficult, and "chaebolism" today is rather characterized by the firms' influence on state policy rather than the other way around.

A model of the Korean market for politics must take into account these changes in the strength of actors. The traditional public choice analysis of the behaviour of parties, bureaucracy and interest groups is the basis for such a model.[113] However, the Korean market for politics, i.e. the determination of Korean politics according to the supply by politicians, bureaucrats and interest groups and the demand by voters, investors, workers, consumers and taxpayers, shows some peculiarities not included in public choice models, which were mostly developed to explain Western markets for politics.[114] First of all, the role of political parties is fundamentally different in Korea than in Western democracies in the sense that parties are basically divided not by ideological bias, but by

112 For a justification of the interventionist state, see the "Invalidation of Neo-Classicism in Korea's Economic Development Process", Mimiko (1997) attempts to show.

113 The change of South Korea from a dictatorship with several opposition parties dependent on the dictators to a full-fledged democracy since 1987 cannot be explored here, but is an important factor in the analysis.

114 The public choice school tries to explain political decision-making by individual utility maximisation and developed models to explain voter and party behaviour, the role of interest groups, and the supply of policies by bureaucrats, largely aiming at explaining the functioning of Western democratic market economies. For an overview see Mueller (1989).

regional interest.[115] While parties are often described as more or less liberal or conservative, the degree of freedom in policy change or pragmatism is much greater than in Western democracies. Ideological positions can be easily changed, as long as regional interests are not affected by these policy changes. Only this can explain the consequent market opening and free trade policy of the Kim Dae Jung government despite its former alliance with left-wing organisations struggling for democracy and trade unions. Also, the alliance between Kim Dae Jung's Millennium Democratic Party with the far right-wing United Liberal Democrats (ULD) can be explained by the lack of ideological orientation of parties.

The role of bureaucracy is also different from public choice models, where bureaucracies act solely as budget maximisers. Due to its strong traditional role, the bureaucracy in a neo-Confucian state, such as Korea, has a much higher degree of discretion than in Western states. While guidance by the state bureaucracy has been weakened through the process of liberalization since the 1980s, still the role of bureaucracy is extraordinarily strong compared with, for example, European or U.S. bureaucracies.[116] Also, frequent changes in government offices weaken the ability of politicians to control bureaucracy. Moreover, the personalization of policy leads to the tendency that individual politicians or bureaucrats are blamed for policy mistakes, while the bureaucracy as a whole remains intact. The collusion between bureaucracy and firms, especially the *chaebol*, remaining from era of 'developmental dictatorship,' is still high. This allows companies to expect support even from a government initially hostile to the *chaebol*, like the government of Kim Dae Jung, while firms themselves support the government policy regardless of this initial hostility. While early in his term Kim Dae Jung's government severed relations with big business, later on cooperation became crucial, because without business support reform policies were futile. But also *chaebol* had to cooperate, because they needed government support to survive after the crisis. For example, Hyundai's politically motivated investment in North Korea, especially its loss-making tour business to Mount Kumgang, was an exchange for implicit support by the South Korean state. Since Hyundai's investment worked as a door-opener for Kim Dae Jung's Sunshine Policy, the government is in a position to take a less hard stance against the *chaebol* in its financial difficulties.

---

115 This became clear again in the parliamentary election of 2000; cf. Seliger (2000b). In Cholla province and Kyongsan province the traditional parties (now renamed MDP and GNP, respectively) could defend their dominant position. Changes in Chungchon province, where the ULD lost its traditional stronghold, show that despite the constancies of the political market described above, also evolution is possible.

116 A recent example is the bureaucratic pressure exerted nowadays on private banks to ease credit restrictions on consumers and companies, which was followed by announcements by major banks of doing so.

The power of the *chaebol* and their interest group, the Federation of Korean Industry, is not only a stronger than their counterparts in Western countries, but of a different form altogether. Much more than in Western countries, the *chaebol* in Korea depend on supportive government action, so lobbying is not only for greater profit, but often for sheer survival.

A similar caution has to be applied to trade unions, whose goals are not fully comparable with the traditional role they represent in public choice models, namely benefit maximisation for insiders. While this role is not entirely absent, especially in the *chaebol* firms where trade union representation is highest and they were powerful enough to achieve wage raises often considerably higher than productivity growth, trade unions still additionally follow their tradition of being a political reform movement. They developed in the time after the Asian crisis into a powerful non-parliamentary opposition, when in parliament both major parties generally agreed to the anti-crisis policy prescribed by the IMF.

The role of the state and the role of the Confucian culture in the economic development of Korea both achieved a prominent but misleading role, since they were discussed in a grossly simplified way. The argument that economic development is either enhanced or prevented by the Confucian culture is problematic, since it greatly underestimates the heterogeneity of the regional cultures. However, it has been important in shaping not only the Western views of East Asian development, but also the views of the actors themselves.[117] It allowed observers and actors to state the 'otherness' of Korea without a need for further justification.

Korea's cultural homogeneity was important insofar as it restricted the possibility of blaming others, such as minorities, for the economic problems, which happened to Christians and the Chinese traders in Southeast Asia.[118] This homogeneity is also an explanatory factor for the relatively decisive action of the Korean government in reforming the economic system after the crisis, compared with other countries of the region. There was no minority to blame for the crisis. This does not mean that Koreans accepted the blame for the crisis entirely. The Koreans' perception of themselves as a unique people – resisting foreign repression for thousand of years and dubbed the "miracle on the Han river" by foreign scholars – left no room for such self-degradation. Their definition of the crisis as the "IMF crisis" suggested a belief in the IMF as a culprit for the country's economic

117 See for example the discussion of the "Asian Business Logic" in Lasserre/Schütte (1995: 115-139). For a more extensive discussion see the study of Couplet/Heuchenne (1998), especially Ch. 1 and 7. The "Confucian argument" is discussed in Chang (1998). Critical is Lee (1996 and 1997). For Korea see the review of Köllner (1997).

118 In Malaysia as well as in Indonesia, occasionally these racial and/or religious discriminations occurred and sometimes were used by the state or parties to deflect the interest from the failure of government, for example after the Asian crisis in parts of Indonesia.

troubles. However, IMF pressure for reforms was welcomed politically, since it helped to overcome domestic opposition. The Korean experience as well as that of Eastern Europe shows the importance of international conditionality for the transformation process (Seliger, 2002c.). Increased international economic integration through organizations such as APEC, the WTO and OECD fosters open markets and a competitive private sector in spite of domestic opposition.

The transformation from an economy characterized by the unique mixture of state influence and markets to an economy more based on markets with a reduced and changed role for the state, according to the structural reform programme proposed by the IMF and to the programme of DJnomics, involved necessarily an additional transformation of the political sector. This transformation began with an important ritual act, namely the self-purification of government. The old government acknowledged its mistakes, and some minor bureaucrats were prosecuted (but not sentenced) for misinformation on the level of foreign reserves in 1997.[119] This act was the precondition for the acceptance of foreign aid and the reform policy by the new government, because it ensured the functioning of the political system. According to the Confucian tradition, economic mishaps are the fault of the ruler.[120] The change of leadership and an acknowledgement of fault by the old leadership meant that the political system itself, which in Korea was a democracy with a short tradition, remained intact. Consequently, unlike Indonesia or Malaysia, where foreign conspiracies or minorities were blamed for the crisis, but the leadership did not take any responsibility, Korea did not experience a crisis of the political system. A second aspect of the transformation is the design of DJnomics as an all-encompassing program for modernization of society involving technocrats and popular movements, which went beyond mere economic reform. The modernization discourse had been used before, for example, in the *saemaul undong* movement of Park Chung Hee.[121] Modernization in the programme of DJnomics was presented not only as a short-term programme to overcome the financial and economic crisis, but as a programme of renewal with

119 This form of self-purification has a long tradition in Korea; see Steinberg (1999). It is linked to the 'mandate of heaven' idea in the ancient East Asian world order. See for the case of Japan Kraus (1994: 50, esp.).

120 In former times this included bad weather conditions or harvest. Rulers lost their 'mandate of heaven' if they could not change the tide.

121 *Saemaul Undong* was a policy of renewal of rural communities to prevent the rising gap between rural and urban Korea in the phase of rapid modernization, especially in the form of infrastructure development, but also with an important ideological superstructure. The term can be translated as "new village movement" or more elaborate as "movement for the progressive renewal based on past experience of rural communities".

far-reaching goals, including the goal to ensure the place of Korea among the wealthy OECD states and as part of the global political community.[122]

The reform policy described above resulted in unintended consequences. While their ultimate impact on the Korean economic system cannot be determined yet, at least three developments seemed to shape the new, post-crisis model. First, the reform of the private sector paradoxically weakened the Korean *chaebol* – for example by ending cross-subsidization, making the whole economy better off but hurt the *chaebol*, which were forced to terminate unprofitable businesses – but at the same time strengthened them with the policy of 'big deals', the forced mergers in industries with overcapacity ordered by the state. The reduction of overcapacity through forced mergers resulted in greater concentration in the already narrow, oligopolistic markets of Korea. This counteracts the effects of market opening through the membership in international organizations.[123]

Second, the freer market, increased FDI inflow, deregulation of overseas studies and the warmer welcome of foreign cultures have more far-reaching effects than the intended ones. The transfer and adoption of a new management style in foreign-invested companies will spread to Korean companies. The inflow of foreign ideas will change the political and economic system in an unpredictable manner. It could lead to greater conformity with the models of capitalism in the investors' countries, notably the U.S. Or, it could lead to the development of a new Korean model of economic and political governance. Increased regional integration also promotes this change, since it additionally means openness for foreign trade and investment and ultimately might even lead to a freer movement of labour, the market still closed in all of East Asia. The third factor is the end of traditional social networks centered around the family. The introduction of new welfare measures, like extended help for the unemployed and extended medical insurance coverage, will increase the speed of this change, making individuals less dependent on families. Rising divorce rates are the most visible effects of this dissolution of traditional social networks. But also, the introduction of the welfare state increases the burden on the state budget already strained by the recapitalization of the financial sector. The new fiscal policy – with all the dangers

122 Participation in international organizations as visible expression of the acceptance of Korea in the international political community is an important goal. Therefore, Korea in the last decade developed a very active programme to chair international institutions (like the UN), host international organizations, like the future Green Climate Fund, and upgrade homegrown institutions to international ones, like the Global Green Growth Institute.

123 Recent data seems to corroborate the persisting closure of the Korean market: For example, LG Electronics reported prices in the domestic market for a range of electronics goods three times higher than in world markets; see Korea Herald (23.4.2001: 8).

inherent in this policy clearly observable in Japan – is another step in the transformation from the former developmental model.

The transformation process of the Korean economic system has not yet ended. An expectation-equilibrium, where expectations of economic and political actors match each other, is not yet reached, as the critical view of the political system by citizens shows.[124] The corporate sector still sees a contradiction between old management practices and increased competitive pressure. The labour market and the structure of society are rapidly changing, but the magnitude and direction of the change is not yet clear. The inherited political structure, including the bureaucracy and the political parties, is increasingly dysfunctional. Transformation theory can help understand these changes by stressing both the transformation that subsystems of the society undergo, and their simultaneous interdependence. Given that, further research on the transformation of the Korean economic system should prove fruitful.

124 Among the signs for a critical view are a low esteem for politicians as exhibited by opinion polls, a high rate of abstention in elections (in recent local by-elections less than 25 percent of voters used their right to vote) and the growing desire to migrate, as it can be seen in the growing applications for permanent living permits, for example in the U.S. and Canada.

Chapter 6: The Interdependence of Economic and Political Systems: Comparing the Cases of Malaysia, Indonesia and Korea

6.1 Introduction – a comparative view of the Asian crisis and the role of the interdependence of order

Thinking about the Asian crisis, in particular in a comparative way, requires an analysis of different economic systems or orders, as the German tradition of order economics (*Ordnungsoekonomie)* did for the past century.[125] When discussing the problem of the interdependence of order in his principles of the economic policy, Walter Eucken (1952: 184) concluded with the words: "We cannot escape the problems of the system anymore." This still holds true today, like the crisis of the East-Asian national economy since 1997 revealed once more. Here, we take a comparative view how this interdependence became important for East Asian countries in the crisis.

Eucken emphasized three aspects in the interdependence of the systems: First, there is an interdependence of the partial systems, the one of the political, economic and social systems. The negative effects of a conflicting political and economic system are made visible in the chaotic transformation processes of the former Soviet Union for instance. Here, too, one has to highlight the divergence of "external" (political and economic) and "internal" (social) institutions (Kiwit/ Voigt, 1995). Second, there is an interdependence of the regulatory system policy. The principles which justify an economic system have to be consistent. Partial interventionism in a liberal economic system leads to a degeneration of that system; the "style-purity" of the market economy (Müller-Armack 1952) has to be granted. The third aspect relates to the interdependence of the national system with the international economic system. This aspect has grown in significance in the last years. Globalization leads to an international convergence of the competing systems. Global trade currents and factor movements are the cause of this competition. The partial opening of countries for such currents is interpreted as a

125 Usually, the German word *Ordnung* is translated to economic system. However, the connotation is slightly different: In the German usage the way has normative implications not seen in the Anglo-Saxon usage. To think about "order economics" is nevertheless useful beyond the specific German context in which it was first applied. Indeed, to understand the Asian crisis as a crisis of its economic order(s) is the gist of this book.

successful integration into the global market. In doing so, one forgets however that integration like that only runs smoothly when the interdependence of both the partial systems and the economic system policy are granted.

The economic development of Asia is a good example of the triple-interdependence. The debate about "Asian values" back in the early 1990s suggested that that any desired mix of elements could exist (Mahbubani, 1998). Authoritarian states (like Singapore, Malaysia or Indonesia) in varying degrees restricted political freedom. At the same time their generally open economies were in a varying degree mixed with more or less strong elements of central planning (like investment plans for selected export industries). Moreover, the mixture can be seen in the transforming former socialist economies of Vietnam and China. On the one hand it is important to acknowledge that every existing economic system is not an "ideal type" in Eucken's sense, but rather a mixed economy. On the other hand this does not mean that every mixture is possible without running into problems. The Asian crisis is a point in case, since some countries enjoyed before a revered status as "developmental dictatorships", where the interdependence of order did not play an important role. The crisis, insofar it was not only a financial crisis, but also a structural crisis of East Asian economic orders, brought this interdependence back to the light. This chapter reviews the answers of three countries, Indonesia, Korea and Malaysia, while in particular looking at the crucial interdependence of orders. All countries had varying answers to the crisis, while being affected in a similar way.

While "East Asian" economic models show a number of similarities after World War II, nevertheless the artificial labelling of "tiger economies" or NICs is problematic, since all economies developed their own order, not the least due to different historical and cultural environments. Here, those factors of the environment directly influencing the economic order and the interdependence of order will be discussed. Malaysia was always a country of different ethnic groups: Malays, Indians and Chinese. During the crisis, capital controls and aggressiveness (mostly as rhetoric) against foreign speculation were a unique answer to the crisis (Section 2). Indonesia, as another multiethnic state, was used to territorial and racial conflict. The financial and later economic crisis brought them again to the forefront, resulting in political strife and later, political change (Section 3). South Korea, which already underwent transformation from an authoritarian state to a democracy in the early 1990s, achieved the first democratic change from the governing party to opposition, together with a comprehensive reform of its economy (Section 4). The last section (5.) reviews the relevance of internal and external institutions and discusses the reform paradox due to the fact that early recovery from crisis might be an obstacle to thorough reform.

6.2 Malaysia – walling-off as answer to the crisis

The economic development of Malaysia before the Asian crisis was largely determined by the fact that three ethnic groups had to live and work together. The Bumiputeras ("sons of the earth"), or the indigenous Malays, were with more than 60 percent of the population, by far largest ethnic group. Thirty percent of the population was ethnic Chinese, and a little more than 10 percent was Indians. When in 1957 the British colonial period ended, the Chinese, as elsewhere in Southeast Asia, were the most important group, particularly in controlling trade. They benefitted among others from existing ethnic trading networks throughout the region. While all three ethnic groups participated in the government after independence, racial strife occurred in 1969. Afterwards Malaysia, in a series of five-year-plans, systematically strengthened under the label of "new economic policy" the role of Bumiputeras. Their share in enterprises rose from a meagre 2,3 percent in 1970 to over 20 percent in 1990. Bumiputeras were receiving preferential treatment through public procurement rules as well as credit allocation, in particular through the newly founded Bumiputra Bank. At the same time they increased their influence in policy making. While formally a coalition government of the Barisan Nasional (National Front) ruled, all ministers came from the Malay party UMNO (United Malays National Organisation). Since 1981 Mohamad Mahathir reigned as prime minister of the state, formally a kingdom. After the policy of import substitution in the 1970s was not successful, Malaysia achieved rapid economic growth with an export-oriented policy comparable to that of other countries in the region and became one of the NICs. In the 1980s real growth (at constant prices) was more than 8 percent annually. At the same time the inflation rate was at less than 3,5 percent. Because of ethnic tensions between Chinese and Bumiputeras, the role models for Malaysia's policy were not the successful neighbouring countries of Singapore or Taiwan, but rather the rapid industrialization of Japan (the so-called "look east" policy). In 1991 the preferential treatment of Bumiputeras was formally given up and a new policy of sustained high growth was introduced. This policy rapidly reduced the share of population under the poverty line. In ASEAN Malaysia enjoyed the highest per-capita GDP after Singapore. With this development, Malaysia is a typical example for the development of Asian growth states. As the World Bank (1993) defined it: Malaysia was able to combine high growth, savings, and investment rates with stable prices and a relatively even income distribution. Thereby, the political approval of the Malaysian policy in the population was ensured. The political stability also led to high appeal among foreign investors.

Despite this exemplary development process, Malaysia's development did not proceed without problems: The Malayan party UMNO, governing since the independence, was able to accumulate a fortune since 1959, but even more so during the time of favouritism. Since the granting of credit followed in many cases not economic but political criteria, the abuse of power knew almost no boundaries. Through this, the freedom of producers was rendered inoperative, and investments were controlled. At the same time, the political granting of credit resulted in periodic breakdowns of banks. The Bumiputra Bank in particular was insolvent repeatedly and could only be saved by massive financial help from the state. Premier Minister Mahathir, governing since 1981, always advocated Asian values abroad, which he contrasted with Western values. An exhausting definition of those values does not exist. Usually, it implies the (neo-) Confucian value hierarchy, which is especially based on the authority of state and family. In the Southeast Asian context, the influence of Islamic moral values is important as well; for example, they were implemented in the Pancasila system in Indonesia. The rigorous elimination of political enemies and the political influence on the justice system and press made democracy in Malaysia, despite the regular elections, only limitedly comparable with Western democracies. Among others, during the Asian crisis Mahathir was called one of the ten greatest enemies of the free press by the Committee to Protect Journalists in Washington.

The interdependence of the systems was thus violated in two ways: The economic system was shaped by the juxtaposition of interventionist and market elements. Here, however, the fact has to be highlighted that the markets had always been open for foreign competition. Therefore, it never came to greater X-inefficiencies like in the completely closed-off socialist economies. Secondly, the political order was also characterized by a mixture of democratic and autocratic streaks.

The Asian crisis started as a crisis of trust of the overrated currencies in Southeast Asia, which were often tied to the dollar. After the devaluation of the Thai baht in the beginning of July 1997, the speculation against the other East-Asian currencies began as well. Although Malaysia's Bank Negara (Central Bank) managed to stabilize the rates of the Malaysian ringgit through backing in the amount of several billion dollars, it had to release the rates of the ringgit in the middle of July. While other East Asian states tried to curb the crisis with the help of the IMF, Malaysia adopted another course: In spectacular announcements in front of the IMF and to the press, Premier Minister Mahathir made international speculators, and particularly the Hungarian-American fund-owner George Soros, responsible for the crisis in Southeast Asia and demanded a ban on any kind of currency speculation. In August 1997, Malaysia imposed capital controls, which, among other things, taxed capital transactions and constrained share sales. The Malaysian ringgit was tied to the dollar after a fall of 40 percent, while most other currencies in the region had flexible exchange rates after the crisis. In the fiscal policy, too, Malaysia followed a different strategy than its neighbours: First, the restrictive monetary policy of the IMF was emulated, but without searching for standby credits of the IMF. The recession following the currency crisis was met with expansive fiscal policy by Malaysia. Negative reports about the economic situation in the press became forbidden.

Although this policy scared away international investors at first, the effects of the recession were significantly lower in Malaysia than in neighbouring Indonesia: The economy shrank about 7 percent, while in Indonesia by twice as much. This was because the banking system was much better regulated in comparison to other Southeast Asian states, and placed the highest capital requirements in the region. The amount of bad credits estimated by the Bank Negara was supposed to have been around 31 billion ringgit (8.2 billion USD). Even if those officially given numbers seem to too low, the amount of problematic credits is substantially lower than in Thailand and Indonesia. After two years, the valley floor of the economic crisis had been reached. The currency, tied to the American dollar, which lay about 10 percent over the current market value, had become undervalued in the meantime.

All other currencies of the region were revalued again after the crisis. For the weak Malaysian exports, this undervaluation is a great help. A different question is however in what way it will affect the price stability and efforts to restructure businesses. Even though many businesses are insolvent, no company crashes happened since the crisis, as had been characteristic for Thailand and South Korea. Contributing to this were credits that banks had been forced to grant insolvent firms. One of the largest conglomerates, Renong, which lay under the direct control of the Premier Minister Mahathir and his former minister of finance, received national credits in the amount of 2.34 billion ringgit. Failure of the management was thus not sanctioned; the danger of future insolvencies remained high. Although the eschewal of aggressive solicitation by foreign direct investors that now has begun in the neighbouring countries does not have any immediate effects, and in many industries overcapacities exist, in the long term the absence of foreign knowledge will indeed have its effects. Contributing to this was the undervalued rate of Malaysian ringgits, making imports of new machines and technology from abroad very expensive. Many replacement investments remained undone, and the capital stock aged.

The effects of the crisis on the political system initially were relatively low; like in Indonesia, the government was put under pressure through protests by the population. However, due to various factors, Premier Minister Mahathir managed to stay in office uncontested. The scapegoat function of foreign speculators is clearly visible. In addition, since the UMNO had an iron grip on the press, political protests could not be articulated easily.

6.3 Indonesia – from economic crisis to political chaos

Indonesia was affected the most by the Asian crisis; here, the economic crisis evolved into a political crisis. This is because of the composition of the Indonesian island kingdom with more than 17,500 islands. Before being combined and colonized by the Dutch East India Company in the 17th century and later on by the Netherlands, there existed a number of Islamic and Hindu kingdoms with different cultures and languages. Even today, over 500 languages and dialects are spoken in Indonesia. The largest demographic group, the Javanese, only make up 45 percent of the population, followed by the Sundanese (14 percent), coastal Malay and Madurese (each 7.5 percent), and Chinese (3.5 percent). The Chinese, who especially benefited as traders in the Dutch times, were, like everywhere in Southeast Asia, disproportionally involved in the economy of the country.

After their bloodily won independence from the colonial regime, the slogan of the state "Bhineka Tunggal Ika" (unity through diversity) was to be seen more as wishful thinking than political reality. There were movements in many parts of the country that wanted to achieve independence from the new state of Indonesia. This is particularly true for Irian Jaya (Western part of Papua New Guinea) and East Timor, a former Portuguese colony that was annexed by Indonesia in 1975. Politically, Indonesia was governed as a so-called "new order", by an autocratic regime under the control of President Suharto since 1967 after a period of an instable democracy. This order was seemingly based on "five principles" (Pancasila): Faith in a single god, a just and humane order, unity of Indonesia, unanimous decisions through negotiations of representatives of the people, and social justice. In reality, Suharto's regime was based on an extensive constraint of democratic rights: The responsibility of the president toward the parliament was abandoned. Only three parties were allowed: The United Indonesian Democratic Party-Struggle, the United Muslim Development Party, and the Party of Suharto, Golongan Karya (Golkar). Golkar was not an actual party but included especially officials, former officers and occupation groups. It served as a pillar of the Suharto regime and is, even today, very influential and well-organized. The loyalty toward tribal elders which were Golkar elders was especially important in remote villages. Bapakism, the Indonesian form of paternalism, is to this day the most important institution which regulates the political and economic life. Like in Malaysia, it helped advance the governing party and particularly Suharto's family.

The economic development of Indonesia is marked by a bad foundation in comparison to the neighbouring state of Malaysia. Only the policy of the new order under Suharto made an opening for foreign investors. The country was modernized through five-year development plans, through which – starting from a low level – it could catch up with the achievements of the other East Asian dictatorships. Before the Asia crisis, the income per capita amounted to less than half as much as in Malaysia. After the Thai currency, the baht, the Philippine peso and later on the Malaysian ringgit were dramatically devalued in July 1997, and the Indonesian rupee had come under pressure as well. While Indonesia was still involved in the bonds of the IMF for Thailand in the beginning of August, the Central Bank Indonesia had to give up its defence on the Rupee a few days later. In October 1997, after the government's austerity plan failed to finish the crisis of the rupee, Indonesia was forced to ask the IMF for help with the replenishment of the exhausted currency reserves and the restructuring of the banking sector, which was marked with ailing credits to a massive extent. Like in Malaysia, the credits could partially be traced back to the politically motivated credit granting; the extent of the problem however, induced through to lax credit supervision, was much bigger. As it stood in 1998, about 60 percent of the credits in Indonesia in comparison to the 33 percent in Malaysia and South Korea each. The external debt of Indonesian companies were estimated to be around 100 bn. USD, and in some cases twice as high by foreign banks. Due to the drop of the rupee, for many firms interest payment and payback wass impossible. In the years of strong growth previous to the crisis, the debt was seen as a minor problem.

The relief program that was enacted in the end of October intended to help Indonesia by providing credits from the IMF, the World Bank and the Asian Development Bank at the level of 21 billion USD. In turn, Indonesia promised to close 16 banks, to strengthen its financial supervision, introduce a modern bankruptcy law, and to deregulate the economy. The evaluation of Indonesia was, under the supervision of the IMF, quarterly, and later on biannual. This evaluation was especially important in crisis economies since government data is often not trustworthy. In spite of the IMF program, the crisis in Indonesia continued. The measures suggested by the IMF led to a "credit squeeze" and, according to critics of the IMF, contributed to the end of the currency crisis as a dramatic recession: The growth of Indonesia fell from about 5 percent in 1997 to minus 14 percent in 1998. About 15 Million jobs were lost. The part of the population living under the poverty level determined by the World Bank rose to over 30 percent. At the same time, inflation surged and lay over 50 percent in 1998.

The economic downfall of Indonesia was accompanied by political unrest. The rise in prices led to pogroms against Chinese which, being the predominant traders, were made responsible for the rising prices. Protests of millions of Indonesians under the slogan "Reformasi" led to the resignation of President Suharto in May 1998. His successor Habibie, under Suharto, promised for June 1999 the first free election after 44 years, 32 years being under Suharto's "new order". At the same time, the greater freedom under Habibie showed the political weak points of Indonesia. In many places emerged new autonomy and independence movements, often linked with religious and ethnic tensions, claiming hundreds of human lives. The settlement policy under Suharto which brought thousands of Muslim settlers into the mainly Christian Irian Jaya for instance, now added to ethnic conflicts. In East Timor, the formerly Portuguese colony, a referendum decided about the independence, which was however overshadowed by the violence of especially Muslim groups.

The reforms enacted by the government were ambivalent. Similarly to the Malaysian "New Economy Policy", there had been a policy of economic preference of the non-Chinese population (the so-called *pribumi*). According to the government, this policy should not serve to the advantage of small groups, as in the reign of the Suharto-family, but should create a new indigenous middle class. Most of the Chinese-controlled conglomerates are said to had a tight entanglement with the Suharto-regime. They had large parts of the domestic economy divided in close oligopolies (for example for the trade with the main food items rice and oil). Now an attempt was made to organize the trade through thousands of independent merchants. Nevertheless every policy of "affirmative action" is exposed to the suspicion of political despotism and the declassing of non-indigenous people. For the parliamentary elections in 1999, in addition to the three old parties, 45 new parties were allowed, of these five workers parties and 19 Muslim parties. The latter at some point in time even called for the holy war against the central government in Jakarta. By then, Golkar joined up with a few moderate Islamic groups and opposed a coalition of nationalistic parties under Megawati Sugarnoputri, the daughter of the first president Sukarno.

Also, economically there were disintegration phenomena in the heterogeneous state. The province Riau on Sumatra, for instance, which is a small province but rich in oil fields, gas and other resources, demanded economic autonomy since it hitherto co-financed a significant part of the central budget. Differently from the case of East Timor, the central government reacted to other autonomy efforts with denial.

Under the supervision of the IMF, numerous reform- and reconstruction measures began in Indonesia, in which the problem of the interdependence of systems became especially clear. The new bankruptcy law, which had been worked out among others by experts of the IMF, was considered to be the core of the reforms. Before, it was virtually impossible to force insolvent firms to bankrupt. Thereby emerged a "moral hazard" problem, since the firms put no value on the payback of their debts. However, even though the new bankruptcy-law corresponds to the standards of the IMF, its actual implementation turned out to be problematic. Out of 55 insolvency cases, only 13 were actually forced to bankruptcy, although many of them could not follow their payment obligations. On one side, this can be explained politically: The conglomerates had formed a loyal fellowship with the Suharto regime; government, justice and administration seats were still occupied by the same followers. In addition, the bankruptcy of the conglomerates led to mass layoffs which could result in political unrest. Another reason for the poor application of the law was the insecurity of the justice system with the new law and the inadequate training of the judges. The most capable jurists did not even pursue the career of a judge as potential earnings were considerably lower than in the private economy. The new insolvency statute should contribute to the attractiveness of Indonesia to foreign investors by granting legal security and solving the "moral hazard" problem of indebtedness. Thanks to a deficient administration and a blend of economic and political interests, it was however not applicable.

Reconstruction had a special meaning in the financial sector. The insolvent Indonesian banks have been combined by the IBRA (Indonesian Bank Restructuring Agency). Particularly affected by the ailing foreign credits were Japanese banks, which lent almost 40 percent of the money. Here the interdependency of the financial systems became apparent as well: As the Japanese banks were in a deep state of crisis themselves, they have refused a write-off of their credit and thus inhibited the restructuring of Indonesian debt.

In spite of Indonesia's deep crisis, the economy recovered in the year 1999. Contributing to this was a policy of unbundling of economic and political interests as well as the privatization or partial privatization of large public firms like PT Telekomunikasi Indonesia and PT Bank Bali (the third-largest private bank which was put under government control due to insolvency), and of infrastructure facilities like port operation associations. Meanwhile, important conglomerates had restructured their foreign debt

Indonesia was an example of the problematic effects of an instable political system on the economic order. In reverse, it also shows that political stability is dependent on an economic order which is not characterized by alleged or actual preferential treatment of certain groups. The pogroms against the Chinese were often co-determined by political consideration. In relation to the political enrichment and corruption in the under former President Suharto, a conflict potential developed which challenged "Unity through Diversity." Nevertheless, from the mid-2000s Indonesia took a very promising turn. After the indecisive government of president Megawati Sukarnoputri (2001 to 2004), a new government under Susilo Bambang Yudhoyono could carry out major reforms which affected the political system, in particular through strengthening judicial oversight, and contained corruption to some extent to make Indonesia a politically and economically dynamic economy increasingly important to the region as a whole.

6.4 Korea – the economic crisis and its political impact

The economic crisis in Korea has been discussed already in the previous chapter. In December 1997, South Korea had to ask the IMF for help. The announced relief program not only wounded Korea's national pride, but also had direct effects on politics: At the parliamentary elections in 1998 Kim Dae-Jung, like incumbent Kim Young-Sam a former dissident who fought against the autocratic South Korean governments, won. Simultaneously, the long-standing ruling party, the Grand National Party, lost its monopoly of power. The radical renewal program of the new government, which constitutes a coalition made up of the National Congress for New Policies (NCNP) and the United Liberal Democrats (ULD), had significant implications for the relationship between economy and politics in South Korea. The over-indebted *chaebol* had to pledge to lower the debt-to-equity ratio to below 200 percent in the course of two years. At the same time, "big deals", mergers *of chaebol* business units, were supposed to ensure the reduction of overcapacities (see Chapter 7). Thereby, the number of manufacturers in the automobile industry was lowered from four to only two. Insolvent banks and parts of *chaebol* were sold to preferably foreign investors. Formerly closed markets – for example in the tourism sector – were opened to foreign competition. Competition authority and banking supervision were strengthened.

The social sector, too, experienced fundamental change. Since the system of help within the family was dissolving more and more with increasing urbanization, and simultaneously the concept of lifelong employment, which was practiced in many large companies, did not apply anymore, elements of the welfare state, for example unemployment insurance or developed health insurance, had been introduced. These reforms had an important function even after the crisis, because on the one hand, no quick restoration of full employment was to be expected when the unemployment rate was at almost 8 percent, and on the other hand the process of dissolution of strong family ties was even more likely to accelerate and seemed to be irreversible. Here, the modernization of South Korea, which required flexible working conditions, had direct influence on the social order. At the same time, the introduction of elements of the welfare state should not to be confused with aiming at developed welfare states, like the ones that are dominant in continental Europe. Instead, social basic insurance could increase the economic performance and acceptance of a greater opening of the country, while avoiding the mistakes of Western welfare states and, for example, making use of the high saving rates of Koreans for its financing. The opening of the country concerned not only the economic sector, but the cultural sector as well, such as the film industry, which had been highly regulated up until then (see

Chapter 13). The previous policy of South Korea to forbid screening of cultural products like motion pictures from the old arch-enemy and simultaneous economic role model Japan has been gradually relaxed. Additionally, the national security law, which for example drastically restricted cultural ties to North Korea, is being relaxed, too.

In South Korea, the success of the policy of openness became soon visible. From an economic point of view, after overcoming the harsh recession, the country's attractiveness to foreign investors in particular could be enhanced. The restructuring of the economy governed by the *chaebol* was still not complete in 1998 and 1999, but had begun properly for the first time. Ultimately, the economic crisis came to the aid of reform politics. Without the crisis, neither the resistance of the completely over-indebted *chaebol*, nor the resistance of the traditionally very powerful and radical unions would have been so low.

6.5 The interdependence of economic systems and the reform paradox

The discussion of the different answers to the Asian crisis shows that the reform of the economic order is a tedious process. Partially, this is because the reforms have been addressed half-heartedly, and partially because the reforms concern institutions that can only be changed slowly. In particular the relationship between external and internal institutions has often become conflicting due to reform steps. Thus, loyalty, based on Confucian logic, frequently opposes the competition logic of the market economy. Although competition is definitely appreciated, seen in the long tradition of entrance exams for the royal court offices still reflected in the entrance exams for schools and universities, loyalty still takes the precedence over profitability. For *chaebol*, which began as family enterprises, and the relationship between bureaucracy and economy, this led simultaneously to corruption and the rewarding of political loyalty instead of economic success. For small enterprises, this was less problematic than for the large conglomerates. On one hand, the middle class always had to adjust to new situations and had no market power, even though the firms are paternalistically organized. The conglomerates in turn, could – for example through the use of their financial power for cross-subsidization – partially escape the pressure of market competition. On the other hand, the political power and thus the opportunity for corruption are much lower. In the Asian crisis, the greater adaptability of middle class firms was visible through the fact that Taiwan, which is based on middle class firms to a great extent, had significantly fewer problems during the crisis than South Korea. An even greater problem is the *bapakisme*, the loyalty to hierarchical networks in the tribal or today quasi-tribal organizations in Indonesia and Malaysia, since it is even less compatible with the impersonality-based market relationships.

In spite of these problems, resulting from the reforms were long-term changes of the systems in East Asian countries. An example of a standard gradual change is the gradual compatibility of traditional norms (labelled Confucian or more exactly neo-Confucian in Korea) with Christian-Western moral values. The Asian self-perception is thus not any longer dependent on the differentiation from Western values but allows its partial assimilation, while retaining positive features of the own set of values. Nevertheless the problems of interdependence of order are significant. In this time of the financial and economic crisis in the U.S. and Europe, again some voices in Asia and the West see state planning and state interventions, not competition in markets governed by a competition order, as the way to achieve sustainable growth. Small interventions are defended as welfare-enhancing. The problem is that such small interventions easily lead to larger ones, a danger called progressive interventionism by Ludwig von Mises (1926).

By this critique, the overcoming of poverty and the high economic growth in the last three decades in the East Asian states are not to be forgotten. In comparison to the states of Latin America or Africa, the East Asian states had a distinctly more positive development. The role of the state in planning is not to be seen as only negative with reason. Despite the discussed flaws of the political system, most East Asian states succeeded in introducing a meritocratic educational system, reaching a relatively even income distribution (also ergarding the rural-urban divide) without diminishing the incentives for economic activity, and achieving a comparatively high amount of legal security in the economic section, making the role of the markets in the production possible in the first place (Hayek, 1944/1994). There, however, where planning did not limit itself to fixing a scope for economic action but directly intervened in the market development, problems arose. The myth of the foresightful guidance by industry ministers was shattered at least since the Asia crisis.

But even the interventions of the state were mostly pragmatic and never ideologically motivated. Since the planning was always seen as only an instrument, there was a distinct advantage as opposed to states, which had planning as a part of their state ideology.

The economic market's purity of style became more important in that way, as they – through their export-oriented growth and later on through their opening for foreign investors – integrated into the world market. Capital controls, for instance, affect the states differently today than in times when they were still much less dependent on the international capital movements. Simultaneously, the economic compatibility of different parts of the economic order became more important today. Thus, the successful performance of the liberalization of the capital markets depends on a functioning bankruptcy act, banking and financial market order. The globalization outright forced this on unwilling countries.

The economic recovery process in Asia led to a reform paradox: Reforms, which were seen as necessary for re-attaining the growth success of the last decades, are threatened by the recovery of the economy. For example, Malaysia's case shows that growth after the crisis made thorough structural reforms unnecessary. Even though this danger fundamentally applied for all three states, there are distinct differences in the reform successes since the Asia crisis. South Korea definitely used the crisis as an opportunity to start long-overdue structure reforms. Indonesia and Malaysia seem to have taken much longer before the unhealthy economic structures exhibited in the crisis led at least to partial reform. The nowadays much more distinct difference in per-capita income among the three countries and the rise of Korea to a diplomatic and economic powerhouse in the region and on the world level shows that decisions taken during the crisis had a lasting impact on long-term growth chances.

Chapter 7: 'Big Deals' – Competition Policy as an Answer for the Korean Crisis

7.1 Chaebol in the Korean economy before the crisis

While the Korean financial and economic crisis of 1997 and 1998 was mainly a debt crisis of the private sector, rather than the previous crises in Latin America, Africa and some other countries, which were driven by state debt, nevertheless the highly concentrated structure of the Korean private sector, comprising the notorious *chaebol*, or conglomerates, did not only survive the crisis, but even was strengthened by it. This is astonishing since the crisis itself was partly a structural crisis and a crisis due to the absence of competition. The Korean government, recognizing this, tried to force companies into mergers, so-called "big deals", in which large conglomerates swap businesses to improve the competitiveness of the Korean economy. This strategy is tantamount to a governmental solution for the development of market structures, which was part of the problem of the crisis itself. Therefore, from the beginning the "big deals" were criticized for offering a medicine which had itself been part of the sickness.

Chaebol (conglomerates, literally "property clan/wealthy faction") developed after the end of the Korean War in 1953, mostly as family-owned and -run businesses.[126] The word *chaebol* itself is identical to the Japanese *keiretsu* business groups, which again are successors of the pre-World-War-II *zaibatsu* groups. However, between the Korean and the Japanese conglomerate model there are important differences, as the following table shows.

Table 3: Comparison of Korean and Japanese conglomerates

	Chaebol	**Keiretsu**
Ownership	Centralized	Decentralized
Management	Founding family (though nominally often no controlling stake)	Professional managers
Production Network	Subsidiaries, before 1997 production mainly in Korea	Subcontractors, with production often in Korea or Southeast Asia, later in China
Finance	Relying on banking system, credit allocation influenced by government	Relying on "house banks" with preferential financing

Source: The author.

126 For an historic overview see Steers et al. (1989) and Choe (1996: 10-51).

In 1997 there were around 80 *chaebol*, eight of which went bankrupt during the crisis years of 1997 and 1998. These 80 *chaebol* had more than 1,100 subsidiaries. The "big five" alone, Hyundai, Daewoo, Samsung Group, SK Corporation and LG Corporation, had more than 100 subsidiaries each; however, only an estimated 10 to 20 percent of them were profitable (Lee Chang-sup, 1998: 2). Over half of Korean exports originated at subsidiaries of the big five (The Economist, 1997: 23-25). The growing importance of *chaebol* before the Asian crisis can be seen over time: In the 1980s and 1990s, around 70 percent of value added came from investments of existing companies in Korea, 25 percent from investments in subsidiaries or joint ventures, and only a meagre 5 percent from independent incorporations of an enterprise (Machetzki, 1997: 175). During their expansion period *chaebol* relied on state-led industrial policy through indicative planning, investment control and credit allocation of state-owned or -controlled banks until the 1980s.[127] In the 1960s and 1970s the Korean government in times of crisis (as during the oil price shocks) forced the larger and more healthy *chaebol* to merge with bankrupt companies, thereby avoiding social problems and rising unemployment during crisis times. However, this irrational growth was not accompanied by efficiency gains and the cross-subsidization of unprofitable subsidiaries became the rule rather than the exception. – Mergers with insolvent companies were sweetened with credit allocation by state-owned banks. A precondition for this was close political contacts between banks and *chaebol* in an often outright corrupt manner.[128] From the 1950s to the 1970s credit allocation worked mainly by state-owned banks; in the 1980s banks were formally privatized, but the politically controlled management and credit allocation remained intact (Frank/Pascha, 1997: 133).

From the point of view of competition policy the growth of *chaebol* was problematic, though conglomerates are not at all typical of the Korean economy alone. Usually, however, the reasons for growth by mergers are economic: vertical and horizontal mergers that result in economies of scale and special sourcing conditions explain the desire for market power and the dynamics of mergers. Competition policy in particular sees this last reason for mergers as a fact warranting regulation. Conglomerates also benefit from economies of scope, e.g. through the joint use of brand names or joint use of management functions (like marketing) in an enterprise. Efficiency reasons were, however, rarely those leading

---

127 On Korea's industrial policy see Yoo and Shim (1986: 95-123), and Lee (1998). On the role of the state in the growth of *chaebol* in detail see Kang (1996: 127-156).

128 For example, the authoritarian presidents Chun Doo-Hwan (1980-1988) and Roh Tae-Woo (1988-1993) during their presidency accumulated, according to some estimates, 900 million USD and 600 million USD, respectively; see Woo-Cuming (1997).

to growth of South Korean companies. Take for example the Jindo group, a mid-size *chaebol* in 1998 ranked as the 37th largest. Started by founder Kim Young-Jin as a fur producer for New York fashion companies, it became in a few years the largest fur merchant in the world. Additionally, the group diversified into unrelated businesses like container construction, retail, as a subcontractor in the automotive sector, and waste management (see Cho, 1998: 1,7). Reasons for uncontrolled growth were the founders' megalomaniac visions, rather than economic benefits. In 1998 the heavily indebted enterprise went bankrupt.

While the extension of the *chaebol* networks did not bring efficiency gains, they also did not bode well in another respect for Korean markets. Many markets in South Korea were divided into narrow oligopolies of a few competing *chaebol*. This was particularly true for all markets with state placements of orders. Also, the profit ratio of Korean *chaebol* was low, since the growth of turnover rather than the growth of profits has been the benchmark for expansion. First, companies wanted to take part in the fast growth of East Asian markets. Profitability was seen as guaranteed through seemingly unlimited growth. Uncontrolled growth, however, needed an ever-faster growing debt to finance new investment, reducing profits more and more. According to estimates by a research institute belonging to the Hyundai Group, the 12 South Korean companies being part of the world's 500 largest companies (as listed in Forbes magazine) only contributed 0.2 percent to their total profit, giving Korea's *chaebol* 26th place out of 27 nations in this listing.

Besides high savings quotas, financing through domestic credit only was the more difficult the more the Korean economy grew. Therefore, with relaxing government regulation and increased access to international capital markets, these markets were more and more important to finance Korean credit, and subsequently Korea's economy became more dependent on trust from international investors. In particular, there was a mismatch between short-term investment by international investors in East Asia and long-term engagement by Korean companies. Uncertainty about the future, but also regulatory hurdles and political issues, were the main reasons for short-term investment. Therefore, the additional financing by international capital markets increased the mismatch between short-term investment and long-term commitment from the Korean side. The debt-to-equity-ratio of 25 of the 30 biggest *chaebol* in 1997 was more than 3 to 1, and for five even more than 5 to 1 (The Economist 1997: 25). This had at the same time negative consequences on the possibility of small and medium enterprises to refinance their investments.

7.2 Crisis of *chaebol* and 'big deals'

While the panic in markets and contagion from Southeast Asia after the outbreak of the Asian crisis in Thailand in July 1997 were partly responsible for the immediate crisis in Korea, already long before, in 1996, the slower growth of the South Korean economy brought economic difficulties for some of the largest *chaebol*. Since most calculations of profitability were dependent on assumed large and constant growth rates, high overcapacity emerged in some markets leading to losses in a slower growing economy. These losses could, due to the high debt-to-equity-ratio, be financed less and less. Already in summer 1997 Hanbo Iron & Steel and Kia Motors, then the eighth largest *chaebol,* went bankrupt. In september 1997, Jinro, the 19th largest *chaebol* and the largest producer of Korean liquor, followed. In the case of Hanbo in particular, collusive relations between government and *chaebol* as well as the misallocation of resources under the drive to expand into heavy industry became obvious; Hanbo built a steel mill in the 1980s wherein costs soared from an estimated 3 billion USD to 6.7 billion USD, leading to a debt-to-equity-ratio of 22 to 1 and annual interest payments of 580 million USD on a debt of 5.8 billion USD (Pollack, 1997). As Feenstra et al. (2001: 75) point out, it was first domestically oriented groups (for example in construction and steel) which went bankrupt, followed by some of the large groups, which led to a third round of bankruptcies among smaller subcontractors.

These bankruptcies, which for the first time happened en masse in the Korean economy, showed a dilemma of Korean growth. By the mid-1990s, *chaebol* became "too big to fail" for Korea, since their bankruptcy brought social and economic problems for the whole economy. This is especially true for the "big five" (Wolf, 1998). Their fate was determining not only the short-term prospects of the Korean economy, but also their long-term growth perspectives. For example, in 1998, 88 percent of Korean private research funds were concentred with the three largest *chaebol*: Samsung, Hyundai and Daewoo (Frankfurter Allgemeine Zeitung, 1998). At the same time the Korean state was no longer – neither with domestic money nor foreign aid – able to overcome the crisis, as in earlier times, through state-led restructuring of the sector structure sweetened by bailouts of non-performing loans. In 1983, for example, after the second oil price shock, a Japanese credit of 4 billion USD helped this restructuring effort, which that time was approximately 13 percent of Korea's net foreign debt, 5 percent of its GNP or 20 percent of its annual investment (Woo-Cummings, 1997).

When Korea asked for an IMF stand-by credit in December 1997, reforming the corporate sector was one of its conditions. The change of government to the new President Kim Dae-Jung also led to a new competition policy trying to tackle the power of *chaebol*.[129] Already in 1994 the government of Kim Young-Sam founded the Fair Trade Commission (FTC) as an independent competition authority. FTC among others had ruled against insider trading and cross-subsidization of insolvent subsidiaries. In 1993 the cross-guarantee of debt was decreased from a legally applicable limit of 200 percent to 100 percent of equity of the creditor's company. However, it was often not easy to establish the ownership relations of companies due to the complex cross-ownership issues, which was another task for the FTC. Since 1996 the FTC was also responsible for consumer protection issues. Nevertheless, policy vis-a-vis *chaebol* was contradictory: On the one hand the government of Kim Young-Sam readily acknowledged that overcapacity could lead to problems in crisis, in particular through ruinous competition in narrow domestic markets, if world markets were not able to absorb Korean goods. Therefore since 1993 the Korean government through the Ministry of Trade, Industry and Energy (MOTIE) tried to implement a plan for industrial specialization (Machetzki, 1997: 179). This plan failed due to opposition by the concerned *chaebol*, which were by now too large for government control, while democratic transition led to a shrinking power of the government to impose its will on *chaebol*.[130] On the other hand, the will to curb the power of *chaebol* was weak in a political system where the ruling party would immensely benefit from "political contributions" by *chaebol*. These were not always outright bribes, but rather since authoritarian times understood as a form of special taxation. Therefore expectations on the new coalition government of Kim Dae-Jung were high to implement (instead of only announcing) a new competition policy. The FTC was a core institution in the early strategy of the Kim Dae-Jung administration to restructure the *chaebol*.[131] Reform was sought in particular for two urgent problems, namely cross-subsidization and cross-guarantees as well as reduction of overcapacity in core markets.

---

129 In the political platform of Kim Dae-Jung (1998-2003), and even more pronounced under his successor Roh Moo-Hyun (2003-2008), this had economic as well as political connotations. *Chaebol* were considered to be part of the long-standing authoritarian system of government. However, ultimately Kim Dae-Jung developed close relations with certain *chaebol*, in particular Hyundai, to forward his policy toward North Korea.

130 The changing power relations of *chaebol* and government are an important aspect of the understanding of the *chaebol* role in the Korean economy: Some authors do not see misallocation and overcapacity as a consequence of industrial policy of the state, but rather as a weakness of the state to curb politically suitable *chaebol* for the ruling party; see Yoo (1995). This reasoning has some benefits in that formal (indicative) planning had lost importance throughout the 1980s. However, *chaebol* always were conscious about government influence on *de iure* independent banks. And decisions to create overcapacity in sectors like the automotive sector were not only based on wrong expectations of market size growth, but also based on an implicit government guarantee for the survival of insolvent conglomerates in the past.

131 See the announcement of the economic advisor to the president, Kim Tae Dong (1998: 7).

First, the government wanted *chaebol* to commit themselves to reduce debt between subsidiaries and to end new cross-subsidization. Second, *chaebol* should commit themselves to the reduction of overcapacity in so-called "big deals" in seven core economic sectors to avoid ruinous competition. Ruinous competition (or cutthroat competition) is defined as a situation "when competition results in prices that do not chronically or for extended periods of time cover costs of production, particularly fixed costs. This may arise in secularly declining or 'sick' industries with high levels of excess capacity or where frequent cyclical or random demand downturns are experienced" (Khemani/Shapiro, 1993). The analysis of ruinous competition is not uncontested, and in particular the conclusion that it represents market failure and therefore warrants government intervention has been criticized (Tolksdorf, 1971). The experience of the reforms was ultimately mixed: *chaebol* opposed all kind of change, in particular forced mergers, and waged a war through the media to undermine reform efforts, showing clear limits to the government's power (Yoo, 1998: 6). At least, *chaebol* began to reduce their debt-to-equity levels. From April to September 1998 alone, the 30 largest *chaebol* reduced their debt levels by 24 percent, a good result given that the deepest recession ever after the Korean War had the country in its grip (Korea Times, 1998b: 9). However, while medium-sized *chaebol* were actively reducing their debt, the five largest *chaebol* even increased their dominance of the credit market by issuing new corporate bonds and other commercial papers. They crowded out small- and medium-size enterprises and saw their debt soaring by another 12 percent (Park, 1998: 9).

Regarding cross-subsidization, the IMF and the Korean government in November 1998, a year after the peak of the crisis, negotiated an agreement to end cross-guarantees and cross-subsidization (Korea Times, 1998a: 9). Also, in 1998 the government designed its strategy for the "big deals". The starting point was the bankruptcy of the two automotive producers Kia and Asia Motors, which forced the car industry to reorganize.[132] This was particularly important, since here competition was almost completely domestic; the share of domestic cars in the market in early 1998 was 99.8 percent. Since then, it has gradually been reduced. Asia Motors Co. Ltd. was founded in 1965 and produced in particular special vehicles (like trucks, military vehicles, jeeps and buses), with a little less than one-third of the company owned by Kia Motors. In 1999, Asia Motors was merged with Kia, which itself had gone bankrupt and by then been sold to Hyundai. Originally, the Korean government wanted to auction off Kia, but several attempts

132 For an overview over the development of the Korean car industry see Lee (2001). For the relation of South Korean industrial policy and the growth of the automotive sector see Auty (1996). For a sectoral overview see Greenbaum (2002).

were unsuccessful, so finally it was sold to Hyundai. The threats and recriminations between the government and Hyundai regarding its acquisition were intent. Only one day after the sales the Korean President Kim Dae-Jung threatened to call off the deal if Hyundai would not participate in further mergers under the "big deal" scheme. The standoff with Hyundai was part of a larger power struggle between the government and *chaebol*, mainly through media announcements. Hyundai group itself became, after a near bankruptcy, split into five parts, among them Hyundai Kia Automotive Group. In the years after the crisis the company has made a spectacular turnaround, and in 2009 had a global turnover of 20.4 billion euros.

The smallest of the competitors, Samsung Motors Inc., was only founded in 1994, in conjunction with Japanese Nissan. From 1995 to 1998 a factory was built. When the first large series, SM5 (based on Nissan Maxima), hit the market in 1998, the crisis already had hit businesses hard. Samsung started to look for a partner, which it found in Renault. Merger talks could be successfully concluded after in 1999 the Renault-Nissan alliance became reality. Renault took over 70 percent of Samsung in 2000 and currently holds more than 80 percent. Daewoo Motor was originally not affected by the merger plans. Daewoo Motor itself had acquired in 1982 a company called National Motor. However, when the bankruptcy of Daewoo emerged in 1998, General Motors started to invest in the company, becoming majority shareholder in 2005 and since then increasing its equity to 70,1 percent in 2009. The case of Daewoo shows how difficult it was for the government to decide about market structures in the midst of an unprecedented economic crisis. The *chaebol* founded in 1967 became bankrupt with a record debt and its founder fled Korea, and after six years abroad finally returned to Korea to become imprisoned for 8.5 years on charges of falsification of a balance sheet.[133] Already in 1997 Daewoo had bought SsangYong Motors. SsangYong Motors looked back on a long history of production since 1954, including production of jeeps for the U.S. Army and some cooperation with German Mercedes-Benz. The merger of SsangYong and Daewoo was in line with the strategy to unify the market and prevent "ruinous" competition. In 2000 however, the bankrupt Daewoo conglomerate had to sell SsangYong again. The company was finally taken over by the Shanghai Automotive Industry Corporation (SAIC), became again bankrupt in 2009, and was in merger talks again with Indian car manufacturer Mahindra Ltd., signing an agreement in late 2010.

After the difficult crisis years, the Korean automotive industry saw a spectacular turnaround. Low export prices due to the devaluation of the Korean won

133 However, his prison term was shortened considerably by President Roh Moo-Hyun, himself often embroiled in power struggles with the *chaebol*. After only 1.5 years in prison, he was set free by special amnesty of the president.

in 1997 as well as increased technology leadership helped, especially for Hyundai-Kia. The original blueprint of "big deals" in the sector, however, was completely abandoned. Market forces shaped the sector. The same is, *cum grano salis*, true for the other six sectors being part of the big deals, namely semiconductors, shipbuilding, petrochemicals, machine building, power stations and aircraft industries. While in some industries, in particular the attempts to build up a functioning aircraft industry, the role of economies of scale is obvious, and overcapacity had to be reduced (however, through which mechanism, market or state, is not implied in this statement), in other industries even the diagnosis that overcapacity existed was contested, since it depended very much in the actual shape of the export markets. For instance, the car and the electronics industries dominating national enterprises was the result of industrial policy (Lee 1998: 84). Fortunately, the outward-looking nature of export-oriented car manufacturers, new competition rules in international organizations like OECD and the WTO, and the growing importance of free trade agreements, among them most prominently the two recent trade agreements with the European Union (in force since July 2011) and the U.S. (in force since January 1, 2012), did a lot to mitigate the effects of concentration on the Korean automotive and electronics market. The goal of achieving an "optimal intensity" of competition, implicit behind the "big deals" policy, was unattainable. At the same time, the use of political power by the government to force mergers also might prejudice later policies vis-à-vis the newly created companies in form of a tacit bailout guarantee. This was for example the intention of Kim Woo-Choong, chairman of the Federation of Korean Industries, the representative group for large *chaebol*, when he demanded state investment "guidelines" for the *chaebol* in the wake of the crisis (Noh, 1998: 8).

Chaebol reform, together with restructuring the financial sector and the labour market and the opening of the economy to foreign competitors, did a lot to reduce the unhealthy debt levels of the *chaebol* and did make some progress, mainly through opening, in increasing competition. Other problems could not be solved, among them the control of *chaebol* by cross-shareholding and shareholding by family members, family-owned charities and senior managers from subsidiaries. Often with a tiny amount of shares, just 1 or 2 percent, owners can still completely control management of *chaebol*. This, however, also might change over time, since the founding generation and also in many cases the second generation of *chaebol* founding families is no longer in control and ownership is dispersing more, leading in some cases to more professional management.

One of the aims of restructuring of the *chaebol*, besides the reintroduction of fresh capital, was the transfer of technology and managerial know-how. This was already stipulated in the bailout agreement with the IMF, e.g. for the banking sector. Some companies sold parts to foreign bidders, like Ssangyong, formerly the sixth largest *chaebol*, which divested in addition to its auto division other parts to multinationals like Procter & Gamble or Hambrecht & Quist (Business Week, 1998). However, the turnaround of the Korean economy from mid-1998 removed a lot of pressure to restructure from the *chaebol*. An ill-defined bankruptcy law was another factor in the lack of motivation for *chaebol* to restructure (Hilsenrath, 1998). The long-standing symbiosis of politics, bureaucracy and *chaebol* could, for example, be seen in the planned split of Pohang Iron and Steel Company (POSCO), which was prevented by the long-standing political ties between a smaller coalition partner the United Liberal Democrats (ULD), and in particular their leader, and the *chaebol* (Sah, 1998: 8). Similarly, in the financial sector the merger of (nearly bankrupt) Cho Hung Bank with bankrupt Kangwon and Chungbuk banks, and the subsequent discharge from state control despite a failure to achieve minimum standards of financial viability set by the government, is an example of the political clout of companies persisting in the post-crisis era (Sah, 1998b: 9).

7.3 Continued *chaebol* reform in the aftermath of the crisis

Enterprise reforms have been a major political goal to overcome the Asian financial crisis and are still not completed. The largest 43 *chaebol* (conglomerates) own 728 units and are, to a large extent, responsible for export performance and the production output of the Korean economy. The former owner-managers of the most exposed ten biggest *chaebol*, among others Samsung, LG and Hyundai (now split into several units) now own a mere 2 percent in capital stock. Yet their influence remains dominant, which can be substantiated with nontransparent business conduct in *chaebol*. This results in exceedingly low international credibility. For instance, in 2003 the prestigious Lausanne, Switzerland-based IMD rated South Korea 47th of 49 selected countries in terms of corporate credibility.

The Roh Moo-Hyun administration attempted to further polish his clean image through reforms of the large conglomerates, the abolition of which Roh as a progressive lawmaker had demanded in the course of the Asian financial crisis. Stronger control and constraints on investment for *chaebol* would be logical indeed if they occurred in a competitive and proper political framework based on rules, not state intervention. However, the alliance with Chung Mong-Joon, who was a majority shareholder of one of the largest *chaebol* corporations, Hyundai Heavy Industries, belied to some extent this intention. The amalgamation with Hyundai, particularly with respect to North Korea policies, was an unfortunate legacy of the Kim Dae-Jung administration. Kim Dae-Jung used Hyundai for putting forth his Sunshine Policy in North Korea.[134] Along with the ability of North Korea to blackmail the government to some extent, this effectuated a strong obligation toward the already bankrupt Hyundai Group, which was accommodated by the government with cash injections.

In 2003, thirteen Korean enterprises were on the Forbes top 500 list, among others Samsung Electronics, Hyundai Motor Co. and SK. Samsung was named with three subsidiaries, whereas Hyundai, SK and LG are named with two subsidiary companies each, which demonstrates the extent of oligopoly existing in the South Korean economy. The ten biggest industrial conglomerates in Korea accounted for 52.2 percent of the total capital in the Korean stock market in 2004. In the previous year, the number was at 51.4 percent. The market capitalization of corporations had reached a value of 152.6 billion USD in December 2003. As opposed to the beginning of 2003, this was an increase of 35.4 percent. Crucial in this aspect was a high demand abroad for Korean stocks. At the same time, in 2003 44.4 percent of *chaebol* stocks were owned by foreign investors (as opposed to 40 percent in 2002). At the peak of the crisis, the biggest *chaebol* had reached a debt-net equity ratio of almost 400 percent due to unchecked growth financed by debt. Then the IMF demanded structural adjustment policies, which decreased the ratio significantly to 135 percent by 2003. While some of the *chaebol* such as Daewoo ceased to exist as corporations, others were able to revive previous export results in the post-crisis period. Nevertheless, the problems of *chaebol* for economic policy making, such as the often criticized lack of transparency, remained.

This became clear for instance in April 2003, when the trade company SK Global, affiliated with SK Corporation, inflated its profits by 1.55 trillion won (1.21 billion USD) in its 2001 balance sheet. Furthermore, according to the state attorney, major stock price manipulation occurred, leading to arrests of high-ranking SK spokespersons. Complicated relations between *chaebol* subsidiaries, which are often merely secured by marginal mutual stockholdings, make dozens of companies liable for their mistakes. The influence of stock owners is often marginal as many *chaebol* are still operated like family-owned businesses.

In his election campaign and during his first weeks of inauguration, President Roh Moo-Hyun named the battle against the oligopolization of the market in South Korea a top priority. Nevertheless, he soon realized that the economic power of the *chaebol* prevented the kind of reforms he had in mind. A more stringent competition policy would be desirable for foreign companies as they are often impeded by numerous regulations, unlike the near-monopolists. But finally, a truce of sorts was

---

134 The policy efforts leading to the first summit between Kim Dae-Jung and North Korea's leader Kim Jong-Il included shady financial transfers, in which a state-owned bank and conglomerate affiliates were also named.

concluded between President Roh and the *chaebol* in face of economic difficulties.

Time also showed that some reforms designed to make *chaebol* more transparent did not achieve the desired result. One of the reform measures under President Kim Dae-Jung had been the introduction of "outside directors" to the supervisory boards of *chaebol*. However, this often leads to the appointment of figureheads (mostly professors) for this lucrative position, who had little control or management experience. An independent small-business sector is completely absent as medium-size companies are bound by exclusive supply contracts with one *chaebol* alone, which therefore renders competition and the possibility to search for new markets impossible. The government is partially responsible for this, as it fails to create and push through a regulative framework and continues to rely on direct state intervention instead. One example is the government's attempt to coerce the *chaebol* to increase loans by the issuance of new shares of their highly indebted subsidiaries in the credit card business in 2003 and 2004. Moreover, some *chaebol* are tightly connected with politics, which results in consistent exemptions or aid, as is the case with the Hyundai Corporation. With a bad economic situation at the beginning of his tenure of drastic *chaebol* reforms, President Roh Moo-Hyun's goal to limit the power of *chaebol* became even less credible, after illegal contributions to his campaign became public.

When President Lee Myung-Bak took office in 2008, many expected an end to *chaebol* reform, since he himself rose through the ranks of Hyundai to become one of the top managers in the country before entering politics. In terms of the fierce anti-*chaebol* rhetoric of his predecessor this is true. However, economic globalization had already transformed many of the *chaebol* into more multinational (instead of national Korean) enterprises. With regards to domestic policy goals, the Lee Myung-Bak government resorted to the same mixture of threats and cooperation also used by his predecessors, for example in the debate about a more equitable share of profits between the *chaebol* and the small and medium components makers often directly dependent on a single conglomerate. Overall, economic opening might have contributed much more to *chaebol* reform than regulatory policies could have done. This does not prevent the continued existence of *chaebol* and this cannot completely eradicate problems like circular shareholding, but it can reduce the effects for the economy as a whole. Today, the list of top groups, according to the FTC, includes a mixture of well-known affiliates of *chaebol*, in particular Samsung, Hyundai, SK, LG and Lotte Co., as well as the large state-owned companies, as the next table shows. Some formerly bankrupt or near-bankrupt companies survived under a new corporate identity. At the same time, former subsidiaries are more independent than before and often act as different companies, like Hyundai Motor Co. and Hyundai Heavy Industries. The overall number of subsidiaries has decreased. Nevertheless, market dominance continues to pose a grave challenge for competition policy.

Table 4: Top 40 companies by subsidiaries and total assets 2011 (in brackets 2010)

Ranking	Name of company	Number of subsidiaries	Total assets in KRW billions
1 (1)	Samsung Group	78 (67)	230.9 (192.8)
2 (2)	KoreaLand & Housing Corp.	4 (4)	148.2 (130.3)
3 (3)	Korean Electric Power Corp.	14 (13)	131.3 (123.5)
4 (4)	Hyundai Motor Co.	63 (42)	126.7 (100.7)
5 (5)	SK Corp.	86 (75)	97.0 (87.5)
6 (6)	LG Corp.	59 (53)	90.6 (78.9)
7 (7)	Lotte Co.	78 (60)	77.3 (67.2)
8 (8)	POSCO	61 (48)	69.8 (52.8)
9 (11)	Hyundai Heavy Industries Co.	21 (16)	54.4 (40.1)
10 (9)	Korea Highway Corp.	4 (4)	47.4 (45.3)
11 (10)	GS Group	76 (69)	46.7 (43.0)
12 (13)	Hanjin Group	40 (37)	33.5 (30.3)
13 (16)	Hanhwa Group	55 (48)	31.7 (26.3)
14 (14)	KT Corp.	32 (30)	28.1 (27.0)
15 (15)	Doosan Group	25 (29)	27.0 (26.7)
16 (12)	Kumho Asiana Group	36 (45)	24.5 (34.9)
17 (17)	Korea Gas Corp.	3 (3)	24.5 (23.0)
18 (18)	Korea Railroad Corp.	11 (11)	23.1 (21.3)
19 (-)	Korea National Oil Corp.	2 (-)	22. 4 (-)
20 (19)	STX Corp.	21 (16)	22.0(20.9)
21 (20)	LS Group	47 (44)	18.0 (16.1)
22 (23)	CJ Group	65 (54)	16.3 (13.0)
23 (22)	Hynix Semiconductor	9 (9)	16.1 (13.6)
24 (27)	Shinsegae	13 (12)	16.0 (12.4)
25 (21)	Daewoo Shipbuilding & Marine Engineering	16 (13)	15.5 (15.9)
26 (25)	Dongbu Group	38 (31)	14.3 (12.4)
27 (26)	Hyundai	14 (12)	13.7 (12.4)
28 (24)	Daelim	19 (16)	13.5 (12.9)
29 (29)	Buyoung	16 (15)	11.4 (9.1)
30 (-)	Daewoo Engineering & Construction	13 (-)	11.0 (-)

Ranking	Name of company	Number of subsidiaries	Total assets in KRW billions
31 (33)	KCC Corp.	9 (10)	10.2 (8.7)
32 (32)	Dongkuk Steel Mill Co.	13 (12)	10.1 (9.1)
33 (31)	S-Oil Corp.	2 (2)	10.1 (9.1)
34 (30)	Hyosung Corp.	39 (40)	9.7 (9.1)
35 (38)	OCI	17 (18)	9.7 (7.7)
36 (41)	Hyundai Department Store	26 (29)	8.4 (6.8)
37 (34)	Hanjin Heavy Industries & Construction Co.	8 (7)	8.2 (8.6)
38 (40)	Woongjin Group	31 (24)	8.1 (6.8)
39 (43)	Kolon Industries	39 (37)	8.1 (6.8)
40 (36)	Incheon International Airport Corp.	2 (2)	8.0 (8.1)

Source: Fair Trade Commission (FTC), internet file: http://www.ftc.go.kr/news/ftc/reportView.jsp?report_data_no=4258 (6 April 2011).

7.4 Competition policy and the lessons of the Asian crisis

The preceding discussion shows that the economic crisis in South Korea was not merely the result of a financial bubble or misallocation in the financial sector, but also the result of wrong decisions and developments in industrial policy, or, in other words, the result of the lack of stringent competition policy not aiming at influencing the market structure, but rather guaranteeing free access to markets and competition. The role of *chaebol* in Korea remains ambivalent. While they are the embodiment of the success of the South Korean economy and today in some cases household brands throughout the world with high brand value, their domestic market power remains problematic and their relation to the government remains close. While the historic pathway of *chaebol*, founded in the Japanese colonial experience, triggered by the Korean War and later the catch-up policy of authoritarian governments, had overall good results, it should be noted that the market structure of *chaebol* was not a necessary ingredient for economic growth, as is sometimes presumed in the literature on developmental states. The example of Taiwan readily shows that other experiences with much smaller and more flexible enterprises can also be successful.[135] In Korea itself, the Asian crisis led to a gradual abandoning of the old relations between government and *chaebol* and new, more professional

135 See the comparison of Taiwan and Korea in Hamilton (1996).

relations. However, all Korean governments, including the latest government of President Lee Myung-Bak, are still conscious of the state influence on the industrial structure and occasionally try to use heavy-handed industrial policy.

Chapter 8: Korea's Economic Development Between the Asian Crisis and the International Financial Crisis 2008-2010

8.1 Macroeconomic developments in Korea in the aftermath of the crisis

In 1999 the South Korean economy recorded double-digit GDP growth, achieving a V-shaped recovery. Consequently, President Kim Dae-Jung, for the first time after coming into power, judged the economic crisis to be "completely overcome". He cited the impressive increase in foreign exchange reserve, the largest-ever surplus in the international balance of payments, record-high foreign direct investment (FDI) and the growth rate. In terms of what the president called – using a popular but misleading Korean expression – the "IMF crisis", i.e. the foreign exchange crisis of 1997, he was right. However, concerning the economic crisis in Korea caused by economic policy choices of Korea, his evaluation for 1999 seemed at least premature. Generally the economic policy of the Kim Dae-Jung administration was very successful, especially compared with the policies of other Asian nations during and after the crisis. The success can not only be shown by the return of confidence (of consumers and investors), the rise of market indices (like the stock market index and other ratings) and the return of growth. One even more important factor is the success of the aggressive wooing of FDI, a new policy of the Kim Dae-Jung era. The record FDI in 1998 and 1999 did not only alleviate some of Korea's crisis problems in the short run, it was a factor in changing the Korean economy in the long run. If the overall reform policy was quite successful, nevertheless important problems remained unsolved. One problem was the decreasing pressure due to the successful development described above, representing a paradox: Because South Korea successfully overcame the crisis, there was the danger of a reduced pressure for reform, as long as it was related to hardship, especially in the private sector. The growth of Korean GDP can be seen in the following table. The crisis certainly has been a turning point for growth. The previous experience of decades of high, often double-digit growth, could, despite the V-shaped recovery, not be prolonged. Growth rates became lower overall, and crises in the world economy, like the terrorist attacks of 2001, the SARS shock in 2003, and the financial and economic crisis of 2008 to 2009, had an immediate impact on the economy. Nevertheless, the growth rate remained much higher than that of most OECD countries.

Table 5: Growth Rate of GDP

Year	Growth Rate of GDP (%)	Year	Growth Rate of GDP (%)
1971	10.4	1991	9.7
1972	6.5	1992	5.8
1973	14.8	1993	6.3
1974	9.4	1994	8.8
1975	7.3	1995	8.9
1976	13.5	1996	7.2
1977	11.8	1997	5.8
1978	10.3	1998	-5.7
1979	8.4	1999	10.7
1980	-1.9	2000	8.8
1981	7.4	2001	4.0
1982	8.3	2002	7.2
1983	12.2	2003	2.8
1984	9.9	2004	4.6
1985	7.5	2005	4.0
1986	12.2	2006	5.2
1987	12.3	2007	5.1
1988	11.7	2008	2.3
1989	6.8	2009	0.3
1990	9.3	2010	6.2

Source: Bank of Korea, www.bok.or.kr

The successful Korean turnaround after the crisis and deep recession of 1998 can also be seen in the development of GDP per capita. In the crisis year, it stood as low as 7,723 USD. By 2004 it had more than doubled, and by 2011, according to an estimate by the IMF, had almost tripled from the crisis level.

Table 6: GDP Per Capita (Current Prices)

Year	GDP Per Capita (USD)	Year	GDP Per Capita (USD)
1980	1,688.84	1996	12,586.60
1981	1,869.65	1997	11,582.11
1982	1,971.31	1998	7,723.84
1983	2,153.89	1999	9,906.40
1984	2,349.78	2000	11,346.66
1985	2.413.94	2001	10,654.82
1986	2,759.69	2002	12,093.73
1987	3.444.80	2003	13,451.10
1988	4,570.73	2004	15,028.82
1989	5,565.10	2005	17,550.88
1990	6,307.69	2006	19,706.60
1991	7,288.83	2007	21,653.274
1992	7.729.97	2008	19,162.04
1993	8,422.05	2009	17,074.48
1994	9,757.50	2010	20,590.96
1995	11,778.76	2011	22,961.25 est.

Source: IMF World Economic Outlook Database (April 2011)

Naturally, this spectacular success in nominal growth rates of GDP does not necessarily say a lot about purchasing power. The deep plunge of the Korean won vis-à-vis the U.S. dollar, which was the immediate effect of the currency crisis, led to a deep plunge of nominal GDP in U.S. dollars. Looking at GDP per capita using PPP data for 2005, the picture gets a little more moderate in the success, but also in the previous crisis. Here, the crisis is only a small indenture in an otherwise fairly constant upwards movement. And, contrary to nominal GDP data, the year 2009 also does not represent a regression of GDP, but in terms of purchasing power also records growth.

Table 7: GDP Per Capita (Using PPP of 2005)

Year	GDP Per Capita (USD)	Year	GDP Per Capita (USD)	Year	GDP Per Capita (USD)
1960	1,877	1978	5,442	1996	16,726
1961	1,929	1979	5,723	1997	17,341
1962	1,914	1980	5,551	1998	16,036
1963	2,032	1981	5,802	1999	17,433
1964	2,171	1982	6,131	2000	18,755
1965	2,238	1983	6,693	2001	19,331
1966	2,448	1984	7,146	2002	20,598
1967	2,533	1985	7,557	2003	21,070
1968	2,755	1986	8,277	2004	21,961
1969	3,066	1987	9,106	2005	22,783
1970	3,263	1988	9,977	2006	23,884
1971	3,463	1989	10,545	2007	25,021
1972	3,550	1990	11,398	2008	25,498
1973	3,908	1991	12,345	2009	27,938
1974	4,117	1992	12,936	2010	29,836
1975	4,290	1993	13,590	2011	31,410 est.
1976	4,668	1994	14,603		
1977	5,055	1995	15,782		

Source: U.S. Bureau of Labor Statistics (July 28, 2009), Year 1960–2008, internet file: http://www.bls.gov/fls/flsgdp.pdf; International Monetary Fund (April 2011), Year 2009-2011, World Economic Outlook Database

What are the macroeconomic determinants of the successful Korean growth performance? Before the crisis, investment and savings rates had been comparatively high, reaching up to 40 percent, as the following table shows.

Table 8: Domestic Investment and Savings Ratios Before the Crisis

Year	Gross Domestic Investment Ratio (%)	Year	Gross Saving Ratio (%)
1970	25.4	1970	17.4
1971	26.0	1971	15.3
1972	21.3	1972	17.0
1973	25.3	1973	22.8
1974	31.9	1974	21.5
1975	28.7	1975	19.1
1976	26.6	1976	24.7
1977	29.5	1977	28.2
1978	32.6	1978	30.6
1979	36.7	1979	29.7
1980	33.0	1980	24.3
1981	30.5	1981	24.3
1982	30.1	1982	25.6
1983	31.2	1983	28.9
1984	31.2	1984	30.9
1985	31.3	1985	31.2
1986	30.5	1986	34.9
1987	30.8	1987	38.4
1988	32.4	1988	40.4
1989	35.3	1989	37.6
1990	38.0	1990	37.8
1991	40.0	1991	37.9
1992	37.0	1992	36.9
1993	36.0	1993	36.9
1994	36.8	1994	36.4
1995	37.1	1995	36.2
1996	38.1	1996	34.8

Source: Bank of Korea, www.bok.or.kr

Surprisingly, this did not change after the crisis, as the following table shows. Investment and savings ratios remained practically unaffected by the crisis. This data does not, however, say anything about the profitability of investment. The credit card business, where one large conglomerate subsidiary (LG Card) went nearly bankrupt, is one of the sectors where overinvestment similar to that experienced before the crisis could be observed. LG Card, the biggest credit card company in Korea with 7 million customers, profited from the boom of consumer credit after the Asian crisis. However, when the boom reversed and customers failed to honour their repayment obligations, only a 4.5 billion USD bailout organized by the government could save the company. In the end of 2004, the former owner of LG Card, LG Group, had to inject another 950 million USD, together with a 480 million USD credit line by other creditors . In 2007 it was merged with Shinhan Card Company, thereby following a typical path of Korean handling of corporate bankruptcies, before and after the crisis.

Table 9: Domestic Investment and Savings Ratio After the Crisis

Year	Gross Domestic Investment Ratio (%)	Year	Gross Saving Ratio (%)
1997	35.6	1997	34.6
1998	25.2	1998	36.6
1999	29.1	1999	34.6
2000	30.7	2000	33.0
2001	29.3	2001	31.1
2002	29.3	2002	30.5
2003	30.0	2003	31.9
2004	29.9	2004	34.0
2005	29.8	2005	32.1
2006	29.7	2006	30.8
2007	29.5	2007	30.8
2008	31.0	2008	30.5
2009	26.2	2009	30.2
2010	29.2	2010	32.0

Source: Bank of Korea, www.bok.or.kr

The external economy remained for Korea of the utmost importance. Export-led growth had been the backbone of the "miracle at the Han river", the rise of Korea from poverty to a modern economy. At the same time, imports also grew constantly and in 1996 were considerably higher than exports, adding together with high external debt to create the uncertainty before the crisis. This can be seen in the following table.

Table 10: Korea's External Economy – Trade and GDP Before the Crisis

	Exports	Imports	GDP	Exports/GDP	Imports/GDP
Unit	Billion USD	Billion USD	Billion USD	Ratio	Ratio
1988	51.811	51.811	192.3	0.269428	0.269428
1989	61.465	61.465	236.3	0.260114	0.260114
1990	65.016	69.844	270.3	0.240533	0.258394
1991	71.87	81.525	315.5	0.227797	0.258399
1992	76.632	81.775	338.1	0.226655	0.241866
1993	82.236	83.8	372.2	0.220946	0.225148
1994	96.013	102.348	435.5	0.220466	0.235013
1995	125.058	135.119	531.3	0.235381	0.254318
1996	129.715	150.339	572.8	0.226458	0.262463
1997	136.164	144.616	532.3	0.255803	0.271681

Source: Bank of Korea, www.bok.or.kr

After the crisis – due to the deep plunge in the value of the currency – imports, which suddenly became much more expensive, plummeted, and exports sky-rocketed. After that, imports recovered, but were for most years, with the exception of 2008, lower than imports, as the following table shows.

Table 11: Korea's External Economy – Trade and GDP After the Crisis

	Exports	Imports	GDP	Exports/GDP	Imports/GDP
Unit	Billion USD	Billion USD	Billion USD	Ratio	Ratio
1998	132.313	93.282	358.2	0.369383	0.260419
1999	143.686	119.752	461.6	0.311278	0.259428
2000	172.268	160.481	533.5	0.322902	0.300808
2001	150.439	141.098	504.6	0.298135	0.279623
2002	162.471	152.126	575.9	0.282117	0.264153
2003	193.817	178.827	643.6	0.301145	0.277854
2004	253.845	224.463	722.4	0.351391	0.310718
2005	284.419	261.238	844.7	0.33671	0.309267
2006	325.465	309.383	951.1	0.342199	0.32529
2007	371.489	356.846	1,049.3	0.354035	0.34008
2008	422.007	435.275	930.9	0.453332	0.467585
2009	363.533	323.084	834.4	0.435682	0.387205
2010	466.384	425.212	1,014.3	0.459809	0.419217

Source: Bank of Korea, www.bok.or.kr

Improvements in Korea's external position became even more visible in the current account (i.e. including factor income, e.g. from loans and investment, and transfer payments). Before the crisis, the current account had mostly been negative. This reversed after the Asian crisis, as the following table shows. While this result should not be over-interpreted, it meant that the trouble leading to the crisis, including the depletion of foreign reserves, became less and less likely.

Table 12: Current Account of Korea

Year	Current Account (Million USD)	Year	Current Account (Million USD)
1980	-5,070.6	1996	-22,953.1
1981	-3,927.4	1997	-8,182.6
1982	-2,133.5	1998	42,644.2
1983	-1,427.5	1999	24,478.7
1984	-385.8	2000	14,802.9
1985	-1,512.5	2001	8,428.1
1986	4,491.9	2002	7,541.9
1987	10,778.9	2003	15,584.3
1988	14,837.8	2004	32,312.4
1989	5,267.2	2005	18,606.5
1990	-1,390.4	2006	14,083.2
1991	-7,511.1	2007	21,769.7
1992	-2,239.9	2008	3,197.5
1993	2,972.9	2009	32,790.5
1994	-3,507.7	2010	29,393.5
1995	-8,012.1		

Source: Bank of Korea, www.bok.or.kr

One of the aspects of the crisis of 1997 and 1998 which changed the life of people most was the emergence of mass unemployment. Before the crisis, Korea had always had, besides a heavily regulated labour market with strong trade unions, a large informal sector, with temporary workers, and from the 1990s increasingly with (often illegal) foreign labourers. In 1998 and 1999 unemployment, which before stood at an obscure 2 percent, suddenly increased to more than 6 percent. However, here also the post-crisis years showed that Korea's policy was, if not completely successful, at least able to reduce official unemployment rates to below 4 percent, though the informal labour market sector grew fast.

Table 13: Unemployment Rates in Korea

Year	Unemployment Rate %
1989	2.6
1990	2.4
1991	2.4
1992	2.5
1993	2.9
1994	2.5
1995	2.1
1996	2.0
1997	2.6
1998	7.0
1999	6.6
2000	4.4
2001	4.0
2002	3.3
2003	3.6
2004	3.7
2005	3.7
2006	3.5
2007	3.2
2008	3.2
2009	3.6
2010	3.7

Source: Bank of Korea, www.bok.or.kr

In recent years the significance of economic data, focusing mainly on GDP data, has been rightly disputed. On the new OECD "happiness indicator" (composed of a number of sub-indicators on welfare) Korea still ranks in the lower third. However, the importance of a growing economy bringing people to work should not be underestimated. If people do not feel improvements, like in the Soviet Union, where for decades growth did not translate into more consumption, or partially in Korea, when growth cannot create enough jobs for job market entrants, lasting disappointment with the economic system can arise; in other words, the expectations-equilibrium is not stable. In Korea, this cannot be said to be the case for most of the population yet. In fact, the macroeconomic development after the crisis was not only the envy of much less fortunate neighbouring countries, but also translated into Korea's rise on the global scene, as the first "successful graduate" from IMF stand-by agreements, and increasingly as a new middle power exerting influence beyond its borders, in regional integration and in international fora, most prominently the G20.

8.2 Korea enters the global governance scene – the successful hosting of the G20 summit

An increasing interconnectedness of economies demands an increasing level of global governance. Nowhere did this transpire more than during the world financial and economic crisis during 2008 and 2009, and the subsequent euro crisis. The euro crisis, however, also shows a tendency to prefer regional solutions (and possibly national solutions) to global ones. It would indeed be a "nirvana approach" to postulate global governance as a demand for a world government. Making an international political order available as a public good has always proved problematic and has only functioned imperfectly, usually under the rule of hegemonic powers. A more efficient way is the formation of clubs such as the EU in which certain rules such as competition rules can be better implemented.

One of the most impressive results of Korea's rise after overcoming the Asian crisis was its increasingly active participation in international fora. The opening policy under the administrations of Kim Dae-Jung, Roh Moo-Hyun and Lee Myung-Bak, different as their policies were, did have some common features, and a more active role on the international scene, including the frequent hosting of international events, was one of them. For economic policymaking, the G20 is to date the most important of these events. Others included sports events (like the co-hosting of the soccer World Cup in 2002 or the successful bid for the Winter Olympics in Pyeongchang 2018), the world exposition in Yeosu 2012, the hosting of the OECD Development Assistance Committee meeting in 2011, the nuclear summit 2012 and frequent hosting of large environmental conferences. All are a sign of a changed Korean confidence level and attitude vis-à-vis the outside world as well as the expression of successful Korean policymaking.

The 2008 G20 summit proved to be a surprisingly well-functioning response to the financial and economic crisis, rising from a relatively insignificant position to one of the most important global governance actors during the crisis. At about 90 percent of global GDP and 80 percent of world trade, the G20 group comes close to a world-encompassing organization and, at the same time, played a more important role during the crisis than the WTO, which officially was in charge of reversing the trend of the dramatic shrinking trade, for instance due to the avoidance of protectionist answers which have led to a global economic crisis in the 1930s. This is probably due to the fact that the format of the G20 is simpler in its composition for reaching a consensus than in a truly global organization of more than 150 members.

In total, the G20 has come a long way. From the beginnings in the Willard Group of APEC since 1997 and since the formal inauguration of G20 with the Berlin summit in 1999, the summit of finance ministers and central bank directors has gained more and more significance over the years. The global financial crisis has led to biannual summits since 2008 and to annual meetings between heads of state today. The rising significance can be noted with the volume of summit documents which, during the Berlin summit in 1999, consisted of six points on one page and increased to 74 points on 17 pages at the Seoul summit, with a 65-page annex. The Seoul summit was almost a failure despite perfect management by the host, due to an escalating currency war between the United States and China, which nearly led to an éclat. Intense efforts by the South Korean summit management headed by President Lee Myung-Bak led to a successful result as the éclat was diverted and some of the most important resolutions were made at the finance ministers and central bank directors meeting in Gyeongju at the end of October 2010.

Among others, they included the reform of the IMF, which changed the distribution of votes in favour of emerging nations such as South Korea and China and in disfavour of the relatively over-represented European countries. The U.S. also conceded a share of its voting weight but still retains a veto as the only country with 17 votes, as a quorum of 85 percent of votes is required for important decisions in the IMF. The second cornerstone of Gyeongju and Seoul was the entering into effect of "Basel III", which basically calls for stricter net equity rules for banks and serves to prevent another financial crisis as the one in 2008. Furthermore, more regulation for globally active banking institutions will be considered in the future. The wish, particularly of South Korea, to grant a loan scheme for the IMF country groups when they have not yet entered a financial crisis also was not yet decided. Such a scheme has already been created in East Asia following the 1997 crisis with the Chiang Mai agreement, which has successively been strengthened. In this regard, an Asian Monetary Fund has been considered on numerous occasions, complementary to the IMF. In the final communiqué in Seoul, the role of regional solutions for the prevention of financial crisis was mentioned. The United States was unable to assert itself with respect to the especially controversial issue of trade imbalance in terms of binding quota for exports (at a high of 4 percent of GDP). The United States especially reproached China for achieving export surpluses by currency manipulation and, to a lesser extent, South Korea and Japan. However, the reproach was returned as the United States attempted to weaken the U.S. dollar, hence the world reserve currency, with a loose monetary policy. In the end, the United States was unable to get its way. In the future, the G20 summit aims to establish a benchmark for measuring trade imbalance on the basis of market economic mechanisms.

Probably the most important positive result of the summit was the unanimous rejection of protectionism as a solution for economic problems. The fear of another great depression, which had been predicted in 2008 and 2009 by a few leading economic scientists, had prevented competitive national depreciation and trade protectionism. Particularly for South Korea, the summit was an important cornerstone for the recognition of its increasing importance to the global economy, but it was also significant for other emerging nations such as China. Moreover, future political decisions will inevitably include the new great powers of the BRIC group (Brazil, Russia, India and China). Nevertheless, important challenges remain for these countries, as well as for the consolidation of the world economy. For that matter, the question in how far the G20 will really become the new coordination instrument and the successor to the G8 of leading industrial nations is particularly relevant. The G8 summit has essentially been created as an informal meeting at the highest political level which addresses important questions and excludes the public to a great extent, while the G20 operates at a more public and political level. Even though the newly emerging economies have the ability to prevent solo attempts by the G8, an informal communication is virtually impossible. The grandeur of the meeting and the political constellation which, among others, requires the presence of an oil country (Saudi Arabia) and an African country (South Africa) prevents the possibility of informal communication. The possibility discussed by some economists and politicians of reducing the G20 to G12 or G14 would not be accepted by countries such as South Korea, which would then be excluded. However, the institutionalization of the G20 itself, which has been decisively pushed by South Korea, will at the same time make it likely that new informal groups will emerge outside the G20. A possible solution would be the grouping of national interests into regional blocks, as already demonstrated by the EU. Yet, to see this as a replacement for national representation is a step too far, even for the leading EU nations such as Germany and would be even less acceptable in other world regions with a low integration rate, such as East Asia.

Hence, it remains to be seen how viable the G20 will be in the future. In the global financial and economic crisis, the format of the G20 has proved to be successful, particularly in the prevention of protectionist measures. Whether this will be the case in the future in terms of preventing new currency crises and reforming the currency regime is yet unclear. Global governance may not be the optimal solution to conflict, but the G20 format proves to be one that incurs less interdependence costs of coordination than a forum with more member states such as the WTO, and frustration of exclusion is relatively smaller than with a smaller format such as the G8, which excludes and therefore frustrates more countries. In this regard, the G20 should be welcomed as an additional feature of global governance.

For Korea, the successful hosting of the G20 summit in 2010 was a clear sign of how different the country was in 2010 from ten years earlier. It was nt longer a newcomer to international government, but truly *inter pares* among the leading world economies. This transformation would have been barely thinkable after the Asian crisis. The next three sections show how reforms in the market for institutions, changes in the country's self-perception through opening, and regional and international efforts to integrate economically contributed to this remarkable development.

Part 3
Transformation and the Relations Between External and Internal Institutions – Institutional Change in Korean Monetary Policy After the East Asian Crisis

Chapter 9: Central Bank Independence and Monetary Policy After the Asian Crisis – the Case of South Korea

9.1 Introduction – monetary policy debates

Monetary policy was one of the most contested fields of economic policy during the financial and economic crisis of 1997 and 1998 in South Korea. After the plunge of the Southeast Asian currencies, beginning in Thailand in July 1997, in the autumn of 1997 the South Korean won also came under pressure. Previously, several Korean conglomerates *(chaebol)*, especially Hanbo Iron & Steel and Kia Motors, had with their bankruptcy added to the economic uncertainty. In December 1997, two aid packages from the IMF with the record size of 58 billion USD were concluded.

The deep plunge of the won exchange rate posed a difficult challenge to monetary policy in Korea (Chopra et al., 2001: 20-26). On one hand, the heavily indebted *chaebol* and the small- and medium-sized companies producing intermediate products for *chaebol* were interested in low interest rates. On the other hand, a large part of the debt was foreign debt, and the depreciation of the won made the interest payment and principal repayment more difficult. The cooperation with the IMF led to a policy of temporarily high interest rates, which was heavily criticized as causing the deep recession of 1998, where the South Korean GDP fell by around 6 percent. However, the goal of this policy was achieved, namely the restoration of trust in the South Korean currency. Already in mid-1998 the level of interest rates was lower than before the currency crisis. Besides this change in monetary policy during the crisis and the cooperation with the IMF, the institutional framework for monetary policy was also thoroughly revised. Specifically the central banking law, the Bank of Korea Act, was revised. In the end of December 1997, the BOK became an independent central bank. Independence of the central bank was no new topic in South Korea. In 1949 the first Bank of Korea Act, which had been formulated with the help of two U.S. experts, had stipulated the independence of the central bank. However, *de facto* the independence was never honoured by the political actors in South Korea, and the military coup in 1961 also resulted in a revision of the act in 1962, formally renouncing the independence of the central bank.

The concept of central bank independence (CBI) is an economic policy originating in the debate of monetary policy in Western industrialized economies (Hetzel, 1990). In South Korea, however, the financial sector and monetary policy always were closely connected under the wings of the government, including under the semi-authoritarian government of Rhee Syngman, the short democratic interlude of 1960 and 1961, especially the authoritarian growth policy of Park Chung-Hee (1961-1979) and Chun Do-Hwan (1981-1987), and the slowly democratizing government of Roh Tae-U (1987-1993). Monetary policy had to accommodate high growth policy, the banking and financial sector was state-owned, and even after denationalization in the 1980s credit allocation was influenced indirectly by the government (Cho/Kang, 1999). The democratization in the late 1980s also brought a new debate about CBI. However, the Ministry of Finance and the Economy (MOFE) prevailed with its opposition to CBI and the maintenance of the status quo, and Maxfield (1997: 120) concludes: "As suggested by the forced resignation in 1993 of Sun Cho, one of Korea's most widely respected and powerful central bank governors, the Korean central bank is likely to continue in its current subservient position until the nation's international economic position deteriorates significantly and/or the country finds itself with a well-institutionalized democracy."

This situation became reality in 1997, when the currency and economic crisis erupted. Shortly before the crisis, in the summer of 1997, a Committee for Financial Reform made proposals for increased independence of the central bank. However, bureaucratic opposition led to the retreat of the Kim Young-Sam government (Haggard, 2000: 57-58). The changes decided during the crisis due to the cooperation agreement with the IMF led to a formulation of independence in the central banking law similar to the laws of the Deutsche Bundesbank or the European Central Bank.[136] This formulation, which is much more clear than, for example, for the American Federal Reserve, has been criticized by some experts of being too single-mindedly focused on price stability (Feldstein, 1998). However, did the new law also bring a change of policies? This question will be discussed in the following sections.

Institutions change economic behaviour. Nevertheless, transformation states in Central and Eastern Europe (CEE) showed that merely to transfer formal institutions is not enough to bring about the desired changes in behaviour. Can a similar failure in the transfer of formal institutions also be observed in the response to the East Asian crisis, in the case of South Korea's monetary policy? To answer this question, the second section briefly discusses the problem of the transfer or imitation of economic institutions with special respect to Korean

136 In Article 1 of the Bank of Korea Act, the goal of the BOK is defined as "the sound development of the national economy by pursuing price stability through the formulation and implementation of efficient monetary and credit policies." In Article 3 under the heading "Neutrality of the BOK", it is stipulated that "the independence of the BOK shall be respected", and in Article 4 it is stated that "the monetary and credit policies of the BOK shall be carried out in harmony with the economic policy of the Government insofar as this does not detract from price stability."

monetary policy, drawing on the debate about the institutional system in previous chapters. Afterwards, Section 3 reviews the historical discussion about CBI in South Korea in relation to the South Korean market for politics, which also sheds some light on the actual situation.

9.2 Institutional imitation and institutional performance – an application to Korean monetary policy

While the transformation of former centrally planned economies in CEE and the transformation of the East Asian "tiger" states after the East Asian crisis are completely different in view of their causes and the responses to the crises, there are still some similarities: In both cases, there had been quite a few critics of the former economic model, but the timing and scope of the crisis were completely surprising. And in both cases, the states affected tried to solve the crisis with the help of institutions imitated from other states, under the guidance of international organizations. Since the transformation in CEE created a lot of "economic systems laboratories", which are perennially plagued with the problem of every social science that there is no possibility for laboratory experiments, it might be interesting to compare the lessons of transformation in CEE with the situation in the crisis states in East Asia.

One of the most important lessons after more than ten years of transformation is the lack of theoretical foundations for transformation: There was no "theory of transformation", and the existing mainstream theory (neoclassical economics) had few things to say about transformation and was, when applied to transformation processes, not very convincing. Theoretically, the lack of institutional factors of explanation led to the change from the theoretical monism of mainstream economics to the flourishing of more heterodox explanations. In transformation policy the expectations of simple and swift institutional renewal after transformation were disappointed (see Seliger, 2002f).

The first question related to institutional explanations of transformation processes is the question of the preferable and advantageous (rather than optimal, in the sense of neoclassical economics) design of formal institutions, i.e. of those institutions enforced by the coercion monopoly of the state. These institutions are formulated in the interplay of demand and supply on a national "market for politics", as it is modelled by public choice theory and constitutional economics. However, additionally these institutions are competing with the institutions of other states in their ability to attract mobile factors of production, especially capital. This leads to institutional imitation and innovation processes, which can improve the position of producers on the national market for politics (politicians, bureaucrats and interest groups). While the competition process is insofar Schumpeterian, due to the characteristics of the produced good and the market structure it should not be confused with economic competition processes (Wohlgemuth, 1995a/1995b).

The orientation toward international, i.e. Western (OECD), standards in the East Asian crisis countries, especially in South Korea, was not only the consequence of an "IMF imposition."[137] It was also an institutional imitation process aiming at improving the South Korean economic system with the help of (really or seemingly) superior institutions. The basis of this imitation is the gradual change of the conviction of economists, and concrete for monetary policy, the large epistemic community of economists convinced of the superiority of independent central banks. The discussions among South Korean economists before the outbreak of the crisis confirm this underlying change. In this, it is not unlike the transformation process in CEE, where also the failure of the economic system, external constraints on economic policy by international organizations and a new orthodoxy in the mechanisms of economic policy, the Washington consensus, came together.

The first problem related to the change of formal institutions is their interdependence with informal institutions, i.e. those institutions like customs or mores, which are not enforced by state power, but by social mechanisms like self-control or social control in communities. The rapid change of formal institutions might now lead to dysfunctional relations between formal and informal institutions. This can be very important for the analysis of monetary policy after the change of the Bank of Korea Act: Will the change of the formal institution (law) also lead to *de facto* independence given unchanged informal institutions, for example the relations of politicians in the BOK with each other and their superiors according to traditional South Korean decision-making mechanisms and political hierarchies? Or will informal institutional change be slower than formal change, thereby blocking *de facto* independence of the central bank?

To answer this question, it is important to observe the cultural context of actors, the embeddedness in a specific culture, since this cultural context shapes the existence and characteristics of informal institutions. South Korea, as a country with neo-Confucian historical background has, for example, a different understanding of the importance and applicability of written law compared with countries with a Western understanding of the role of written law and the rule of law. This cultural context again determines the perception and self-perception of actors. A central bank known as the "Namdaemun branch of the Ministry of Finance"

137 In fact, the responses to the East Asian crisis were heterogeneous, and South Korea has been the country most eager to adopt new formal institutions; see Seliger (2000c).

(named after the district of Seoul where the central bank building is located) might also be dependent from the government, if formal institutions (the Bank of Korea Act) seem to guarantee their independence from the government. Figure 2 shows the elements and influence factors important to understanding the outcome of the market for institutions.

Figure 2: The Market for Institutions and Korean Monetary Policy

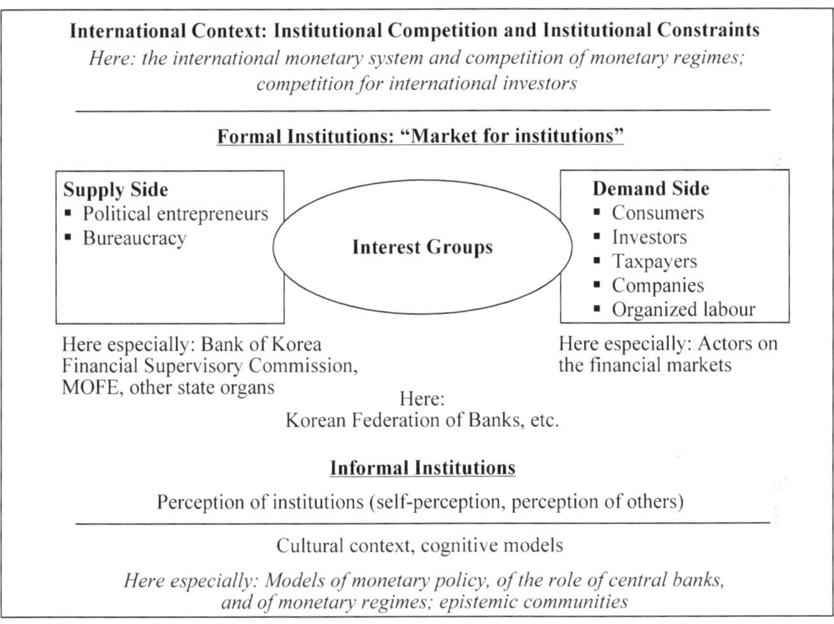

Source: The author

So, to understand the consequences of the reform policy in South Korea after the East Asian crisis, especially on monetary policy, the introduction of new formal institutions in international institutional competition and the international monetary system must be analysed in relation to informal institutions, along with the embeddedness of institutions in their specific cultural context. This analysis can answer the question of institutional viability, i.e. if on the market for institutions an "expectional equilibrium" of actors exists, and whether the expectations of actors are more or less matched by the new institutional setting. Furthermore, the question can be answered, if this new situation also coincidences with the results desired by the reform policy or if not. In the case of important unintended consequences of reform policy, alternatives or amendments to the reform can eventually be derived.

9.3 The Bank of Korea and South Korean monetary policy – an overview

The history of modern Korean central banking begins with the rise of Japanese influence, ultimately leading to Japanese colonization of Korea. In July 1909 the Korean Empire and the Japanese general resident in Korea concluded an agreement on the founding of the Bank of Korea (BOK) to issue money and handle the state treasury, a job formerly done by the private Japanese Daiichi Bank. Throughout Japanese colonialism, from 1910 to 1945, the bank, then called the Bank of Chosun (the former name of Korea), held this position. In this time the bank became also heavily involved in monetary affairs in the Japanese-dominated Manchuria after World War I. 1945 brought independence from Japan and the Bank of Chosun acted for the newly emerging Korean state, soon confined to South Korea only. Since 1947, the government and the political parties began to debate the future of monetary policy, during a time when Korea was beset with inflation. After several drafts of a central bank law were written, two American experts were invited to draft a new central bank law. Despite of opposition of the Ministry of Finance, which saw its powerful position undermined by an independent central bank, the draft became law March 14, 1950, shortly before the outbreak of the Korea War.[138]

The Bank of Korea Act defined the role of the central bank as issuing money, carrying out monetary policy, as a bank of banks (lender of last resort), treasury of the government and regulating authority for the financial sector as well as manager of official reserves. Monetary policy was decided by the Monetary Policy Committee (governing council of the central bank). This committee consisted of the Minister of Finance as chairman, the governor of the central bank, as well as five additional member, one each recommended by the minister of the Economic Planning Board, the minister of Agriculture and Forestry, two members selected by financial institutions, and one member recommended by the Korea Chamber of Commerce and Industry. This composition guaranteed close relations between the Monetary Policy Committee with the government. Nevertheless, the BOK was independent and the governing council not dominated by the government.

However, the history of the BOK is a history of conflicts between central bank leadership and government. During the semi-authoritarian government of Rhee Syngman, these conflicts emerged, when the government or the governing

138 The two American experts were Arthur I. Bloomfield and John P. Jensen of the Federal Reserve Bank of New York. For the history of the BOK see Bank of Korea (2000: 9-13); Lee (1991b: Ch. 2), and Kim (1965: Ch. 3 und 4).

(Liberal) party tried to abuse the BOK for the financing of the party and to cover up financial scandals of the party. During the short democratic interlude of Chang Myong (1960-1961), these conflicts did not stop and two governors of the central bank resigned due to conflicts with the Liberal party. After the military coup of 1961, a revision of the Bank of Korea Act was prepared and came into power on May 24, 1962. This revision determined Korean monetary policy despite some minor later revisions until the financial crisis of 1997. It was an adjustment of monetary policy to the institutions of the "development dictatorship" aiming at high economic growth of Park Chung-Hee.[139] The revision enlarged the Monetary Policy Committee to nine members. Five of them were recommended by the government, namely one member by the minister of the Economic Planning Board, while two members were recommended by the minister of Agriculture and Forestry, and two members by the minister of Trade and Industry. Additionally, the Minister of Finance was still the chairman of the committee and the governor of the BOK, also a member of the committee, was appointed by the prime minister on a second motion by the minister of Finance and approved by the cabinet council. The other two members were recommended by financial institutions. The role of the committee was reduced from the formulation of monetary policy, credit policy and foreign exchange policy to the implementation of monetary policy and credit allocation. Foreign exchange policy was handled by the government. The subordination of the Monetary Policy Committee was completed by the newly introduced veto right of the Minister of Finance for decisions of monetary policy, leading to a final decision by the cabinet council.

After 1961 a long phase of high growth in South Korea began, which was accompanied by equally persistent high inflation rates, which averaged 12.2 percent from 1961 to 1991 for consumer prices.[140] During this time on the South Korean market for political decisions, none of the relevant groups was deeply interested in low inflation rates. The government was interested in high growth rates, which were the basis of its legitimacy vis-à-vis the communist North Korea government (which until 1960 had seemingly greater success in rebuilding the country from the Korean War and even could offer – at least in its rhetoric – food aid to the South!) and also vis-à-vis the government of Rhee Sygnman and the economic chaos of the short democratic period. Growth policy made control of the financial sector necessary to achieve credit allocation in the export industries. The banks were nationalized until the 1980s and dependent on the low-interest

139 For the meaning and theory of "development dictatorship" see Adamovich (2001).

140 High growth in East Asia was not necessarily linked to high inflation rates: At the same time the inflation in Malaysia averaged 3.4 percent, in Singapore 3.6 percent, in Taiwan 6.2 percent, and in Hong Kong 8.8 percent; see World Bank (1993: 110).

political credit of the central bank. The companies again were dependent on equally subsidized bank credit, so that all relevant actors had no interest in inflation-fighting (Maxfield, 1994). Consumers, mostly hurt by the rise in prices, were unorganized and had no possibility of influencing monetary policy. This resulted in high inflation rates.

Several phases of inflation can be distinguished in South Korea. In the 1960s and 1970s inflation with one exception (1973) always was higher than 10 percent. The two oil price shocks had a deep impact on Korea, which is completely dependent on energy imports, and brought inflation to levels above 20 percent. After the political confusion after the murder of Park Chung Hee in 1979 and the second oil price shock in 1981, the economic situation stabilized until the mid-1980s. In the late 1980s, democratization and the legalization of labour unions led to wage increases far above productivity growth, which again triggered higher inflation. After a peak in the early 1990s until 1997, inflation was in the 5 percent range. The first crisis year, 1997, brought about the devaluation of the won and price increases of 7.5 percent. Afterwards, inflation reached historically low levels, as can be seen in the following table.

Table 14: Consumer prices in Korea 1980-2011

Year	Percent Change	Year	Percent Change
1980	28.697	1996	4.925
1981	21.353	1997	4.439
1982	7.19	1998	7.513
1983	3.421	1999	0.813
1984	2.274	2000	2.259
1985	2.459	2001	4.067
1986	2.75	2002	2.762
1987	3.05	2003	3.515
1988	7.146	2004	3.591
1989	5.7	2005	2.754
1990	8.573	2006	2.242
1991	9.334	2007	2.535
1992	6.212	2008	4.674
1993	4.801	2009	2.757
1994	6.266	2010	2.956
1995	4.481	2011	4.5 (est.)

Source: IMF World Economic Outlook Database (April 2011).

While the monetary order and monetary policy institutions remained almost unchanged from the first revision of the central bank law in 1962 to the sixth revision in 1997, the Korean financial sector experienced important changes in this period. Originally, all banks were state-owned and supported political credit allocation by the government.[141] Foreign banks were admitted specifically to carry out foreign exchange operations.[142] Political credit allocation reached its peak with the heavy and chemical industry (HCI) drive in the 1970s. Since the late 1960s, the government had planned an "industrial upgrading" program. A National Investment Fund (NIF) was established in 1973. It provided selected *chaebol* with low-interest loans.[143] Ultimately, this policy led to serious macroeconomic imblanaces, and the government was forced to abandon the HCI drive and adopt a macroeconomic stabilization package in 1979 (see Stern et al., 1995). The confusion following the murder of Park Chung-Hee and the second oil price shock further changed opinions about successful state intervention in credit allocation and so paved the way for less dirigisme (Bank of Korea, 2000: 185). The financial sector was slowly deregulated and most of the banks were privatized. However, even after the democratization in the mid-1980s, personal relations between bureaucracy and now private banks allowed the state a form of indirect control over credit allocation.

Democratization also led to a new debate about CBI. The higher management of the BOK saw the independence of the central bank as a corollary to a democratic government in South Korea. However, neither the political parties nor the BOK employees were strongly favouring changes. Ultimately, the Ministry of Finance and a desire for the status quo prevailed (Maxfield, 1994: 115-119). During the Kim Young-Sam government (1993-1997), the liberalization and deregulation of the financial sector was accelerated in the name of globalization and admission to the OECD. However, deregulation was not accompanied by sufficiently increased monitoring of banking and financial activities. In the banking sector as well as in the private sector debt levels were dramatically increasing, ultimately reaching unsustainable levels and leading to the bankruptcy of several of the *chaebol* in 1997, when conditions for refinancing worsened and international rollover of short-term credit stopped. Financial supervision was insufficient. The restructuring of the

141 The development of special banking institutions like development banks, which were exempt from the financial sector supervision of the BOK, was one of the debated issues on the independence of the BOK in the 1950s.

142 On the one hand these banks were privileged compared with domestic banks due to the favourable conditions for currency swaps, but on the other hand they were heavily restricted in the kind of business they could engage in; see Müller (1996).

143 The rate for loans was set in 1974 at 9.0 percent, when the prevailing three-year interst rate on bank loans was 15.5 percent. Given the high inflation rate of the 1970s, this meant a significantly negative real interest rate; see Lim (2000: 38).

monetary order and the financial sector was one of the most important parts of the IMF program in South Korea in 1997, as well changing the status of the BOK and introducing an improved form of supervision of the financial sector.

As mentioned before, the proposal by the Committee for Financial Reform under the Kim Young-Sam government had been abandoned after strong opposition and could only be introduced after the IMF programs of December 3 and December 24, 1997, which were linked to a number of conditions. One of these conditions was a revision of the central bank law, which was carried out in record speed and enacted at the end of 1997 (Bank of Korea, 2000: 27-34). The sense of urgency for these reforms was increased by a public dispute between the BOK and the Ministry of Finance about the causes of and parties responsible for the financial crisis (see Chosun Ilbo, 18.11.1997; Kim, 1999). The reform of the monetary order brought a clear assignment of a goal, namely price stability to the central bank. The revision of the Bank of Korea Act guaranteed independence from the government, and the government's influence on the Monetary Policy Committee was considerably reduced. The Ministry of Finance lost its veto ability for monetary policy decisions. Also, the internal organization of the BOK, which had occasionally been changed for disciplinary actions against the BOK, became more independent from government. Finally, for the supervision of the financial sector, the Financial Supervisory Commission was established. Thereby, the tasks of controlling monetary policy (price stability) and financial stability, which might be conflicting goals in the short run, were separated. An overview over the changes is given in Table 15.

Table 15: Changes in the Bank of Korea Act in the Sixth Revision, December 31, 1997

BOK Provisions	Until 1997	Since 1998
Objective of Monetary Policy	Stabilizing monetary value and mainting the soundness of the bank and credit system.	Price stability.
Monetary Policy Committee	Nine members, two of them independent from the government.	Seven members, two of them independent from the government.
Chairman of the Monetary Policy Committee	Minister of Finance and Economy.	President of the BOK.
Monetary Policy	Undetermined.	Annual inflation goal (inflation targeting).
Conflicts in Monetary Policy	Ultimate decision made by the government.	Ultimate decision made by the BOK.
Bank Supervision	The Office of Bank Supervision in the BOK.	The Financial Supervisory Service, with only limited rights for the BOK.

BOK Provisions	Until 1997	Since 1998
Accountability	Undetermined.	Annual reports on the implementation of monetary policy to be submitted to the National Assembly, and accountability of the BOK president.
Internal Organization	Supervised by the Ministry of Finance; controlled by an Auditor; change of articles of incorporation require approval by the Minister of Finance and Economy.	Controlled by Board of Audit and Inspection; articles of incorporation changed by deliberation of the Monetary Policy Committee.

Source: Bank of Korea, 2000: 31-34

These changes will be discussed in Chapter 10 in relation to concepts of the measurement of CBI.

Chapter 10: Central Bank Independence in Korea Before and After the Crisis

10.1 The concept of central bank independence

The idea that an independent central bank outperforms a dependent central bank in guaranteeing price stability is not new. Indeed, many central bank laws are based on the belief, for example in the Federal Republic of Germany, where ordo-liberals saw a close relation between the functioning price mechanism as the "basic law of the market economy" and the primacy of monetary policy (Eucken, 1952). The primacy of monetary policy, i.e. the price stability necessary to guarantee the functioning price mechanism, implies an independent central bank as the guarantee of price stability (Dehay, 1995). The Deutsche Bundesbank (German central bank), emerging after explicit discussion of this function, has often been discussed as a prototype of independent central banks (Berger, 1997; Maier/Haan, 2000; Buchheim, 2001). The question of an independent central bank has also been debated as part of the problem of how much institutions have an impact on economic volatility and growth (see the literature review in Hanaki, 2000).

From the 1970s through the 1990s, three reasons can be cited for an increasing interest in central bank independence (CBI). First of all, in the 1970s and 1980s the end of the Bretton Woods system made the subordination of monetary policy under currency stability goals less important and allowed governments to use monetary policy in the form of short-term Phillips curve effects. This brought considerably higher inflation rates and a greater interest in institutional safeguards of monetary stability. Second, in the 1990s the discussion of a common European currency involved a debate about the optimal design of a central bank which allowed countries with a low inflation record to pool their currencies with countries with a high inflation record. Third, the collapse of centrally planned economies, economic transformation and the political changes in the former Soviet bloc, together with the trauma of hyperinflation in many transformation countries, increased demand for policy recommendations on the design of an independent central bank.

The theoretical debate about CBI names three reasons for the government's interest in inflation: short-term Phillips curve effects, seigniorage (i.e. the financing of budget deficits), and a balance of payment motive, namely the easier surprise devaluation in the situation with a strongly negative current account (Botzenhardt, 2001: 4-5). As an institutional solution for this problem the hypothetical "conservative central banker" (Rogoff, 1985) was discussed. The independence of the central bank was seen as a safeguard against surprise inflation, since the central bank has a different time preference than politicians.[144] Also, the clear orientation of monetary policy through inflation targeting and the accountability of the independent central bank toward the National Assembly were discussed.[145] Theoretically, this was modeled on principal-agent models. Empirically, the relations between CBI and inflation and CBI and long-term growth were analyzed. Most studies determined a clearly negative relation between CBI and inflation in industrial states, while the studies for growth were inconclusive.[146]

The establishment of this seemingly clear relationship is based on a number of assumptions, which are not trivial. First of all, it requires an operational definition of CBI. Usually, independence is measured using various dimensions.[147] The dimension of constitutional independence (Forder, 2002 speaks of statutory independence) is measured by the constitutional position of the central bank in the economic constitution of a country. In particular, the question of the strength of the commitment to an independent central bank is interesting. For example, in the Federal Republic of Germany the independence of the central bank (Deutsche Bundesbank) could be changed by a simple majority vote in parliament. In the European Economic and Monetary Union the independence of the European Central Bank is protected by a treaty, which only can be changed by a unanimous decision of the signatory states.[148] The dimension of political independence measures how far political decision-makers can directly or indirectly influence monetary policy decisions. An example for direct influence is the veto right of the Minister of Finance and the Economy before 1998 in South Korea. An example for indirect influence is the appointment of members of the Monetary Policy Committee. The dimension of economic independence measures to what degree the central bank can be forced to accommodate fiscal policy of the government and cover a budget deficit, for

144 The fact that central bankers are independent from politics and political considerations does not imply that they are interested in maximisation of a social welfare function through price stability. Central banks follow their own, bureaucratic agenda. Only an independent central bank designed in a way where bureaucratic interest and price stability coincide can be expected to fullfil its task. In this case, the price stability record of the central bank leads to higher prestige, more power and, eventually, higher incomes (or discretionary spending) for central bankers; for the European Central Bank as bureaucracy see Forder (2002).

145 Inflation targets are a form of commitment, which is seen as necessary to reduce inflation expectations.

146 See the overview in Eijffinger/De Haan (1996: appendix), Solveen (1998: 26) and Botzenhardt (2000: 55-56). See also the discussion in Cukierman/Webb/Neyapti (1993), Alesina/Summers (1993), Cargill (1995), Haan/Kooi (1997), Kissmer/Wagner (1999), and Borrero (2001).

147 See Alesina/Summers (1993), Eijffinger/Schaling (1995), Neumann (1996), Fujiki (1996), Eijffinger/Hoogduin (1998), Sergi (2000), Botzenhardt (2001) and Dvorsky (2000) for transformation states.

148 Artis (2002) complains about a "democratic deficit" stemming from "exterme central bank independence" in the case of the European Central Bank. A similar view is maintained by Bibow (2002).

example through automatic buying of government bonds which can not be sold on the free market. Lastly, financial and organizational independence measures the degree of financial and organizational autonomy of the central bank, for example in the approval of the central bank's budget or the use of the bank's profit. The literature on CBI tries to compile (non-weighted or weighted) indices of CBI using these dimensions to achieve the comparability of the status of central banks.

10.2 The development of central bank independence in Korea 1950-1997

In this section, these dimensions will be discussed for the Korean economic constitution of 1950, 1962 and 1997 with the help of three widely used indices: the index of political independence of Bade and Parkin (1985), the index of political independence of Eijffinger and Schaling (1993) and the indeces of political and economic independence of Grilli, Masciandaro, Tabellini (1991).[149]

The index of political independence of Bade and Parkin (1985) comprises the three questions in Table 16, which can be answered with yes or no and result in a ranking from 1 (no yeses, lowest degree of independence) to 4 (three yeses, highest degree of independence).

Table 16: Measurement of Political Independence According to Bade and Parkin (1985)

1. Does the Central Bank ultimately have the competence to decide monetary policy?
2. Does the central bank's governing council (monetary policy decision-making body) include representatives of government?
3. Are fewer than half of the members of the central bank's governing council (monetary policy decision-making body) appointed by the government?

Source: Solveen, 1998: 16.

For the three South Korean monetary constitutions of 1950, 1962 and 1997 the ranking is as follows:

149 This choice follows Solveen (1998). It is appropriate, since these indices are widely used in the literature on central bank independence and thereby also gained an important influnce on the political discussion, including the discussion in South Korea.

Table 17: Ranking of South Korean Central Bank Independence According to Bade and Parkin (1985)

	1950	1962	1997
1.	Yes	No	Yes
2.	No	No	Yes
3.	No	No	Yes
Rank	2	1	4

Source: The author.

Eijffinger and Schaling (1993) take the same index of political independence as Bade and Parkin (1985). However, they weight the ultimate competence for monetary policy decisions as the single most important criterion and accordingly give 2 points for independence (yes), 1 point for a competence invested equally in the central bank and the government, and zero points for a competence completely invested in the government. For South Korea this means a ranking as shown in the following Table 18.

Table 18: Ranking of South Korean Central Bank Independence According to Eijffinger and Schaling (1993)

	1950	1962	1997
1.	2	0	2
2.	No	No	Yes
3.	No	No	Yes
Rank	3	1	5

For Question 1, three answers are possible.
Source: The author

Grilli, Masciandaro and Tabellini (1991) measure political as well as economic independence of the central bank according eight dimensions, which are simple added, giving ranks between 1 and 9 (for the last question in the measurement of economic independence, three answers between zero and 2 points are possible). Political independence is measured by the questions below in Table 19.

Table 19: Measurement of Political Independence According to Grilli, Masciandaro and Tabellini (1991)

(1) The governor (president of the central bank) is not appointed by government.
(2) The governor is appointed for five years or more.
(3) No executive (of the monetary policy decision-making body) is appointed by government.
(4) The executives are appointed for five years or more.
(5) On the executive body there is no mandatory government representative.
(6) No government approval of monetary policy decisions is necessary.
(7) Statutory (constitutional) requirement exist for the central bank to pursue price stability.
(8) Explicit conflincts between central bank and government are possible and are solved according to a statutory procedure.

Source: Solveen, 1998: 17.

For the three South Korean monetary regimes, this produces the ranking shown below in Table 20.

Table 20: Ranking of South Korea central bank independence according to Grilli, Masciandaro and Tabellini (1991)

	1950	**1962**	**1997**
1.	No	No	No
2.	No	No	No
3.	No	No	No
4.	No	No	No
5.	No	No	Yes
6.	Yes	No	Yes
7.	No	No	Yes
8.	Yes	Yes	Yes
Rank	2	1	4

Economic independence is measured by Grilli, Masciandaro and Tabellini (1991) by answering the questions in Table 21.

Table 21: Measurement of Economic Independence According to Grilli, Masciandaro and Tabellini (1991)

(1) Government credit from the central bank is not automatic.
(2) Government credit from the central bank is extended at market interest rates.
(3) Government credit from the central bank is extended for a temporary period only.
(4) Government credit from the central bank is limited in amount.
(5) The central bank does not take up government bond issues which are unsold in the private market.
(6) The discount rate (main refinancing rate; in Korea, the overnight call rate) is set by the central bank.
(7) The central bank is not responsible for banking supervision (i.e., it does not assume a position of lender of last resort).
(alone = 0 points, together with government = 1 point, only government = 2 point)

Source: Solveen, 1998: 17-18

For the three South Korean monetary regimes, the resulting ranking is shown in the table below.

Table 22: Ranking of South Korea central bank economic independence according to Grilli, Masciandaro and Tabellini (1991)

	1950	1962	1997
1.	Yes	Yes	Yes
2.	No	No	No
3.	No	No	No
4.	No	No	Yes
5.	No	No	No
6.	Yes	Yes	Yes
7.	No	No	Yes
Rank	3	3	5

Source: The author

The results of the three studies (if the indices of Grilli, Masciandaro and Tabellini are taken together) coincide with the finding that the Bank of Korea (BOK) originally enjoyed a medium degree of independence, followed by a lower one, and since 1997 the relatively highest degree. However, this does not yet indicate if the degree was overall high or low. An international comparison of CBI as shown in Table 9 might help to answer this question.

Table 23: International Comparison of Central Bank Independence

	South Korea 1950	South Korea 1962	South Korea 1997	Germany	U.S.A.	Japan	EU
BP	2	1	4	4	3	3	4
ES	3	1	5	5	3	3	5
GMT pol	2	1	4	6	5	1	6
GMT ec	3	3	5	7	7	5	8

(BP=Bade and Parkin (1985); ES = Eijffinger and Schaling (1993); GMT pol = Grilli, Masciandaro and Tabellini (1991) political criteria, GMT ec=Grilli, Masciandaro and Tabellini (1991) economic criteria)

Source: For South Korea the author's calculations; for other countries Solveen, 1997: 22.

This comparison shows that the degree of political independence of the BOK since 1997 was very similar to other OECD countries, and that also the degree of economic independence increased.[150] All dimensions discussed here relate to the

150 An interesting exception among the OECD countries is Japan with its low degree of political independence and a record of low inflation. This confirms the assumption that a country's market for politics has to be taken into account in the interpretation of the indices, which in the following analysis will be done for the case of South Korea.

economic constitution of a country, the constitution or constitutional treaties (in the case of the EU), the central bank law and statutes of the central bank, plus related laws. The advantage of such a measurement is that it is relatively simple and allows a comparison of different countries and monetary regimes. However, only the degree of legal independence (*de jure* independence) is measured, while not the degree of real independence (*de facto* independence). This means a clear restriction to such criteria which can be traced in the constitutions, central bank law, statutes, etc. While – as seen in Figure 2 – the relation of average inflation and CBI measured with such indices is closely negative (and statistically robust), this is not the case for a larger number of countries including developing countries (see Blinder, 1998: 56), and an overview over various studies (in Botzenhardt, 2001: 56-61).

To solve the problems of discrepancy between *de jure* and *de facto* independence, Cukierman, Webb and Neyapti (1992) tried to measure the independence of central banks in developing countries with a questionnaire aiming at detecting differences between law and reality and with an additional measurement of the turnover rate of the central bank governor. The turnover rate of central bank governors might affect the monetary policy and ultimately inflation rate of a country in two ways. First, a central bank governor who carries out tight monetary policy against the will of the government expecting lax policy will eventually be forced to resign. Second, because of this threat, central bank governors will prefer to accomodate the policy desired by the government. So a higher turnover rate of central bank governors means more government intervention in monetary policy as well as a more credible threat to do so and should be related to higher inflation rates. This last index is for OECD countries not significant, where central bank governors change sometimes only after very long periods of time, however it is significant as a measurement for *de facto* independence in developing countries. The following Table 24 shows the turnover rate of central bank governors and the average inflation rate for various East Asian countries for the period of 1980 to 1989.

Table 24: Turnover Rate of Central Bank Governors and Inflation 1980-89

	Turnover Rate of Central Bank Governors	**Average Annual Inflation Rate**
South Korea	0.50	8
Indonesia	0.20	9
Malaysia	0.20	4
Thailand	0.10	6

Source: Anyadike-Danes, 1995: 337

This index is, however, quite different from the legally oriented indices, insofar that no simple policy conclusion is possible. This describes the core problem for changes in the formal institutions of a country like Korea: Will the legal changes also bring *de jure* independence to a country, and if so under what circumstances? While the literature on the measurement of CBI grew enormously in the past years, criticism of the indices also grew strongly.[151] Even those authors developing the indices are aware of possible flaws and weaknesses and the resulting restricted meanings of the indices. This problem especially exists for the comparison of various monetary regimes with regard to CBI. If one measures too few criteria, some criteria important in the specific context of a country might be neglected. For example, usually the organizational and financial independence of a central bank are seen as less important than political and economic independence. However, in South Korea in the 1970s under Park Chung-Hee, the restriction of organizational and financial independence (especially of privileges concerning the salary of BOK employees) was used to discipline the BOK (Maxfield, 1994: 114-115). This was one indicator of the low degree of *de facto* independence of the central bank. If too many criteria are used to measure CBI, then inevitably the problem of weighting criteria arises. Many criteria do not use any weighting, thereby implicitly weighting all criteria with the same weight (for example the indices BP and GMT discussed above). Eijffinger and Schaling (1993) increase the weight of ultimate monetary policy independence, but the weight (50 percent) is not scientifically justifiable. Solveen (1998: 22) therefore uses an additional indicator with the overall criterion of dependence and independence of monetary policy and thereby leads the discussion of a meaningful index *ad absurdum*.

The South Korean case is revealing with respect to the problem of measuring CBI. Some criteria discussed above seem to contradict South Korean economic policy practice. For example, the larger degree of separation between central bank function and financial supervision introduced in the revisions of the Bank of Korea Act in 1962 and 1977 (4th revision) was a sign of a restricted CBI. According to Grilli, Masciandaro and Tabellini (1991) it should have increased CBI, because it reduced the possible conflict of interests in the central bank. Another part of criteria is not clearly determined: According to the act and its interpretation by the BOK (2000), only three members of the Monetary Policy Committee are appointed by the government, which means a majority of members are not appointed by the government. However, this calculation excludes the governor (president) of the BOK himself and another member appointed by the governor. Both are also directly or indirectly dependent from the government, which makes a clear calculation impossible. Similarly, the banks in South Korea were until the early 1980s nationalized. Nevertheless, the representatives of financial industry in the Monetary Policy Committee were considered independent

151 An extensive discussion of these criticisms is not possible here; see instead Forder (1996), Forder (1999) and Mangano (1998).

from government. Another example of unclear measurement is the existence of many ambiguous criteria concerning the economic independence of the BOK. For instance, interests and conditions for the extension of credit to the government and governmental agencies are decided by the Monetary Policy Committee (Article 75 and 77). Thereby, the criteria 2 and 3 of the index of Grilli, Masciandaro and Tabellini (1991) must be answered with "no", but *de facto* it is still possible that interests are extended at market rates and only temporarily. In another example, the amount of credit to the government is restricted in South Korea by the Parliament (and thereby criterion 4 is fulfilled), but this restriction is very general and the restrictive effect of it is unclear, given the relatively weak position of the Parliament in the Korean market for politics.

Some other criteria are not meaningful in South Korea. For one, the accommodation of government budget deficits is an important problem for many developing countries suffering from chronic debt crises, but in South Korea this criterion is not important since the 1960s, when Korea's budget had low deficits or even surpluses.[152] Accordingly, seigniorage has been not an important source of government finance, as the following Table 11 shows in an international comparison for the years 1980-1995. [153]

Table 25: Seigniorage, Inflation and Public Deficit in an International Comparison

	Seigniorage			**Inflation (Consumer Price Index)**			**Public Surplus/Deficit**		
	1980-1991	1992-1995	1980-1995	1980-1991	1992-1995	1980-1995	1980-1991	1992-1995	1980-1995
South Korea	0.79	1.12	0.87	8.5	5.4	7.7	- 1.2	0.1	- 0.9
12 Southeast Asian states	1.34	1.57	1.39	7.8	6.5	7.5	- 3.3	- 1.2	- 2.8
U.S.A.	0.35	0.44	0.37	5.4	2.8	4.8	- 3.5	- 3.3	- 3.4
Germany	0.48	0.30	0.44	2.9	3.5	3.1	- 2.4	- 1.6	- 2.2
Japan	0.63	0.32	0.55	2.6	0.9	2.2	- 3.1	- 3.0	- 3.1

Source: World Bank (1998), internet file: http://www.worldbank.org/fandd/english/0398/articles/0100398.htm

Other important characteristics of the South Korean monetary regime, like the still existing political influence on credit allocation and banking, are not measured in the indices discussed above.

152 From 1980 to 1988 the public deficit in South Korea averaged 1.89 percent of GDP, while the OECD average was 2.82 percent; see World Bank (1993: 109).

153 Seigniorage here is defined as annual growth of base money divided by nominal GDP.

Not only is the measurement of *de jure* independence difficult, but equally so the measurement of *de facto* independence using the turnover rate of central bank governors.[154] An argument against this method is the use of historical data, which in the case of South Korea can not be used to interpret the changes after 1997 (for the use of historical data in a similar context see Smithin, 1994: 74-75). Another problem is that the turnover rate of the central bank governor cannot be considered unrelated to the turnover rate of other government employees. In South Korea, where the turnover rate of ministers is high, even a relatively short duration of job can be long compared with the counterpart in the Ministry of Finance and the Economy (MOFE). The biggest problem, however, is the interpretation of a long office term of the central bank governor, which can either indicate a very strong position vis-à-vis the government or a very weak position, where every wish of the government is fulfilled. For example, in the 1970s the turnover rate in South Korea would only be 0.1, since governor Kim Sung Whan as the only governor until now acted for two full periods of five years, from May 1970 to May 1980. However, this obviously has no relation to the independence of the BOK (which was low) and to the inflation rate (which was high).

This criticism of the indices does not mean that the indices are not useful for comparative studies of legal and *de facto* independence. However, the criticism means that the interpretation of indices for individual countries must be cautious, even in those cases, where the results of indices on average are statistically significant and robust. Furthermore the criticism reduces the normative meaningfulness of indices. Policy recommendations with respect to the monetary constitution of a country and the results to be expected from these changes can be tentative at best. In the following section, South Korean monetary policy after the 1997 crisis is discussed to investigate the differences between *de jure* independence and *de facto* independence of the BOK.

10.3 Central bank independence and monetary policy since the financial crisis

The economic and monetary situation in South Korea in the end of 1997 was characterized by the following symptoms of crisis:[155]

154 Indeed, a newer study that includes the 1990s does not find a statistically significant influence on the inflation rate; see Sturm/de Haan (2001).

155 The economic and financial crisis of South Korea and its causes cannot be discussed here extensively; see Choi (1999), IMF (1999) and Haggard (2000).

- The official currency reserves sank to a minimum in November 1997.[156]
- The South Korean won had to be floated (after a quasi-fixed exchange rate with the U.S. dollar) and drastically depreciated.[157]
- The South Korean sovereign rating was lowered.[158]
- The last two factors increased the difficulty of repaying credits, which often were denominated in foreign currency, for the over-indebted *chaebol*. The nonperforming loans of banks increased from 3.1 percent in December 1996 to 10.2 percent in June 1998.
- The stock market crashed like the exchange rate.[159]
- The roll-over of credit by foreign creditors was drastically reduced, which was especially problematic since most of the debt was short-term.[160]
- The current account deficit was increasing from 3.9 billion USD in 1994 to 8.5 billion USD in 1995 and 23 billion USD in 1996 (Bank of Korea, 2000: 227).

The goal of stabilizing the currency and to regaining the trust of foreign investors presented the South Korean authorities with a dilemma in terms of monetary policy. On the one hand, high interest rates were necessary for regaining investor trust, but on the other hand they augmented the crisis for many companies and led South Korea into a recession. The IMF rescue package included a stabilization program, which prescribed strongly increased short-term interest rates. The overnight call rate (OCR), the most important short-term interest rate, increased from 12 percent in early December 1997 to 32 percent on December 26, 1997. On January 8, 1998, for the first time the IMF and the South Korea government decided on macroeconomic and monetary targets for the future. Following that these targets were revised five times until February 1999 (see Table 26). The high interest rate policy and the plunge into recession in 1998 led to a backlash

156 The official reserves of South Korea sank from 33.2 billion USD in 1996 to 24.4 billion USD in November 1997 and 20.4 billion USD in December 1997. Since, however, a large part of reserves was deposited in banks overseas, the usable reserves sank from 29.4 billion USD to a minimum of 7.3 billion USD in November 1997; see Choi (1999: 15). Until the end of 2001, the official reserves continuously rose to a record sum of more than 100 billion USD.

157 At the end of 1996 the exchange rate was 844 won/USD, and afterwards the won depreciated to 1,965 won/USD on December 24, 1997, and then appreciated at the start of the new year, after the announcement of the IMF rescue package, to 1,415 won/USD, which still was a depreciation of 40.3 percent compared with the end of 1996; see Bank of Korea (2000: 236-238.)

158 Moody's lowered the rating from A1 (January 1997) to Ba1 (December 1997), and S&P lowered the rating from AA- (January 1997) to BBB- (December 1997).

159 The Korea Composite Index fell from the last quarter of 1996 to the last quarter of 1997 by 32.21 percent, and the KOSPI 200 fell in the same time by 37.67 percent; see Lee (2000: 6).

160 The roll-over ration of short-term foreign borrowings by domestic deposit banks had been more than 100 percent before June 1997, and afterwards was around 80 percent, falling to 30 percent in December 1997; see Bank of Korea (2000: 234, 238)

movement criticizing the IMF as the main culprit of the economic crisis and demanding a more lax monetary policy. The labeling of the crisis as "IMF crisis" is symbolic of the protest.

Table 26: Macroeconomic Targets Defined by the IMF and South Korean Government

	8.1.1998	17.2.1998	22.5.1998	28.7.1998	18.11.1998	2.2.1999	Actual value in 1998
Inflation (%)	9	9	Single-digit	9	5	ca. 3	7.5
Growth (%)	1-2	1	-1	-4	Positive growth	2	-6.7
Short-term Interest (OCR)	High	Careful lowering	Additional decrease	Flexible adjustment	Low and stable	Low and stable	–

Source: The author after Choi, 1999: 17; KDI, 2001

As the target show, the inflation prognosis became more optimistic in the end of 1998, i.e. for 1999, and the growth prognosis also became more optimistic after the deep recession of 1998, which was overcome in the last quarter of 1998. The interest rates, which had risen strongly, in mid-1998 already reached lower levels than in the before the crisis (see IMF 2000: 49).

In 1999 the BOK for the first time published an inflation target. This was in accordance with the change of the BOK Act prescribing after the revision of 1997 in the new Article 6 an inflation target. But also the impact of financial innovations, which made the steering of monetary aggregates more difficult, was a justification for the inflation target. Indeed, the monetary targets were changed from M2 (until early 1997) to MCT (M2 and certificates of deposit and money in trust) and at the end of 1997 to M3 (for inflation targeting in Korea; see Oh, 1999).

Table 27: Inflation Target, Monetary Target and Actual Values 1999-2001

	1999	2000	2001
Inflation target (%)	2-4	1.5-3.5	2-4
Actual inflation (%)	0.8	2.3	4.8 (bis 7/2001)
Monetary target (M3) (%)	13-1	7-10	6-10
Actual growth of M3 (%)	8.0	7.1	8.8 (bis 9/2001)

Source: The author after data of BOK and KDI, 2001

As table 27 shows, in 1999 inflation was lower than the goal, in 2000 within the goal and in 2001 over the inflation target. Compared with historical data, inflation was extraordinarily low. However, the inflation target, which plays an important role in the monetary policy discussion after 1999, has to be interpreted cautiously. In 2001, it was changed from the measurement of consumer price inflation to "core inflation", excluding more volatile food and energy and raw material prices. The political dimension of this index becomes even more clear by further recommendations to exclude government-fixed prices like medical treatment prices, since increases in these prices are administered; see Huh (2001, p. 8). Also the growth rates of M3 were in 1999 and 2000 low and then slowly increasing, while M2 and MCT were characterized by a much higher volatility. The moderate development of monetary growth and inflation together with the deep recession of 1998 also led to a continously decreasing BOK OCR, which was followed by the market OCR. Because of the high growth rates of GDP in 1999 and 2000, the OCR was increased slightly in 2000, before the slowing growth in 2001 and later the political and economic worsening of the world economy after the terrorist attacks in September 2001 led to a new round of interest rate decreases, as shown in the following table.[161]

Table 28: Monetary Policy Decisions of the Monetary Policy Committee 2000-2001

	September 2001	**August 2001**	**July 2001**	**February 2001**	**October 2000**	**February 2000**	**1999**
Change of OCR (%)	- 0.5	- 0.25	- 0.25	- 0.25	+ 0.25	+ 0.25	-
OCR	4.0	4.5	4.75	5.0	5.25	5.00	4.75

Source: The author after data from BOK

In this section the decisions by the Monetary Policy Committee will be analysed according to the political influence by the government, to gain some idea of the *de facto* independence of the BOK, after it gained *de jure* independence in 1998. The first year of independence, 1998, will not be included in this analysis, since monetary policy in 1998 was clearly determined by the targets of the IMF program. It is noteworthy that already in 1998 there are signs for still-existing strong government influence on the BOK. In particular the president, Kim Dae-Jung, often intervened in the monetary policy decision-making process by issuing public statements on monetary policy. But at the same time, the IMF program

161 In September 2001 the ordinary session of the Monetary Policy Committee decided to maintain the current OCR. An extraordinary meeting after the terrorist attacks, on September 19, 2001, decided to lower the OCR by 0.5 percent.

restricted the policy choices of South Korea. It is more interesting to analyse the functioning of the new formal institution "independent BOK" after the relaxation of outside constraints. Such an analysis can only rely on hints of government influence without presenting a general indicator or index of influence, since neither the government nor the BOK is interested in publicizing such an influence, at least as a rule.[162] First, direct pressure by the government will be analysed. Then, indirect pressure on the BOK and the countering strategies of the BOK will be discussed. Finally, the influence of fiscal policies and exchange rate policies of the government will be discussed. All this leads to a better understanding of the role of the BOK in the South Korean market for politics, which will be reevaluated in the following section.

While the GDP growth in South Korea in 1999 was 10.9 percent and in 2000 was still 8.8 percent, among the highest in the world, nevertheless the government continously pressed the BOK to lower or maintain a low interest rate. Already in February 1999, only one year after the revision of the BOK Act, President Chon Chol-Hwan complained publicly that the legal conditions for autonomous monetary policy were created, but that practically the BOK could not fulfil its tasks because of constant government intervention (Chosun Ilbo, Feb. 25, 1999). In May 1999 President Chon announced, contrary to remarks of the MOFE, plans to shift from the policy of lowering interest rates of 1998 and early 1999, since it led to a bubble in the share market (Korea Times, May 3, 1999: 1). The KOSPI increased to more than 810 points, reaching a three-year high. The then Minister of Finance and the Economy Lee Kyu-Sung before stressed that the MOFE saw no speculative bubble and that no hike of interest rates was necessary (Korea Herald, May 7, 1999: 1). Chon admitted that every governmental agency is free to issue its opinion on monetary policy, but that the ultimate decision is made by the Monetary Policy Committee. In this case the BOK – also mentioning the revision of the act – could prevail (Chosun Ilbo, May 6, 1999). At the end of 1999, another conflict between the MOFE and BOK broke out with respect to the evaluation of the economic and monetary perspectives for the year 2000 and the issuing of contradicting press statements. The government announced plans to follow a policy of fiscal expansion and low interest rates, because it saw no risk of monetary expansion (Chosun Ilbo, Nov. 1, 1999). In February 2000 the BOK, MOFE and the Financial Supervisory

162 The government has no interest in making its influence public, since this might have a negative impact on its image with voters, who were historically in favor of less influence, the international organizations and the international investors, who might loose their trust in South Korean monetary policy. The BOK also is generally not interested because of the latter two reasons. However, occasionally it can try to counteract hidden government pressure by publicizing it. In the 1950s Kim Yu-Taek tried to counteract the influence of the government of President Rhee. However, he failed and resigned in 1956; see Maxfield (1994: 112).

Commission (FSC), the financial market watchdog, could not achieve a common view on monetary policy. After a coordination meeting discussing the widening gap between short-term and long-term interest rates, FSC Chairman Lee Yong-Keun demanded either lower long-term interest rates (which are not to be manipulated by the government) or higher short-term interest rates. The MOFE consented. The BOK, however, argued that a policy of low short-term interest rates was necessary due to the disturbance of financial markets after the bankruptcy of the Daewoo *chaebol* in the summer of 1999, and generally criticized the intervention by the government (Chosun Ilbo, Feb. 7, 2000). This is an interesting case for two reasons. First, it is the only case where the MOFE and the FSC did not demand lower short-term interest rates. However, the argument of the FSC that either lower long-term interest rates or higher short-term interest rates are necessary can also be interpreted in a different way: Since many of the banks are quasi-public due to the injection of public funds during the financial crisis or an ongoing degree of considerable dependence on the government in the highly regulated Korean banking sector, it might be less a call for higher short-term interest rates for the independent BOK, but more a call for lower long-term interest rates for the banks. Second, the meeting of the BOK, MOFE and FSC is interesting as part of the informal policy coordination between governmental agencies (including the BOK). This conflicts with the idea of a clear separation of competencies as envisaged by the revision of the BOK Act. It is part of the conflict of new formal institutions and old informal behaviour after the crisis.

When in September 2000 the BOK planned to increase the OCR due to increased signals for inflation, the Minister of Finance and the Economy, Jin Nyum, tried to prevent this by a public announcement that no such move would happen or was necessary. Indeed, the OCR was not increased and the BOK president had to face allegations in the Korean media, that he submitted to the pressure of the government (Korea Herald, 8.9.2000: 1). The decision not to raise interest rates only could be taken after a tumultuous Monetary Policy Committee meeting. In 2001, the pressure on the BOK to lower interest rates was increased because of the worsening economic situation, while at the same time monetary growth and inflation potential were increasing, as can be seen in Table 29.

Table 29: Consumer Price Inflation and M3 Growth November 2000 – July 2001

	Nov. 2000	**Dec. 2000**	**Jan. 2001**	**Feb. 2001**	**March 2001**	**April 2001**	**May 2001**	**June 2001**	**July 2001**
Inflation	2.6	3.2	4.2	4.2	4.4	5.3	5.4	5.2	5.0
M3 Growth	6.6	6.7	8.2	8.4	7.9	7.7	8.2	8.8	9.8

Source: The author after KDI (2001) and BOK

One of the most visible signs of the crisis had been the depletion of foreign currency reserves. The course chartered by the BOK and the government, first under the guidance of the IMF, showed how successful Korea was in reversing this course. Indeed to an extent, that the inflow rather than outflow of currency reserves had to be reviewed, due to the accompanying upwards pressure on the currency. The next table shows the development of reserves of Korea, from a meager 23 million USD in 1949 to almost 300 billion USD in 2010. While these reserves should not be confounded with a sufficient shield against currency crises – indeed, they were not sufficient to fend of market movements, as the past crisis showed – they nevertheless have a great significance as a sign of trust in the Korean economy.

Table 30: Foreign Exchange Holdings (International Reserves)

Year	Million USD	Year	Million USD
1949	23	1980	2,956
1950	27	1981	2,714
1951	38	1982	2,838
1952	83	1983	2,378
1953	109	1984	2,785
1954	108	1985	2,901
1955	96	1986	3,351
1956	99	1987	3,615
1957	116	1988	12,378
1958	147	1989	15,245
1959	147	1990	14,825
1960	157	1991	13,733
1961	207	1992	17,153
1962	169	1993	20,262
1963	132	1994	25,673
1964	136	1995	32,712
1965	146	1996	34,073
1966	245	1997	20,405
1967	357	1998	52,041
1968	391	1999	74,054
1969	553	2000	96,198
1970	610	2001	102,821
1971	437	2002	121,413
1972	527	2003	155,352

Year	Million USD	Year	Million USD
1973	889	2004	199,066
1974	282	2005	210,391
1975	786	2006	238,956
1976	1,975	2007	262,224
1977	2,973	2008	201,223
1978	2,794	2009	269,995
1979	2,990	2010	291,571

Source: Bank of Korea

At a cabinet meeting in July 2001 the South Korean President Kim Dae-Jung demanded expansive fiscal and monetary policy measures to revive the ailing economy. In his statement the lack of understanding of a separation of tasks of private sector, government and central bank was very clear. A newspaper article states (Chosun Ilbo, 16.7.2001): “President Kim Dae-jung ordered his cabinet to stimulate domestic consumption to revive the nation's economy. ... In another move, the government will operate its monetary policy more flexibly and may, depending upon more recent market developments, lower further the inter-bank call loan rate in the near future.” This shows clearly that he sees the BOK as mere part of the government. This perception of the government’s position vis-à-vis the BOK and the private sector already in 1998 led to criticism, when frequent demands of president Kim Dae-Jung to the banks to lower interest rates occurred (Song, 1998). This interest rates were called “DJ interests”, after the initials of the president, who also labeled the economic program to counter the financial and economic crisis “DJnomics.” While such a tactic of “moral suasion” is part of the standard repertoire of economic and monetary policy-making in other countries, it has a different weight in South Korea, where the capital injection in the financial crisis led to quasi-public ownership of most banks. The government no longer enjoys the direct influence of the time before the privatization in the 1980s. However, the management of the quasi-public banks has to face restructuring and at least partly the exchange of management. So, in the time before re-privatization it will be highly responsive to government desires.[163]

In August 2001 the Minister of Finance and the Economy, Jin Nyum, declared before the Monetary Policy Committee meeting that he was of one opinion with the BOK about the necessity of lowering of interest rates. Other members of the decision-making body contradicted him on the condition of anonymity, itself

163 Similarly to the government, the BOK also tried to influence the behaviour of banks reluctant to follow the downward tred in interest rates of the central bank; see Korea Herald (Aug. 18, 2001: 14).

an indicator for asymmetric power relations in the Monetary Policy Committee (Chosun Ilbo, Aug. 8, 2001). In July as well as in August 2001, the interest rate steps downwards were barely reconciliable with increasing inflation and increasing M3 growth, which reached 10 percent in August 2001. While the time lag in monetary policy transmission does not allow a direct relation of actual data and policy decisions, nevertheless the trend of inflation and M3 growth was cleary upward. The political motivation for the decisions can be seen in the political situation in South Korea at the time: The government of Kim Dae-Jung faced severe crises, namely the stalemate in its most important policy, the Sunshine Policy toward North Korea, frequent corruption scandals increasingly close to the president, a loss of parliamentary majority leading to the blocking further policy initiatives, and a leadership crisis in the governing Millennium Democratic Party (MDP) due to the preparation for the next presidential election in 2002. At the same time, the reform of the financial sector was still not completed, and the growth success of 1999 and 2000 dwindled. Given the strongly pro-growth policy orientation of South Korean governments, the last point was especially important and will be further discussed in the next section in relation to the South Korean market for politics.

The terrorist attacks of September 2001 worsened the economic situation of South Korea, which is strongly dependent on exports. The main target country for those exports is the U.S. In the ordinary meeting of the Monetary Policy Committee in early September before the attacks the OCR had been maintained at 4.5 percent despite renewed government pressure for a lower rate (Korea Herald, 5.9.2001). After the attacks. in an internationally coordinated move interest rates were lowered to improve the world economic outlook. In a special meeting on September 24, 2001, the Monetary Policy Committee for the first time decided a "big step" of lowering rates by 0.5 percent. Usually, increases or decreases were only by 0.25 percent. Shortly before the extraordinary meeting the president of the BOK testified in the Parliament about interest rate policy. Some members of the National Assembly pointed out that before all four interest rate steps in 2001 the government or the ruling party MDP voiced their desire for such steps. The answer of the BOK president was ambiguous: He denied having met government official before Monetary Policy Committee meetings. But he also demanded the end of government pressure, thereby indirectly confirming the suspicion of the National Assembly members (Chosun Ilbo, Sept. 24, 2001).

The controversy surrounding the government and BOK reached a peak in 2001 before the terrorist attacks on September 11, when the economic outlook rapidly worsened. One of the arguments of the BOK against the low interest rates was that the low nominal interest rate paired with increasing inflation led to real interest rates close to zero or even lower. This leads first to lower interest income, which is especially problematic in South Korea, where the coverage of social security is not very dense and where therefore not all elderly people are included in social security and instead dependend on life savings. Second, the trend of a lower propensity to save was increased by negative real interest rates. And third, the danger of a speculative overheating in the share market and real estate market increases, which indeed could be seen in the rapidly rising real estate prices in Seoul (Chosun Ilbo, Oct. 29, 2001). Historically, interest rates in South Korea have mostly been stable and positive and were cited as one of the reasons for South Korea's growth and development performance (see Figure 7; see also World Bank, 1993: 111-112). Since April 2001 the real interest rates for bank deposits became negative, which also reduced the attractiveness of the South Korean bond market for foreign investors (see Park, 2001: 9).

Besides the direct influence on monetary policy by public statements before the meetings of the Monetary Policy Committee, indirect influence through public institutions also can be seen. An example of this is the call for lower interest rates by the public Korea Development Institute (KDI) in March 2001. KDI is the largest and most important economic research institute in South Korea, and its publications have an important impact on the public policy debate. KDI is not necessarily a government-controlled institute.[164] However, the president of KDI in 2001, Kang Bong-Gyun, was a close advisor to the government. Already his appointment led to a discussion about government influence on economic research. In March 2001, Kang Bong-Gyun publicly pleaded for lower interest rates to increase the effect of the interest rate decision of February 2001, when the OCR had been lowered to 5.0 percent (Dong-A Ilbo, March 27, 2001). The reaction of the BOK is a clear indicator of the seriousness of the impact of the KDI publication. Only shortly after the discussion, the BOK published a comparison of the status of the BOK and the U.S. Federal Reserve Bank, comparing the similarities in the legal situation, but the differences in *de facto* independence (Bank of Korea 2001). At the same time, the BOK denounced the "continuous intervention of the government in monetary policy." This shows that the demand of the president of KDI was seen as tantamount to government demands (Chosun Ilbo, March 28, 2001). In this case the public discussion had the effect that for three months, until July 2001, no further interest rate steps were taken.

Another form of indirect influence is the discussion of scenarios by the MOFE in informal meetings with the financial industry about possible interest rate steps, which are incorporated in the financial industry's expectations and make a contradictory policy decision less likely (Korea Herald, Oct. 9, 2001: 10).

---

164 For example, in October 1999 there was a controversy about interest rate policy, were KDI sided with the BOK for stable instead of lower interest rates; see. Chosun Ilbo, Nov. 11, 1999.

Also the already mentioned informal coordination among the BOK, the government (MOFE) and FSC is part of the indirect government pressure. Generally such coordination seems to be desirable, since it guarantees non-contradictory monetary, fiscal and financial policies. Nevertheless, this coordination easily can lead to subordination to the most powerful participant of meetings, especially if the importance of personal relationships in the Korean market for politics is taken into account (See the discussion in the next section.). In particular, coordination leads to blurred responsibilities of the organizations involved. But accountability, based on clear responsibilities, is one of the main reasons for independence of the central bank, since it is expected to lead to a desired change in behavior. The meetings between the BOK and MOFE are regular and have a long tradition and can be interpreted as a traditional mechanism to transmit the government's policy targets to the BOK, in the time when the BOK still was labelled unofficially as the "Namdaemun branch of the Ministry of Finance."

One example of the possible lack of a clear separation of competencies is the common growth initiative taken by the MOFE, the BOK and the FSC for the bond market and share market in November 2001. The state-controlled Korea Development Bank provided credits in an amount of 1 trillion won (770 million USD) for subsidized interest rates for domestic firms. Additionally, guarantees for credit, especially technology credit, were extended, and 1 trillion won was injected into the Seoul Guarantee Insurance Company as new capital for the financially unsound investment trust management companies to buy in the stock market. Additional measures on the bond market and for risk capital were also planned (Chosun Ilbo, Nov. 7, 2001). While these measures were part of a government package, they were decided by the three organizations together. Naturally, the government expense also had an influence on monetary policy and the inflation target. This shows the problematic relationship between monetary policy and fiscal policy, which are interdependent in their consequences, but should be carried out transparently and separately, to make both accountable.[165]

Fiscal policy can become a problem in the long run, which did not exist in the past because of traditional budget surpluses and orthodox fiscal policy. Even after the financial crisis, the Korean fiscal position was still sound in an international comparison and its fiscal policy stance was still conservative compared with other East Asian states (see The Economist, Aug. 16, 2001). The political

165 A similar case of coordination happened directly after the terrorist attacks of September 2001, when the BOK, MOFE and FSC approved another subsidized credit amount to 1 trillion won to help ailing companies in the wake of the crisis. But while that case could be justified with the instability of the financial market and the role of the BOK and the FSC as lenders of last resort, in November 2001 the interests of MOFE and FSC were not the stabilization of the financial market, which was not endangered by special instability, but rather improved economic figures for political reasons.

stalemate in the National Assembly, where the government lost the majority, even led to a delay of planned spending in 2001 and to the call by the IMF for a more expansive fiscal policy, because despite a planned budget deficit for 2001, South Korea ended up with a budget surplus situation in the autumn of 2001 (Korea Herald, Nov. 27, 2001/Dec. 5, 2001). However, the public debt since 1997 had more than doubled.[166] Even more important are indirect guarantees given by the government or government-led institutions like the Korean Development Bank and other quasi-national banks and investment trusts, which cannot fully be evaluated in their uncertain impact. The Hyundai crisis of 2001 showed again that the problem of "too big to fail" still exists despite vows of the government to respect market solutions.[167] While the restructuring of the financial sector began much more swiftly than in Japan, especially furthered by the establishment of an asset management corporation to assume non-performing loans, the incomplete restructuring process further burdens monetary policy. A last point is the massive purchasing of government bonds by the BOK, like after the terrorist attacks of 2001 in the U.S., amounting to 1 trillion won (770 million USD), or after the Daewoo crisis in November 1999 (Chosun Ilbo, Nov. 23, 2001). While this can well be justified with the stabilization of financial markets, it also has implications for the future independence and room for independent decision-making of the BOK.

Another potential and actual source of conflict between government and the BOK is the exchange rate policy. This is the case in many countries, where (like in the EU and before in Germany) exchange rate policy competency is a domain of government policy. South Korea has an active exchange rate management vis-à-vis the U.S. dollar and the Japanese yen, after abandoning in the financial crisis the quasi-fixed exchange rate with narrow margins vis-à-vis the U.S. dollar. The dollar is especially important for South Korea, since the U.S. is the main export target country, and the Japanese yen is important, since Japanese and South Korean exports are fiercely competing on export markets. Historically, the won-USD rate had been fixed to the dollar from 1974 to close management under a quasi-fixed system until 1997. After the initial plunge in 1997, the rate rose again; however, despite record inflows of foreign currency, Korea managed a renewed steering of

166 The data about public debt is inconclusive due to divergent measurement: While the government officially estimates the public debt as 23 percent of GDP, which is very low in an international comparison, an estimate by an investment bank, J.P. Morgan Chase, which is cited in The Economist (Aug. 18, 2001), figures at more than 40 percent.

167 Another example of government influence on credit decisions by banks is the government 'recommendation' to extend credit to companies in the government-led restructuring process, which amounts to an implicit guarantee of this debt; see Korea Herald (Nov. 12, 2001: 11).

the rate away from undesirable (in the point of view of policy-makers looking to increase exports) low levels in 2006-2007, as the following table shows.

Table 31: Won-USD Exchange Rate

Year	Won per USD	Year	Won per USD
1948	0.4	1980	659.9
1949	0.9	1981	700.5
1950	2.5	1982	748.8
1951	6.0	1983	795.5
1952	6.0	1984	827.4
1953	18.0	1985	890.2
1954	18.0	1986	861.4
1955	50.0	1987	792.3
1956	50.0	1988	684.1
1957	50.0	1989	679.6
1958	50.0	1990	716.4
1959	50.0	1991	760.8
1960	65.0	1992	788.4
1961	130.0	1993	808.1
1962	130.0	1994	788.7
1963	130.0	1995	774.7
1964	255.8	1996	844.2
1965	271.8	1997	1,695.0
1966	271.2	1998	1,204.0
1967	274.6	1999	1,138.0
1968	281.5	2000	1,264.5
1969	304.5	2001	1,313.5
1970	316.7	2002	1,186.2
1971	373.3	2003	1,192.6
1972	398.9	2004	1,035.1
1973	397.5	2005	1,011.6
1974	484.0	2006	929.8
1975	484.0	2007	936.1
1976	484.0	2008	1,259.5
1977	484.0	2009	1,164.5
1978	484.0	2010	1,134.8
1979	484.0	2011	1,130.5

Source: Bank of Korea

Despite the prolonged economic crisis of more than ten years during the period of 1990 to 2001, the Japanese yen did not show a weakness before 2001, when it began to depreciate against the US dollar. The South Korean competitiveness in export markets is closely related to the Japanese Yen. However, a depreciation of the won also brings the danger of imported inflation, which in 2000 and 2001 also was given due to rising energy costs. Therefore, for several months in early 2001 there was a controversy between the BOK and the government about the danger of imported inflation due to a possible depreciation to revive Korean exports. Another debate was brought about by the depreciation of the Japanese yen at the end of 2001. In 2001, the yen lost around 10 percent vis-à-vis the U.S. dollar, to around 127 yen/USD, representing a three-year low. The South Korean Minister of Finance and the Economy, Jin Nyum, in a press statement spoke of the danger of a round of competitive devaluations, which was understood as a threat against Japan (Korea Herald, Dec. 14, 2001/ Dec. 15, 2001). At the same time the government signaled to financial markets to not tolerate a won/yen exchange rate of less than 10 won/yen (Korea Herald, Dec. 17, 2001 a). The president of the BOK, however, favoured the imported price stability through a stable exchange rate with the U.S. dollar (Korea Herald, Dec. 19, 2001). These contradicting views were part of a new controversy internally fought between the BOK and government.

The discussion above shows that the *de facto* independence of the Bank of Korea is continuously challenged and restricted by government pressure, directly or indirectly, in influencing decisions by the Monetary Policy Committee and through fiscal and financial policies. The next section will analyse how the position of actors in the Korean market for politics led to such a contradiction of formal and informal institutions, and what consequences this has for the policy options and future development of the BOK.

10.4 From 'gatekeeper of growth' to 'gatekeeper of stability'? –Changes in the BOK Act and the Korean market for political decisions

In Chapter 9, the Korean market for politics as a framework of analysis for the study of CBI in Korea was briefly discussed. In this framework, the revision of the Bank of Korea Act in 1997 represents a change in a formal institution, namely the monetary policy regime, which affects the organization implementing this regime, the Bank of Korea, and all other actors related to it. To understand the change implied in the BOK revision, the following dimensions are important:

The revision of the act affects the organization of the BOK, directly by changing the legal definition and decision-making processes (constitutional or statutory dimension), as well as possibly indirectly by changing the self-perception of the BOK and the perception of the BOK by other actors, notably MOFE and other governmental agencies. However, both changes do not automatically occur, and indeed the dysfunctionality arising from a change of formal institutions, when informal institutions are unchanged or only slowly changing, has been widely discussed (Mummert, 1995/1998). The revision of the act is related to the underlying policy models, which – in the form of systems of belief and ideology, economic mainstreams or schools of thought, or epistemic communities – shape the formal institutions and actions of policy-makers.[168] The policy itself is again shaped by the cognitive models of the actors. Besides, the development of formal institutions and the impact of their change is externally constrained. In the case of the BOK Act revision, the change itself was clearly defined in the IMF rescue packages. Finally, all the changes mentioned above are necessary to understanding the behaviour and policy direction of the BOK.

As we saw in the preceding section, the change of the formal institution, i.e. the increased independence of the BOK, did not lead to independent decision-making by the BOK. Two possible reasons for this can be cited: First, the constraint can be external. Indeed, in the immediate time of the crisis, the impact of international policy recommendation was important. However, for this reason, the first post-crisis year (1998) was excluded from the analysis.[169] The second possible reason is the mismatch of formal and informal institutions, leading to a discrepancy between the BOK Act revision and BOK policy. This discrepancy can be based on power relations in the Korean market for politics and organizational constraints in the Korean bureaucracy, both of which lead to the subordination of the BOK under other governmental agencies despite formal independence. It can also be based on self-perception and the perceptions of others diverging on the description of goals implied in the BOK Act. Self-perception shapes the policy horizon of an actor, the perception of others is important to their view

168 The role of ideas is as important at the national as at the international level. As mentioned, the emergence of the idea of CBI is related to the three challenges posed by the demise of the Bretton Woods model, the European Economic and Monetary Union, and the introduction of new currencies and monetary regimes in Central and Eastern European transformation states. Thus the Korean discussion of CBI must be seen in relation to an emerging epistemic community. For the impact of epistemic communities see Haas (1992), and for an analysis of ideas on the national and international level Milner (1993).

169 Even an inclusion of this period, however, would not change the result of the analysis: Rather, the external constraint meant constraints on the MOFE and other government organizations, which increased the policy discretion of the BOK in terms of upward interest movements.

of their mutual relationship, and thereby the acceptance of the goals of an actor. In this section, first the power relations of actors in the market for politics and the organizational relations of BOK and MOFE are reviewed. In a second step, the perception and self-perception of the BOK is analysed.

While a general analysis of the Korean market for politics and the power relations is beyond the scope of this paper, it is useful to recall three important aspects of the Korean development model influencing these relations, which have a direct impact on the two main actors, namely BOK and MOFE: The first aspect is the historical continuity of the political culture in Korea, from the neo-Confucian Chosŏn period (1392-1910) through Japanese colonial rule (1910-1945) to today. In the highly homogenous and atomistic society attracted to the vortex of society, the power center in Seoul, factionalism substituted for non-existing cleavages, leading to a political culture based on the importance of personal relations in clans and fiefs, especially the "three relations" of kinship, region and school (see Henderson, 1968). The second aspect also concerns political culture, namely the relation between political actors and bureaucracy in the Korean model of politics. Both inherited the function of decision-makers in the neo-Confucian state to act righteous, a category which could be measured by economic success.[170] Given the political instability and factionalism, the role of the bureaucracy, which regularly outlasted the political decision-makers with their much higher turnover, became more important. This fostered the role of the bureaucracy as an agent for the guarantee of economic success, as measured mainly in growth. The third aspect again confirmed this role, namely the impact of the development model of government-led growth in East Asia (Haggard, 1990; Pascha, 1997). In particular, this took the form of a military growth dictatorship in Korea, where growth was the justification for the coup d'état and military rule as well as an ideological justification against the hostile communist North Korea.[171]

To understand the resulting power relations in the Korean market for politics, it is useful to interpret the relations of BOK and MOFE and their employees in terms of the organizational model of Boisot (1995) as a hybrid form of bureaucracy and fief relationship: In this relationship, information is concrete (personal knowledge in the sense of Polanyi 1966) and uncodified as well as undiffused in society. This results in the importance of personal relationships and identity.

---

170 In the past, this concerned the responsibility for good harvests as the sign from heaven. Today, this can be translated into "good economic results." The assignment of responsibility could clearly be seen in the dispute between BOK and MOFE for the failure of currency policy and the "ritual retribution" after the crisis; see Steinberg (1999).

171 For the role of the military in South Korea's growth policy see Huer (1989).

While coordination is hierarchical and formal in the bureaucracy, and goals are generally imposed from above, the importance of loyalty to organizations as a core value is persisting even in the case of changes in formal descriptions of goals and may lead to conflicts between loyalty and a new job description.

This is especially important for the BOK in its relations with the MOFE, since the MOFE is by far the more important and larger institution, and flows of employees have led usually from the MOFE to the BOK. The "double loyalty" of members of the BOK had historically been a problem for those members appointed by the government. Therefore, the revision of the act changed the status of the Monetary Policy Committee members to a full-time appointment. Nevertheless, in the Korean market for politics also career history is important. Of the seven members of the Monetary Policy Committee in 2001, four have served a part of their career on the Economic Planning Board (the Ministry of planning, formerly the agency for indicative planning central for public growth policy and predecessor of the MOFE) or the MOFE. Three members came from universities, the financial industry or the BOK itself.[172] One should not directly jump to the conclusion that this automatically signifies a dominance of the MOFE. Indeed, the BOK president tried to defend the independence of the BOK on numerous occasions, as discussed above. But it shows the personal interdependence of the BOK and MOFE, which is in South Korea linked to the much stronger bonds of loyalty than in many Western states.[173]

The selection of central bank personnel is an important determinative factor for the policy of the central bank, without that there is any mechanistic relation.[174] According to Grilli, Masciandaro and Tabellini (1991), the appointment of the central bank governor and members of the monetary policy decision-making body is important for the independence of the central bank. In fact, almost no government renounces the right to appoint the central bank president. In South Korea, the appointment of members of the Monetary Policy Committee is

---

172 The president of the BOK, Chon Chol-Hwan, and Chang Seung-Woo served on the Economic Planning Board, Kang Yung-Joo and Hoon Namkoong in the MOFE. Hwang Eui-Gak came from a university, Yoon Jong-Yong from the financial industry (Securities Dealers' Association) and Kim Won-Tai from the BOK.

173 Simple conclusions might be misleading, since many members of the Monetary Policy Committee had diverse academic and political functions linked with many intertwined loyalties. For example, BOK president Chon had been at a university before the BOK, so not directly sent from the MOFE to the BOK. And the non-MOFE-related members nevertheless occasionally held other posts in public institutions, for example Kim Won-Tai, who began his career at the BOK as director of the public Finance Training Institute.

174 This has been confirmed in studies of the relation of political party affiliation and monetary policy decisions in the Bundesbank, where affiliation gave no indication of a "hawkish" or "dovish" stance at the Deutsche Bundesbank.

the right of various organizations.[175] The importance of the nominations and the political influence of nomination can be seen for example in the public debate about nominations before the parliamentary election in April 2000. At that time the government, facing a difficult election, waited a long time before presenting new candidates in the hope of not sparking a new controversy over the nominations (Chosun Ilbo, April 7, 2000/April 11, 2000).

An improved understanding of the relation between government and BOK has to be based on an analysis of the perception and self-perception of the BOK in the Korean market for politics. The self-perception of an actor is embodied in a central idea (*leitmotif*) or ideology, which is protected by an 'institutional aura.' For the central bank, the institutional aura means the transcendence of the central idea from the realm of politics and economic policy, specifically, to the realm of the unquestionable truth, which can empirically no longer be challenged (Weinert, 1999). The institutional aura itself can be much more important than the competencies of the formal institution and organization of the central bank.[176] The self-perception of the BOK becomes clear in the following statement of the BOK: "Over this half-century, the Bank has endeavoured to help the Korean people shake off the vestiges of colonialism and recover from the disaster of war, and it has made every effort to lay the cornerstone of sustainable growth for the nation's process of economic development" (Bank of Korea, 2000: 3). Two central ideas are voiced here, namely the goal to overcome the colonial tradition and burden and the goal of high growth rates. Thereby, monetary policy is not visibly defined by its own realm, price stability, but as part of the overall government function.

This definition is shared by the government, which usually does not at all separate the functions of monetary policy and the functions of fiscal policy and other government policies, but only refers to the "monetary policy of the government." For example, the Minister of Finance and the Economy, Jin Nyum, as well as his deputy, Kim Jin-pyo, announced in the end of 2001 that the government would maintain the flexible monetary policy, i.e. the policy of low interest rates, for the coming year (Korea Herald, Dec. 11, 2001/Dec. 17, 2001 b). This is a fundamental difference between the perception of the role of the BOK and the

175 One each by the MOFE, the central bank president, the chairman of the FSC, the president of the Korean Chamber of Commerce and Industry, the chairman of the Federation of Korean Banks and the chairman of the Korean Securities Dealers Association (Article 13 Bank of Korea Act). The nominations are confirmed by the president as head of the government.

176 Weinert (1999: 343) in this respect discusses the position of the Bank of England, which form 1694 until the end of World War II had been organized as a private institution. The difference between the formal institution and institutional aura can also be seen in the positions of the Bank of Japan and the Bank of Thailand, which both enjoyed a relatively high *de facto* independence despite their organizational role as dependent government agencies.

role which central banks play in Western OECD countries, where CBI enjoys a high level of importance, like in the U.S. or in Germany before the introduction of the euro. Private actors also maintain this view of the BOK as part of the government. For example, a statement by a researcher at a private economic research institute is revealing: "The economic circumstances in and outside Korea are saying that the priority for the Korean government *or* the central bank should be economic growth rather than price stability" (Sim, 2000: 15, author's italics). Accordingly, the pressure to take specific monetary policy steps is not directed toward the BOK, but toward the government. For example, the Federation of Korean Industries, the interest group of the *chaebol*, called in a meeting with members of the ruling party (which at that time was called National Congress for New Politics) in May 1999 to call for further interest rate cuts, while the BOK just had announced a possible end to the policy of low interest rates (Korea Times, 12 May 1999: 1).

In South Korea the central idea (*leitmotif*) of 'growth' is related to success as well as a sign of 'righteous policy' as centerpiece of the developmental dictatorship since Park Chung-Hee. The growth ideology was central to the Economic Planning Board, which was responsible for the five-year plans during the time of record high growth rates in the 1960s and 1970s. The MOFE, the successor of the Economic Planning Board, therefore represents the growth-oriented technocracy or, in the words of Weinert (1999: 354-355), the "expertocratic interest neutrality." It is part of a bureaucracy characterized by administrative elitism in a government as a "unit of purpose for economic growth" (Kim/Kim, 1999: 150). The BOK is merely part of this technocracy.

This analysis is somehow a simplification, since there had been always conflicts between the BOK and the government, showing a certain independence of the BOK and allowing the BOK to present itself as an apolitical body interested in price stability. However, the self-perception of the BOK was clearly dominated by the same growth ideology as that of the MOFE. Even the introduction of a single goal of price stability in the BOK Act in 1997 did not change this dominating goal. Price stability enters the ideology of the BOK only as a precondition of growth. In an interview on the economic outlook of Korea at the end of 2001, BOK President Chon explained the importance of price stability in the following way: "Once price stability takes hold in the economy, it is easier to absorb and ease the impact of external uncertainty" (Korea Herald, Nov. 29, 2001: 14). Price stability is instrumental to achieving other goals of growth and external stability.

This compares to a different understanding of price stability for example in the German Deutsche Bundesbank. In the ideology of the Deutsche Bundesbank, price stability (in the form of the 'primacy of monetary policy') was part of the economic constitution of the country, but not instrumental. This may seem to be similar at the first glance, but the important difference is that the instrumental function of price stability in South Korea allows a subordination under other goals (for example credit expansion), if this goal is deemed politically more important. When, like in the case of the Deutsche Bundesbank, price stability is part of the (unquestionable) institutional aura, it can not easily be substituted or subordinated to other goals. So the perception and self-perception of the Bundesbank as the technocracy compared with the political Ministry of Finance or Ministry of the Economy in Germany was therefore quite different than in South Korea. As ideal types, two models of central banks can be imagined, namely central banks as gatekeepers of growth versus central banks as gatekeepers of price stability. It is obvious that the Bank of Korea, despite the change in its legal status, still corresponds with the former.

10.5 Conclusion: Central bank independence, the transformation of economic systems and three scenarios for the BOK

The preceding analysis shows that the BOK through the change in legal status did not automatically gain *de facto* independence, but has had to face continuous conflict over monetary policy. In these conflicts the legal status was, however, an important argument for the BOK to defend its decisions against government influence. Therefore, it can be said to have raised the costs for the government to intervene in monetary policy decisions in terms of public allegations of disregarding the legal procedures of monetary policy making. In some cases the intervention even failed. So, from the point of view of economic policy making, the revision of the act led to greater independence of the BOK. Additionally, a change in the central idea occurred, from a pure growth orientation to an understanding of price stability as a precondition for growth. In the long run this could lead to a more and more prominent role of price stability. At the same time, open conflicts between the BOK and MOFE can lead to a change in the perception of actors with new roles, namely monetary technocracy (BOK) versus political actor (MOFE).

However, the analysis also showed that the change of the BOK Act alone was not sufficient to secure *de facto* independence. This also is the experience of many transformation states in Central and Eastern Europe. Wagner (1999) sees the danger that formally independent central banks, which are *de facto* still dependent, are made responsible for unsuccessful disinflation policy, a situation he calls "institutional cheating." For South Korea in this situation three developments seem to be possible.

A negative scenario could bring increasing conflicts between the government and central bank. Only in the first years after the financial crisis and the change of the act, the deep recession of 1998 opened the road to price-neutral growth due to the low degree of capacity utilization. Monetary and fiscal expansion leads eventually to higher inflation. At the same time, growth is sluggish in the medium term, when low nominal interest rates and negative real interest rates can no longer work as an incentive to invest, as in the case of Japan. The inflation targets of the BOK are regularly surpassed and loose their credibility. Foreign investors loose their trust in the Korean economy and a new financial crisis results from their withdrawal from the Korean market. When the BOK calls for higher interest rates, the government can deny the responsibility for inflation and even blame the BOK and, ultimately, reverse the act of 1997. This scenario is, however, not very probable for now. First, the symbolic value of BOK independence for the whole governmental reform policy is important. Second, a reversal of the act of 1997 would trigger the loss of trust by foreign investors. Only during the period of a new crisis it might be possible, under the pretext of weak performance by the independent BOK.

A second scenario is the maintenance of the *status quo*, with a formally highly independent central bank, which is informally still strongly influenced by government. This influence leads to an asymmetric monetary policy, where signals for growth weakness and signals of price stability allowing interest rate decreases are weighted higher than signals for economic overheating, and where accordingly monetary policy tends to be expansive. Interest rates are downwards flexible, but upwards sticky.

A third possible scenario is the development of the *leitmotif* of the BOK in that sense that price stability indeed will be evaluated as central not in an instrumental sense for some other policy goal, but for the functioning of the economic order of South Korea. This leads to a consequent policy of price stability and successful conflicts with the government. Nationally and internationally, the BOK would accumulate credibility, allowing even lower interest rate spreads to major currencies. The institutional aura of the BOK as the monetary technocracy compared with the political MOFE would improve its position in policy conflicts. The successful bureaucracy of the BOK would attract more and more able employees, leading to a new network of loyalties, this time in favor of price stability orientation. A clear separation of tasks between the MOFE (growth), FSC (financial stability) and BOK (price stability) would develop: Eventually, the "gatekeeper of growth" would become a "gatekeeper of stability".

The case study on monetary policy after the Asian crisis in South Korea can contribute to increase understanding of recent monetary policy debates, in particular the debate on the relations among inflation targeting, CBI and central bank reputation. Critics of the model of CBI have pointed out that formal CBI is neither necessary (as, for example, the case of the Bank of Japan shows) nor sufficient (as the track record of the U.S. Federal Reserve in the 1970s shows) for price stability (Cargill, 2001: 10-12). Reputation, rather than a pre-commitment to price stability, was seen as determining the success of fighting inflation (Blinder, 1998: 49). However, the constraining function of inflation targets and CBI on discretionary behaviour to overcome the time inconsistency problem of monetary policy still seem to be favourable institutional arrangements (Kydland and Wynne 2002). The case of Korean monetary policy shows why CBI might be not sufficient, but nevertheless desirable as a new institutional arrangement to borrow credibility in the time of crisis: It is not sufficient, since it needs to be complemented by informal institutions.[177] As long as these are not in place, elaborate prescriptions for monetary policy regimes also might fail. Khan (2003) for example enumerates several preconditions for successful inflation targeting systems: commitment to price stability (not multiple goals); instrumental independence of the central bank; public accountability and a sufficient degree of transparency for major aspects of policy design and implementation (credibility and central bank discipline); and the announcement of clear inflation targets, including sufficient information and the early announcement of changes, ex-ante indication of a breach of the targets, as well as ex-post comprehensive analysis of monetary policy. These preconditions indeed are important (and have been, by and large, successfully implemented in South Korea), but they do not yet guarantee the expected outcome of price stability. In the light of this case study, CBI should rather be evaluated not by its intrinsic value only (legal ability to ward off governmental pressure), but also by its value as communication tool, signalling policy commitment to inside and outside actors of monetary policy.[178]

The case study of the BOK did not aim at formulating a completely new theory of central banking, but rather to help explain the paradoxes and shortcomings in the recent debates on monetary policy, in particular CBI. While some authors have recently discarded the notion that CBI is a successful institutional arrangement, the context of CBI, i.e. the relations between formal CBI and informal institutions, the cultural embeddedness of the central bank, and the perception and underlying cognitive models of central bankers are important for explaining

177 Hayo and Voigt (2005) analyse independence of the legal system and public trust in the legal system as such institutions. Thies (2004) analyses what he calls "conceptual complexity", as a measurement of cognitive ability of central bankers through the analysis of bankers' speeches and publications.

178 Miller (2002) speaks critically about "myths" of central banking, e.g. with regard to price stability as the sole goal. However, these myths can at least partly be understood as their defence against outside pressure on monetary policy.

the relation between CBI and price stability. CBI then can no longer be viewed as a question of optimal central bank design in the tradition of Rogoff's conservative banker and public choice models like incentive contracts.

In the case of South Korea, institutional transformation toward a more independent central bank has been successful overall. A longer term perspective largely confirms the results of the case study for 1999-2001. Policy conflicts over monetary policy outcomes did not end. However, the BOK could indeed slowly build up its reputation as a new, independent body, while still retaining features of the old decision-making model. The revision of the act in 2003 fostered the independence of the bank, by giving it the right to nominate one more person on the Monetary Policy Committee. Historically low inflation rates helped to strengthen the new expectation-equilibrium, which established CBI as the core of the new monetary policy regime. However, the post-crisis macroeconomic situation as well as the low international inflation environment in recent years were conducive to the ability of the BOK to maintain price stability and historically low interest rates at the same time. One result is a developing asset price bubble, especially in real estate in South Korea. Though the BOK warned various times about the bubble, it has not been able to take decisive steps against this bubble, other than slowly convincing the government to act fiscally. Analyzing the development of the institutional culture of BOK, one finds many features of the former, growth-oriented framework remaining. This can also be seen in the composition of the Monetary Policy Committee being still strongly dominated by decision-makers close to MOFE or with MOFE and Economic Planning Board background. Therefore, rather than seeing CBI only through the lense of legal independence, the BOK can be best understood as a hybrid institutional arrangement. This hybrid form of institutional arrangement will prevail for the time being, making it an interesting study object with lessons for a wide range of similar situations.

Part 4
Cognitive Models and the Changing Perception of FDI After the Crisis

Chapter 11: Cognitive Models and Self-Perceptions and the Role of Korea's History

11.1 History wars in East Asia and the self-perception of Koreans

"Postage stamp disputes" and the "Wiki war", demonstrators who cut off their own fingers, a Ministry of Education which by decree antedates the Bronze Age by 1,000 years – in East Asia, a fierce debate is going on about a subject, which elsewhere is usually met with an indifferent shrug, namely the 'correct' portrayal of history. Emotions can run high not only with regard to the recent historical experiences of World War II (which is emotionally charged elsewhere, too) and the previous period of the Japanese expansion, but also with regard to the existence of a Northeast Asian kingdom which was extinguished several thousand years ago.[179] A correct understanding of history as the basis for good governence in the present and the future, and the basis for good relations between states, is by no means a new idea, and is upheld in the (neo-) Confucian heritage of Northeast Asia. However, only recently have disputes arisen simultaneously among all Northeast Asian states: Japan, the People's Republic of China, Taiwan, South Korea and North Korea.

Nevertheless, the three disputes over the interpretation of history that had prevailed since World War II have faded into the background. One reason is that they were oriented along the ideological frontline of the Cold War (Japan, South Korea and Taiwan against the People's Republic of China and North Korea) and – next to the systematic conflict itself – pertained, for example, to the correct comprehension of the (neo-) Confucian heritage. Secondly, there was a dispute which could be simplified as 'East vs. West,' the subject of which was the self-assertion of specifically Asian models of society and values against the intrusion

179 The "postage stamp dispute" refers to the issuance of Dokdo stamps by South Korea and Takeshima stamps by Japan in 2003. The "Wiki war" was the competitive editing of entries in Wikipedia on the subject of the Goguryeo kingdom (until the provisional labeling as controversial issue). The cutting off of one's own extremities during protests has a certain tradition in Korea and was, for example, performed at the Korean protests against Japanese claims to the Dokdo or Takashima Island in 2005. The antedating of the Bronze Age by decree to explicitly counter Chinese "claims" on this period occurred in February 2007.

of Western culture.[180] Thirdly, there was the simmering conflict about the heritage of the Japanese occupation and expansion, which culminated in the Pacific War, and which again could be simplified as "Japan against the rest."[181]

The reasons for the new conflicts are complex and have to be analyzed individually. There are ostensible political conflicts which also have an economic component (such as the dispute about territorial claims of the sea between Japan and Korea as well as between China and Japan). There are questions which are political-territorial in character (the conflict about the so-called Kando Treaty, in which Japan and China recognized Chinese territorial sovereignty over a region also populated by Koreans in exchange for concessions for Japan for railway construction). At the same time, these are to be understood as instruments for domestic presentation in Korea and as part of the minority policy of China. Other questions, however, such as the one about the heritage of Goguryeo (or Gaogouli), are of more cultural nature and part of the quest for a cultural self-conception of Korea, while for China, it is determined by the potential threat to the Chinese unity through its minorities.

Simultaneously, collective memory can be utilized as a (domestic or international) political or economic weapon (with Japan often described as "playing the history card"). In order to get reparations from wealthy Japan, this strategy has often been used in the economic sector. In relation to China and Korea, Japan accepted this strategy for a long time, and it did yield successes as 'checkbook diplomacy' (including developmental aid for China). In the consumer and trade policy sector (particularly import policy), one's own identity is often the topic of advertisement with ethnocentric undertones, which frequently constitutes barely veiled protectionism in favor of domestic industries.

However, it would be wrong to conclude that in general the question of identity is a feigned argument used to attain political or economic advantages. In fact, on one hand economics and politics are behind certain seemingly cultural conflicts, while on the other hand cultural questions likewise determine economic and political conflicts. The role which cultural identity plays in the economic and

---

180 The politically most relevant article on this topic was "The Japan that Can Say No" by Ishihara/Morita (1989). A more philosophical approach can be found in the essays of Mahbubani (2001). This line of conflict also has a significant economic component, for example in Malaysian Premier Mahathir's "look East" policy, launched in 1982, which he summarized during his visit of Japan in 2002: "This then is the challenge for Japan in a globalized world, to lead and not to be led" (Mahathir, 2002).

181 Of course, while these disputes have neither been resolved nor completely replaced by the new debates about the understanding of East Asian history, at the moment they are clearly overshadowed. However, elements of all three older disputes are influencing the new debates, especially the conflict over Japan's modern history and its effects on East Asia.

political conflicts in the case of Korea is the subject of this discourse. In this respect, Korea as the "shrimp between two whales" is interesting because it did and still does maintain intensive but asymmetrical relations with China and Japan, which promoted self-assurance through strong emphasis of its own cultural identity.[182]

In the self-perception of Koreans three widely prevalent stereotypes can be found, which are important to the political and economic development and interaction with other nations: Korea as victim of foreign aggression, Korea as nation with a 'pure,' unique culture which resists foreign influences ("Hermit Kingdom"), and Korea as the nation of the East Asian economic miracle ("tiger economy"). The role of Korea as victim of foreign aggression is historically rooted in the relations with China and especially Japan, but also in the later development of Korea as pawn in the hands of foreign powers, as Japanese colony, and finally as country which was divided during the Cold War. Certainly, the biggest collective trauma developed through the colonization and Japanization of Korea from 1910 to 1945 as a Japanese colony. The role as "Hermit Kingdom" (originally a term for the Chosŏn dynasty in the 19th century, which refused all contact with foreign powers), refers to Korea's long history as a homogenous kingdom. The preservation of this (racially and culturally founded) unity is an important paradigm in economics, politics and cultural politics. The role as prototype of a "tiger economy" refers to the experience of having the highest economic growth rate worldwide since the 1960s, which was expressed metaphorically as the East Asian economic miracle or the "miracle on the Han River" (which passes through Seoul). This stereotype leads to a special, positive view of the role of the economy and to opposing trends with regards to the idea of the "Hermit Kingdom", because in this case globalization is perceived quite positively as Koreanization, for example through exports and Korean investments in other countries, but also by the success of Korean culture abroad.

To this day, these stereotypes in the self-perception of Koreans have significant effects on political and economic decisions. This will in the next chapter be explored in detail with regard to foreign direct investment (FDI) policies in South Korea. In this chapter, the connection between historical experience and its reappraisal (culture of remembering and the creation of cognitive models, which condense the historical experiences) and present-day political and economic questions will be examined. To this end, the policy toward Japan (con-

182 If not explicitly mentioned, in this modern context "Korea" always refers to the Republic of Korea (South Korea). Although the Democratic People's Republic of Korea (North Korea) is part of the debate, especially in the context of China's supposed expansion plans after a fall of the Kim regime, it is markedly less involved in the debate, due to its own political system of isolation and mainly through official statements of North Korean's Korean Central News Agency.

flicts overhistory books and territories in the Sea of Japan/East Sea), ethnocentricity in consumer behaviour, as well as the conflict with China about the interpretational sovereignty of the history of Northeast Asia will be analyzed.

In the second part of this chapter, the role of collective memory and of cultural self-conception (self-perception) will be discussed. The third part concerns itself with stereotypes, which play an important role for the Korean self-conception and help to better understand the current disputes. These will be discussed in the fourth section, by reference to the relation to Japan (in the political sector), consumer-ethnocentrism (in the economic sector) as well the relation to China (in the historical sector). Even though not all aspects of the Northeast Asian relations can be extensively dwelled upon with this method, the presentation of the causes, instruments and effects of these conflicts in the light of the previously presented stereotypes of self-perception clarifies the roles cognitive models play for the comprehension of these relations. The final part concerns itself with the normative question to what extent a new identity policy can help in overcoming problems in the relations of the Northeast Asian states and to what extent economic development facilitates a new cultural identity.

11.2 *La mémoire collective*, cognitive models, identity and self-perception

The analysis of the significance of cultural self-conception for political and economic decisions requires that the often only vaguely defined term of cultural identity is made practicable. On one hand, the cultural self-conception of a person is created by cognitive processes (such as knowledge, memory and forgetting), but on the other hand, it is also influenced by social processes (such as interaction and rules). According to Fraas (2005), the central question is the socialization of knowledge, which can only be solved when mental aspects of collectivity and sociality are combined. This is the reason why insights of cognitive science into knowledge structures and knowledge processing and the sociological concept of collective memory are relative to each other (cf. Fraas). An encompassing understanding of the creation of cultural self-conception requires the cooperation of cognitive science, psychology and social sciences, but this cooperation has only recently begun. In his book "The Sensory Order", Friedrich August von Hayek (1952) examined cognitive psychological principles for human actions which also had implications for his social science-based research: for example, with regards to microeconomic coordination and social institutions (Horwitz, 2000). Nevertheless, the integration of cognitive and social science-based research remains a desideratum (North, 1996), especially with respect to the practicability of such research.

Cognitive processes concern individual knowledge processing, or in Neisser's words (1976: 1) "the acquisition, organization, and the use of knowledge."[183] Cognitive schemes can be understood in the sense of Gagné (1985) as a "network of interrelated propositions." When new information is gathered, it is processed and categorized with the help of mental scripts (cf. Bruner/Goodnow/Austin, 1956). Changes in mental scripts can occur, for example, when the existing scripts keep 'failing' and yielding flawed results. This can lead to an extension or even a total change of cognitive schemes, or to an addition of auxiliary conditions or *ad hoc* explanations, which are supposed to lead to more plausibility.

Mental scripts do not develop on a *tabula rasa*, since they are created by the social interactions of humans, who in turn are influenced by rules (institutions). These in turn are expressions of cognitive models, which people have created of their environment. Groups (such as national, religious, regional, tribal, etc.) share a common understanding of the world, which is learnable (transferable), cross-generational, symbolic and structured.[184] This understanding includes value judgments (convictions of right and wrong, important and unimportant, etc.) and is the basis of all language and communication, institutional systems and decision-making systems, concepts of time, and relationships with others.

Two aspects are important for this: Firstly, culture is transferable and cross-generational through education, but nobody is programmed through culture. Secondly, culture is defined by comparing and differentiating the 'we' group with the group of the 'others', but there are no 'pure' cultural groups. Instead, every individual is distinguished by an overlapping of cultures, including national, religious, and workplace cultures. The misunderstanding which developed, for example, with regards to the the ability of Confucianism to explain the East Asian economy is strongly determined by a narrow definition of culture (Tu, 1996). Culture helps individuals to generate a worldview by reducing the confusing complexity of external signals and information. Because information is unlimited but the capacity to process it is not, cognitive models (schemes) for routinely grouping and processing information are necessary. These, in turn, are the basis for informal institutions of a social order, which are not (like formal institutions) enforced through the state monopoly of the government, but through voluntary cooperation and social control. Cognitive models and social interaction amount to the "identity" of a human being, which can be understood, for example, culturally or nationally. The common fixation on national culture might also be due to the fact that the most data exists for this without being considered *a priori* to be of special importance toward religious, workplace and other group-specific cultures; oftentimes, overlapping terms are also being used (see Rauscher, 2006).

183 For an introduction to cognitive psychology, refer to Reed (2007).

184 Cf. Hodgetts/Luthans (1997: 95-126) for an introduction.

According to Delanty (1995), cultural identity is expressed in so-called "codes". Delanty had a notion of a progressive development of primordial codes (social identity through random formation of groups) from traditions and origin myths as determining codes over religious and transcendental codes, and finally, codes related to everyday life (e.g. privileges) and discursivity as the code with the highest level of reflexivity. Such a progressive, optimistic notion, which was chiefly developed for Western societies, cannot be universally valid. Especially in the debate about the identity of the East Asian states, in countries such as China and North Korea, a return to origin myths as one of the important identity-political strategies becomes apparent. For example, in North Korea, the legendary foundation in 2333 B.C. through Dangun, the son of the "Heaven King" and a bear is represented as historical fact in order to legitimize the current regime. Dangun was born as the son of a god on Baekdu Mountain (the highest mountain of Korea), allegedly just like Kim Jong Il, current North Korean leader as son of Kim Il Sung, who is the "eternal President" despite his death. According to mythology, Dangun founded Pyongyang, just as Kim Il-Sung founded Pyongyang as modern city for a second time after the Korean War (according to modern North Korean mythology), and an old mound is shown to be Dangun's grave. In reality, Kim Jong-Il was born in Khabarovsk, Russia, and bore the Russian name Yura for a long time as a child. The wooden hut, in which he was allegedly born, is a later creation in line with the Dangun myth and one of the most important places for the god-like veneration of the leader. Thus, on the one hand, the Dangun myth is historicized, while on the other hand, the story of Kim Jong-Il's birth is mythologized. In China, the myth of the Yellow Emperor, the legendary forefather of the Han Chinese (the dominant group in China), is being cultivated at the moment. Although there is no archeological evidence, his reign is fixed at 2700 B.C., turning him into the "evidence" for the oldest continually existing civilization in the world (Hilton, 2007).

Hence, cultural codes coexist, and since the identities of individuals and groups as well as subgroups (such as dissident parties or social classes) are not always uniform, they are sometimes compatible, but sometimes they are not. They are being passed to proceeding generations, and thus form a 'collective memory,' which is either passed on verbally, or more importantly through relics (buildings, paintings, etc.) and in writing (cf. Assmann, 1997). Of course, the distinctiveness of this memory varies from individual to individual and it is always a subjective image, filtered through cognitive schemes. This category (which is useful for analysis) does not lead a separate existence, independent from the individuals.[185]

185 Thus, if identity is socially determined through necessity and not by an isolated individual, then one does not depart from the foundation for the methodological individualism. Refer to

In psychology and sociology, the term *mémoire collective* was first used by Maurice Halbwachs (1925).[186] According to Halbwachs, societies neither passively adopt relics, symbols, publications and ideas nor attempt to apprehend them as objectively as possible like a historian would, but create something new, namely a collective memory which is affirmative toward the society's existing aims. Therefore, Halbwachs understood self-perception as a significant part of the explanation for collective action. The components of the collective memory are often archetypical and mythological; if they facilitate the giving of meaning, vagueness, projections and undifferentiated reflection accepted (Nora, 1990).[187] On one side, the thus created collective memory serves to determine the affiliation with a certain group (for example religion, nation or social rank), but on the other side also serves reciprocally for the demarcation to other groups. Therefore, in addition to self-perception, a perception of the 'other' takes place, too: The self and the other as terms exclude one another. This so-called "othering", the differentiation between the self and the other through categorization, identification (with a group) and comparison with other groups, is a practice that can be documented even in cases of randomly formed groups.[188]

In terms of the relations among states and cultures, which relations exist between one's own group and the other is central once the identification is fixed. Bitterli (1992) refers to the experiences of the European and non-European powers of cultural touch (first exchange without reciprocal pervasion), cultural collision (suppression of indigenous cultures) and cultural relations (reciprocal exchange

---

the critical comparison of individual memory in cognitive psychology and biology with the "collective" memory in the social sciences of Wilson (2005).

186 Halbwachs is most widely known because of his contributions as sociologist; however, his election to the Collège de France in 1944 shortly before his arrest and death in a concentration camp, was as a specialist in collective psychology (cf. Marcel/Mucchielli, 1999).

187 With his large-scale project "Les Lieux de Mémoire" (Nora, 1997), in which all material and immaterial heritage sites of France were registered by a prestigious group of historians from 1984 to 1992, Nora tried to establish a sort of "history of the second-degree". Likewise in Germany, the research on memory and collective memory as part of historical sciences has become very important (for an introduction, refer to Wischermann 1996 and Jaeger/Rüsen 2001). For this, Rüsen (1992/1994) developed the term historical culture, which does not denote a "counter-history", but an expansion of traditional history with regards to the the reappraisal of the past in everyday life.

188 To this end, Tajfel and Turner (1986) formed random groups on students. Even despite a hint regarding the highhandedness of the formation of groups, one's own group was preferred *a priori*. In the normative sense, the term "othering" is usually used pejoratively, since it led to discrimination. Nevertheless, for the purpose of evolutionary theory it can be classified as a cognitive procedure, with which the complexity of the world is reduced and which, depending on the imposed standards (i.e. economic efficiency or moral judgments), is permissible or impermissible.

relations with mutual influencing) as the three basic types of such relations. The type of cultural collision was analyzed at length by Huntington (1996).[189] Therefore, self-perception and perception of the other are decisive in forming an opinion about the other and therefore also in the dealing with other. However, they are not separate processes because the experiences in dealing with the other in turn influence the perception of the other and of the self. These experiences occur for example, between nations (i.e. in diplomatic dealings), but mainly between individuals such as traders, investors, employees of foreign enterprises, overseas students, consumers who buy foreign products, travelers, etc. These experiences, in the way that they are perceived by individuals and then processed via memory routes (for example, through travel reports, handbooks for investors, etc.) lead to a reformulation of the perception of the other, but also of the self. A central element of the passing on of such experiences is the educational system, which first creates a uniformity of opinion through state regulation (i.e. through a canon of predetermined texts and admission criteria for school books), and second is experienced by almost all, or even, in case of compulsory education, by all members of society. Therefore, it often is the focal point of domestic or interstate controversies.

Like individuals, governments, religious communities and other groups are interested in the formation of a collective memory which matches their own ambitions. They pursue a policy of memory and a policy of identity. But the collective memory does not let itself be freely manipulated, even though at the same time it is not free from manipulations. This holds especially true the more potential sources of input in the collective memory exist, which is exactly why dictatorships like that of North Korea attempt to control those sources. Thus, one can view self-perception as a significant category for the understanding of collective action. It is not possible to directly observe it, but one can approach it using, for example, surveying people's attitudes and evaluating important sources of communication and memory. The first method is used in for example, social studies (i.e. long-term studies of certain social groups) and in marketing (in consumer surveys), and the second one is used in political and historical analyses.[190] However, in this case the word approach has been used deliberately, since the vagueness of the term identity as well as differing individual characteristics, which all overlap and are subject to different cultural influences, do not allow an exact definition of for example, "the self-perception of Koreans" or "the self-perception of neo-Confucian, employed family fathers." Despite this, self-

189 Huntington's exaggerated theses shall explicitly not be assessed here.

190 Regarding the attitude towards foreign direct investments in South Korea, refer to Seliger (2005a).

perception is a useful category for analysis, which in the following section shall be used in an analysis of Korean relations with the outside world, especially with neighbors in the economic sector.

11.3 Stereotypes in the self-perception of Koreans

National stereotypes (of oneself or of the other), self-perception and collective memory describe that which is historic, passed on. However, they are not static categories, but variables which are in a constant state of flux. While there are times in which people's expectancies by and large match the actual results of their actions ("equilibrium of expectation") and therefore, change in self-perception are only minimal, there are other times in which rapid changes ("transformation") comes about. Regarding the culture of memory, this has been established as a "decrease in assuredness" (Seybold, 2005). But this should not be understood as a quest for the lost previous harmony, because this assuredness itself is *ex post* – a reconstruction in the present time. In this sense, the present debates in Northeast Asia, which were mentioned at the beginning of this chapter, can be understood as a sign of reappraisal and change of identities (cf. Höpken/ Lackner/Richter, undated).

Polemically and often politically motivated in the sense of "Japan against the rest", these are often seen as Japanese historical revision and the consequently provoked reactions of China and Korea. In fact, there are more profound underlying causes. These conflicts are connected to globalization and the consequent questioning of cultural identities; to the secular trend of the economic rise of East Asian states; to the discontinuation or reduction of old lines of conflict of the Cold War, which led to new conflicts, for example through questions of minorities; and to the East Asian economic and financial crises and the new beginning after it. But these changes did not lead to a completely new perception of self and image of the other. Thus, the perception of Japan remains a basic constant in the self- perceptions of China and Korea. Despite the economic rise and the new role as a major power of China, its victimhood in relation to Japan remains important, and it is merely being newly interpreted, here as legitimization of its role after the Cold War. This is not only a 'toolkit' for political actors, which can be used to gain diplomatic or economic advantages, but it is part of the old and new identity of China, as it views itself (Suzuki, 2007).

Due to the historical experiences of isolation and colonization, a strong nationalism developed in South Korea, which influenced the decisions of politicians and bureaucrats as well as consumers. In comparative international surveys about nationalism in East Asia, through the Political and Economic Risk Consultancy from Hong Kong, South Korea has been identified as one of the most nationalistic countries, on a regular basis (Korea Times, 23 February 1999: 12). Foundational to this nationalism is the historical experience of threats to Korean culture and statehood by foreign influences.[191] In the 5,000 years during which, according to Korean popular opinion, Korea has existed, even if in a line of predecessor states whose affiliation with modern Korea is partially controversial, the Korean states have, for the most part, not been completely independent. For a long time, the Korean predecessor states, especially Chosŏn which existed from 1392 to 1910 under the rule of the Yi Dynasty, as vassal states were more or less dependent on their powerful neighbor China. Partially, this dependency was merely nominal and exhausted itself in yearly symbolic tribute payments, and in some cases (i.e. under the Mongolians and Manchurians) invasion occurred.[192] China was, at the same time, the most important source of new cultural influences, such as Buddhism, Confucianism, writing, and later Christianity.

Equally formative and equally paradoxical in terms of cultural and political relations was the relationship with Japan. On the one hand, Korea was the cultural bridge that brought Chinese culture to Japan, and was also connected to mutual influences culminating in territorial overlap of South of Korea and the Japanese islands. On the other hand, Japan was seen as aggressor, especially because of the major invasion from 1592 as well as 1597 under Toyotomi Hideyoshi. This invasion, whose actual aim was the conquest of China, could only be ended by the intervention of the Chinese army and the death of Hideyoshi in 1598. In the national culture of memory, however, it is reappraised as part of Japan's plan of Korean submission, parallel to the later colonization, which was defeated by the Korean's heroic resistance.[193] The colonization itself, which began with a constantly growing Japanese influence in Korea since the last third of the 19th century, and finally formally from 1910 to 1945, is the most important memory moment in the relations between Korea and Japan today.

---

191 A detailed account of Korean history cannot be given at this point. Refer to Eckert et al. (2002).

192 Under the Mongolians in six larger invasions from 1231 to 1273, and under the Manchurians, against whom Korea fulfilled its vassal obligations towards the Ming state, in 1627 and 1637.

193 This took place in the "three major victories", at sea (in front of the island Hansan through Admiral Yi Sun-Shin with the turtle boats, a form of pre-modern ironclads) and ashore (through the generals Kwon Yul in Haengju and Kim Shi-Min in Jinju). While these battles are historical, their influence on the outcome of the war was rather marginal, especially for the land battles. However, important is the national collective memory, which was brought about by the war against Japan (*Imshinhwaeran*) in Korea, which was formerly weakened by fractional battles, and which included Buddhist monks as well as (neo-) Confucian noblemen and led to the appearance of "just armies" (*uibyeong*), in which slaves as well as noblemen fought.

The colonization has had ambivalent results. It was clearly interested in the suppression of Korean nationalism, insofar it questioned Japanese authority. For Koreans, the colonization was the trigger moment of a modern nationalism which was catching up, as was also typical for European nations that emerged or became independent late. While the political movement against Japan failed, especially in the defeated demonstrations in and after March 1, 1919, but also later in the exile movement such as the exile government in Shanghai and the guerilla units in Manchuria, cultural and economic nationalism experienced a significant movement, which influences the self-perception of Koreans today. Cultural nationalism, cultural movement (*munwha undong*), expressed itself in, for example, the reflection of one's own culture and language and the collecting and publishing of old texts. More political methods, such as the publishing of newspapers were not impossible, but were often prevented by the Japanese authorities. Economic nationalism expressed itself in for example, the Korean production movement, which promoted the existence of Korean products, but following some successes was also suppressed by the Japanese authorities. The suppression of national culture culminated in the 1939 instruction to adopt a Japanese name. This was enforced for approximately 80 percent of Koreans until the end of World War II. Particularly in the family-oriented Korean society, this aroused outrage. Thus, Japanese attempts after the revolutionary movement of 1919 to paint the connection between Korea and Japan as harmonic alliance of convenience (*Nissen Yuwa*) failed completely.

The colonization, and before that the protectorate situation of Korea since 1905, when Japan took over the foreign policy representation of Korea with the Eulsa Treaty, also had territorial consequences, which are controversial to this day. For example, an uninhabited group of rocks, which are named Liancourt Rocks after a French whaler, but known as Dokdo in Korea, was formally incorporated as not yet exactly determined state territory in the Japanese prefecture of Shimane under the name Takeshima. The Kando Treaty of 1909, with which large parts of Manchuria were permanently given to China, has already been mentioned above.

Next to these consequences, the Japanese colonization also undeniably brought about a major push for modernization. This mainly concerns the economy which, although strongly focused on the needs of the Japanese motherland, also experienced a major upswing and improved living standards in colonized Korea. The subsistence economy, known as as *chakeupjajok*, meaning frugal, self-sufficient economy, which was the rule during the Chosŏn Dynasty (until 1910) and which was almost philosophically elevated as "happy poverty" (*kanan*), was replaced by industrialization and a market economy. In North Korea, the idealized *chakeupjajok* was later revived in the *Juche* ideology, but was also interpreted as an economy free from foreign influences in South Korea.[194] Next to the economic upswing, it was the education system which despite the Japanization effect played a major role in the modernization of Korea. Part of this was the opportunity for a large number of Koreans to be exposed for the first timeto new ideas (technical, economic, cultural and political) at Japanese universities. The ambivalence of the Japanese occupation remains a controversial subject in Korean society to this day. The fact that administratively and economically many Koreans played a role which inevitably led to collaboration with the Japanese most clearly expresses this.[195] To this day, this is the subject of debate and can still end the careers of politicians if the collaboration of their parents with the Japanese occupation force is made known.[196]

The World War II or the Pacific War was surely among Korea's darkest times. The mobilization of all forces in the territory occupied by the Japanese brought along a more strict control and expansion of the loathsome Shinto cult. The controversy about the mass recruiting of Korean women (along with Chinese, Japanese and Southeast Asia women and a few European women) as so-called "military comfort women" *(jugun-ianfu)*, forced prostitutes who were treated like slaves, persists today. At the end of the war, their recruiting was notably forced and organized or tolerated, respectively, by the Japanese military (Yoshimi, 2001; Tanaka, 2002). After the Japanese government for a long time denied responsibility for the military brothels. which were organized by private operators, its attitude changed after the discovery of new documents. While even in 1990 the government denied responsibility and various lawsuits were dismissed at court in Tokyo, apologies were offered repeatedly, including by Chief Minister Kiichi Miyazawa during a trip to Seoul on January 17, 1993, and by Yohei Kono, chief secretary of the Japanese Cabinet on August 4, 1993. Later, this apology was reiterated several times, among others by the chief ministers Ryutaro Hashimoto and Keizo Obuchi.[197] In 1995, the Asian Women's Fund for the compensation of

194 A detailed account of the *Juche* ideology cannot be given here, but for an introduction, refer to Seliger (2002d).

195 Refer to de Ceuster for details (2001). For him, the collaboration was "the fall" of Korea, from which, in the Korean self-perception, the division of Korea and military dictatorship with strong foreign (American) presence in South Korea are explainable.

196 For example in August 2004, Shin Ki-Nam, Chairman of the governing Uri-Party, had to resign after it became known that his father had collaborated with the Japanese. Kim (2004) predicted a gradual ending of the debate with Kim Dae-Jung's taking office, but this did not happen. Anti-collaborations laws, which were introduced by the following government under Roh Moo-Hyun and which are supposed to support the confiscation of unlawfully obtained property of collaborators and their descendants, have even promoted this debate explicitly.

197 For a discussion on the wording of these letters, which were meticulously watched politically, refer to Soh (2001).

the comfort women was set up using private Japanese funds. Since they were not official funds, primarily Korean women and their supporting lobbies declined to accept the money and demanded official apologies.

The end of the Japanese occupation in August 1945 did not lead to complete independence but to division between American and Soviet spheres of interest, which in the systemic conflict soon led to two opposing systems, that for four years in a bloody fratricidal war caused a total destruction of Korea and took a huge human toll. While a totalitarian system that endures to the present day was introduced in North Korea, in South Korea lasting democracy was established only at the end of the 1980s after a series of authoritarian and military leaders with brief democratic interludes. For the authoritarian and military leaders as well as their opponents, invoking nationalism was the rule. This holds especially true for the North Korean leaders and their ideology, after the conflict between the Soviet Union and China broke out in the 1960s and North Korea tried to attain equidistance between the two powers on which it depended through its own, nationalistic ideology. In South Korea at the end of the 1980s, not only was democratization attained that later stabilized itself further and led to one of the liveliest civil societies in Asia, but also an enduring growth period was initialized from the 1960s onward, with the highest economic growth worldwide for almost 30 years. This was viewed not only as the success of a superior economic system, especially in comparison to the neighbor North Korea that was continuously falling behind, but also as a sign of national strength of Korea. Accordingly, nationalism dominated in all political factions and thus, such varied governments as the dictatorships of North and South Korea, the opposition powers, and finally the South Korean democratic government accepted nationalism and used it to dominate the academic discourse. Korean nationalism was not critically analyzed until the late 1990s and, in one of the first attempts at critical judgment of the nationalistic collectivist memory of Korea, it is stated that "even now there are not many scholars in Korean Studies, whether on or off the Korean Peninsula, who have attempted to systematically contest any of these nationalist narratives" (Pai/Tangherlini, 1999: 11). The relationship with the neighboring states of China and Japan, which shall be elaborated on in the following section, was affected by this nationalism, as was the relationship with the U.S.[198]

198 In 2002, according to a study by the Pew Research Center, 44 percent of Koreans had a negative attitude toward the U.S., significantly more than in France, Germany or every other European and East Asian country (cf. Woo-Cumings 2003). The relationship with the U.S. demonstrates a similar paradox to that of Japan and China, since it, too, deals with a large and important power on which Korea is dependent, not the least because of the military alliance, and which strongly influenced Korea after the World War II, which is the same reason why Korea rejects it. While Korean anti-Americanism cannot be discussed here in detail, the discussion of

The collective experiences of Koreans discussed above, their individual and collective processing of memories, have led to the development of three common stereotypes in the self-perception of Koreans which are important for their view of political and economic development and interaction with other nations: Korea as victim of foreign aggression ("victim nation"), Korea as nation with a 'pure', unique culture which resists foreign influences ("Hermit Kingdom"), as well as Korea as the nation of the East Asian economic miracle ("tiger economy"). The role of Korea as victim of foreign aggression is historically rooted in relations with China and especially Japan, but also in the later development of Korea as pawn in the hands of foreign powers, as Japanese colony and finally, as country divided during the Cold War. Certainly, the biggest collective trauma resulted through the colonization and Japanization of Korea from 1910 to 1945 as Japanese colony.

In the Korean shame culture, failing to fulfill other's expectations (*changpi*), to which the loss of the own statehood in 1910 clearly belongs, since here, the entire people "failed" to defend its own continuance, is not a morally internalized problem (such as guilt in Christianity) that can be atoned for through internal acts of contrition, but an external, public problem that can only be solved through public redemption such as apologizing (*sagwa*) or revenge. This is the crux of the matter of Japanese apologies for the aggression against Korea, which damaged the national honor (*myeongye*) as a whole. The repeatedly demanded apologies lack sincerity (*chinshim*) and, due to a continuous grudge (*wonmang*), they are not being accepted. This grudge as a feeling of bitterness (*han*) has virtually become a topos of Korean self-imagery, for example in literature, social studies, political theology and the workers' movement.[199] Politically less regarded and less adopted, especially in social and human sciences, is the term of the unrelenting resistance (*ogi*), which is a type of double term. For example, it expresses itself in the symbolic and real acts of vengeance (*pa*) in social relationships, but also between states, or sporadically in erupting violence (*pongnyok*).

The continuous feeling of being discriminated against or oppressed or not sufficiently rehabilitated for past oppression leads – in combination with the experience of centuries-long dominance of other powers in the cultural and the political and economic sector – to a minority complex (*yeolteungeuishik*), which in turn is compensated in the sense of *ogi* by inflexible demands for historic justice.[200] It then turns into the feeling of being constantly underestimated by foreign powers (*yatpoda*). The constant emphasis on the civilizing achievements

---

the stereotypes in this chapter and the next one can help in understanding. For an introduction refer to Kim Seung-Hwan (2002).

199 Koo (2001) examines the term in detail with the example of the workers' movement. *Han* can be understood as a feeling of lack of power and cultural and symbolic surrender.

200 Cf. the analysis by Kim (2002) for the American–South Korean relations.

of Korea and on Korean top positions in various sectors is one of the results. Differentiated analyses, which potentially could be an obstacle to the politically and also the morally desired rehabilitation, are rejected. This results in, for example, a publication by the Korean Educational Development Institute on the analysis of the image of Korea in foreign school books interpreting tribute payments to China as friendly gestures and as "a form of barter". This conveys a very dubious interpretation of at least large parts of Korean history. Another result is that the role of Japan in the industrialization process is judged as completely negative (Sohn/Kim, 1998).[201] While such a hypothesis is by all means legitimate in the scientific discourse, it is being presented as undeniable truth (fact or fallacy), or as twisted truth which has to be corrected.

The role as "Hermit Kingdom" (originally a term for the Chosŏn dynasty in the 19th century, which refused all contact with foreign powers), refers to Korea's long history as homogenous society. The already mentioned legendary foundation of a Korean empire (Ko-Joseon) in 2333 B.C. is the starting point from which the entire history of the Korean peninsula is interpreted as Korean history. Normatively, this leads to the negation of every form of foreign influence and to the demand for a Korean unity, probably also because politically this unity does not exist. The maintenance of the (racially and culturally founded) unity is also an significant paradigm economically and politically. For example, Rupert Murdoch's media company's attempt to enter the South Korean satellite TV market in 2000 was branded as "cultural invasion" which would destroy the national, unique culture (Korea Herald, 19 February 2000: 11).

In various ways, respect for Korean culture (*chongyong*) is demanded. Part of this is the already mentioned study of school textbooks from foreign countries which are then notified regarding the faulty interpretations. On behalf of the NGO Voluntary Agency Network of Korea (VANK), an entire network of volunteer so-called "cyber-diplomats" sends out chain letters calling for the correction of false portrayls of history, especially in Japan, but elsewhere, too. The topics are always the same: The great achievements of ancient Korea, the inseparable history of Korea for 5,000 years, the wrongdoings of foreign powers, especially China and Japan, and the role which is befitting Korea, namely as the centre of Asia and gateway to Northeast Asia (VANK, undated).

Korea's uniqueness also has another aspect, namely that of inherent racism (*minjokchuui*). This racism resulted in the centuries-long discrimination of mixed-race children, even after the end of the World War II as the everyday culture was

201 It is stated verbatim that "[t]he legacy of the Japanese occupation left nothing but negative practices in Korea …."

strongly Americanized.[202] In many other areas of daily life discrimination was and is not a rarity, especially against the oftentimes illegally working migrant workers from Southeast and South Asia. The classification into one's own groups (*chung*) and foreigners does not, despite the common kinship, stop at North Korean defectors, who are by no means welcomed with open arms, but rather often encounter problems with integration due to their dialect and their unfamiliarity with the South Korean lifestyle. Of course, the stereotype of Korean uniqueness is not to be understood as a fixed, unchanging attitude. Especially the experiences of the South Korean economic upswing since the 1960s, and in particular the globalization of the last 20 years, have brought about many changes. Nevertheless, it remains a significant explanatory approach for the attitude of Koreans in political, cultural and economic matters.

South Korea's role as "tiger economy" refers to the experience of having the highest growth worldwide since the 1960s, which was expressed metaphorically as "East Asian Economic Miracle" or "miracle on the Han River" (which passes through Seoul). This stereotype leads to a special, positive view of the role of large-scale enterprises (*chaebol*), as well as the possibilities of the guiding economic policy of the state, but in particular of the importance of growth and exports. Of course, such a perception is not static. The economic crises resulted in a very negative attitude toward the *chaebol* and general uncertainty regarding the South Korean governance model. The policy for the preparation of globalization since Kim Young-Sam (*seghewa*) and the forced opening of many sectors after the economic and financial crises of 1997 and 1998 also led to a change of attitudes in the economic sector. Despite this, the unique position of South Korea has remained a common stereotype, which found new variations in the subject of the first successful completion of the IMF aid program in East Asia and also of Korea as the economic hub of East Asia.

It is important to realize that, of course, perception may vary among different groups. For example, in relation to the scientific assessment of FDI, toward which Korea has traditionally followed a very reserved policy, it is possible to discern the influence of an international "epistemic community", a community of like-minded scientists who have been positive about FDI since the 1980s and who well can exert great influence on the country's elites.[203] This also means that the perception of the Other, in this case the view of foreign observers on the role

---

202 This is even more the case in North Korea, where one major reproach towards South Korea is that it tainted its pure bloodline by getting involved with Americans.

203 This influence overtly showed itself in the case of Singapore, whose authoritarian ruler Lee Kuan Yew, according to his own statements, gained significant insights about the effect of FDI when he worked with Raymond Vernon in Harvard; cf. Lee (2000).

of FDI in South Korea, is adopted as the self-perception. This was the case in, for example, the debate about the reasons for the economic and financial crises of 1997 in South Korea, where the independent development involving very established, narrow oligopolies under the guidance of the state was seen as a failure, or at least no longer passable, both by external observers and by Korean scientists, and where stimulus through foreign competitors was discussed as way out of the crisis.

If prior to the crises there had been an equilibrium of expectation with regards to the high economic growth and fast development under guidance from the state in which FDI was of no significance, this changed now in favor of an equilibrium of expectation in which the roles of foreign investors were increasingly regarded as positive. But this change in perception of FDI did not pertain to all layers of the population in equal measure. It depends on the individually expected advantages and disadvantages of FDI, which can be specific to layers (i.e. a well-educated student with knowledge of foreign languages will expect different advantages than an uneducated worker), but it also depends on the different views of FDI, meaning the underlying cognitive schemata.

The perception of Korea as the prototype of the tiger economy expresses itself in, for example, a close national symbiosis of products and companies in advertisement, such as the advertisements of Uri Bank (*uri nara, uri unhaeng*), which could be freely translated as "fatherland, bank of the fatherland". The SUV made by the company SsangYong, which ironically now belongs to the Chinese automobile manufacturer SAIC, is named "Korando", which is an abbreviation for "Koreans can do". The drawback of the trust in the economic power of Korea is a strong economic nationalism and protectionism (*pohojuui*), which will be addressed in the next section.

The previously outlined stereotypes must not be misunderstood as fixed characteristics of every Korean. They do not exist in all people in equal measure, since individual and collective differences in the sense of the above discussed overlapping cultures also lead to very different images of self. In some cases, the stereotypes reinforce each other. For example, Korea's economic success as part of Korea's uniqueness has been understood as being based on its homogeneity and long history. However, the stereotypes are not free from contradictions. Korea's economic success and the trust in Korea as economic power are not compatible with the historically rooted minority complex. All in all, these stereotypes are constructs of social science that do not lead an existence independent from the observer. But they are helpful for the understanding of collective action in Korean economy and politics. In the following, this shall be demonstrated with three examples, namely economic nationalism, relations with Japan and relations with China.

11.4 Three examples of the role of national stereotypes: Economic nationalism, relations with Japan and relations with China

Though the significance that cognitive schemata have for the theory and politics of economic order has been increasingly recognized in the last years, operationalisation has not yet occured. While cognitive schemata that lead to the formation of hypotheses about the economic order cannot be observed directly, the perceptions can be recorded, for example through surveys. In international marketing and management this has been an important instrument for a long time, especially in relation to the already discussed category of economic nationalism. Economic nationalism can be found not only in state politics, but also in the economic decisions of enterprises and consumers.

The latter has been examined in detail as consumer ethnocentrism in the literature of international marketing (Cf. Shimp, 1984; Balabanis et al., 2001). The theory of consumer ethnocentrism examines in how far nationalism influences the individual in his economic decisions. Consumer surveys attempt to measure the degree of nationalism. To this end, Shimp and Sharma (1987) introduced the so-called CETSCALE that includes the different dimensions of consumer ethnocentrism. On the bases of these dimensions it is examined how nationalism is reflected in an individual's economic decisions. The CETSCALE has proven itself to be better suited empirically than other variables such as marketing-mix or demographic variables for the predictions of imported goods (Herche, 1992/1993). Economic nationalism has proven itself to be closely connected to a general nationalistic attitude, whereas economic crises can lead to an increase in economic nationalism (cf. Baughn/Yaprak, 1996). Conversely, open-mindedness is connected to a positive attitude toward foreign products (cf. Rawwas et al., 1996).

Strong consumer ethnocentrism was prevalent in Korea at least until the economic and financial crises of 1997 and 1998, when its importance diminished with the greatly changed economic-political parameters and also the new economic-political theoretical influences. Generally, consumer ethnocentrism expressed itself in the purchasing attitudes toward foreign products as measured for example by the CETSCALE. One of the larger manifestations was the strong resistance to the introduction of American cigarettes in 1988, along with several "frugality campaigns", such as the one shortly before the Asian crises which criticized the supposedly excessive consumption of foreign luxury goods. Government agencies directly or indirectly supported such campaigns. For example, owners of foreign automobiles, which had a tiny marketshare in Korea until 1997, were especially subject to tax investigations for a many years. Companies reacted to the "buy Korean" campaigns by hiding foreign partnership that elsewhere was seen to helps sales. Such behaviour can be explained by Korea's role as "Hermit Kingdom" and the previously discussed self-sufficiency in the economic sector. Simultaneously, in times of crises the Korean victimhood repeatedly becomes the centre point of discussion, i.e. during the economic and financial crises, in the form of a supposed conspiracy of foreign capital against Korea with the aim to destroy Korea or cheaply buy Korean companies. This becomes apparent also in the repeated protests against the opening of the agricultural commodity market, which is seen as the source of pure Korean culture and the victim of "ruthless" foreign interests.[204] Of course, such an explanation is not mono-causal. For example, oftentimes simple lobbying is a sufficient explanation for economic barriers to foreign products. But that does not explain why a Korean demonstrator killed himself at the protests against the opening of the agricultural commodity market at the meeting of the WTO in Cancun in 2003.

Korea's victimhood in economic questions of everyday life can be demonstrated also when one reverses the question of consumer ethnocentrism and applies it to the products of other nations. This "animosity model" then measures the animosity that products of other nations are apportioned, regardless of their quality. In a study with South Korean students Shin (2001) demonstrated clearly that there is a resistance toward Japanese products in the purchasing behavior, although the superior quality of Japanese products is acknowledged.

Economic nationalism can be demonstrated in Korea also on the level of state regulations. For a long time, Korea pursued a defensive strategy of selective liberalization for foreign imports, namely for such products that were necessary as raw material or intermediary goods for the export of domestic products. Foreign capital also was only selectively permitted into the country, for example in connection with desired technology transfer. When with increasing export successes and growing prosperity, the policy of selective liberalization was no longer possible, the Korean government oftentimes tried to enforce exceptions with reference to its unique culture.[205] But with the growing prosperity and acknowledgment of the underlying model of the tiger economy, an increasingly offensive economic policy, in large parts supported by the population, manifested itself. For example, the policy toward FDI changed dramatically, not only as a result of a foreign dictate like it was at first presented during the financial crisis of 1998, but also as a result of a new search for identity of Koreans, who

---

204 For a detailed discussion of the influence of globalization on the Korean agricultural commodity market, refer to Feffer (2004).

205 For example, in April 2007 with the exceptions for the agricultural and educational sectors in the FTA with the United States.

suddenly no longer saw themselves as the victims of foreign economic policy but as the catalyst of East Asian integration and as the economic hub of Northeast Asia. This will be explored in the next chapter.

The turbulent and tragic history of the Korean-Japanese relations has been hinted at in the previous section. After World War II, there was hardly any Korean-Japanese contact for almost twenty years, until in 1965 the establishment of diplomatic relations was declared. This was desired by the U.S., which during the course of the Vietnam War wanted a consolidation of the alliance system and increased participation of Japan (in the logistics sector) as well as of Korea (with ground troops). The Japanese government gave 800 million USD of development aid to South Korea, which in return renounced additional claims for the compensation of forced labourers.[206] While contracts between Japan and Korea were labeled as null and void even before the colonial rule (therefore before 1910), there was no agreement on the territorial dispute over Dokdo/Takeshima Island, instead only the affirmation of the desire to peacefully solve this dispute. No real reappraisal of the past or attempts to answer controversial questions occured, even more so since in South Korea under the reign of Park Chung-Hee, no free political debate was possible.

After the establishment of diplomatic relations, the economic ties with Japan strengthened steadily and the cultural exchange grew gradually stronger, at first particularly through Japanese tourism. While in 1965, 10,000 tourists visited Japan and South Korea per year, nowadays this number holds true for a single day. Nevertheless, for almost 40 years, Japanese cultural products, especially products of mass culture (such as movies or pop music) remained blocked from the South Korean market, where nevertheless a black market flourished. Despite the strengthening ties and the apologies for the colonization, war and the consequences of war, which have been mentioned above, ultimately, controversial questions remained in abeyance.

When with the change of the geopolitical situation after the end of the Cold War more and more people in Japan demanded an end to the "apology policy" (or "masochistic interpretation of history"), many in South Korea understood this as revisionism. The Korean victimhood was conjured up and there was wholesale talk of the revival of Japanese militarism, for example in Lim (2006). Here it was demonstrated that all apologies until then did not alleviate the *wonmang*, the bitter grudge about the Japanese role in Korea. The sentiment of sincerity (*chinshim*)

206 However, only a small portion of the money was actually used for compensations, which led to considerable debates in South Korea after the negotiation protocols that were secret until then became known in 2005. The biggest portion of the money went to the very successful economic development of South Korea, which was beginning at the time.

was missing. Lim (2006: 14) for example, demands a "sincere apology from the bottom of the heart." In what way the sincerity of this apology can be ascertained is completely unclear. But the more often apologies were rejected, the more people in Japan called for an end to the apologies. When in 2005, for example, protests in China as well as South Korea over controversial subjects in school books, such as territorial claims, did not end, the Japanese Premier Yunichiro Koizumi once again apologized for Japan's role in the World War II. At the beginning of the Asia-Africa-Summit in Jakarta, Koizumi declared live on camera to feel "deep regret" for the war history of his country and gave a "deeply felt apology". Koizumi said that especially in Asia, Japan "caused enormous damage and suffering" through its colonial rule and aggression. While this apology of Koizumi did not go beyond previous declarations, according to observers it was unusual for an international summit. Hence, both China and South Korea appreciated Koizumi's words but also declared that this alone as insufficient. Rhetoric must be turned into action.

In the 2000s, there were five main matters of dispute, namely the controversy about Japanese school books and the interpretation of history in general, the visits by Japanese politicians to the Yasukuni shrine, acknowledgement and compensation for comfort women, territorial affiliation of Dokdo or Takeshima, as well as the naming of the Sea of Japan (Korea's East Sea). The school books dispute, concerning the revisionist interpretation of history that since the mid 1980s, is finding more adherents in Japan, in particular high-profile politicians.[207] One particular school history book by a nationalistic historians society has become the centre of criticism, although it is only being used by an extremely small handful of Japanese students. In Japan, also there is indeed no widespread approval of the revisionist interpretation of history; rather, it is a controversial minority opinion. Therefore, it is less about the actual cultural memory in Japan, but rather a symbolic dispute in which Korea's victimhood that continues until Japan corrects its history is demonstrated.[208]

On the one hand, the textbook dispute resulted in major resentment in South Korean-Japanese relations, but on the other hand, it also led to noteworthy initiatives. Joint bilateral and trilateral (involving China) historical commissions attempted to find a consensus on the interpretation of history (cf. Fuhr, 2005). The overcoming of "offender-victim-patterns" can only be successful when it is not a unilateral recrimination of Japan, like it happens in some cases even when historical commissions are staffed with Japanese historians who are interested in composing a Japanese counter-history. Korea's role as the victim of forced recruiting in

207 For a more detailed account refer to Saaler (2005).

208 Regarding the role of the media in Korea in this discussion refer to Lee (2002).

World War II has already been discussed. Again, the same holds true as with Japan's general apology for colonialization: Not sufficiently acknowledged in its victimhood, South Korea does not think itself capable of accepting the apologies as sufficiently sincere. According to many Koreans, the missing sincerity of Japan in the reappraisal of the past manifests itself in the visits to the Yasukuni shrine by leading Japanese politicians, especially the former Premier Koizumi. At the shrine not only are millions of war dead commemorated, but also convicted war criminals. Visits to the Yasukuni shrine is seen by China and Korea not without good reason as unnecessary provocation and has regularly resulted in protests by these countries.[209]

While the human stories behind the colonial experience, forced labour and prostitution in World War II, of course make the sentiment of *han*, or bitterness, comprehensible, it is a different case with the dispute about Dokdo/Takeshima island and the naming of the sea between Korea and Japan. Here the symbolic value that the victimhood has for Korea becomes apparent, regardless of the actual suffering. Dokdo or Takeshima or the Liancourt Rocks, as they are often called on international maps, are a group of basically uninhabited rocks in the sea between Japan and Korea. In 1905, they were incorporated into Oki Island (and thus, the Shimane Prefecture) of Japan, that regarded the island as *terra nulla*. However, this was denied by Korean nationalists, without them being able to effectively protest the situation at the time. In the Peace Treaty of San Francisco in 1951, the issue of the rocks was not conclusively settled, but one year later South Korean President Rhee Syngman proclaimed the "Rhee line" outlining an exclusive zone of 60 sea miles, within which Dokdo was located. At the time, Dokdo was used as a target for practice bomb droppings by the U.S. Air Force. When the diplomatic relations were established, no solution for the problem was found (the parties agreed on the formula of "agree to disagree"), and in the Fisheries Agreement of 1998, the rich fishing grounds around the rocks were marked as neutral territory. The actual sovereignty of the island clearly lies with South Korea which by now even has permanent inhabitants and continuously expanding harbor facilities there, albeit mostly because of symbolic reasons.[210]

Although the Japanese attitude toward Dokdo/Takeshima is extremely reserved and only clings to the legal position that the island is Japanese, the disagreement, after alleged attempts by Japan to re-Japanize the island, has repeatedly escalated. When asked by journalists Tokyo's ambassador confirmed the claim on the island in

209 This was also the reason why the former emperor as well as some premiers stopped visiting the shrine. For a more detailed account, refer to Hundt/Bleiker (2007: 77-80).

210 Refer to the legal analysis by Fern (2005), who concludes that the actual sovereignty of Korea is a strong argument for the legally unequivocal sovereignty of Korea.

2005, and a Japanese prefecture initiated a "Takeshima Day." This triggered a wave of anti-Japanese protest in South Korea. Demonstrators burned Japanese flags while others cut off one finger as (traditional) sign of protest in front of the Japanese embassy. Here the role of Dokdo as a place that symbolizes Korean suffering due to the repeated desire for expansion by Japan becomes apparent. The justification for the ownership of the island on the Korean side is historically rooted with the argument that the island has been an "integral part of Korean territory" (according to the Korean Overseas Information Service, 2005) for centuries. Important is not the question of the actual ownership of Dokdo – which clearly lies on the Korean side – but the historical clarification that this has continuously been the case and it was only the Japanese aggression that ended the situation. It is accepted that the transfer of present-day laws to nations which have been formed with entirely different (for example territorial) principles (ultimately the model of the Westphalian sovereign state) and the dubious interpretation of maps, which according to today's standards are much too imprecise, by no means reinforces the legal status of ownership of Dokdo, which is actually clear, but rather undermines it.

This becomes even clearer in the attempt to name the Sea of Japan (the most common geographical designation) in accordance with the Korean language "East Sea", an attempt which has been pushed ahead privately and for some years now. Again, this clearly demonstrates the self-centrism in the self-perception of many Koreans (as the Hermit Kingdom), which simply geographically argues that a sea to the east of Korea must be named East Sea. On another level it is being argued that the term "Sea of Japan" could result in territorial claims by Japan. President Roh Moo-Hyun of Korea even suggested a coining a new name of "Peace Sea". Again, as evidence for the "historical correctness", old maps are referred to, even though they appear to use various terms such as Korean Sea, but not East Sea.

The discussion of the controversial issues in light of the stereotypes in the self-perception of Koreans is not supposed to mean that the single issues do not relate to important questions in the bilateral relations to Japan. They are not supposed to be evidence for unilateral irrational policy making of Korea when compared with its neighbors.[211] However, they can help in explaining why categories of historical science, political science or economic science are not sufficient to explain the conflicts, and can even be wildly misleading sometimes. This also can be seen in conflicts over historical interpretation with Korea's other neighbor, China.

211 In many respects, Japan itself has stereotypes of self-perception similar to those of Korea, starting with the concept of *nihonjinron*, the unique culture of Japan.

After the establishment of diplomatic ties between the People's Republic of China and South Korea in 1992, relations both in the political and the economic sector developed very quickly and successfully over the course of ten years. China became the main trade partner of South Korea and an important destination for South Korean foreign investments, and China played and still plays an extremely significant role in the question of overcoming the division of Korea and the future of North Korea.[212] However, in the recent years the difficulties emerging from the status of the border region between China and North Korea grew. In this border region a Korean minority resides, mainly in the Korean autonomous region Yanbian, which has long served an important link between China and North Korea through relational and economic connections. In the first few decades after the division of Korea, this link, especially the minor border traffic, was essentially problem-free. During the period of the "Great Leap Forward" (in late 1950s), Chinese and Chinese of Korean ethnicity went to North Korea in order to seek food, but since the 1990s, it is the other way around with thousands of North Koreans crossing the border in search of food, and in some cases freedom. The situation of these Koreans was the first problem area between both states, since North Korea constantly demands more efforts from China to catch and repatriate defectors, while China in turn is afraid of a real mass exodus. This relates exclusively to the relations between China and North Korea.

Chinese relations with South Korea developed a rift when South Korea issued a special law pertaining to the rights and the legal status of overseas Koreans in China. At the same time in North Korea, graves from the Goguryeo era (37 B.C. to 668 A.D.) were added to the UNESCO World Heritage List. The Goguryeo Empire stretched across huge areas of today's Manchuria as well as North Korea. According to Korean interpretation, it is one of the predecessor states of present-day Korea, and with its capital in Pyongyang is of course especially significant in the (completely distorted) North Korean historiography. Less bothered by possible territorial claims of North or South Korea, China was more bothered by the growing national consciousness of the Koreans in the Yanbian region. After all, South Korea economic success was becoming clear, through investments in the region by South Korean *chaebol*. In the People's Republic of China with its extremely difficult ethnic relations, a Northern border with a divided ethnic identity was not at all desirable.

Thus, China answered with a historical interpretation: Goguryeo (or in Chinese *Gaogouli*) was, as well as Barhae (in Chinese *Bohai*) and the legendary Go-Joseon, two other predecessor states of today's Korea, a provincial state, based on an ethic group, within Chinese territory and in a kind of fealty to the Han Chinese

212 Please refer to a detailed discussion in Kim (2005).

state, and therefore not a territorially independent entity but part of the Middle Kingdom.[213] In simpler terms, Goguryeo developed out of a Han Chinese command post in Xuantu. Moreover, the Three Kingdoms, which were unified in Korea because of their racial homogeneity as descendants of the Yemaek tribe, were in fact characterized only through the common adoption of the Han Chinese culture. In spring of 2003, as a first step toward the acknowledgment of this view of history, China, too, registered graves from the Goguryeo era with the UNESCO World Heritage List. Simultaneously, China initiated a politically motivated research project, the Northeast Project (*dongbei gongcheng*), which was intended to reinforce the Chinese interpretation. The corresponding school books were changed on governmental order – as even Koreans noticed – a more drastic step than the longstanding opposition to the governmental permission, but not order, to use Japanese school books which did not correspond with the Korean view of history.[214] The Northeast Project is no isolated project but mirrors the so-called West Development Project, which covers the Western areas of China, especially Tibet and East Turkistan (the country of the Uyghurs). It is about economic development (the Northeast Project was supplemented with a Northeast development strategy), but also about historical-political assurance.[215] After the end of the concept of history from Mao's era, which was based on the Marxist interpretation of history as a class struggle, such assurance surely has become necessary. It can be found, on the one hand, in the fallback on Confucian and other pre-Communist traditions, and on the other hand, also in a reinterpretation of China's relation with its border regions.

The "multiethnic unified state" is the perception that Han Chinese as dominant group together with other Chinese form the Chinese nation (*ZhonghuaMinzu*) and share the Chinese civilization (*Zhonghua wenming*). This is a marked departure from for example, the conception of history of the 1950s until the 1980s, during which Goguryeo was always described as part of the "Three (Korean) Kingdoms" in Chinese history books. According to South Korean press reports, China spent up to 2 billion USD for the Northeast Project. Correspondingly large was the outcry in South Korea, which then initiated a long series of conferences and research activities and founded the Goguryeo Research Foundation (*goguryeo*

213 For a detailed discussion of the Chinese and Korean positions compare Ahn (2005) as well as Leonard (2007).

214 The scientific reinforcement of this process came about through a five-year-long governmental research project, the Serial Research Project on the History and Current State of the Northeast Border Region, which began in 2002 at the new Centre for the Study of Borderland History and Geography of the Chinese Academy of Social Sciences.

215 As Yoon (2004) states, it is not about an expansive but rather about a defensive new conception of history, which preserves the *status quo*.

yonku chedan). The "falsehood" of the Chinese conception of history was criticized on conferences and a "historical correction" was demanded, for instance in Lee (2004).

The conflict, which until then still could have been dismissed as a historical dispute, took full effect in 2004, when more and more politicians accused China of falsifying history, and in their turn enumerated supposed or real mistakes by China in history, among them the annexation of Korean territory through the so-called Kando Treaty. In 1909, Japan and China signed a contract that acknowledged China's sovereignty over the Kando region, which for the most part is inhabited by Koreans, and in return Japan received concessions for mining and railways. In September 2004, at least 59 assembly men of the government and opposition submitted law in the South Korean National Assembly asking for the repeal of this treaty. While the South Korean government, like the Chinese government, tried to downplay the conflict as meaningless, a serious rift developed in the relations of both states.

Again, it is possible to discern that the role of South Korea as having national unity and integrity through the millennia (as in the question of the Goguryeo dispute) is an important component of the Korean understanding of the conflict and also of victimhood (in terms of the Kando Treaty). Korea's victimhood in relation to China is once again projected into the future, since many Koreans suspect that with a transition of the present North Korean regime to a new regime, possibly controlled by the military, incorporation of North Korea into China could happen as a "fourth Northeast province", or in form of a protectorate. To reinforce both the Korean and the Chinese claims and positions, archaeology and scientific research have been mobilized, along with popular culture (such as soap operas about Goguryeo in Korea). Once again, it is not about a differentiated conception of history but the affirmation of a role which matches the self-conception of both nations (cf. Hays Gries, 2005).

11.5 Final reflections: Identity and identity policy and economic and cultural development

Stereotypes in the self-perception of groups and states help to understand their political, economic and cultural actions and attitudes. Nevertheless, they are necessarily vague because of the overlapping of cultures and cultural heterogenity. The identification of stereotypes can be effected through surveys and analyses of political, economic and cultural discourses.[216] The collective memory also

216 Both were also the basis for the selection of the three stereotypes in this discourse.

can be specified through the analysis of material and immaterial "places of memory." The fact that it is cross-generational must not be misunderstood in the sense that it is a fixed, unchanging variable.

This assessment opens up the possibility for a conscious policy of remembering. The more stereotypes are known, the greater the possibility of organising a differentiated view of controversial matters. However, especially for regionally working social or human scientists, it is not exactly easy to research these stereotypes since opposition from the society is to be expected, which, while fostering the existence of these stereotypes, at the same time denies them.[217]

An example of a policy of remembering that tries to overcome stereotypes are the mixed historical commissions that in Europe, and to some extent also in East Asia, successfully try to make compatible the national and the regional history through a joint interpretation of sources. However, there is also a policy of remembering which rather hinders such processes. In 2005 for example, the talks about a free trade zone were halted as "sanctions" by Japan against Korea, as with previously when the student exchange between both states was suspended as a sanction. Such a policy ruins the acquisition of mutual knowledge, and thus the possibility to overcome stereotypes. Hundt and Bleiker (2007) name three different preconditions for successful joint activities for the overcoming of stereotypes: They must not be started as an attempt to restore a previous, at some point lost "harmony", but necessarily remain an incomplete process. Thus, a "historical correction" of all controversial matters is impossible. They should try to expand the dialogue where it is successful. For example, among Northeast Asian states, economic cooperation, which is successful and useful for all states, should expand. While this cannot completely compensate for the lack of a historic consensus, it can contribute to mutual understanding in a significant way. Finally, a promising joint policy of remembering must accept a different conception of history which, at least in part, is contradictory to one's own conception of history.

In relation to the stereotypes of Korea discussed here, one can add that their weakening and the rise of alternate hypotheses have significantly increased with Korea's success in the economic sector. This becomes apparent for example in *hallyu* (the Korean Wave) in popular culture. In South Korea, foreign cultures were for a long time perceived as a threat to the Korean lifestyle which, in the sense of the stereotypes about Korea's uniqueness (Hermit Kingdom) and Korea as victim state, brought along a hyperxenesis or colonization. This was plainest in the cultural relations to Japan. Although since 1965, relations with Japan had normalized, Japanese technology and Japanese capital played a significant role in

217 This is a general problem for critical area studies for researchers who come from or work in such a region or culture, cf. Seliger (2004b).

the South Korean economic development, and both countries closely followed the United States, there were absolutely no cultural imports from Japan until the end of the 1990s. Only on black markets it was possible to buy pop music that was popular with teens, Japanese adult comics (mangas) and cartoons. Moreover, the American influences, that were noticeable everywhere, were repressed on the part of the government, for example through a film quota in the film market. To this day, a quota for Korean film productions is supposed to strengthen the domestic film industry. The increasing prosperity of South Korea and the ripening of the market for cultural products were accompanied by an increased composure and Korea began to liberalize Japanese cultural imports. Today, as will be explored in Chapter 14, the Korean Wave is rather understood as part of a new narrative of Korean success vis-à-vis the outside world, and cultural competition is seen as beneficial in this context.

For the future formation of East Asia as a region in which common stereotypes no longer prevent the joint shaping of the future, the *hallyu* phenomenon could have a significance that is not to be underestimated: Apart from the nationalistic interpretations of the cultural superiority of Korea, which was what originally inspired it in Korea, the fact that Korea, after the political and economic emancipation, also emancipates itself (pop-) culturally from the Western or Japanese role models, is remarkable. Above all, it allows for more composure in the contact with the neighbors, against whom it no longer is pitted only as victim and beleaguered state.[218]

218 The question of whether *hallyu* is as sustainable phenomenon is of secondary importance since it is precisely not about lasting dominance in an area, but only about emancipation.

Chapter 12: FDI Policy and the Perception of Korea's Economic Model Before and After the Financial and Economic Crisis

12.1 The Asian crisis as the turning point in Korean FDI policy

The strong increase in foreign direct investment (FDI) was one of the most obvious results of the Korean economic development after the economic and financial crisis of 1997 and 1998 and a policy for attracting FDI was widely discussed. However, already in the time before the crisis there were changes in FDI policy, in particular during the Kim Young-Sam presidency (1993-1998) and his *segewha* (globalization) policy. In the Korean market for institutions, 1997 was a turning point regarding FDI, since now explicit openness to FDI and wooing of investors became an institutional innovation. It was part of the answer to formerly disregarded structural problems made apparent by the crisis, like the lack of competition in domestic markets, the lack of modern forms of corporate governance, and the inflow of short-term capital used for long-term investment projects. Second, in 1997 external influences in institutional competition were most obvious, including in the imitation of foreign policies on FDI, partly in accordance with liberalization conditions of external actors (namely the IMF). Thirdly, the new policy could also be seen as a change in perception based on cognitive schemata with regard to foreign capital no longer matching reality. To understand the resulting changes, an institutional economics viewpoint is more useful than traditional theories of FDI, like models of the optimal regulation of FDI by host countries (Seliger 2004c).

The discussion of FDI in economic science began with the study of the impact of FDI on technical progress and skill development in the labour force in developing countries and the impact of multinational companies on economic development (the "dual economies" debate). Optimal regulation of FDI by the host country was modeled in a way to ensure maximum welfare gains in a static-neoclassical model.[219] The theory of comparative advantage was applied to East Asia by the wild geese model (Hiley, 1999; Dowling/Cheong 2000). Later, when the debate about globalization and locational competition was ongoing, attracting

219 See for example the use of the model for Korea in Koh (1993).

FDI was understood as an important ingredient in the "catching up" process. The much-discussed analysis of Dunning (1993/2002) puts firm-specific, locational and internalization advantages of foreign investors in the spotlight. However, not only were microeconomic advantages like technological change and increased worker skill level or macroeconomic advantages like positive effects on growth, employment and the current account considered important, but so were institutional changes, like improved corporate governance and management structures. This also has consequences for the host country institutional structure, as well the public and private sector. In this way, FDI becomes relevant to institutional economics. Transformation processes in Central and Eastern Europe shed a new light on the role of FDI, in addition to being instrumental in preventing monopolistic market structures and in relation to long-term, sustainable growth.[220] The experience of CEE was also important in the study of various competing institutional frameworks aimed at attracting FDI, political and cultural obstacles to FDI, as well as the impact of FDI on the results of domestic companies.[221]

In South Korea's economic policy FDI for a long time played only a marginal role. Until the 1990s South Korea was among the countries with the lowest level FDI. This changed under the administration of Kim Young-Sam (1993-1997), who saw FDI as part of his globalization strategy. Under the administration of Kim Dae-Jung (1998-2003) Korea began to woo investments aggressively, in particular by pointing out institutional changes in the Korean economy. Crisis and post-crisis times also saw a renewed interest of academic research into the effects of FDI in Korea.[222] This chapter discusses how the changes to external institutions (for instance the legal and taxation issues of foreign investors in South Korea) and internal institutions (e.g. the treatment of foreigners by tax authorities, attitutdes of consumers on the market for consumer goods, job seekers on job markets, and regulatory authorities on licensing and supervisory processes) are dependent on the change of the perception of the role of FDI, and thereby influenced by cultural factors. The changes in these cultural factors have been

---

220 It is important to stress that to date the causal relation between FDI inflows and long-term growth is subject to debate. FDI can be seen as an indicator of sucessful institutional arrangements (e.g. a stable economic policy framework set by the state) and/or it can direclty affect growth.

221 See Lankes/Stern (1997), Claessens et al. (1998), Meyer (1998) for an analysis of the institutional determinants of FDI in CEE, and Meyer (1996) for a comparison of FDI in East Asia and CEE. Vlachoutsicos (1999) analyses specifically cultural barriers in managment of transformation companies in companies with FDI.

222 See for example Cho/Kim (1998) on FDI policy, Ruffini (1999) on FDI in the banking sector, Park/Yun (1999) on FDI and the privatization of state-owned enterprises, Hong (1998) on technology-transfer and FDI, and Kim (1999), Ahn (1999) and Kim (2000a) on FDI policy and the role of the new ombudsman system for FDI.

discussed in-depth in the previous chapter. The question of resulting institutional change will again been discussed in the framework of the by now well-known institutional framework of the "market for institutions" model. Here, cognitive models regarding the effects of foreign economic activity in Korea and their evolution are of particular importance. The second section of this chapter looks into FDI policy and economic policy in Korea. The third part discusses the role of FDI in the market for institutions model, and the fourth part discusses attitudes toward FDI, followed by a short conclusion.

12.2 FDI and economic policy in South Korea – an overview

Direct investment long stood in the background of South Korea's economic policy. Until the late 1990s, South Korea was one of the market economies with the lowest FDI. Moreover, South Korea explicitly opposed the entry of foreign investment for a considerable period of time.[223] From a cultural perspective, this can be explained by South Korea's historically linked ethnocentrism, which, politically speaking, carried with it strong economic nationalism.[224] But also, economic considerations were relevant, such as the question of how to control companies with foreign ownership in the specifically South Korean form of developmental dictatorship.[225] The South Korean experience from 1910 until 1945 as a Japanese colony with an economic structure solely adjusted to Japanese interests and largely consisting of foreign (Japanese) ownership resulted in a period of radical economic nationalism. It is ironic that nevertheless only Japanese direct investment carried certain significance due to historical relations, geographical proximity, and the development of differences in factor prices and technological advancement following the rapid reconstruction of Japan.[226] Economic nationalism is a phenomenon which had always existed and already played an important role in Aristotle's essay, *Politeia*, but which gained specific

223 For early Korean FDI policy see Park (1986).

224 The concept of ethnocentrism has been developed by Sumner (1906: 13). Sumner defines ethnocentrism as follows: "Ethnocentrism is the technical name for this view of things in which one's own group is the center of everything, and all others are scaled and rated with reference to it."

225 For the concept of developmental dictatorship see Adamocvich (2001). For an application to Korea see Lee (2003a).

226 See Castley (1996a and 1996b), Köllner (1998) and Castellano (1999). Between 1972 and 1976 more than seventy percent of FDI originated in Japan, including an important share of FDI from the Korean minority in Japan.

weight during the decolonization period following World War II (Heilperin, 1960). Economic sovereignty became an important instrument for creating a new sense of nationality in the newly founded states or former colonies which were declared independent, such as in South-Saharan Africa, or for strengthening national consciousness vis-à-vis minorities, such as the Chinese minority in Southeast Asia. Similarly, economic sovereignty was an instrument for recovering the national pride of nations which suffered humiliation during the colonial era, as in South Korea.

The most important form of economic nationalism was the nationalization of foreign companies, in particular raw materials industries. For that matter, regulatory policies were introduced for new FDI which, among others, restricted property rights and determination over domestic management participation and required local content specifications for produced goods. Soon thereafter, models of optimal regulation of direct investment developed, promising maximum utility without letting run dry the necessary influx of capital and technology. Moreover, the economic policy of economic nationalism was aimed at the achievement of autarky in the field of agriculture and targeted at import substitution in the field of industry and export control.[227] While economists were wary about economic autarky, they often advocated the possibility of optimal FDI regulation policies.[228] As late as the 1980s and the early 1990s, when for the first time successful growth was observed in states which conducted open market policies toward foreign investment, economic nationalism as a strategy lost its appeal.[229] In this regard, South Korea is an exception in the sense that a change in FDI policy was considered a consequence of successful growth rather than a precondition. Following the Korean War, South Korea was subject to significant influence of American development aid, but this nevertheless did not lead to a lasting development process. The participation of foreign investors was especially rejected during the authoritarian regime under Park Chung-Hee (1962-1979) as well as Chun Do-Hwan (1982-1987), in which economic autonomy was considered an expression of political sovereignty (Lee, Doowon 2003: 86). Because of these factors the inflow of foreign investment remained marginal until the end of the 1980s, as indicated in the table below.

227 For an overview see Burnell (1986). Since the strategies mentioned are explicitly national, they were different in each country.

228 On autarky, see the articles in Johnson (1968). Early models try to optimize regulation in terms of export quotas, technology transfer, reinvestment versus profit transfer, etc. Later models, which view FDI overall much more positively, try to optimize the amount of subsidies necessary to attract FDI.

229 The first Asian country to radically change its FDI policy was Singapore in 1961.

Table 32: FDI in South Korea 1962-1989

Time	FDI (registered) in Millions of USD
1962-1981	93 (annual average)
1982-1986	354 (annual average)
1987-1988	1,174 (annual average)
1989	1,090
1990	803

Source: Park, 2003, after data of the Bank of Korea

Even though two special export zones for foreign investors were put in place in the 1970s in South Korea, local production was strictly limited by coercive export quotas, local content requirements and technological transfer regulations. In the late 1980s and early 1990s, a tentative opening to FDI occurred (see Kim, Il-Hwan, 1987; Lee, Kyoung-Ryoung, 1991). At the same time, the Korean stock exchange was opened to foreign portfolio investments, first by the Korea Fund (1984) and the Korea Euro Fund (1987), and later to direct portfolio investments as well. One reason was the failure of the national development strategy in the heavy and chemical industries in the late 1970s.[230] Furthermore, the worldwide crisis of highly indebted developing countries led to the new perception of FDI as an alternative to debt. In addition, on the one hand the strong export-based growth of South Korea led to demands that the newly industrialized country opens its market, and on the other hand the willingness to do so grew from the country's desire to prove its competitiveness on the world market. Overall, South Korea's attitude changed from a determined rejection to a more tolerant attitude until the economic and financial crisis from 1997 to 1998; however, it did not lead to a more active procurement policy. The following table gives an overview of the liberalization path.

Table 33: Liberalization of FDI in Korea Before 1997

Date	Policy Measure
1960	The "Foreign Capital Inducement Promotion Act", with the goals of productivity growth, employment, and improving the current account.
1965	Normalization of relations between Japan and South Korea and the beginning of Japanese FDI.
1970	Creation of a special export zone in Masan open to FDI in the consumer goods industry strictly regulated in terms of export quota, local content and technology transfer.
1974	Creation of a special export zone in Iri open to FDI in the consumer goods industry strictly regulated in terms of export quota, local content and technology transfer.

230 The heavy and chemical industry (HCI) drive led to an even more restrictive position toward FDI, to decrease the possibility of external shocks; see Sakong (1993: 114-115).

Date	Policy Measure
1984	Transitioned from a positive list of allowed FDI to a negative list of prohibited sectors.
1989	Abolition of regulations for FDI on export quotas, local content and technology transfer.
1991	Introduction of a registration system for FDI, rather than permits, in selected sectors.
1992	Registration system becomes the rule, with the permit system the exception.
1993	Five-year plan for attracting FDI in 132 (out of a total of 224) formerly restricted sectors.
1994	Extension of licenses for trade with foreign currency to banks
1995	"Five-Year Foreign Investment Liberalization Plan" of the Ministry of Finance and Economy
1996	Korea becomes an OECD member with the consequence of adjusting FDI rules to fit OECD standards.
1997 (before the crisis)	"Act on Foreign Direct Investment and Foreign Capital Inducement" for FDI liberalization in 47 of 81 still-restricted sectors over three years.
1997 (after the crisis)	Permission given for friendly takeovers (with the consent of the board of directors); previously only new investment was possible.

Source: Sakong, 1993; Park, 2003: 225-226; Baang/Kim, 1996; Seong, 1996

President Kim Young-Sam (1993-1998) and his policy played an important role in elevating South Korea into the ranks of OECD states and in preparing South Korea for globalization. In this regard, *segewha* (i.e. globalization) became a crucial economic vision. International competitiveness of South Korean industries, an improved national image as well as the opening of Korea to other cultures, such as by intensifying the instruction of foreign languages, were the preconditions. This was supported, among other measures, by the introduction of internationally oriented study programs (area studies or international studies). There were many economic preconditions for entering the OECD, such as the introduction of real name accounting in 1994, which abolished anonymous accounts that were widely used at the time.

Of particular importance for the new FDI system was the possibility of takeovers instead of only new investment introduced the same year as the crisis. This measure – later hotly debated in high-profile cases of corporate takeovers after the crisis – which by some commentators was seen as a bargain-sale against national interest, showed the transformation toward a more market-based system of attracting FDI. In addition, the liberalization of the early 1990s brought about an imbalance. While the former state governance of large conglomerates was put to an end, a new alternative institutional system was not yet introduced to replace the former industrial policy. The government's industrial specialization plan, which sought to reduce over capacity (e.g. in steel production), failed in 1994. In this scenario, a dilemma of rapid growth occurred. The outdated model in which the state governed the *chaebol* was no longer possible, due to the sheer size of the *chaebol*. On the other hand, the *chaebol* were still tied to the government and were able to coerce government support, as they were "too big to fail". The lack of more stringent competition laws and transparency in the executive branch were two of the greatest structural weaknesses which were unveiled by the Asian financial crisis of 1997 (Seliger, 1999d).

While the table 23 shows clearly that FDI liberalization was well underway before the crisis, the economic and financial crisis between 1997 and 1998 nevertheless signified a watershed with respect to the inflow of FDI. The new Kim Dae-Jung administration made aggressive attempts to attract FDI. For one, this was a tool for improving the balance of payments crisis which occurred mainly due to short-term capital drain. Secondly, another reason constituted the obligation to the IMF to open diverse markets for foreign competitors, in particular the obligation to sell two banks to foreign holders. Moreover, the opening of markets was an important part of the propagated "DJnomics", the government policy of modernizing the labour market, the public sector, the private sector and the financial markets.[231] The unconditional fulfillment of the IMF conditions was the fundamental tenet of the reform package, which was constantly adjusted to South Korea's real economic situation. However, the core principle of the reforms was the "four plus one" policy, which required simultaneous labour market reform, reforms of the financial, public and private sectors, together with the opening of the oligopolistic Korean markets for competition. The opening of the market for foreign competitors was supposed to coerce reforms in the four sectors. To do so, FDI was massively accommodated, as can be seen in the following table.

Table 34: Policy Measures for Liberalizing FDI in South Korea 1997-2003

Date	Policy measure
1997	Economic and financial crisis, with stand-by agreement of the IMF in December: Among the conditions are the sale of two South Korean banks to foreign investors and further opening for FDI.
1998	Attracting FDI is one of the most important policy fields of the new Kim Dae-Jung administration (opening for FDI in almost all fields except radio and TV, and restricted opening in 27 remaining sectors like agriculture and energy).
1998	Foreign Investment Promotion Act, further liberalization of FDI.
1998	Introduction of an ombudsman system for FDI (as a channel for complaints and review of policy measures).

231 This was also clearly stated in the programmatic statement of MOFE; see Ministry of Finance and the Economy (1998). See also the discussion in Seliger (1999c) as well as Chopra et al. (2002).

Date	Policy measure
1998	Reformulation of the Foreigner's Land Acquisition Act (liberalization of ownership of land and buildings by foreigners).
1998	Permission given for hostile takeovers.
1998	Introduction of the Korea Investment Service Center of the Korea Trade and Investment Promotion Agency as one-stop service center for foreign investors.
1999	Participation of foreign investors in infrastructure projects is partly liberalized (foreign capital is not automatically classified as risky).
2002	Kim Dae-Jung announces plans to make Korea the "Hub of East Asia"; debate about special investment zones for foreign investors.
2003	Announcement of a system of cash subsidies for foreign investors (of up to 20 percent of the investment value).

Source: Park, 2003: 226-227

A combination of deregulation, improved macroeconomic conditions, drastically decreased costs of acquisitions and an advantageous exchange rate led to a strong influx of FDI after 1998. In 1999 and 2000, FDI inflows reached a peak at above 15 billion USD (Seliger, 2001d: 5-7). This can be explained in part by cheap firm prices in the wake of the economic crisis. A strong depreciation of the South Korean won and the necessity for quick sale of many companies or company branches ("fire sales") in the course of the liquidity crisis contributed to this development. Secondly, the IT boom led to a strong increase in foreign investments, particularly in 2000. However, global and South Korean conditions deteriorated soon after due to uncertainty over the development of the global economy, the regression of the stock market bubble – especially in the IT sector – the gradual appreciation of the South Korean won, and the end of company "fire sales."[232] The most attractive investments were already executed with the market opening. The level of FDI dropped below 1997 levels in 2003, although South Korea made continuous efforts to improve general conditions for foreign investors. FDI trends from 1991 to 2002 are summarized in the table below.

Table 35: Development of FDI 1991-2002 (in USD millions)

Year	Total	Japan	U.S.	EU	Others
1991	1,396	226	297	749	124
1992	894	155	379	242	118
1993	1,044	286	341	299	118
1994	1,317	428	311	393	184
1995	1,947	418	645	461	423

232 See the analysis of takeovers after the crisis by Goydke (1999) and Freund/Djankov (2000).

Year	Total	Japan	U.S.	EU	Others
1996	3,203	255	876	892	1,180
1997	6,971	266	3,190	2,305	1210
1998	8,853	504	2,973	2,885	2,491
1999	15,542	1,750	3,739	6,251	3,802
2000	15,217	2,448	2,922	4,391	5,456
2001	11,292	772	3,889	3,062	3,569
2002	9,101	1,403	4,500	1,663	1,535

Source: Korea International Trade Association (2003) after data of the Ministry of Commerce, Industry and Energy (1991-2002: 53)

This demonstrates that the measures taken by South Korea to improve its attractiveness as a location for FDI were not entirely in vain. Nevertheless, after the initial boom of FDI due to fire sales after the crisis, the trend partially reversed. The banking and financial sector is a particular example for this ambiguous trend in South Korea. In the old development model of South Korea prior to the financial crisis between 1997 and 1998, banks played an important role, as the government extended loans via the banks in accordance with political and economic criteria, with the former having a priority in case of doubt. The democratization process of the 1980s and 1990s led to a liberalization of the banking sector, with banks no longer subject to direct state intervention. At the time, unrestricted loan extensions did not provide for government guarantees against bankruptcy and were one of the reasons for the financial crisis. During the Asian financial crisis from 1997 to 1998, part of the agreement with the IMF was to sell at least two of the bankrupt banks to foreign competitors. This process took years and proved partially unsuccessful. Nevertheless, new regulations allowed foreign banks to continuously expand their marketshare. With the entering of Citibank into consumer banking via the takeover of KorAm bank for 2.7 billion in November 2004, there were three banks (together with Korea First Bank and Korea Exchange Bank) which were controlled by foreign capital.

Nevertheless, foreign banks were facing a number of difficulties. Cash injections in other domestic banks during the crisis led to the de facto nationalization of all banks (save the above mentioned banks that were sold). While the government had promised to stay away from the management of banks, this proved to be difficult. In the case of Kookmin Bank, Kim Jung-Tae, the chairman, was denied a second term by the government due to some differences on how to manage the bank. While there might have been good reasons for that it was the government influence in such decisions per se which was problematic (not necessarily the sinlge decision). Ironically, Kookmin Bank was the bank which, together with foreign banks, had opposed the bailouts of domestic bankrupt companies such as LG Card, SK Global and Hynix Semiconductor over the previous few years by amortization. This type of bailout under state pressure before 1997 was typical, but later was rightfully rejected on the basis of profitability. Moreover, banks which are controlled by *oegukjabon* (foreign capital) also experienced increasing pressure by the state in shape of the Financial Supervisory Commission (FSC). The FSC chairman contended that it is not acceptable for those banks to make profits like blackmailers, while denying loans to small and medium-sized companies. To decrease foreign influence in banks, a law was prepared in 2004 to prescribe banks to occupy at least half of the board with Korean members, as they are supposedly better positioned to comprehend the mentality and challenges of the Korean market. It is in this atmosphere of tension over increasing internationalized practice and, at the same time, continuing economic nationalism, that not only banks and the financial sector are caught up in, but generally all foreign companies in South Korea.

While the growth (and subsequent decline) of FDI inflows can be partly explained by macroeconomic and microeconomic factors (exchange rate developments, change of company valuations in the economic crisis etc.), this cannot be said for the changes in FDI policies. Institutional changes can rather be understood as the supply of a new form of FDI policy on the South Korean market for institutions. This will be discussed in the next section.

12.3 The market for institutions model and FDI in the Korean economy

The market for institutions model has already been discussed above (see Section 5.2). The expectations equilibrium, which is not the normative (optimal) outcome, but rather the match of expectations and economic outcomes, ensures that in a world of bounded rationality people can carry out their economic plans. If there is a grave mismatch, a crisis of the economic system (*Ordnungskrise*) ensues. And this crisis leads to a new policy, which again has intended and unintended consequences, which are among others caused by the mismatch between the old informal and new formal institutions and the expectations people have with regard to changed institutions. Perception of the FDI regime is therefore an important factor to take into account. Communication about the economic system is a key element of the perception, a point largely neglected until now (Wentzel, 1999). This can be explained by Figure 3, which combines the international context of FDI policies, changes in formal and informal institutions and the cultural context of FDI policies.

Figure 3: The Market for Institutions and Korea's FDI Policy

International Context: Institutional Competition and Institutional Constraints

Here: FDI attraction through locational competition; international framework for FDI through the WTO and OECD; (regional) integration of markets for goods and factors

Formal Institutions: "Market for institutions"

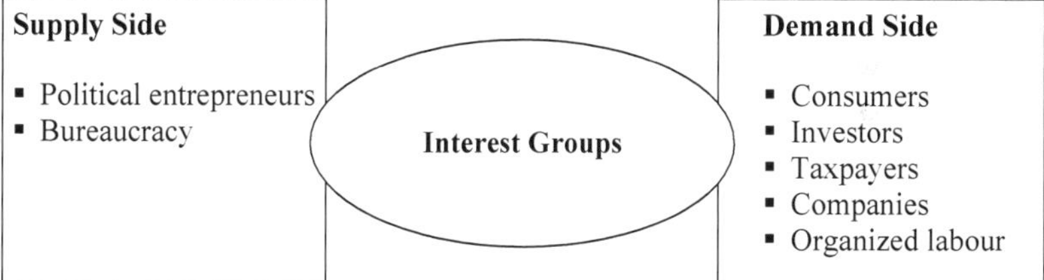

Here:
Domestic and foreign business associations

Informal Institutions

Here: Praxis of tax and customs authorities, local authorities, and courts;attitudes of domestic competitors, job seekers

Perceptions of institutions (self-perception, perception of others)
Here: Perceptions of the impact of FDI on the domestic economy, national sovereignty, and cultural preservation

Cultural context, cognitive models
Here especially: Consumer ethnocentrism, economic nationalism, models of globalization

Source: The author

The international dimension involves institutional competition of FDI regimes. As mentioned above, since the late 1980s and during the 1990s, the positive impact of FDI on economic development became visible in the most open East Asian economies like Singapore and Hong Kong, and later also in mainland China. At the same time, state-led development in Korea experienced problems, first in the HCI drive, and culminating in the economic crisis of 1997-1998. The policy of opening to FDI can be understood as an institutional imitation of a policy already successful abroad. Some elements, like the new FDI ombudsman system aiming at unbureaucratic aid for foreign companies in case of disputes, were even institutional innovations. Second, the international context of Korea's FDI policy includes external pressure to change former FDI policies: this included the membership conditions for admission to international institutions like the WTO and OECD. More contested and painful were the conditions of the IMF standby agreement mentioned before. Third, already since the early 1990s trade integration in East Asia had accelerated, leading also to demands for a more liberal investment regime from trading partners. An institutional answer to this was the start of functional integration processes like the ASEAN Plus Three – process proposed by President Kim Dae-Jung and discussed in some detail in chapters 14 to 17.

Institutional change again is a concequence of changing formal and informal institutions. Changes in formal institutions result from competition in the market for politics, where suppliers and the demand side of certain policies interact (being neither homogeneous nor mutually exclusive). On the supply side, during the presidential campaign of 1997 Kim Dae-Jung was successful in cementing his reformist image, including as a reformer of politics-business relations and the failed economic system.[233] This included a new attitude toward FDI. The highly publicized campaign of "DJnomics" (much more popular than the later, less credible drive for "DJwelfarism") as well as the later campaign for a positioning of Korea as a hub of East Asia (see Chapter 16) increased this openness. It is important to see that external pressure as defined above was not unwelcome in this context. Many changes in the Korean economy could only become politically palatable once they were presented as outside demands and not under the control of domestic economic policies. The role of bureaucracy was quite ambivalent with regard to FDI. While in particular the Ministry of Finance and the Economy (MOFE), but also other government ministries and agencies, were involved in the formulation of new FDI policies and "DJnomics" in general, traditional close relations with *chaebol* also led to inertia or even covert opposition, leading to a divergence of formal and informal institutions. For example, the bureaucracy tried to slow down market opening by making public (i.e. informing the press, usually on condition of anonymity) alleged exorbitantly disproportionate demands of for-

233 As Robert Myers (1998) wrote: "The new president, long-time dissident opposition leader, Kim Dae-Jung, seemed to be just the man to right the wrongs of the past and lead Korea into a free-market economy and democracy."

eign investors or foreign business associations. A typical case occurred in March 1999, when a confidential paper by the U.S. Chamber of Commerce (AmCham) in South Korea regarding progress and desiderata in economic reform was published by civil servants from MOFE (Korea Times, 16 March1999: 9). In particular with regard to the sales of two bankrupt banks to foreign investors (a condition of the IMF standby agreement), ever new demands by Korean authorities led to frustration and in some cases failure of negotiations (Korea Times, 1 May 1999: 9). While on the national level markets were liberalized, this policy was often undermined by regional or local opposition. In several cases the opening of affiliates of foreign chain stores like supermarkets was rendered impossible by local bureaucracy (Korea Herald, 28 April.2001: 13). In particular, tax authorities were seen as being discriminating in their practice against foreign companies as well as against owners of high-profile foreign goods, such as cars.[234]

On the demand side of policies interests were widely diverging. Voters were interested during the crisis in economic stability. Some welcomed the inflow of foreign capital for this reason, while others saw it rather as a weakening of the national economy. Equally ambivalent were the workers: Often FDI inflows were seen as foreshadowing job losses. While logically FDI should have had a positive impact on jobs (all other things equal), this was not the case since FDI often went into those sectors or companies already bankrupt or having difficulties. In the old Korean political-economic system, the government had forced healthy conglomerates to merge with such bankrupt counterparts. This was neither possible after democratization, nor feasible in the economic crisis, which involved some of the largest *chaebol* like Daewoo. In the case of the sale of Daewoo to General Motors there were month-long strikes, though most of the jobs were indeed saved by the sale. Trade unions especially rejected any foreign participation in the Korean economy. The *chaebol* themselves were also divided: for some foreign investors were key to survival, while for others they were seen as bringing a loss of power, in particular for the founding families. In between the supply and demand side of politics are the interest groups, which possess asymmetric information necessary to the formulation of policies and at the same time mediate these policies vis-à-vis the demand side. They include chambers of commerce, professional associations, lobbying groups, etc. While their attitude toward FDI depends on their political outlook, during the crisis there was a range of views on market opening. It was favored by foreign chambers of commerce, many professional associations, as well as, at least immediately during the crisis,

234 This includes the habitual special tax audit for owners of foreign cars deemed to be luxury goods. In 1999 one-third of complaints with the ombudsman for FDI concerned tax problems, 17 percent were related to problems with customs authorities regarding exports and imports, and nine percent to health, safety and environmental standards (Kim, 2000b).

by many of the new citizens groups interested in curbing the influence of *chaebol*. Though groups like the People's Solidarity for Participatory Democracy came from a position of economic nationalism, by championing the rights of minority shareholders in Korea's business conglomerates and filing lawsuits against executives for illicit transactions and insider trading they actually aided the opening process.[235] The changes in formal institutions (the revised FDI policies after the crisis, as discussed above) also depended on changes in the cultural context, in which FDI policies were formulated. The strong economic nationalism as a result of historic experiences of isolation and colonization and the resulting stereotypes in Korea's self-perception have already been discussed in the preceding chapter. While this perception is not static and policies before the crisis already signaled change as well as triggering more change, they were still dominant. After the economic crisis they could not remain unchanged, but were reformulated, for example by integrating the concept of being the first and most successful graduate of an IMF program into the narrative of Korea as an exceptional economic power, or in justifying a new, unique role by claiming the position of hub of East Asia.

As culture is heterogeneous and overlapping, there is no single perception of the role of FDI in the economic system. Regarding the academic evaluation of FDI, in the 1970s and more so in the 1980s, a new epistemic community emerged that saw FDI as a necessary and positive ingredient of economic reform and catch-up programs. This also had a lasting impact on national elites.[236] This means also that the perceptions of Korea and the role of FDI in the Korean economy by foreign observers were reflected in South Korea's self-perception. This was visible in the debate on the reasons for the economic and financial crisis of 1997 and 1998. Suddenly Korean and foreign economists shared the perception that the traditional economic system based on oligopolistic conglomerates closely related to the government was a failure, and stimulus through foreign competition became a widely accepted remedy. Before the crisis, the expectations-equilibrium was based on a model of high economic growth rates and rapid development driven by the state. In this model, the role of FDI was marginal. The new expectations-equilibrium included an increasingly positive view of FDI. This means that the demand for policies accommodating FDI was increasing as well as the supply of such policies. However, not all social strata shared this view: They

---

235 Directly, through the advancement of foreign minority shareholders, as well as indirectly, by depicting *chaebol* and their influence as main targets of economic policy reform, which logically includes the admission of competitors as one relatively easily available remedy.

236 This was made explicit for example in the case of Singapore's legendary leader Lee Kuan Yew, who in his autobiographical record of Singapore's economic rise mentioned the formative influence of Raymond Vernon of Harvard regarding the effect of FDI on the economy; see Lee, K.Y. (2000).

differed depending on individual advantages and disadvantages expected from FDI. For example, a worker might see foreign investment mainly resulting in future job losses due to corporate restructuring. A highly qualified student with foreign language knowledge at the same time might see it as an opportunity to get a job in times of high unemployment among graduates. The following section discusses attitudes toward FDI in social strata based on empirical results.

12.4 The perception of FDI in South Korea – empirical results

The significance that cognitive schemata have for the theory of economic order and the policy of economic order has been increasingly recognized in recent years: North (1996) assigned them a central function for the advancement of new institutional economics (NIE). This was particularly emphasized in studies of the transformation of economic orders (Herrmann-Pillath, 1998/1999; Rosenbaum, 1999). But for the East Asian national economies, too, the importance of cultural factors for the development of the economic order was emphasized (Pascha, 2002; Lee, 2002). However, an operationalisation of cognitive schemata for use in the theory of economic order and the policy of economic order has not yet been achieved. While cognitive schemata that lead to the formation of hypotheses about the economic order cannot be observed directly, the perception can be recorded, for example through surveys. In international marketing and management this has been an important instrument for a long time, especially in relation to the already discussed category of economic nationalism, which is central for the judgment of FDI. Economic nationalism cannot only be found in state politics, but also in economic decisions of enterprises and consumers. The latter has been examined in detail as consumer ethnocentrism in the literature of international marketing (Shimp, 1984; Shimp et al., 1995; Balabanis et al., 2001). The theory of consumer ethnocentrism examines in how far nationalism influences an individual's economic decisions. Attempts to measure the degree of nationalism are made using consumer surveys. To this end, Shimp and Sharma (1987) introduced the so-called CETSCALE that includes the different dimensions of consumer ethnocentrism. The CETSCALE has proven itself to be better suited empirically than other variables such as marketing-mix or demographic variables for predicting sales of imported goods (Herche, 1992). Economic nationalism has proven itself to be closely connected to a general nationalistic attitude, whereas economic crises can lead to an increase in economic nationalism (Baughn/Yaprak, 1996).[237]

237 A particularly highly developed, morality-based economic ethnocentrism could be verified in Southeast Asia; cf. Hewstone/Ward (1985).

Conversely, open-mindedness is connected to a positive attitude toward foreign products (Rawwas et al., 1996). A second major group of studies on the cultural context of economically relevant decisions hails from management literature, in which culture is analyzed as factor in the management of international enterprises (Webber, 1969; Hofstede, 1991; Hampden-Turner/ Trompenaars, 1993).[238] In these studies, special focus is placed on analysis of the effects of polycentric (decentralized) vs. ethnocentric (based on national superiority) management systems. The costs of a change in management systems depends on, among other things, whether the according (national, regional, or religious) value systems are affected, on how much changes are met with opposition and on how far opinion leaders can play an important role in the change process.[239] In relation to FDI, the studies examined whether cultural differences caused different forms of market entry. However, it was not clear if major cultural differences between investors and recipient countries favor total control rather than joint ventures.[240] For the theory of economic order with regard to FDI, it is of particular interest whether state policies have the potential to change the perception of FDI. If the aim of a state policy is larger receptiveness to foreign investments, but the policy also requires, next to changes to formal institutions (such as the liberalization of FDI, as discussed in the second section), changes to informal institutions (which in turn are based on the perception of FDI), a new category of economic political measures is necessary – namely measures that belong to the area of communication policy. The aim of new training for opinion leaders to be more open-minded and eloquent was part of the previously mentioned opening program under Kim Young-Sam with respect to globalization. As part of the program, nine Graduate Schools of International Studies received specific government support for a period of three years. They are a part of a larger network of similar schools that offer students in all departments the ability to earn a Master of International Studies or Master of Area Studies (usually with specialization in economics, politics or culture). Have these programs also resulted in a different perception of FDI?

In order to examine this question, a questionnaire on attitudes toward FDI that was compiled out of a representative cross section of the population by the opinion research center ORC Korea (2001) on behalf of the Korean Foreign Company As-

238 The problem of overlapping cultures as already discussed above results in substantial measuring problems; cf. Adler/Villafranca (1983).

239 For South Korea it was assessed that opinion leadership in enterprises is closely connected to seniority; cf. Marshall/Gitosudarmo (1995).

240 The articles of Kogut/Sing (1988), Eramilli/Rao (1993) and Lachman et al. (1994) that initiated the debate argue in favor of shared control, since missing knowledge about the recipient country can be acquired through joint ventures. By contrast, Padmanabhan/Cho (1996) and Anand/Delios (1997) argue in favor of 100 percent ownership, since this could lower the transaction costs for enterprises. Additionally, Kim/Hwang (1992) refers to the signal effect of 100 percent commitment.

sociation (KFCA) was compared with the results of an identical questionnaire, which was completed by students of the Graduate Schools of International Studies.

Box 1: Comparison of Survey by ORC Korea and Poll of Students[241]

On behalf of the Korea Foreign Company Association, ORC polled 1,000 Koreans aged 20 to 59 via a telephone survey in the cities of Seoul, Busan, Daegu, Gwangju and Daejeon. 54.7 percent of those polled were from Seoul. Those polled represent a random sample, with 50 percent males and 50 percent females. The survey took place from 29.11. – 3.12.2001. The survey of students was completed with the aid of a questionnaire among students at Seoul National University, Korea University, Ewha Womens University and Hankuk University of Foreign Studies in Seoul. All four schools were a part of the project supported by the Kim Young-Sam government for the establishment of graduate courses specializing in the study of globalization. A total of 71 students were polled (52.1 percent male and 47.9 percent female). 81.7 percent were 20-30 years old, while 18.3 percent were older. 26.8 percent studied international business or international politics, and 73.2 percent majored in area studies (for example European or Latin American studies). The survey took place in June 2002. 64.8 percent of those polled were from Seoul or Gyonggi Province nearby Seoul.

In the survey, some distinct differences can be seen between the students and the total population. An interesting fact is that decidedly positive attitudes in particular, but also markedly negative attitudes, are more distinct among the students.

Table 36: Question: How Is Your Attitude Toward Foreign Enterprises in Korea?

	Total Population (%)	Students (%)
Very positive	3.9	22.5
Positive	57.9	60.6
Negative	34.0	7.0
Very negative	3.0	8.5
Not specified	1.2	1.4

Source: KFCA and the author

The students were also asked about the reasons for their attitude. The contributions of foreign enterprises to the advancement of entertainment culture, technology and economic development, as well as the systematic management of human resources, and high, performance-based wages were named most frequently. Most often cited by the total population were the strengthening of Korea's competitiveness through foreign enterprises, the positive impact on employment, and

241 Special thanks to the Korea Foreign Companies Association for their permission to use the data.

good product quality. Both students and population based negative assessments on the self-serving aims of foreign enterprises, the outflow of profits to the home countries of investors, as well as the possible dominance of domestic markets. Additionally, the students named the lack of the Korean customary retirement or severance payment as aspect of working for a foreign company. The question about the contribution of foreign enterprises to the economic development of Korea received a slightly more positive response from the students.

Table 37: Question: How Much Do Foreign Enterprises Contribute to the Economy in Korea?

	Total Population (%)	Students (%)
Very much	7.2	9.9
Much	63.4	66.2
Little	26.7	16.9
Very little	1.7	0.0
Not specified	1.0	7.0

Source: KFCA and the author

Students as well as the total population ranked employment effects first, and then technological characteristics like product quality. Moreover, the students also named the aspect of stimulating competition through foreign enterprises. As negative aspects, the outflow of capital and the self-interest of foreign enterprises were named by both groups. On the question of the future role of foreign enterprises, distinct differences can be discerned: The students demand a much stronger role of foreign enterprises.

Table 38: Question: Should There Be More Foreign Enterprises in Korea in the Future?

	Total Population (%)	Students (%)
Very much	12.7	26.8
Much	44.9	66.2
Little	35.9	5.6
Very little	6.0	0.0
Not specified	0.5	1.4

Source: KFCA and the author

When asked for the reasons, the national competitiveness, employment effects, as well as the contributions to economic development were positively cited as main reasons by both groups. Reasons for rejecting a stronger foreign commitment are in particular protecting the domestic market as well as the outflow of capital to foreign countries. Interesting is the question about the status of globalization in South Korea. Apparently, the students of international studies think that Korea is globalized to a much greater extent than the wider population, because at least 8.5 percent of the students deem Korea to be sufficiently globalized, and more than 50 percent fairly globalized, far more than the total population.

Table 39: Question: In Your Opinion, How Far Is South Korea Globalized?

	Total Population (%)	**Students (%)**
Sufficiently	1.5	8.5
Fairly	40.1	53.5
Little	54.5	25.3
Not at all	3.6	0.0
Not specified	0.3	12.7

Source: KFCA and the author.

This is probably also related to the environment of the students, in which globalization is more distinctly perceived than, for example, in a provincial town, so that the opinion about the status of globalization is more positive. The acceptance of economic and political measures which aim to support foreign enterprises, such as subsidies for research and development costs, depends on, among other factors, how the previous policy of the government was perceived. Although in both groups an obvious majority is of the opinion that the state rather supports the domestic enterprises, the total population rather than the students also thinks that there is positive discrimination of foreign enterprises.

Table 40: Question: Does the South Korean Government Support More Domestic or Foreign Enterprises?

	Total Population (%)	**Students (%)**
Domestic enterprises	61.0	50.7
Foreign enterprises	34.0	12.7
Undecided	5.0	36.6

Source: KFCA and the author.

In total, students have a significantly more positive attitude toward foreign enterprises and their role in South Korea than the total population. If one takes into account the effect of age group as well as the regional composition and the level of education, this difference is a little less marked but is, in particular on the question of what the role of foreign enterprises should be in the future, very differenciated.

Table 41: Question: Should There Be More Foreign Enterprises in Korea in the Future?

	Total Population (%)	**Students (%)**	**20s Age Group (%)**	**Population of Seoul (%)**[242]	**Population with a University Degree (%)**
A great many	12.7	26.8	15.2	62.2	63.7
Many	44.9	66.2	47.9		
Few	35.9	5.6	33.9	37.5	36.0
Very few	6.0	0.0	2.4		
Not specified	0.5	1.4	0.6	0.3	0.3

Source: KFCA and the author

In total, men were more positive toward the role of foreign enterprises than women, younger South Koreans considerably more so than older ones, the population of the capital more so than the provincial population, richer people more so than poorer people, and those with international experience more so than those with no international experience. But the attitude of students was significantly more positive than all of the other groups. The positive attitude of the students is mirrored in the professional aims of the students.

Table 42: Question: Where Would You Like to Work in the Future?

Chaebol	19.8
Foreign enterprise	67.6
Small business	4.2
Own company	7.0
Other	1.4

Source: KFCA and the author.

Furthermore, more than 60 percent of the students stated that they can imagine working abroad. It fits that mainly positive characteristics were stated in association with the term foreign enterprise. Categories important to macroeconomics such as rational management, technological level and financial stability were named alongside individual advantages such as high, performance-based wages,

242 For Seoul as well as the group of graduates only the summarized categories were made available.

a liberal work climate, in particular in comparison with the work climate in Korean companies, and also better conditions such as shorter working hours.

It is not the objective of this section to verify the verisimilitude of the attitudes of both the total population and the students in international courses of study. Rather, the point is to examine in how far education with explicit focus on globalization influences the perception of FDI. This is clearly the case, although the information of the students could be entirely different from that of the rest of the population. Even if a different level of information regarding foreign enterprises and other valuations (for example by foreign professors) played a role, this does not seem altogether plausible because one could then expect a similar level of information from other groups (such as the graduates, the richer people, and the population of the capital). It is likely that there are other cognitive schemata with regards to the role of foreign investments.

Now, two different possibilities should be considered: Firstly, the different cognitive schemata could be a result of the self-selection of students. The students of the Graduate Schools for International Studies usually enter graduate study with a preselected professional aim (different from undergraduate study which in South Korea for a long time had more to do with the results of the national university entrance exam than with individual professional aims). Moreover, there is another selection process of the Graduate Schools themselves, which have a kind of filter, through which the most 'internationalized' students surely slip the easiest. Secondly, the most different cognitive schemata could also be a result of the formation of these schemata through the course of study itself. With such relatively short terms of study (two years) and a small number of students, such a change in schemata certainly is not easy to measure. This change is of limited interest to the success of the Graduate Schools of International Studies. The aim was to qualify a group of students who were supposed to represent the idea of the opening of Korea (*segewha*) as conscious and visible multipliers. This has come about through the establishment or support of the according institutions. If the change of the cognitive models is a result of these programs, and thus, the differences are not completely brought about by self-selection or pre-selection of the students in the admission process, then this means that the change in cognitive models can become a variable of the policy of economic order. If this (preliminary) result is correct, some conclusions for the theory of economic order and the policy of economic order can be drawn.

12.5 The lasting success of Korea's FDI policy after the crisis and some theoretical conclusions

As mentioned above, the role of cognitive models for the emergence and acceptance of economic systems in the sense of North (1996) is a decisive factor. This had been recognized by NIEs, but not really operationalized. The last two chapters analyzed it as theoretically as well as empirically. For economic systems theory and policy there are several implications. With regard to the theory of economic systems it is important to understand the system as a complex phenomenon which cannot be reduced to its formal institutions. Changes in formal institutions can easily be tracked, as has been done here for FDI policies. Equally important is the influence of informal institutions. They are embedded in a cultural system emitting innumerable signals which are reduced by cognitive schemata to enable human beings to process them given bounded rationality.

In terms of attitudes toward FDI, they were clearly more positive for students of international studies than for the professionally active population. Since in Korean management the seniority principle still holds, this means that there are not necessarily immediate effects of changed attitudes, even when they slowly become a majority perception. While consequently there were still many complaints among investors after the changes to formal institutions were enacted, nevertheless FDI played an ever-more important role in the expectations-equilibrium of Koreans after the crisis. The old equilibrium where "Koreans on the whole still have a rather narrow perspective on international matters" and "maintain a highly mercantilistic mentality", as former Minister of the Economy Sakong (1993: 175) expressed before the crisis, was shattered. A new equilibrium was slowly built up, going first through a phase of economic policy activism before taking a more settled course. In terms of economic policy-making, this means that economic policy should and can include measures regarding informal institutions. This was until recently a desideratum of evolutionary economic policy-making and NIEs (Pelikan/Wagner, 2003). Communication and education play an important role in this respect. This should not be misinterpreted as mere economic policy propaganda, neither in the media nor in schools and university education. However, a long-term vision of economic policy is necessary. In this sense also attempts by the Kim Dae-Jung and the Roh Moo-Hyun administration can be understood to make Korea a "hub of East Asia". This vision allowed for a number of reforms not popular with the domestic population and economy. While a vision can help to overcome political resistance, it has to be credible; if not, it can even be counterproductive, as might have been the case with the Korean hub vision (Seliger 2002b; Krause 2003).

Free trade policy is one policy area where the leadership's vision and popular perception are far apart, and this is one reason why in an economy as open and trade-dependent as the Korean economy is nevertheless opposed to (certain) trade deals to a surprising degree, a point discussed in Section 5. At the same time, a self-perception that is more confident regarding the ability to withstand foreign competition can be the result of economic policies allowing for FDI and achieving success. This can be seen for example in the cultural sector and will be discussed in the next chapter.

Chapter 13: From Ethnocentrism and Cultural Nationalism to Globalization and *Hallyu* (Korean Wave)

13.1 Culture as the core of economic nationalism in Korea

The cultural sphere and cultural businesses have been to some extent the core of economic nationalism in Korea, since the justification for protection of Korean markets have been cultural rather than economic. The experience of Japanese colonization (1910-1945) as well as the contested identity as the "true" Korea through the Korean division and Korean war are equally responsible for this as the neo-Confucian heritage of the "Hermit Kingdom", when Korea (Chosŏn) was the last country in East Asia to open up to Western influences. Therefore, it is no wonder that the cultural markets have been especially highly protected, against the dominant Japanese market as well as against the U.S.-dominated Western influences.

From the time of the Asian crisis, however, there has been more and more pressure to remove this last bastion. While normalization talks with Japan began in the 1960s, only the East Asian crisis brought a sense of urgency to extend friendly relations with neighbours. The resulting free-trade talks during the Kim Dae-Jung and Roh Moo-Hyun administrations led nowhere, but they were accompanied by a gradual relaxing of the ban on Japanese cultural goods, for which a thriving underground market existed anway. The negotiations with the U.S. for a bilateral investment treaty at the same time put pressure on the Korean screen quota for locally produced movies. Last but not least, the huge educational market (especially for higher education) began to open as part of the commitments under the Doha Development Agenda of the WTO. Also, the impact of the EU-Korea free-trade agreement, which came into force in July 2011, and the Korea-U.S. FTA, which came into force in January 2012, will lead to further opening of cultural markets.

While there is still considerable opposition to the opening of cultural markets, forces in favour of greater openness have also emerged. These are (consistent with what theory predicts and also what other OECD economies in early stages of development experienced) not so much consumer groups potentially benefiting from lower prices and greater access to foreign culture and ideas due to market opening, but rather entrepreneurs benefiting from the popularity of Korean culture abroad: the K-pop wave in East Asia's music market and the domestic and international success of the Korean movie and soap opera industry (*hallyu*) are examples of cultural market opening.

13.2 Culture, globalization and the Korean Wave

It is ironic that besides the U.S., Japan has been since World War II the most important partner nation for South Korea, especially after the normalization of diplomatic relations in 1965. Japan remains an important source of foreign investment as well as of imports, especially of machinery with high-tech content. Culturally, however, after World War II exchanges were completely banned in the beginning. While most Koreans at that time had grown up speaking Japanese in schools, its language and culture were now extinct from South Korea. With growing economic success and growing interdependence with the world economy, exchanges with other countries increased. The fight for democratization in the late 1980s was a hallmark of this trend, allowing, for example, in 1989 for the first time South Koreans to freely engage in travel overseas; moreover, not only was it allowed, but growing numbers of middle class citizens were able to afford such travel.[243] At the same time, there was growing concern for the introduction of world culture into Korea. World-class facilities for opera, concert and theatre were built and international orchestras and troupes regularly visited Seoul. Even traditional Japanese performing arts like *bunraku* (puppet theatre) and *kabuki* (traditional theatre) were allowed in Seoul, and in 1994 Korea admitted a large cultural promotion mission from Japan, after itself sending one to Japan two years earlier.

The Seoul Olympics of 1988 were certainly a major trigger not only for democratic development, but also for a changing attitude toward the outside world. When autocratic governments were overcome in the late 1980s and in 1993 the first civilian government of President Kim Young-Sam (1993-1997) began, there was already a major imbalance between Korea's inward-looking cultural policy and its outward-looking trade policy. A new policy of globalization (*segewha*) was designed to overcome this imbalance. For Korea to become a truly globalized economy, increased industry competitiveness had to be matched by an improved national image and the opening of Korea to foreign cultures, for example through learning foreign languages and educating international specialists.[244]

---

243 It should be noted, though, that democracy activists often had an extreme nationalist and anti-foreign (especially anti-American, but also anti-Japanese) outlook and at the same time tried to preserve national culture, e.g in the form of the *samulnori* ("four instruments"), a form of revived and modernized popular folk music based on percussion which played a major role in the demonstrations of democracy activists and was a popular form of university-based protest, and today remains an element of university culture.

244 For this purpose, specialized international graduate schools were promoted at major universities, educating students in foreign politics, economy and culture to become international and area specialists.

Still, in this time opening was slow and careful and fully controlled by the government. OECD membership in 1996 brought new obligations for liberalization. But a major force for opening was the Asian crisis, which brought South Korea to the point of near-bankruptcy and led Korea to accept large loans from international financial institutions. These loans were conditional on far-reaching institutional changes, among them the opening for foreign investment in many formerly closed fields. While these fields did not directly affect the cultural market, they fundamentally challenged the self-perception of Koreans as discussed above and introduced the possibility of a much bolder opening of Korea's culture to foreign influences.

At the same time, the renewed necessity for support from the large though mistrusted neighbour Japan led to further gradual market opening. At the heart of Korea's fear of "cultural contamination" (Cha, 2004) was the onslaught of Japanese popular culture. While Japanese "high" culture could be consumed by a minority elite like Western high culture before it, it was feared that the immensely popular underground market for Japanese music, video and especially animation would expand even more once the market was legalized. Japanese songs were for the first time in 53 years legally performed at a concert in Gwangju in October 1998 (Web Japan, 1998). Gradually, first movies which won prices at international film festivals, "J-pop" (music) and other cultural activities, then Japanese broadcasting and cable TV were allowed as well as other movies. Final restrictions concern the particularly strong Japanese animation film industry. While Japanese culture had finally reappeared legally in Korea, it had by no way an overbearing influence, but rather made a "soft landing" (Shim, 2005).[245] Certainly, the passing of time (and the slow disappearance from active life of people themselves suffering from Japanese colonization) helped the acceptance of liberalization. But, moreover, there was a new attitude of Koreans toward cultural opening which was maybe the most important long-run result of the shake-up of Korea's society during the Asian crisis and its aftermath.

How did this change happen? It was not so much the pressure itself, which opened up Korea's cultural markets, but rather a new feeling of confidence, after Korea emerged from the crisis in relatively short time as a successful economy again. In the field of the economy, market opening through foreign pressure and changes in the traditional Korean developmental state model led not to a decline, but rather to a rejuvenation of the economy. Especially in the field of popular culture, technical developments led to market pressure, more than direct political lobbying by foreign culture industries for access to the Korean market. Digitalization

245 Of the 35 Japanese TV dramas (soap operas, serials) shown in Korea in 2005, only four made it to the top in terms of audience, among them foremost "Gokusen" (gangster teacher).

rendered national quota systems often ineffective, the internet allowed for worldwide access to movies and music. Korea's fascination with technology meant an enthusiastic adoption of these technologies, but this also meant much more pressure for innovation by domestic cultural industries (see Feigenbaum, 2002).

Suddenly, market opening in the field of culture was not seen as a threat to Korea, but rather as an opportunity for Korea to spread its culture, more and more also its popular culture, to other countries: *hallyu*, the Korean Wave, was born. Korea began to market its popular culture abroad and had, especially in East Asian countries, great success, foremost with its TV soap operas, but also with movies and pop music, computer games and fashion items. The term *hallyu* (Korean wave or fever) was first used in China and Taiwan for the fondness for Korean popular culture, but soon spread to Hong Kong, Vietnam, Singapore, Thailand and Japan (see Korea National Tourist Organization, 2005). The Korean actor Bae Yong-Joon, known in Japan as Yonsama, epitomizes the Korean wave by drawing enthusiastic crowds wherever he goes or is aired in Japan. Since the turn of the century, *hallyu* has also been used to promote Korea as a tourist destination, the Korean fashion industry and Korea as a shopping country (so-called new Korean wave or *shin hallyu*). According to one opinion poll, two-thirds of visitors from East Asia to South Korea are influenced in their decision to visit South Korea by a prior experience with Korean popular culture (Korea Net, 2005).

Cultural opening in the context does not mean bringing global culture to Korea, but rather spreading Korean culture abroad. While this has been also the aim of the *segewha* policy, it only became successful when Korean cultural industries themselves were under greater competitive pressure from market opening and had to conquer new markets to survive.[246] Before 1998, exports in cultural products were so insignificant that no figures were provided for cultural industries by the government. In 2003, South Korea exported 650 million USD worth of cultural products; the size of the entertainment industry jumped from 8.5 billion USD in 1999 to 43.5 billion USD in 2003 (Onishi, 2005). More than 150 movies were exported alone, according to the Korean Film Council under the Ministry of Culture and Tourism, 80 percent of which went to East Asia (Koreacontent News Team, 2005). Film directors like Kim Ki-Duk, Bong Joon-Ho, Lee Myeong-Se and Park Chan-Wook won international acclaim. Korean popular culture, once seen as threatened by its Japanese counterpart, became domestically as well as internation-

246 This understanding of globalization, by the way, is not unique to Korea: indeed, it can be said that it is at least to some extent derived from the Japanese understanding of *kyosei* (living in harmony, i.e. integrating into the world community), by which in the 1980s Japan's policy discourse on globalization began. As a further step, this harmony was interpreted as a re-focusing of globalization, from the West to Asia, and, more specifically, Japan (Iwabuchi 2002).

ally much more potent, leading to the headline in New York Times: "Roll over, Godzilla: Korea rules" (New York Times, 2005).

Besides movies, Korean TV programs were also an increasingly attractive export product, as the following table shows.

Table 43: Export of Korean TV Programs

Year	Exports (1,000 USD)
2001	21,383
2002	27,141
2003	35,559
2004	70,306
2005	121,763
2006	133,917
2007	150,953
2008	160,120
2009	170,228

Source: Korea Information Society Development Institute

While the South Korean movie industry as well as popular culture in general was on the rise after the departure from old exclusionism, the way of expansion followed again the more traditional way of Korea's development: In 1998, the year the opening to Japanese culture began, the Ministry of Culture and Tourism saw an important increase of its budget to finance a five-year-plan for the development of cultural industries.[247] The study of culture industry in universities became popular and in half a decade almost 300 departments of culture industry had opened in South Korea, which contributed enormously to popularizing the culture industry sector in the country in accordance with its Confucian tradition of highly valuing formal university education (see Seliger, 2003). Also, the promotion of exports of cultural goods was supported by the Korea Culture and Content Agency since 2002. The Ministry of Culture and Tourism and the Korean National Tourism Organization were also active in organizing trips to Korea as part of the *shin hallyu* mass tourism.

The one remaining barrier, which has been much debated, is the screen quota for Korean movies. Since the mid-1980s the cinema has been gradually liberalized, but a quota for Korean movies at 120 days per year (i.e., Korean films are guaranteed to

247 As with most cultural policies, there was a previous, though much less bold, cultural five-year plan in 1996 titled the "Five-Year Plan for New Korean Culture."

run at least two-fifths of the year in Korean theatres) is in place, and is similar to provisions in France, Australia and Canada. The reasons for the quota were mainly formulated in terms of Korea's "infant movie industry" needing protection from the Hollywood movies, which enjoy much larger economies of scale (in terms of audience) and investment, though there are also some advantages for local content, given the language and culture barrier (Kim, 2004). Not only did Hollywood films dominate Korean audiences (e.g., in 1995 there were 65 Korean movies and 358 Hollywood movies, which was a 15-fold increase over the mid-1980s), but also Korean movies clearly imitated Hollywood style, as content analyses show (Oh 2005). But after the Asian crisis, a number of Korean blockbusters challenged American dominance at the box office, while at the same time Korean directors like those listed above developed a unique Korean aesthetic and style.[248] On secondary markets, translations or subtitles made these movies also available as DVDs to an international audience.

Until now there are no concrete plans when to scrap the screen quota. However, the defenders of the screen quota are now more often found among the directly affected industry associations and some political groups concerned about cultural diversity and generally opposed to globalization (e.g. Yang, 2004), and less so among successful actors and directors, who are quite confident about competing with other cultures and culture industries.

13.3 Outlook – will Korean culture survive in a globalized world?

"Koreans on the whole still have a rather narrow perspective on international matters" and "maintain a highly mercantilistic mentality", the former Minister of the Economy Sakong (1993: 175) wrote. Nowhere has this dictum been truer than in the sensitive field of cultural industries. But today, it far from describes the actual situation. The Asian crisis fundamentally shook the old model of the developmental state and the underlying perceptions of Korea as a victim of foreign aggression and a pure state needing to be preserved with as little contact with the outside world as possible. The new South Korea is much more confident about the exchange with other cultures, still maintaining an aggressive outward orientation concerning the sale of Korean culture, but also accepting the inflow

248 Berry (2003) writes of the de-Westernization of blockbusters, a development also taking place in China. The first such blockbuster was the spy movie "Swiri", followed, among others by "Shilmido" and "Taegukki."

of foreign cultural content.[249] Regarding one of its hottest competitors, Japan, it can be said that Korea's cultural industries have survived market opening, and, contrary to expectations, the flow of cultural content was stronger from Korea to Japan than vice versa. This has nothing to do with the preservation of the status quo. New products and content developed abroad will always be a potential threat for domestic producers. But this, instead of eliminating domestic producers of cultural content, forces them to constantly innovate (or, if foreign ideas are good, imitate) to stay in the market.

Still, some questions remain open. One hotly debated topic in the case of Korea is the market for education, which is still relatively closed to foreign competition. Being at the core of cultural understanding, schooling and higher education are rigidly controlled by the administration. An opening of these markets might have a major impact, as shown by the "voting by the feet" of Korean students, who in record numbers try to escape the rigid school and university system for destinations abroad. But perhaps the situation is quite similar to before the opening to Japanese cultural industries. Ultimately, opening might speed reforms of the education sector which now are being imposed by the administration at a slow pace.

Another open question concerns the traditional Korean culture. While the cultural industries, the popular music, TV and movies, might fare well under market competition, does the traditional culture survive? Given the technical aspects of globalization one can say, luckily, that chances for surviving are better than ever. Not in the sense that South Korea remains a museum, where people live, as in ancient times, in Eastern decorum, but in way such that smaller, more specialized forms of digital broadcasting make programmes for much more specialized audiences feasible. Traditional culture will survive, though not as a mass market, but rather for a minority in Korea and abroad. Rising incomes also lead to a greater appreciation of the cultural heritage, as a recent movement to preserve the few remaining traditional houses (*hanoak*) in Seoul and elsewhere shows.[250] And, at the same time, Korea's new confidence in its own culture, far from the fear of cultural repression so pronounced before, leads to a new confidence in playing with elements of traditional culture. The boom of historical soap operas, taking place during the times of Chosŏn or earlier and also enjoying a phenomenal success as exports to China, are an example of how traditional culture can be a source of new endeavours to popularize Korean heritage domestically and

249 This new attitude is also increasingly shared by Korean politics and administration, as demonstrated by a number of reform bills, which were debated in mid-2005 in the Korean Parliament and which were aimed at promoting cultural industries instead of restricting them (Kim, 2005).

250 The same it true fort he living environment. The recent restoration of an old river flowing through downtown Seoul, which for decades had been buried under a double row of highways, the Cheongyge Stream, is a prime example of this greater care.

abroad. In this sense Korean culture is not a victim of globalization but truly reaches beyond national borders. This can also be observed in the trend of intercultural marriages seen in the table below.

Table 44: Intercultural Marriages in Korea 1992-2008

	Total Marriages Unit: Cases	**Intercultural Marriages Unit: Cases**
1992	419,774	5,534
1993	402,593	6,545
1994	393,121	6,616
1995	398,484	13,494
1996	434,911	15,946
1997	388,591	12,448
1998	375,616	12,188
1999	362,673	10,570
2000	332,090	11,605
2001	318,407	14,523
2002	304,877	15,202
2003	302,503	24,776
2004	308,598	34,640
2005	314,304	42,356
2006	330,634	38,759
2007	343,559	37,560
2008	327,715	36,204

Source: Korea National Statistical Office

An interesting aspect of the globalizing effect of marriages is the gender composition – formerly, mainly Korean women married foreign men, but now the trend has reversed – and the rural-urban divide: Today most marriages occur in the countryside, with brides coming from Southeast Asia or China, making the rural areas a new and unexpected arena for globalization.

Part 5
Institutional Competition, East Asian Integration and Korea's Future in the World Economy

Chapter 14: Trajectories of Economic Integration in East Asia During the Kim Dae-Jung Government

14.1 Introduction: Economic integration in East Asia and the crisis

When the leaders of the Southeast Asian and Northeast Asian states met in November 2001 for the 'ASEAN plus three (China, Japan and Korea)' meeting in Bandar Seri Begawan in Brunei, President Kim Dae-Jung of South Korea proposed the exploration of an East Asian Free Trade Area and thereby opened a new chapter of East Asian integration. The special Northeast Asian perspective on regional cooperation became clear by the simultaneous agreement with the Japanese Prime Minister Junichiro Koizumi and the Chinese Prime Minister Zhu Rongji to hold annual meetings among their finance and trade ministers. At the same time, bilateral agreements like the FTA between Japan and Singapore, the tentative large free trade area between ASEAN and China, and the work-in-progress on a Japan-Korea Free Trade Agreement showed the new-found devotion with reaching regional trade agreements (RTAs). It seems the Asian crisis finally brought regional integration on the Northeast Asian agenda.

After researchers as well as politicians maintained throughout the 1990s that economic integration in East Asia was something apart from integration processes in Europe or America – namely "open regionalism" or a search for "de facto" instead of "de jure" integration – suddenly it seemed that the race for integration based on free trade treaties was unstoppable.[251] This marks another change in the process of East Asian integration in addition to the last decade's two major changes. In the early 1990s, East Asian regionalism, which before only existed rudimentarily, was discussed as a collective answer to growing regionalism elsewhere. Existing organizations like ASEAN focused more on economic issues. The Asia-Pacific Economic Cooperation (APEC) emerged as the leading, trans-Pacific organization for economic integration, but inter-regional cooperation in the form of the Asia-Europe Meeting (ASEM) was also explored. However, after the Asian crisis this trans-Pacific approach in the wake of serious trade conflicts and difficulties with an ever-growing membership of APEC lost much of its appeal. Only very recently did political, rather than economic, considerations

251 For the distinction see Yamazawa (1998: 181-182) and Higgot (1998: 339-340); for a comparison of the European and Asian forms of integration see Seliger et al. (1999).

lead to a rebirth of trans-pacific discussions in the form of the Trans-Pacific Partnership (TPP) – mainly as a tool to check Chinese influence.

When the Asian crisis broke out in 1997 and the national responses to the crisis were quite heterogeneous, many observers predicted an end of East Asian regional integration. While this did not happen, the crisis was nevertheless a turning point. The flow of goods and factors had been the focus of economic integration before the crisis; afterwards, increasingly macroeconomic cooperation and a common framework for financial stability were sought after. The results of that discussion were until now limited to an extension of a network of regional currency swap and repurchase agreements. But in the long run, the aspect of monetary cooperation could change the previous direction of integration.

Regardless, the Northeast Asia integration can only be called nascent since no exclusive RTA binds China, Japan, and Korea together as of now. South Korea is geo-politically in an exposed position between Japan and China. Until now, the trilateral political problems made an economic integration comparable to Southeast Asia's Asian Free Trade Area impossible. The division of the Korean peninsula and the precarious situation of the Russian Far East add to the multitude of unresolved problems in Northeast Asia. Economically and politically, the dependence on the United States and the fear of Japanese dominance are factors determining South Korea's interest in regional economic integration. China and Japan again watch each other with a mixture of interest and mistrust as potential hegemons in the East Asian region. The free trade agreements of other countries also have a strong domestic policy impact; popular support for free trade is limited due to the difficulties to conclude even minor bilateral negotiations like a Korea-Chile FTA.

In this chapter we will discuss the preconditions and perspectives of economic integration in Northeast Asia after the Asian crisis. Since economic integration is linked to political factors in various ways, the second section discusses the geo-political situation of Northeast Asia today. The third section deals with the economic perspectives on different forms of trade integration, followed by an analysis of various attempts for greater macroeconomic and financial cooperation in section four and a short conclusion.

14.2 The geo-political situation of Northeast Asia and East Asian economic integration

Economic integration is not only an economic phenomenon, but also closely related to political developments. Therefore, the geo-political situation in East Asia is one of the determining factors for economic integration. East Asia has been a latecomer in economic regionalism, and the region developed its specific form of 'open regionalism' based on voluntary integration and non-intervention in domestic affairs. Political factors first led to cooperation in Southeast Asia. The Southeast Asia Treaty Organization (SEATO) of 1954 as well as ASEAN of 1967 was motivated not by common features of the political systems of these countries, but by a common external threat. Internally, the countries were autocracies of different degrees. The common threat was the existence of communist movements and the possibility of a spill-over from the Vietnam War. The countries considered the possible 'domino effect' from Vietnam more important than the goals first mentioned by ASEAN – namely wealth, growth, and the peaceful development of the region. Economic development and the development of a Southeast Asian identity ('think ASEAN') were instrumental in stabilizing the ruling regimes in ASEAN states.

Two additional factors were catalysts of ASEAN integration, namely the importance of the Japanese economy for all ASEAN states and the existence of ethnic Chinese trading networks. Japan was by far the biggest economy in the region in terms of size, with a weight of approx. 80 percent in East Asia until the mid-1990s. Since the 1980s, Japanese capital flows and Japanese technology played a growing role in economic development of the region. Rising labour cost in Japan and the yen appreciation made Southeast Asia a main target for Japanese foreign direct investment (FDI). Not only did Japanese multinationals invested in Southeast Asia, but they were followed by a number of smaller enterprises producing intermediate products for the multinationals (Yamashita, 1991; Tokunaga, 1992; Doner, 1993). Investment led to a transfer of Japanese technology and Japanese management know-how. The 'look East' policy of Southeast Asian states furthered the transfer of Japanese management style, seeing it as a role model of non-Western economic development.[252] Besides Japanese FDI flows, Japanese lending also made Japan the biggest investor in the region. For example, Japan accounted for around 40 percent of all Indonesian debts in 1998, compared with 8 percent for the United States (Asia Wall Street Journal, 1998: 1). Investment and lending often targeted state companies and Chinese trading companies, which increased its influence in the region.

The trading networks of ethnic Chinese in Southeast Asia are considered a second factor leading to 'de facto' integration in the region. The ethnic Chinese often make up a tiny portion of the population, such as two percent in the Philippines and thirty percent in Malaysia. Yet their share in private business is much greater, from anywhere between forty percent in the Philippines and eighty-five

252 Originally, this has been a policy of Malaysia, which preferred looking to Japan as an Asian model of development rather than to the equally successful policy of Singapore and Taiwan, two countries dominated by ethnic Chinese; see Smith (1996).

percent in Thailand. Networking between their companies also leads to increased demand for regional institutional integration. However, in times of crisis like the Asian Crisis, the situation of the Chinese minority is endangered. The alleged cooperation of Chinese companies with the Soeharto regime led to ethnic tensions in Indonesia. Despite these circumstances, the role of ethnic Chinese has been important for economic integration in Southeast Asia.

In Northeast Asia, the political situation has been much less conducive to integration.[253] In Southeast Asia, communist threat and civil war in some peripheral states like Vietnam, Laos and Cambodia led to closer integration of the rest of the region. In Northeast Asia, tension existed directly in the center, namely in China and on the Korean peninsula. Political confrontation among the People's Republic of China, Taiwan and the United States in addition to Maoist central planning made economic integration difficult. Even after the economic 'open policy' in China, increasing economic ties, and FDI, political problems remained where the idea of institutional integration giving the same political status to Mainland China and Taiwan was inacceptable to the former. Only semi-official contacts in the APEC were tolerable. At the same time, the People's Republic remained skeptical about the economic imperialism of Japan and the United States, as well as their dominance in regional organizations, until the mid-1990s. On the Korean peninsula, China's role is important as the only important partner for North Korea (International Crisis Group, 2006). For South Korea's economic relations with China, increasing ties with China in the Yellow Sea region show some positivity, while the increasing competition especially after the WTO accession of China in 2001 is a concern.

From an economic point of view, China recently seemed content with secured domestic economic growth and record FDI. However, the sheer size of its economy does not guarantee continued growth and, indeed, it seems that the Chinese transformation process until the Asian crisis left out problems, which one day painfully must be solved. As Jha (2002) analyzed in line with many Korean commentators of China's economic development, the most important of these problems is the dual economy problem with the thriving private sector and the large bankrupt, state-owned sector whose transformation will bring mass unemployment, unresolved debt problems, and the end of current pump priming measures. Therefore, the shift in policy to a FTA with ASEAN can be explained. However, integration with the rivaling Japan and Korea will be much more difficult for political reasons. Also, embracing regionalism would open the possibility for China to become a regional hegemon while sharing its power with Japan.

253 While geographically, Southern China including Hong Kong and Taiwan are part of Southeast Asia, here they are treated as part of Northeast Asia, since they are part of the Northeast Asian geopolitical theatre.

The historical legacy of the Japanese concept of a "Greater East Asia Co-Prosperity Sphere" (*Daitoa Kyoeiken*) under Japanese leadership from World War II hampered the role of Japan in Northeast Asian integration.[254] The colonial experiences of South Korea, Taiwan, and parts of Mainland China add to the problem, making a 'look East' policy hard to realize. Japanese economic engagement suffered from the still lingering suspicion from its neighbors. Japan's relation to the neighbouring countries is extremely complex. Since it was by far the largest economy in the region, the most successful and the first Asian modernizer of the countries in the region, Japan could play a more important role, even a leading role in economic integration in the area. But as well as ancient fears, decades of economic stagnation seem to prohibit such a role for Japan.

In terms of culture, while in many ways related to China and Korea (which has been a cultural bridge to the mainland) (Sasse, 1988), Japan nevertheless qualifies in the terms of Huntington as a "lonely" state, not part of any larger cultural area.[255] This also means that the neighbors put a lesser amount of trust into Japan. While a role as regional hegemon becomes improbable for this reason, Japan, according to Huntington, has four different strategic possibilities: to become the "United Kingdom of East Asia" and to take the role of France, Switzerland, or Germany in East Asia. The first option would mean a close alliance with the U.S. and would mainly be interpreted in the regional context as an anti-Chinese solution. Indeed, the alliance between Japan and the US became strengthened after tensions relaxed in the 1990s (Green et al., 1999). Seeing from a decade later, this trend might be even more pronounced with the secular decline of Japan in Northeast Asia and the world's economy along with a more aggressive Chinese foreign policy. The second option would be a close alliance with China (like the French alliance with Germany) and a common strategy for the future of East Asia. This option is regarded skeptically by Japan, which, according to Professor Yukiko Fukagawa, was reluctant and cautious about closer economic ties with China (Korea Herald, 9.11.2002). Even more, it is also viewed extremely

254 It is not possible here to discuss the still debated role of Japan's imperialism in detail here. Growing out of an desire to maintain autonomy vis-à-vis the other Imperial powers (Crowley, 1966), it embraced all of East Asia in a more and more aggressive way, belying the intentions of creating a more harmonious East Asia liberated from Anglo-American imperialism; see Jones (1974), Beasley (1987), Peattie (1988). While the experience of Southeast Asia was brutal, but short (Benda, 1967; McCoy, 1980), especially in the colony Korea and to some extent in the quasi-colony Manchuria/China it was a form of integral colonization, with the ultimate goal of complete assimilation.

255 Huntington (2001: 139) He refers, in the general context of his theory of the role of culture for international relations in the post–Cold War times, to the specific Shintoist background of Japan. However, this view contrasts with the view of Japan as part of a larger Chinese-centered Confucian culture. The role as part of a "Chinese World Order" is at least historically justified.

skeptical by the Chinese, which, after a phase of admiration for Japanese modernization in the early 1990s and a willingness to accept Japanese capital and development aid, grew in fear of the possibility of Japan's regional hegemony through regional institutions (Moore et al., 1999; Rozman, 2002).

The third strategic possibility for Japan is to take on the role of a neutral, benevolent state like Switzerland, remaining outside the quest for regional integration, but eager to keep good relations with all neighbors. This role is still open to Japan today, but its political and economies woes in the decade after the Asian crisis have made it less engaging with the neighbors. The last role is comparable to that of Germany in Europe, namely to develop an active diplomacy – with the help of considerable funding as an incentive for more reluctant partners – to achieve a form of integration acceptable to all partners. While so far a close alliance with the U.S. was the cornerstone of Japan's foreign policy in East Asia, Japan in the wake of the Asian crisis have become "reluctantly realist" (Green, 2001) about its role in East Asia.[256]

The geopolitical role of South Korea did not become easier in the last years. China is no longer a political enemy, but now a potential rival in many markets, including its rise as a shipbuilding nation. The rise of bilateral trade and FDI did not end, as many hoped, China's alliance with North Korea. Recently, the more aggressive Chinese foreign policy also points to potential conflicts in the West Sea. For South Korea, this situation between two economically and politically far bigger countries, poses a historical trauma as "a shrimp between whales". Occasional nervous reactions, like those concerning the textbook conflict or the garlic trade conflict with China, show the growing South Korean uneasiness. However, this could also lead to a greater South Korean desire for regional economic integration.

Despite its Far Eastern provinces with huge raw material potential, Russia plays only a minor role in East Asian integration. The political relations with Japan and South Korea improved dramatically after the end of the cold war, but the hope for economic integration did not materialize (Seliger, 1999f). This is partly due to the unresolved problem of North Korea caused in part by the internal instability in Russia – which for a long time was a particular problem of the Russian Far East. De facto, there had been a disintegration between the European part of Russia and the Far East Russia, with the European side dominating the Federation and the Far Eastern provinces. This leads to an often chaotic situation concerning the administration of the Far Eastern provinces. Such situation was a major problem in attracting Korean and Japanese FDI, even in highly profitable businesses like oil and gas exploitation at Sachalin Island. Territorial dispute

256 It should be noted that the choice of a role is not an autonomous choice of the country's leaders, as Huntington sometimes seems to assume, but decisively influenced by the people, as Rozman shows for the Chinese attitude towards Japan in the 1990s (Rozman, 2002: 98-101).

about the Kuril Islands also affecting South Korea's fishery industry adds to the problem. APEC membership and the improved economic and administrative situation under the Putin government did change the prospects for the Russian Far East to some extent, and the APEC summit planned in Vladivostok in 2012 is an expression of this change. Nevertheless, Russia's interest in the Far East is mainly a mild strategic interest plus a strong focus in the resources of the region and not so much in becoming a more active player in Northeast Asia.

The United States is an indirect political and economic factor in Northeast Asian integration. Politically, the U.S. is indispensable for Taiwan and South Korea as a guarantee power for these states but poses a problem to achieving greater integration. Economically, most states of the region still rely heavily on the United States as an important market for exports, after China and in competition with the EU. This common interest in East Asian states can lead to closer cooperation, but also puts the East Asian states in a competitive situation. Also, the importance of the American market limits the form of regional economic integration, making more protectionist forms of integration unlikely. 'Open regionalism' therefore is partly a result of trade dependence.

Overall, the geopolitical situation in Northeast Asia is much less conducive to the economic integration than that of Southeast Asia. Political and territorial conflicts are unresolved, regional factors facilitating integration do not exist and the increasing political role of Japan as well as the increasing economic power of China pose a challenge for the necessary atmosphere. Both states can either attempt to lead economic integration in the region or to prevent it, while South Korea, stuck in the middle, can only try to take an active role as a catalyst for regional integration. In the next section, the possibilities for trade integration and factor market integration will be reviewed.

14.3 Perspectives of Trade Integration and Factor Market Integration in East Asia

The possibilities of economic integration in East Asia can be analyzed from a normative and positive point of view. The normative question is the size and depth of the optimal integration area, i.e. the question of advantages in multilateral, regional, and subregional integration. The positive analysis focuses on the interests of the actors in the 'market for politics' with the actors in the region.[257]

257 This means that the decision about integration, as mentioned above, is to a large extent dependent on internal power and interest constellations; for the model of a market for politics in South Korea (Seliger, 2000e).

Here, the first question is especially of interest. While by now the original concept of APEC's open regionalism lost much of its appeal, it is nevertheless a good starting point for discussion. Therefore, the existing integration in the APEC framework is discussed first, then the policy of FTAs, and lastly the possibility of a greater East Asian free trade area in the form of ASEAN plus three (China, Japan, South Korea).

The intensity of regional economic integration can be measured by the degree of importance for intra-regional trade, and its relatively minor significance is an indicator of a low level of regional integration. According to this indicator, South Korea as well as Japan and Taiwan were characterized by a relatively low level of regional integration compared with their Southeast Asian and Chinese neighbors, in the wake of the Asian crisis. In 1998, the share of East Asia in Korean exports was 39.1 percent, compared with 34.9 percent in 1980.[258] The share of East Asia in Korea's imports was 37.3 percent, compared with 29.9 percent in 1980. The share of exports in the region was more than fifty percent for Southeast Asian states and 46.6 percent for China; a similar situation existed for the imports. South Korea's trade structure can be compared with Japan, while China's trade structure is mostly complementary. A decade later, the situation had completely changed, with China the largest trading partner for all economies in the region – a result of modernization from free trade policies.

Since APECs inauguration in 1989, the forum was informal at first and later fostered more and more of an institutionalized framework for economic integration in the Asia Pacific Region (Ahn, 1999; Pascha et al., 1999). Originally, the cooperation was born out of the Australia and New Zealand's desire for escaping the periphery of the world economy and the desire of the United States and the East Asian states to counteract the increased economic integration in Western Europe, specifically the Western European role in the Uruguay Round of world trade negotiations. In the early years, APEC states explored the possibilities of increased cooperation. In 1994, the Bogor Declaration formulated the goal of free trade between developed countries in 2010 and for all other states in 2020. This was a major step toward serious economic integration. The Osaka Action Agenda of 1995 and the Manila Action Plan of 1996 made the efforts more concrete and precise, both defining the steps toward liberalization and their implementation. Since 1997, the member states decided Individual Action Plans (IAP) to guarantee national implementation of the APEC liberalization plans. This phase of APEC was characterized in part by the low level of institutionalization, the dominance of national sovereignty, and consequently, the voluntary characterization

258 Measured was the share of Japan, China, Taiwan, Hong Kong, Indonesia, Malaysia, the Philippines, Singapore, and Thailand.

of liberalization instead of fixed time-tables and goals, and the openess for non-member states in the form of most favoured nation rules.

However, since the Asian crisis, APEC lost its dynamics and some analysts even spoke of the death of the APEC process. The first problem of APEC was the growing heterogeneity of its member states. Today, membership ranges from the original founding states in the Asia Pacific region to some states of Latin America (Chile and Peru) and Russia, effectively including parts of North and South America, most of East Asia, parts of Central Asia due to Russian membership, and even Europe. In that sense, APEC became a victim of its own attractiveness. The goals of member states after the Asian crisis were much more diverse than the original focus on trade liberalization and integration (Lee et al., 2001). Secondly, the process of fast-track liberalization for advanced member states and slower integration of the rest of APEC did not lead to sufficient 'peer pressure'. This became clear at summit meetings of APEC, where the programmes of Early Voluntary Sectoral Liberalization (EVSL) found no majority and where support for additional liberalization steps was lukewarm at best, as the slow progress of IAP implementation showed. In South Korea, where liberalization was rapid after the economic crisis, the catalyst was the IMF conditionality and the crisis situation rather than the APEC process (Ahn et al., 1999).

While the goal of an Asia Pacific-wide free trade still nominally exists, APEC lost its role as a leading organization in regional integration. In world trade negotiations, as well as in the failed Seattle Round of the Doha Ministerial Meeting, South Korea took a hostile stance toward inclusion of agriculture into trade liberalization negotiations, together with Japan and the European Union. Therefore, the future role of APEC seems to be limited. It is important insofar, as it links East Asia with the Pacific region, allows a geographically wide integration area to be possible, and serves as a semi-official point of contact between Mainland China and Taiwan. The possibility of a common APEC market, however, seems unlikely. As mentioned before, one reason is that a new instrument, the Trans-Pacific Partnership, gained more prominence in the late 2000s. Today the Partnership is driven by much politics and focuses on attempts to check the rise of China than pursuing the desire for free trade.

The decreasing dynamics of APEC as well as the proceeding economic integration in other parts of the world, including Southeast Asia where the Asian Free Trade Area was inaugurated, were probably the most important reasons to look for substitutes in the form of bilateral integration. According to their proponents, FTAs are not thought to be substitutes for open regionalism, but rather as complements (Cheong, 1999a). FTAs in East Asia could enhance the process of greater East Asian integration, while FTAs in other continents could overcome the problem of regionalism posing increasing trade barriers to outsiders. However, much of the validity of this reasoning depends on the kind and the number of bilateral trade agreements.

RTAs have always been seen as analogous to potential stepping stones or stumbling stones on the way to free trade (Lawrence, 1991/1995; Anderson et al., 1993). Taking the reality of increasing RTAs into account and hoping for a "domino process", regional agreements would attract more and more members, ultimately creating a worldwide free trade (Baldwin, 1995). International Organizations also saw the RTAs more positively in the mid-1990s (Frankel, 1997; OECD, 1995). Among the Northeast Asian states, first Japan and Korea took steps for integration, not between each other but rather with states that are relatively insignificant from the perspective of bilateral trade, such as Singapore and Chile. These RTAs, according to the Singapore's Trade Minister, George Yeo, were driven by "fear and insecurity" (De Jonquires, 2001) and were more or less "test balloons" on the way to forming more important RTAs, such as a possible FTA between Japan and Korea. Also, Korea's RTA with Chile was especially meant to minimize possible conflict areas by choosing a country with an economic structure which is complementary, not competitive, to the greatest extent. However, it was questionable whether this form of RTA showed the road for the future, since in the beginning increased intra-industry trade in an RTA with two or more similar partners experienced pain in terms of economic adjustment processes; it was not certain whether the form might, in the long run, allow any such benefits through increased competition, innovation, and product quality. Indeed, it gradually proved to be a stepping stone for negotiations with more important nations and economic blocs, and finally with the USA and the EU.

For Korea, pursuing bilateral agreements had various reasons: to secure export markets through overcoming trade barriers, to counter economic regionalism in other parts of the world by enhanced negotiation power of a regional trading bloc, to enforce economic restructuring in the domestic industry, to curb regional overinvestment in competitive industries, and to achieve cooperation in a wide range of topics related to the economy but needing political coordination, such as pollution issues (Sohn, 2001: 4-5). Only the first of these arguments points in the direction of RTAs with remote countries.[259] All other reasons rather support RTAs with competitive, regional partners, in which China, Japan and ASEAN are strong candidates. The important question of bilateral trade deficits could lead to a gradual liberalization strategy, but it is not a general argument against such an RTA (Cheong, 1999b: 33). Also, for Japan, the reasons for a closer regional integration point in the direction of an RTA to enhance dynamism

259 The original Korean strategy under the Kim Dae-Jung administration to establish RTAs with at least one country in each continent came out of this reasoning.

and competitiveness: This could help overcome the Japanese "Asia-sclerosis" (Seliger, 2001b) and paralysis of the political-economic system (Cheow, 2002: 149-150) characterized by deflation, financial and political crisis as well as social transformation.

A bilateral FTA, while possibly beneficial to the concluding partners, need not be beneficial to world trade at the same time. Both the Japan-Singapore FTA and the Korea-Chile FTA have considerable areas excluded from free trade, like financial services and agriculture. If a cobweb of more and more FTAs is woven in East Asia, this might be difficult to entangle when assuming that region-wide free trade is the goal. Barfield (2002: 7) demands a number of preconditions for FTAs compatible with the goal of region-wide and international free trade: The baseline for tariffs should always be the lowest of the two countries' tariffs (so that no other trading partner is worse off in terms of tariffs after the FTA)[260], the agreement should be monitored by the WTO, and the agreement after some time should be opened to all other participants willing to enter it (a form of open regionalism). However, such a form of bilateral free trade compatible with international free trade would meet severe opposition from special interest groups lobbying for protection. Another way, in which even a bilateral arrangement with exceptions could become beneficial in the long run, would be the "peer pressure" created by an agreement; other states in the region would be attracted to the FTA so that the bilateral agreement would multilateralize. One problem in bilateral trade negotiations is the strong and concentrated position of possible losers of integration.[261] The case-by-case removal of trade barriers is rarely successful, since the costs of protection are dispersed among consumers or taxpayers, while the gains of protection are concentrated to industries – giving them a much greater interest in lobbying efforts to secure protection.

The Western European experience of the 1970s demonstrates the same kind of experience, but also shows a possible way out of it. In the 1970s, Western Europe attempted a case-by-case discussion of trade barriers which failed, and the European Community slipped into "euro-sclerosis" (Seliger, 2001c). However, in the 1980s, a program to create a common market at the same time attacked 279 different main barriers to trade, including non-tariff barriers, and national protection and controls. Thereby, in a bargaining process, where all nations had to give and take, the obstacles of trade barriers could be overcome. A similar situation exists in East Asia today. Here, the barriers to integration are partly political, as discussed above, and partly economic. The integration project should be big

260 It should be noted that from the point of view of economic theory, even this does not preclude the possibility of trade diversion through the FTA.

261 It is the problem already identified by Mancur Olson (1965) in his "Logic of Collective Action".

enough to overcome concentrated opposition of small groups, but small enough that it does not fail due to heterogeneity like APEC. The decade after the Asian crisis saw the rise of trilateral China-South Korea-Japan cooperation, with currently more than 150 different regular annual meetings on the ministerial or working-level and the opening of the trilateral office in Seoul in 2011. Private initiatives, studies of think tanks and cooperation on the level of business representatives supplement these efforts.

From an economic point of view, even more promising is the approach of ASEAN plus three (China, Japan, South Korea). Since 1997, this group meets to this day without a formal institutional framework. The group has two political advantages compared with APEC: First, since Taiwan is not a member of the group, the problems of Taiwanese-Chinese relations is not a stumbling block in the way to integration. Second, the inclusion of many smaller states as well as both big states from Northeast Asia (China and Japan) is an important aspect to counteract the possible tensions over either Chinese or Japanese domination of their neighbors.

South Korea's President Kim Dae-Jung first proposed the study of closer economic, political, and cultural ties on the ASEAN plus three Summit in November 2000 in Singapore. Afterwards, a study group discussed plans for integration. In November 2001, it was again Kim Dae-Jung who, in the summit meeting in Bandar Seri Begawan in Brunei, proposed a regional free trade area. The response from Kim's counterparts was generally cautiously optimistic. While calling it a 'bold yet feasible' plan (so did Brunei's Sultan Hassanal Bolkiah), they voiced fears of too fast-paced ASEAN plus three free trade negotiations. The ASEAN states were reluctant to give up the lead in integration, which they had with the opening of the ASEAN FTA in 2002 as well as the initial agreement on an FTA with China. Kim Dae-Jung additionally proposed regular ministerial meetings between China, Japan, and South Korea. This showed that South Korea itself considered as well the greater ASEAN plus three option as the Northeast Asian option. The success of both integration processes is dependent on the development of a true regional identity. This was stressed by the Asian crisis, which on the one hand was perceived as a collective threat to the economic position of East Asia, but on the other hand resulted in divergent national responses instead of greater East Asian cooperation.

For South Korea, the options of multilateral trade liberalization through the WTO and APEC, regional integration of ASEAN plus three and bilateral FTAs are some of the various options for mutual reinforcement. Bilateral FTAs can be used as promoters of regional integration. ASEAN plus three and APEC can be a fora for trade negotiations overcoming bilateral political or economic problems.

For the success of regional economic integration, the domestic acceptance of liberalization is very important. The strong position of concentrated business and of farming lobbies in South Korea can counteract the intentions of liberalization. The willingness to assume the political risk to be in favour of liberalization and possibly hurting domestic producers is low. However, in South Korea some factors also favor free trade acceptance. First, the strong position of the ministerial bureaucracy compared with the relatively weak position of political decision-makers is a factor contributing to free trade. Bureaucrats are less dependent on interest groups and have a strong position vis-à-vis political leaders due to the frequent changes in office of the political leadership. Also, the relatively low intensity of ideological conflict about free trade is important for the general Korean political acceptance of free trade. Due to ideological opposition, no important political group is principally rejecting free trade. This became clear when an administration rather reluctant to uphold the traditional alliance with the US, the Roh Moo-Hyun administration, ironically became the administration finally concluding FTA negotiations with the US. At the same time, this did not prevent those lawmakers adhering to the same ideological camp in 2011 from showing violent opposition to this same FTA agreement when the agreement was to be ratified by the Parliament.

A second important factor conducive to free trade is the strong political position of the export sector in South Korea. Together with the bureaucracy, export industries generally favour trade liberalization. Therefore, in South Korea, there is an all-encompassing interest group in favour of free trade. This makes South Korea a possible promotor of regional integration even in times when worldwide protests against globalization and free trade are increasing. However, South Korea's interest in regional integration also has a second source, namely the possibility of greater economic policy coordination. This became very clear after the Asian crisis and will be discussed in the next section.

14.4 Perspectives of Monetary and Macroeconomic Coordination in East Asia

The East Asian Economic and Financial Crisis of 1997 and 1998 have been widely discussed from two different points of view: One group of economists stressed the role of structural weaknesses in the national economy as a fundamental factor for the Crisis. In South Korea, the system of corporate governance, including high concentration of *chaebol*, intransparent management, overcapacities, and low profitability have especially been identified as structurally weak points. However, other economists discussed the Asian crisis mainly as a problem of international and regional financial stability. The question of monetary cooperation as a possible remedy was raised and this discussion was increased by the Western European movement toward a single currency and the discussion of the dollarization in Latin American economies.

Besides Malaysia, all East Asian states in the crisis decided against the imposition of unilateral capital restrictions and indeed, South Korea proceeded with capital flow liberalization. However, monetary cooperation was always perceived as a possibility to achieve better regional control of capital flows, prevent competitive devaluation, and ultimately, develop into a monetary system in East Asia. And the international financial crisis of 2008, which also showed the vulnerability of South Korea, was another factor strengthening Korea's interest in regional financial cooperation. In the following, the possibility of an Asian Monetary Fund (AMF), a common Asian Monetary System (AMS), and the greater coordination of fiscal policy will be discussed.

The introduction of an AMF was first proposed by the Japanese Finance Minister, Hiroshi Mitsuzuka, in September 1997 in Bangkok, at the most dramatic moment of the Asian financial crisis. This fund should fulfill the role of a regional lender of last resort and complement the IMF, whose role was widely perceived to be insufficient among the East Asian finance ministers. Japan was willing to contribute half of the necessary funds. Implicitly, the fund was designed to circumvent the conditionality of IMF structural adjustment programmes, which were deemed to be unacceptable. The lack of structural adjustment programmes in the AMF design and the weakening of the IMF were exactly the reasons why the United States, as well as representatives of the IMF, strongly rejected the possibility of supporting an AMF. This would increase the danger of 'moral hazard' which is the irresponsible behaviour of creditors and debtors in the region. If creditors and debtors could implicitly count on a bailout by the states through the AMF, there would be no incentives to introduce the urgently needed and improved rules for corporate and financial management, especially prudential rules in relation to borrowing and lending.

When the AMF was rejected, the representatives from East Asian states, the World Bank, and the Asian Development Bank in November 1997 in Manila installed the 'Manila Framework Group' to discuss the stability of an international and regional financial architecture. APEC, on the other hand, where monetary cooperation in the crisis years of 1997 and 1998 also became a debated topic, stressed the importance of domestic structural reform, for example, financial sector reform and prudential regulation. They introduced a programme to improve the education of financial regulation authorities in states facing a crisis.

In October 1998, when the financial crisis was overcome and the region was still in a grave recession, Japan funded the so-called new 'Miyazawa Initiative' with USD 30 billion. Half of the money was used to finance East Asian trade and half of the money was used as medium or long-term credit. Trade in East Asia, especially in Southeast Asia, had suffered from underfinancing due to a lack of pre-financing possibilities. Occasionally, states had even resorted to a highly inefficient barter system. The idea of AMF was not revived. Opposition to it not only came from the United States and the IMF, but after the worst of the crisis was over, the East Asian states also saw the proposal of an AMF as strengthening the role of Japan and therefore not desirable. In May 2000, the finance ministers of ASEAN plus three in Chiang Mai, Thailand decided on the 'Chiang Mai Initiative,' a system of regional bilateral currency swap-and-repurchase agreements. These agreements widened the scope of the ASEAN swap arrangement through the inclusion of the three regional states with the strongest reserve positions.

The 'Chiang Mai Initiative' could become the seminal decision for an East Asian monetary system. In the 1970s, when the Bretton Woods system collapsed, one answer was the introduction of a European Monetary System (EMS). Similarly, the Asian crisis led to a collapse of the dollar pegging of most East Asian states before the crisis, and the search for a new, more stable exchange rate system began. East Asian states prefer exchange rate stability due to their trade dependence and alleged positive effects on trade and growth through the reduction of currency risk, the alleged better defence of currencies against speculative attacks, once currency reserves are pooled and also the prevention of competitive devaluation rounds (Fukasaku et al., 1998: 134-6; Kim et al., 2000: 49-51). An AMS can take on a similar form of quasi-fixed exchange rates, like the EMS or even the form of an Asian Monetary Union (AMU) with one currency.

The AMS' first decision is to decide about an anchor currency or a currency basket, for example, an Asian Currency Unit (ACU). Empirical analysis showed that as of now in East Asia, the US dollar is by far the most important currency (as a transaction currency, a vehicle currency, and a reserve currency) despite the greater internationalization of the yen since the 1980s, and also that the United States is the most important trading partner. Therefore, East Asia is more a dollar-bloc than a yen-bloc. An important question faced by the AMS is the decision of central parities (bilaterally between the participating currencies or in relation to the ACU), the allowed margins of deviation from the central parity, and the conditions of interventions by central banks to defend central parities. The experience of the EMS is not very encouraging: Independent central banks cannot always achieve internal stability and exchange rate stability at the same time without policy conflicts. If interventions by the central banks to defend parities are not accompanied by reforms, they are ineffective in the medium term. This was the lesson of the crisis faced by the EMS in 1992 and 1993. Structural reforms, however, are very difficult to enforce in the absence of a hegemonic power, like the IMF, with the strong political backing of the United States. A credible committment or strict conditions, however, would lead to the question what additional value an AMS would have when compared with the IMF with the same characteristics.

Even more problematic seems to be the introduction of a common Asian currency or AMU. According to the theory of optimum currency areas, a currency area is characterized either by the absence of asymmetric economic shocks or by sufficient shock absorption capacity of factor markets, especially labour markets. Asymmetric shocks (i.e. supply or demand side shocks either occuring in only a part of the participating countries of an AMU or shocks affecting some countries positively and others negatively) are less probable among the more advanced countries of the region, like Japan, Taiwan, South Korea, and Singapore. These countries are characterized by a higher amount of intra-industry trade, i.e. trade between the same industries, which makes asymmetric shocks less probable (Kwan 1998). However, such a monetary union would clearly miss the goal to strengthen regional financial stability. A larger union however, including most Southeast Asian states, would be more prone to asymmetric shocks.

The shock absorbtion capacity of the labour market seems to be decreasing in the last decades, especially in Japan. Other possible shock absorption mechanisms like migration or fiscal federalism are largely absent in the region and can hardly be introduced into the area due to a lack of political will (Sakong et al. 1999: 44). This leads to the main problem in achieving AMU, namely the lack of political will to give up a part of sovereignty to a supranational monetary institution and the lack of political will to come to greater fiscal coordination. Therefore, despite convergence of some macroeconomic indicators (like inflation rates), AMU does not seem to be feasible.

Finally, macroeconomic coordination became another topic of policy initiatives after the Asian crisis. In 1998, Kim Dae-Jung proposed to his colleagues in ASEAN plus three a concerted lowering of interest rates and programs to stimulate consumption through the easing of credit (Korea Times, 17. November 1998: 1). The same idea, suggesting that the Asian crisis was mainly an issue of trust which could be solved by deficit spending, was also prevailing in the new 'Miyazawa Initiative.' However, Japan's experience with deficit spending was not very successful; as long as structural reforms were lacking, especially the cleaning of the banking sector haunted by bad debts, even giant consumption programs leading to record levels of debt to GDP in Japan did not pull Japan out of the crisis. Also, it allows for considerably limited room for additional fiscal action by the state with every new program.

For these reasons, monetary and macroeconomic coordination or integration in East Asia only promises success, if at the same time necessary structural reforms in the financial and corporate sector are enforced. But then, the political attractiveness of coordination is greatly reduced, since structural reforms mean adjustment costs – for example, when insolvent companies are forced into bankruptcy. In the long run, coordination used to delay structural adjustment will fail. South Korea, who might eventually be forced to finance the North Korean transformation process besides its own restructuring process, should therefore prefer the liberalization of trade, leading to a more competitive economic structure, to the possibilities of monetary and macroeconomic cooperation.[262]

As mentioned above, the international financial crisis of 2008 and the subsequent crisis in the Euro-zone again changed the Korean and East Asian view on macroeconomic policy coordination. It became clear that successful monetary integration needs, in absence of economic homogeneity, a strong integration of fiscal and regulatory policies. And even then, giving up the exchange rate as a tool of economic policy-making might be costly. China, with its managed exchange rate, as well as Korea, with occasional interventions, is not willing to bear these costs. This makes monetary integration even less attractive and thereby less likely than before.

14.5 Conclusion

With the reform policy after the Asian crisis, economic integration in East Asia was finally on the agenda. As the discussion above showed, those parts of the agenda focusing on trade and investment seem to be most successful. While trade and investment opportunities are the basis for economic integration, all forms of integration needing stronger regional, supranational or intergovernmental institutions are only possible after the development of a strong, regional identity. Such an identity, however, cannot be constructed by the state, but rather has to develop spontaneously. The Asian crisis was a possible catalyst for the development of a common identity. Until now, the evolution of East Asian integration followed the model of 'open regionalism.' Politically, other forms of integration were not feasible. From the perspective of institutional development, this allowed for institutional flexibility and competition.

However, without a minimum of institutionalization, 'market-driven' integration will come to an end. This does not mean that strong supranational institutions are necessary, but that at least common competition rules for competition in the markets of goods and services and also for regulatory competition are necessary.

262 In this book, the impact of the unresolved divide on the Korean peninsula cannot be a topic due to space limitations. But it should be noted implicitly that all integration steps of Northeast Asia also have effects on its relations to North Korea. While economic integration on a regional instead of national scale might be politically more acceptable to North Korea, currently, the political isolation of the North prevents both.

This poses two challenges to future research of East Asian economic integration: First, the forms and size of integration areas should be understood not exclusively as an economic problem, but the explanation must be interdisciplinary, including the cultural as well as political factors shaping integration. Second, the dichotomic discussion of 'open versus closed regionalism' is no longer appropriate for the discussion of East Asian regionalism. Instead, the role of clear and enforcable competition rules (institutionalization) without supra-nationalization must be clarified.

The current reality of a network of bilateral RTAs seems less conducive to such a market-preserving integration process. Market-preserving integration would rather mean a more encompassing, ASEAN plus three approach. This would be able to overcome the stumbling blocks of bilateral free trade such as concentrated losses and dispersed gains, by giving countries enough incentives to design a bolder approach of region-wide free trade. South Korea is a relatively small country in Northeast Asia and can, due to the historical position, have a key role in East Asian economic integration if it overcomes the obsession with historical "rectification" and convincingly solves its own economic problems. The more South Korea can implement the domestic reform agenda, the stronger its role in regional integration will be. If South Korea fails to restructure the domestic economy, not only will the country fail to have a leadership role in East Asian integration, but will also become a factor of dangerous instability among a bankrupt North Korea and the two Northeast Asian giants, China and Japan.

Japan again can achieve a leading role in economic integration when it makes more serious efforts to understand the historical trauma of its neighbors. From an economic point of view, such a turnout seems clearly desirable for Japan given its own domestic economic stalemate. A large-scale cultural exchange program could be the beginning of such an effort.[263] While money cannot buy trust automatically, a compensation fund for war atrocities might help these efforts. China, which is now the most uncertain factor in East Asia's economic integration process, is preoccupied with the unresolved domestic reform process and has the chance to use closer regional cooperation for a more rapid modernization process.

For the three Northeast Asian countries, China, Japan, and Korea, a future without economic integration is at worst antagonistic and full of conflict and at best a future in "splendid isolation". The sharing of power necessary in an economic integration process, again, does not really diminish the power of individual countries, but rather bundles their power, allowing the three countries a common and harmonious future. A bilateral FTA between Japan and South Korea, designed as an "open" form allowing the accession of other states and with a minimum of exceptional areas, could be a first step to that future.

---

263 In this way, for example, Franco-German understanding began in the post-Second World War time.

Chapter 15: The option of Bilateral Free Trade Agreements

15.1 Introduction – why did bilateral agreements fare so well after the Asian crisis?

While regional economic integration has been widely discussed in Korea and its neighbouring states after the Asian crisis, progress has been most pronounced elsewhere, namely in bilateral trade integration; and such step forward did not take place here with the neighbours, but rather with distant but important trading partners. This result could not be expected after the crisis. First, the sense of joint policy challenges was strong enough to make East Asian states explore the potential of integrating into a wider economic and political bloc. However, policy heterogeneity gradually became more important again. After the Asian crisis, China was still regarded as a transformation country and not yet ready for integration, being an economic and political stumbling bloc to East Asian integration Korea, after its V-shaped recovery, was more interested in securing access to international markets which made up the bulk of its trade. When multilateral trade negotiations in the Doha round successively failed, Korea began to turn its attention to free trade agreements. These had also become more acceptable internationally. Not all of FTA negotiations were successful, but in 2011 Korea successfully entered a high profile FTA with the European Union and could, after a four-year stalemate, finally ratify the FTA with the USA, thereby achieving free trade with an area representing sixty percent of world GDP. In this chapter, the unsuccessful attempt to negotiate an FTA with Japan is juxtaposed to the successful conclusion of an FTA with the European Union.

15.2 The difficulties of coming to terms with neighbours – the Japan-Korea Free Trade Agreement

Economic integration in Northeast Asia has been inhibited by the historical legacy of the Japanese concept of a "Greater East Asia Co-Prosperity Sphere" in World War II. However, the weaknesses of Asian economies exhibited in the Asian crisis as well as the growing feeling of isolation in a world increasingly characterized by trade blocs that are no longer counteracted by a strong multilateral trading dynamics put pressure on Northeast Asian nations to enhance cooperation.

In this situation, regional approaches like the emerging ASEAN plus three (China, Japan, South Korea) as well as bilateral approaches like a Japan-Korea Free Trade Agreement (JKFTA) gained attention. An agreement had officially been proposed by Japan's Prime Minister Obuchi in 1999. In 2002, both countries concluded a bilateral investment treaty and Prime minister Koizumi as well as President Kim Dae-Jung spoke in favour of a JKFTA. Also, big businesses of Japan and Korea in the Korea-Japan Business council's 18th annual conference in November 2001 endorsed a JKFTA and even invited China to join such an undertaking.

Japan was of utmost importance as a partner for South Korea, being an important trading partner and especially the prime source for technology transfer. At the same time Korea was traumatized by the colonial experience of 1910 to 1945, when Japan tried nothing less than to erase South Korean national identity, even forcing Koreans to take Japanese names. After World War II, Japan in a development called "miracle" rose from the ashes to become one of the most modern economies worldwide in the span of four decades. In the 19th century, Japan was already the most successful among Asian countries in adapting modern Western technology and administration during the Meiji Restoration. This was on the one hand seen with admiration by struggling East Asian states forced to open to Western influences; on the other hand, however, Japanese expansionism was soon feared, rightly, in East Asia. The rise of Japan to become the dominating power in East Asia was abruptly stopped with its defeat in World War II. Industry and basic infrastructure was widely destroyed, the territorial acquisitions after 1894 were separated from Japan, and the United States governed the country through the Supreme Command of the Allied Powers (SCAP). Millions of ethnic Japanese settling formerly in the colonies had to be reintegrated.

The powerful prewar industry conglomerates, the *zaibatsu*, were dissolved as part of the Japanese war machine. Inflation, unemployment and shortages threatened the stability of Japan. However, after SCAP backed the recovery of the economy and in particular with the onset of the Korean War, Japan's economy began to grow at a rapid pace. Industrial production increased by 36.8 percent in 1951 alone. Overall, the Japanese economy expanded by almost 10 percent a year from 1950 to 1973. In the 1970s, it still grew by an average 5 percent a year and in the 1980s by 4 percent a year. Among the characteristics of the Japanese postwar economy was the strong influence of industrial planning by the state particularly by the Ministry of International Trade and Industry (MITI); the reemergence of dominant business groups, *keiretsu*, with strong horizontal and vertical integration as well as house banks catering for the needs of industry; a labour market with enterprise unions closely interested in the fate of their companies; lifetime employment; and the rapid adaptation of technology. In the period from 1950 to 1973, the strong contribution of productive factors to the growth was particularly remarkable (Valdés, 2003: 69, table 1).

Explanations for the Japanese economic miracle have always been competing. In the 1950s and 1960s Japan was seen as a successful model of modernization thanks to US-led economic and political reform, massive inflow of American aid, and low defense spending due to the alliance with the US (Allen, 1958; Forsberg, 2000). Japanese economists challenged this view and referred to the modernization success in the 19th century as the cultural roots of Japan's economic miracle (Hein, 1996,). A key factor of growth was the export orientation of Japan's industry, which at the same time was protected by selective liberalization, allowing the free importation of inputs and intermediate goods, but closing the market for consumer goods of foreign countries. The low entry rate of the yen into the international monetary system, which until 1973 was a system of fixed exchange rates (Bretton Woods) helped Japan to accumulate large trade surpluses. International economic integration into the GATT (1963), the IMF and the OECD (1964), where Japan soon became a major player, aided the internationalization of Japan's economy. In particular Chalmers Johnson (1982) stressed the role of the MITI and sparked a debate about Japan's success as a developmental state. Others were skeptical on the almost mythical power of foresight attributed to industrial policy of the MITI (Okimoto, 1989). Mancur Olson (1982) saw the destruction of powerful distributional coalitions at the heart of the growth success of Japan in the post-war period, a record which is consistent with the later decline of growth rates.

While the Japanese economic miracle had enormous impact on its East and Southeast Asian neighbors, through direct investment (the so-called "flying geese model", Ozawa, 2005) and as well as a model of development, the initial virtuous circle of accumulation became a vicious circle of debts in the 1980s for companies too big to fail; and prolonged existence of these so-called *zombie* companies lead to two lost decades for Japanese growth in the 1990s and 2000s, greatly diminishing the appeal of the Japanese economic model.

For Korea, Japan was not only an important neighbour in terms of trade and source of technology, but also, despite all bitterness from colonial times, a model to be emulated and admired. Korean *chaebol* were in many respects (though not all, see chapter 7) copies of the Japanese *zaibatsu*. Korean indicative economic planning closely followed the Japanese experience, and Korean exposure to international science, technology and culture went to a large extent through Japanese intermediaries, together with US influences. The attempt to conclude an FTA was a culmination point of a long history of antagonism, based in the colonial experience of Korea from 1910 to 1945. When in 1965 diplomatic relations between both countries were normalized (Oda, 1967), it was accompanied by strong protests of students reluctant to forgive Japan's role as colonizer (Mobius, 1966). While the soft loans of 800 million USD by the Japanese government helped Korea's economy to take off, resentment over the lack of additional, individual compensation in particular for war crimes and forced labour still remains great. While FTA negotiations were explored, nationalism flared up again. In 2002, the joint hosting of the World Cup soccer seemed to confirm the possibility of improved ties. But the "Japan-Korea friendship year of 2005" did not result in more understanding, but rather brought old grievances to the forefront again (Card, 2005).

Table 45: Chronology of the JKFTA 1999-2004 (see Seliger 2005b for details)

Chronology of the JKFTA 1999-2004	
March 1999	Prime Minister Obuchi Keizo visits Seoul and proposes JKFTA
October 2000	President Kim Dae-Jung visits Japan and calls for overcoming historical tensions; beginning of liberalization of culture market in South Korea for Japanese products
May 2000	Joint report of Japan External Trade Organization's Institute of Developing Economies (IDE) and the Korean Institute of Economic Policies on the Feasibility of a JKFTA
September 2000	summit meeting Prime minister Mori Yoshiro and President Kim Dae-Jung, proposal of a JKFTA business and scholarly forum
September 2001	Joint study for a RTA between Mexico and Japan begins
January 2002	Joint communiqué of the JKFTA business forum requires early conclusion of FTA agreement
March 2002	summit meeting of Prime minister Koizumi Junichiro and President Kim Dae-Jung, joint government-level study group (Ministries of Economy, Foreign Affairs, Finance, Agriculture and Fisheries), three meetings of the study group in 2002 Signing of a Bilateral Investment Treaty (BIT)
Summer 2002	Co-hosting of the Soccer World Cup by Japan and Korea
October 2002	After four years of negotiations, Korea signs the first FTA with Chile; however, important sectors are excluded from the FTA due to political reasons
June 2003	Visit of President Roh Moo-Hyun in Japan is criticized in Korea; no concrete date set for negotiations
December 2003	six rounds of JKFTA negotiations start
November 2004	negotiations frozen after difficulties to overcome differences on market access for sensitive goods

Not surprisingly, an opinion poll by the Korea Economic Research Institute (KERI) in October 2001 showed that among the 154 Korean corporations, fourty percent favoured a FTA with the United States and around thirty percent for a FTA with China, but only eight percent picked Japan. The main concern was the doubt of whether Korean products will be competitive in the Japanese market, in addition to the existing huge trade deficit with Japan. But still more important is the historically rooted fear of Japanese domination. Cultural exchange, especially the lucrative market of popular culture like comic books and the movie industry, has been the area where opening to Japanese products has been slowest. The controversial textbook issue with the alleged whitewashing of Japanese past in some government-approved textbooks and the equally controversial visit of Koizumi to the Yasukuni shrine showed the sensitivity of Northeast Asia to the historical legacy. An immediate reaction was the freezing of cultural, rather than economic, exchanges.

Both Japan and Korea experienced rapid economic development through trade expansion, a fact that influenced their preference of multilateral free trade negotiations, thereby securing open markets especially in the US, over possible bilateral or regional free trade arrangements. However, the rise of "new regionalism" since the 1980s and the growing difficulties of successful multilateral negotiations in a growing WTO changed the perception that multilateral free trade negotiations were the best way to achieve national goals of uninhibited export markets. By 2001, 152 active regional trade agreements (RTAs) were notified by the WTO, among them 108 FTAs and 13 customs unions. Additionally, not only the factual rise of RTAs furthered a new view of Japan and Korea, but also a different view of RTAs as possible catalysts for international free trade. The proliferation of RTAs led to the growing feeling of isolation of Northeast Asian countries, which soon became the only countries without any RTAs.

Given the geographic closeness and the mutual economic interdependence, a FTA with Japan is an important option for South Korea and vice versa.[264] The Asian crisis, which left the formerly successful "Asian tiger" states deeply distressed, led additional urgency to the importance of closer regional ties, especially with Japan, which was seen as an alternative to the strict conditionality of the IMF. After the South Korean president Kim Dae-Jung prepared the ground in his visit to Japan in 1998, where he declared that historical legacy should not interfere with future bilateral relations, Prime Minister Obuchi of Japan proposed the formation of a Japan-Korea FTA in 1999. A joint report of Japan External Trade Organization's Institute of Developing Economies (IDE) and the Korean Institute of Economic Policies on the Feasibility of a JKFTA in 2000 concluded that overall, the introduction of a JKFTA would increase welfare for both countries (Yamazawa, 2001). Also, a newly introduced joint business forum called various times for early conclusions of a JKFTA. Nevertheless, the eruption of the controversy over Japanese history in 2001 proved to be a set back for the project. In 2002, a Bilateral Investment Treaty has been concluded, where Korean companies in Japan and Japanese companies in Korea were granted domestic treatment. While Korea concluded BITs with more than 70 countries, the number for

264 The interdependence is in many respects rather one-sided, e.g. in terms of exchange rate movements and business cycle in the direction from Japan to Korea; see Kang/Wang/Yoon 2002.

Japan is only ten. Among them, the Korean-Japanese BIT is insofar far reaching, as it grants national treatment even before the actual investment takes place in the partner country (for an analysis see Mok, 2003). This circumvents otherwise strict investment regulations. After President Roh Moo-Hyun's inconclusive visit to Japan, serious negotiations on an FTA began in December 2003, with six rounds of talks taking place over the course of the following year. The talks came to an abrupt stop in November 2004 over how to open sensitive trade sectors, namely Korean marine and fishery products in Japanese markets and Japanese capital goods and machinery products in Korea. Attempts to start negotiations since then regularly failed, always frustrated by new (or rather, old) historic controversies. The latest call of the Japanese ambassador to Korea, Masatoshi Muto, in September 2011 to restart negotiations did equally fail, though the successful conclusion of the FTAs with the USA and the EU gave the discussion of new FTAs a potentially new dynamic. One of the most difficult problems preventing a more optimistic Korean view of the JKFTA is the large and persisting trade deficit with Japan, as the following table shows. That fact that it increased from less than 5 bn. USD in the wake of the Asian crisis to more than 36 bn. USD in 2010 does not bode well for Korea's interest in taking up bilateral negotiations.

While the future of negotiations remains open, the joint studies provided a lot of insight into the economic effects of the JKFTA (see Korean Institute for Industrial Economics and Trade, 1999; Cheong, 2000; Sohn, 2001a; Yamazawa, 2001; Japan Korea Joint Study Group, 2003). What are then the effects of JKFTA on welfare in Japan and Korea? The answer of this question is crucially dependent on the design of the models to measure these effects. The most common measurement is the application of CGE (computed general equilibrium) models. However, it should be noted that such CGE approaches are based on extremely restrictive assumptions, namely neoclassical (equilibrium) states of the economy, including full employment of all factors of production. However, economic integration is rather driven by disequilibria, explaining the Schumpeterian dynamics of competition. Even the so-called 'dynamic' CGE models, which are simulations based on increased productivity due to increased competition, fail to represent adequately an economy characterized by Knightian uncertainty rather than probabilities. Bearing these limitations in mind, the existing studies should be read very carefully. The results of the study of IDE as presented by Yamazawa (2001: 27-32) show that based on trade in the year 1995, the static effects calculated in four simulations do not lead to a change of real income in Japan, but a slightly higher income in Korea (by 0.3 percent). The Japanese trade surplus, however, will increase by 34.5 percent. Based on productivity increases of 30 percent for goods with intra-industry trade, 10 percent in textile and other manufacturing, and zero in primary industries, the dynamic effects of a JKFTA will lead to a real income increase in

Japan by 10.45 percent and in Korea by 9.11 percent. However, the Japanese trade surplus is also increasing by 59 percent. A similar dynamic study by McKibbin et al. (2002), with an intertemporal dynamic model, also sees long term economic benefits for both countries from a JKFTA.

Table 46: Korea's Trade (Im)-Balance with Japan

Year	Export	Import	Balance	Year	Export	Import	Balance
1965	45	175	-130	**1988**	12,004	15,929	-3,925
1966	65	294	-229	**1989**	13,457	17,449	-3,992
1967	85	443	-358	**1990**	12,638	18,574	-5,936
1968	0	623	-623	**1991**	12,356	21,120	-8,764
1969	113	754	-640	**1992**	11,599	19,458	-7,858
1970	234	809	-575	**1993**	11,564	20,016	-8,451
1971	262	954	-692	**1994**	13,523	25,390	-11,867
1972	408	1,031	-623	**1995**	17,049	32,606	-15,557
1973	1,242	1,727	-485	**1996**	15,767	31,449	-15,682
1974	1,380	2,621	-1,240	**1997**	14,771	27,907	-13,136
1975	1,293	2,434	-1,141	**1998**	12,238	16,840	-4,603
1976	1,802	3,099	-1,297	**1999**	15,862	24,142	-8,280
1977	2,148	3,927	-1,778	**2000**	20,466	31,828	-11,362
1978	2,627	5,981	-3,354	**2001**	16,506	26,633	-10,128
1979	3,353	6,657	-3,304	**2002**	15,143	29,856	-14,713
1980	3,039	5,858	-2,818	**2003**	17,276	36,313	-19,037
1981	3,444	6,374	-2,930	**2004**	21,701	46,144	-24,443
1982	3,314	5,305	-1,991	**2005**	24,027	48,403	-24,376
1983	3,358	6,238	-2,881	**2006**	26,534	51,926	-25,392
1984	4,602	7,640	-3,038	**2007**	26,370	56,250	-29,880
1985	4,543	7,560	-3,017	**2008**	28,252	60,956	-32,704
1986	5,426	10,869	-5,444	**2009**	21,771	49,428	-27,657
1987	8,437	13,657	-5,220	**2010**	28,176	64,296	-36,120

Unit: mill. USD
Source: Korea National Statistical Office

What are the dynamic effects leading to higher productivity? Increased sales between the two countries will lead to increased competitive pressure, which again might result not only in lower prices, but also in innovations on product markets and production processes. Given the market structure in Korea and Japan – dominated by large companies with oligopolistic power – these (not exactly predictable) effects might be among the most important effects of JKFTA. Also,

Yamazawa (2001: 33-34) considers the possibility of a strategic collaboration of Japanese and Korean companies as well as the increased attractiveness of the JKFTA for foreign companies and the increased personnel exchanges.

The study of Nakajima (2002) comes to similar results. Nakajima uses a static GTAP CGE short run model and a long-run model allowing for capital accumulation. In his analysis of a JKFTA, the short term effects on real GDP are small but positive in the case of Korea (0.29 percent increase), while the long-run effects are somewhat higher (1.09 percent). This is the result of a higher rate of return on capital after the removal of tariff barriers and subsequently, capital inflow to Korea. For Japan, with lower initial tariffs, the effect on real GDP is not measurable in the short run and only at 0.02 percent in the long run. In this model, productivity increases are not measured. However, the results on a JKFTA are not unambiguous. The Korean Institute for International Economic Policy (2001) concludes that a FTA would reduce Korea's GDP by 0.07 percent and worsen the trade balance, with a contraction in major industries like electronics, heavy industry and chemical industry (see Cheong 2002). In Cheong's (2002) study, which allows for capital accumulation and economies of scale and at the same time integrates the effects of the reduction of Non-Tariff Barriers and services, positive results of an FTA can be predicted for Korea. Sohn (2001a and b) also calculates gains in GDP (2.81 percent) and in welfare (11.24 percent) for Korea, again based on the assumption of productivity gains. So, the positive effects of an FTA for Korea seem to be largely dependent on productivity increases. While these increases cannot be measured from the beginning (in the models, they are rather assumptions; for example, of annual increases of productivity by one percent due to an FTA), the data gives important insight into the design of an FTA: the FTA should lead to increased competition, meaning that it should, besides the removal of tariffs, also consider the removal of the non-tariff barriers. Mutual market access, together with openness (since increased competitive pressure can come from partner countries as well as from foreign competitors), should be at the center of the FTA; the ultimate goal should be a common market.

However, all studies agree that Korea's trade balance with Japan is negatively affected by the removal of trade barriers, the static effects of an FTA. This last result can be explained by the existing differences in tariffs between both countries. In 1978, Korea tried with the Import Sources Diversification Program to reduce the import of Japanese goods, a policy which was gradually abolished until 1999. However, as can be seen from table 47, Japan gains more from tariff removal than Korea, since Japanese tariffs are already low or even zero for some categories of goods.

Table 47: Average tariff rates per sector in bilateral trade of Japan and Korea

	Japan	Korea
Average Tariff	3.6	7.9
Textile Products	6.4	8.4
Chemical Products	5.9	7.6
Iron & Steel Products	2.5	3.9
Nonferrous metals	2.1	6.0
Metal products	2.2	8.0
General Machinery	0.4	7.5
Electric Machinery	0.0	7.8
Transportation Equipment	0.0	3.6
Precision Machinery	0.0	7.6

Sources: KIET (2001), A Study on Free Trade Agreement and Investment Agreement as a new External Economic Policy Instrument.

The possible static effect of a JKFTA that increases the bilateral trade deficit of Korea concerns among others apparel, leather products, agriculture and fishery products, while Japanese exports will gain in sophisticated machinery, metal, and chemical products (see Fukagawa, 2000). However, important effects also concern those categories of goods, where the industry structure between Korea and Japan is highly competitive, among them shipbuilding, steel, petrochemicals, semiconductors, electronic appliances, telecom equipment and automobiles.[265] Here, strategic alliances among companies of both countries, leading to a greater horizontal divison of labour are possible as well as the restructuring of over-capacities. The last point is especially critical in the question of political support from interest groups and workers of the concerned industries. The large and consistent Korean trade deficit is a grave burden for progress in FTA talks, since it seems to confirm the negative outlook for a number of industries in competition with Japanese companies.

Overall, the presented studies are inconclusive: Mostly, the dynamic studies that allow productivity gains from increased competition result in increased welfare (as measured by gains in GDP and real income). However, they do not discuss the desirability of JKFTA for regional and world trade. A bilateral FTA, while possibly beneficial to the concluding partners, need not be beneficial at the same time to regional or world trade. This is especially an important point to consider for JKFTA, since both countries are leading economies in East Asia

265 For an analysis of competitiveness and complementarity of the industry structure see Lee/Shin (2000), Kim (2001).

with a combined GDP of 5 trillion USD. The effect on world trade is dependent on the trade diversion effects of bilateral free trade as well as on the attitude of the new trade bloc on progress in regional and multilateral free trade negotiations.

The economic discussion of a JKFTA shows varied shortcomings: First, the use of CGE models for predicting effects of integration uses a model of the economy failing to grasp the complexity of real world markets: Markets are modelled to be in equilibrium, actors are rational and factors are fully employed. The results are crucially dependent on the manipulation of data, especially productivity gains. Even more problematic is that economic institutions in the sense of North (1990), important for the economic performance in a national and international context, are absent from equilibrium models. All economic institutions are assumed to work frictionless, non-tariff barriers due to differences in economic culture do not exist. For example, the impact of corporate governance styles cannot be represented in the models. This means the models are as well limited in a normative sense, as guiding economic policies, as in a positive sense, as explaining economic outcomes. The stalled FTA negotiations between Japan and Korean clearly show that such an equilibrium view, while being able to support economic decision-making, cannot substitute an institutional and political-economic analysis.

15.3 Concluding FTAs in other world regions – the EU-Korea FTA

The negotiation of KORUS, the FTA with the United States, was a milestone in Korea's way toward a global network of FTAs, after similar trade pacts with Chile, Singapore and ASEAN (without Thailand). Much less in the spotlight were the FTA negotiations which began almost immediately after the conclusion of a much heralded pact with the US – the negotiations with the European Union. Though politically less controversial, the economic significance of the pact with the EU should not be underestimated; in 2006 the EU states together accounted for 78.6 bn. USD of trade volume, lagging clearly behind China (with more than 118 bn. USD) but beating Japan and the US. Additionally, the EU is one of the largest investors in Korea and held the top position again in 2006 with around 5 bn. USD.

To understand the position of the EU toward FTA on the global level, it is important to see that the history of the EU itself is the history of an integration area (beginning not as an FTA, but as a Customs Union with a similar effect on world trade) and that the EU has been linked to a number of countries particularly in its neighborhood through special economic agreements. Currently, agreements cover four different types of countries, namely other Western European states (the old EFTA group), other European states (mainly in Eastern Europe, or what is left of that after most countries joined the EU), with Middle Eastern and Northern African states, and finally with the rest of the world (Woolcock, 2007). From the beginning of European integration, the tension between multilateral free trade and closer economic integration with the potential negative effects of trade diversion was present. The decision of the United Kingdom to abstain from European integration in the 1950s and the subsequent foundation of EFTA as a more open alternative were motivated by this tension. After the inclusion of most of the EFTA in the European Community (EC) in various rounds of enlargement (1973, 1995), the remaining EFTA states, in particular Norway and Switzerland, are related to the EU today through the European Economic Area, a de facto FTA between the EU and the EFTA states. By and large, the free trade and preferential trade agreements of the EU can be divided in those driven by political factors, in particular in its near neighbourhood, and those driven by economic factors. With the end of the Cold War in Europe and the breakdown of the socialist commonwealth in 1989 and 1990, the need for a new political and economic order in Central and Eastern Europe (CEE) was a driving factor behind a model of trade and political agreements aimed at stabilizing the region as well as binding it closer to the European Communities. Soon, the ultimate goal of EC membership became the core question of these agreements. Already in the very early phase of transition, the EC concluded trade and economic cooperation treaties with Hungary (1988), Poland (1989) and Czechoslovakia (1990) based on art. 113 EC Treaty. In December 1991, the first association treaties (so-called Europe agreements) were concluded with these states, based on art. 238 EC Treaty. These stipulated a step-by-step approach to free trade between the transition states and the EC, with basically unequal liberalization (the EC liberalized its market faster than the transition states), with the exception of certain sensitive sectors (like steel and agriculture), where the EC states feared for negative consequences. Additionally, the transition states had by and by to adopt EC norms and standards. For the industrial markets, the Europe agreements meant that for most goods, free or nearly free trade existed throughout Europe relatively soon.

While ultimate EC membership was the goal and was vaguely mentioned in the treaties, automatic membership was not foreseen. This was rather decided based on the Copenhagen criteria of 1993, which comprised as well criteria of political maturity (democracy, human rights, rule of law), as economic criteria (market-based economy;, competitiveness in the common market, acceptance of the *acquis communautaire*, i.e. the rules of the EC including those of monetary and political union), as necessary, but not sufficient membership criteria. The EC explicitly, similar to its current approach to trade policy, encouraged regional or subregional economic integration in the so-called Viségrad group (Poland, Hungary, Czechoslovakia) since 1992 and the later Central European FTA between these states. The Central European states were, however, reluctant to cooperate and rather tried as fast as possible to qualify for full EC (and later EU) membership. They did not like the idea to be put together in the "anteroom" of European integration. In 1993 Europe agreements with Romania and Bulgaria were concluded, in 1995 Europe agreements with the Baltic states (Estonia, Latvia, Lithuania) and finally in 1996 with Slovenia. The EU reserved the right to reject enlargement based on its own readiness for enlargement.

In fact, however, the political forces were so that – while there was no automatic membership and theoretically a case-by-case decision on membership –enlargement happened rather fast in two steps. By this, the original framework of preferential agreements disappeared. However, in the meantime a second wave of much more difficult enlargement candidates from the Balkans (emerging from a bloody civil war and generally economically much more backward) as well as the FSU emerged, which now again is linked to the EU by preferential agreements. Moreover, in the case of Turkey, the country applied for EC membership but has been rejected largely on political criteria and had to find a solution. All these agreements are economic in nature, but rather political in their intention.

This is also true for the various forms of Euromed partnerships between the EU and the Mediterranean states. Here, the EU tries through its neighbourhood policy to stabilize a region potentially threatened by radical Islamism as well as prevent mass migration of Africans via the Mediterranean Sea. Similarly to its strategy in CEE, (sub)regional integration among the Mediterranean states is promoted as one way to foster growth and development; and similarly to the situation in CEE, the partners are not thrilled by such a perspective but rather are interested in bilateral agreements with the EU.

Finally, the preferential trade agreements with the so-called ACP (African, Caribbean and Pacific) states are also politically driven. They focus on development goals for former colonies and are motivated by a mixture of guilt (about former colonization), leading to large and often weakly controlled – therefore ineffective – forms of aid and self-interest to preserve the exclusive nature of economic relations with the former colonies. In particular the rise of China as a new partner for these states in exploiting natural resources has led to a more active ACP policy. From the perspective of multilateral trade, the ACP agreements were clearly harmful, leading to economically suboptimal forms of economic specialization, e.g. in agricultural markets like the sugar market (Busche-Jerosch, 2007). This led to demands by other countries to modify ACP agreements. Since 2003, the second phase of ACP agreements has been negotiated, with a scheduled end of negotiations in 2008.

Besides the more politically motivated agreements – though economic factors always play an additional role in these agreements – there are those trade agreements clearly motivated by economic considerations, in particular those with the Central and Latin American states. Here, the EU negotiations can also be seen as an answer to concerns of being isolated or victim of trade diversion, like in the case of Mexico, where originally the NAFTA brought a fall of European trade. Only in the mid-2000s, negotiations were proposed or began with Asian states, among them India, South Korea and ASEAN. With ASEAN plus three (China, Japan, Korea), the EU is also linked through the ASEM process, though this is rather limited in effects for trade. The variety of economic agreements and motivations behind them make an evaluation in terms of multilateral free trade – the original goal of the WTO process as well as the announced goal of the EU itself – very difficult. While some of the agreements seem to directly or indirectly (through political stabilization) enhance free trade on a global level and while many of them include elements of capacity building for worldwide free trade (e.g. through training for officials in trade matters), the ACP agreements are clearly less than welfare enhancing and are hindering structural change in some of the poorest economies on the globe.

The tensions between multilateral free trade and a multitude of bilateral agreements also led to the de facto moratorium on new economic agreements during the early phases of the current round of world trade negotiations, the Doha round and the previous Millenium round, from 1998 to 2006. A comprehensive world trade round addressing as well concerns of the EU (like investment, competition and transparency in government procurement, the so-called Singapore issues) as those of developing countries seemed to promise more benefits than additional FTAs. According to estimates by the World Bank, the successful conclusion of the Doha round could elevate between 66 and 95 million people over the poverty threshold of 2 USD per day, while other estimates are much higher. Not development aid or global re-distribution create wealth, but rather the successful implementation of free trade. The "aid for trade" initiatives of the WTO follow this philosophy. Also, on a more practical level scarce resources on the EU level as well as the level of member states in trade diplomacy had to be used for alternative uses.

However, negotiations of the Doha Development Agenda (DDA) are slow, marred by political inconclusiveness and a generally much more distanced and negative public opinion on the prospects for globalization and the benefits of free trade. In Cancun in 2003, the EU dropped the Singapore issues. The proliferation of new bilateral agreements on the global level added to the growing feeling of being left out and isolated among the EU decision makers. This is particularly true for the more aggressive US stance on bilateral agreements, as in the KORUS

FTA (European Commission, 2006b: 14). Finally, in particular East Asia seemed to be a challenge for the EU. The rise of China meant that a formidable new competitor was active on many markets. To secure traditional markets for EU products was a goal of new protectionist and new "bilateralist" thinking as well as to secure access to the vast Chinese market itself. The promotion of Pascal Lamy as the WTO director and the subsequent changes in the EU personnel related to international trade issues might have added to a less multilateral and more bilateral view (Woolcock, 2007: 5). All these factors led to the decision of the EU to open new FTA negotiations, among them those with Korea, which will be discussed in the next section.

In October 2006, the EU Commission published the new trade doctrine in the communication "Global Europe: Competing in the World" (European Commission 2006a). In essence, the strategy stipulates: *"We need to open markets and create new opportunities for trade and ensure European companies are able to compete fairly in those markets .... Under the Global Europe framework, in Autumn 2006 and Spring 2007, I will set the agenda for EU trade policy with a series of linked strategies on market access, trade defence instruments, protection of intellectual property rights, EU policy on China and a new generation of bilateral trade agreements to complement the EU's commitment to the WTO."*

While rejecting the idea that this is a shift from multilateralism to bilateralism, it is difficult to see it in a different way, more benign to multilateral liberalization. In essence, the new strategy is a shift to new bilateral agreements with a clear economic focus, or "hardnosed focus", as trade commissioner Peter Mandelson described it. This approach can be distinguished from the rather more asymmetric trade liberalization of the EU under agreements within its neighbourhood and with the ACP states, where the focus was more political or developmental. The new approach is in particular important for trade agreements with the successful East Asian trading nations, among them Korea.

In the communication "Global Europe" of October 2006, the EU Commission identifies the market potential (economic size and growth) as well as the level of protection against EU export interests (tariffs and non tariff barriers) as key economic criteria for new FTA partners, additionally with the negotiations with EU competitors (like the KORUS negotiations in the case of Korea), the likely impact on EU markets and economies and the impact on current beneficiaries of preferential agreements (mainly ACP states). Korea was, together with ASEAN and Mercosur, among the priority candidates, due to high levels of protection and large market potential. India, Russia and the Gulf Cooperation Council were runners-up (with the last one, the EU is already negotiating), China fulfills the same criteria, but was put in a different league due to the challenge of its size. Implicitly, also the stance of the potential partners to conclude such an agreement was evaluated. It is a stated goal of the new bilateral agreements to be comprehensive in coverage, leading to the highest possible degree of trade liberalization, including services and investment, but also tackling non tariff barriers, IPR and competition issues, public procurement. Rules of origin should be simplified, an issue, which the EU itself has to tackle urgently. Effectively, with the bilateral partners the Singapore issues, where no consensus could be reached on a multilateral level, are re-introduced. Table 48 shows the calculations of the market potential of possible FTA partners.

Table 48: Market potential according to the EU

	Market Potential (2005-25) (€ bn.)	**GDP 2005 € (bn.)**	**Annual average growth rates 2005-2025 (in %)**	**Trade with the EU (2005, € bn.)**	**Share of EU trade (2005, %)**
USA	449	10.144	3.2	412.7	18.5
China	204	1.573	6.6	209.4	9.4
Japan	74	3.920	1.6	116.4	5.2
India	58	607	5.5	40.0	1.8
ASEAN	57	714	4.9	115.1	5.2
Korea	45	598	4.7	53.3	2.4
Mercosur	35	677	3.6	51.0	2.3
Canada	28	849	2.6	40.8	1.8
GCC	27	412	4.3	87.6	3.9
Russia	21	526	3.0	163.0	7.3
Taiwan	18	268	4.3	36.5	1.6
Australia	17	526	2.5	30.1	1.4
Hong Kong	12	149	4.8	31.1	1.4
Iran	10	151	4.3	24.2	1.1
Ukraine	5	61	4.9	20.7	0.9

Source: European Commission, 2006a: 16 (according to World Bank, Global Insight and EU Commission calculations)

With Korea, already two important agreements were in force, namely the Framework Agreement on Trade and Cooperation (since April 1, 2001), i.e. an agreement aiming at fostering trade and investment as well as political dialogue, and an agreement on cooperation and mutual administrative assistance in customs matters since 1997. At the same time, the EU and Korea faced each other occasionally in the WTO dispute settlement bodies, e.g. in 2007 in four cases, three of them being related to shipbuilding and one related to DRAM memory chips. In December 2006 the EU proposed FTA negotiations with South Korea and on April 23, 2007, the Council authorized the Commission to start negotiations on an FTA. An earlier approach by Korea in 2004 had been rejected by the EU. On May 6, 2007, the negotiations for the FTA were launched in Seoul, while both parties stressed their continued commitment to the DDA round of multilateral trade liberalization.

After eight rounds of talks, the FTA has been initialled by both sides on 15 October 2009. On 16 September 2010 the European Council approved the FTA, and the Agreement has been officially signed on 6 October 2010 in the margin of the EU-South Korea Summit in Brussels. It is provisionally applied since July 1, 2011. Non-tariff barriers, in particular in the automotive industry, the inclusion of goods of the North Korean Gaesong Industrial Complex into the FTA coverage, and the time for phasing out tariffs have all been issues of discussion in the negotiation rounds. Moreover, the KORUS FTA showed that political majorities and political consensus for FTA can rapidly change and therefore, besides economic benefits and discussions, political leadership is important in concluding negotiations.

What was the expected economic impact from the EUKOR FTA? The EU commissioned two studies, a quantitative study using a CGE model (Copenhagen Economics, J.F. Francois 2007) as well as a qualitative study by the Centre for European Policy Studies – Korean Institute for International Economic Policy (2007). The quantitative study shows that both economies gain economically from all levels of trade liberalization, but those benefits are unevenly distributed; Korea, the previously much more protected area, will gain most. For the EU, especially liberalization in services proves to be beneficial, where now high hurdles exist. What are potential dynamic effects leading to higher productivity? Increased sales between the two countries will lead to increased competitive pressures, which might result not only in lower prices but also in innovations in product markets and production processes. These effects might not be directly measurable, but they might well be much more important than the static effects. The qualitative study of the CEPS and KIEP (2007) identifies four challenges, namely the elimination of non-tariff barriers (e.g. in the automotive sector), the liberalisation in the services sector, the removal of barriers to investment (especially in the service sector) and transparency in the regulatory environment. Additionally, the protection of intellectual property rights was one of the most important problems in Korea, as Korea is the world's largest exporter and producer of counterfeit goods. Close regulatory cooperation and the introduction of a dispute settlement agreement are ways identified to help achieve the ambitious goals of the FTA.

Table 49: EU-Korea Economic Relations 2009-2010

	EU to Korea	Korea to EU
Trade in goods (2010)	€28 billion	€38.7 billion
Trade in services (2009)	€6 billion	€3.9 billion
Investment flows (2009)	€0.5 billion	€1.0 billion
Investment stock (2009)	€28.9 billion	€9.9 billion

Source: European Commission, 2011

Among the changes remarkable in the EU-Korea FTA is the opening of the market for certain services, like legal services. Here, lobbying and resistance was traditionally very high. The change in this area can be understood in two ways, both showing the change of Korea after the Asian crisis. The opening of Korea can be seen as a concession or adaptation to global trade standards, and this is certainly the driving force behind many changes. But it can also be understood as the result of greater Korean confidence to compete in such markets, thereby underlining the successful globalization Korea already underwent. This is particularly interesting in view of markets still largely closed, like the agricultural market. Preparing for opening can offer new chances on international markets and can be much more successful than fighting it off.

15.4 Conclusion – bilateral agreements as the finale of trade integration, or as a stepping stone to regional integration?

The conclusion of successful agreements with the EU and the USA seems to swing the pendulum of Korea's integration policy clearly in favor of bilateral agreements. The number of agreements concluded or under negotiation is impressive, as the following table shows.

The next agreements could again be concluded more close at home, maybe in form of another attempt with Japan, maybe as an agreement with China, or maybe even in form of the trilateral agreement currently studied. Other agreements are considered, often already in various planning stages (like joint economic study groups etc.), targeting Mercosur, Russia (Bilateral Economic Partnership Agreement or BEPA), Israel, Vietnam, Mongolia, the Southern Africa Customs Union, Indonesia, Malaysia and Central America. For the time being, a concentration on bilateral agreements seems to consume most of the diplomatic resources and efforts. However, these bilateral agreements might themselves be only stepping stones to a more comprehensive regional approach. First, this might be result of institutional learning. Starting with an FTA with a relatively minor trading partner, Chile, going to the more complex task of tackling FTAs with major trading partners (the US and EU), and finally going to FTAs with regional large partners might equip Korea with the necessary knowledge and understanding to achieve the more difficult task of negotiating comprehensive regional integration. It might also be related to the fact that trade integration alone is only one of the potential benefits of economic integration. Others, like monetary integration, which is maybe approaching as seen by the increased facilities under the Chiang Mai Initiative, might lead to regional approaches. Finally, especially bilateral agreements with much larger economies might also bring difficulties. As long as the partners are allies or benevolent, this might not be so difficult, but integration with Japan or China might lead to fear of hegemony. In this relation, region-wide integration might become a new alternative. This interaction between economic, institutional and political aspects of integration, which is typical for South Korea after the Asian crisis, will again be discussed in the next section.

Table 50: The Network of Korea's FTAs in 2011

FTAs in effect (in brackets date of coming into force)	Korea – Chile FTA (April 2004) Korea – Singapore FTA (March 2006) Korea – EFTA FTA (September 2006) Korea – ASEAN FTA (May 2009: FTA Trade in Services, September 2009: FTA Investment) Korea – India Comprehensive Economic Partnership Agreement (January 2010) Korea – Peru FTA (August 2011) Korea EU – FTA (July 2011 provisionally in force)
Concluded FTA	Korea – US FTA (ratified December 2011, in force from 2012)
FTAs under negotiation	Korea – Canada FTA Korea – Mexico FTA Korea – Gulf Cooperation Council FTA Korea – Australia FTA Korea – New Zealand FTA Korea – Columbia FTA Korea – Turkey FTA

Source: Ministry of Foreign Trade, 2011

Chapter 16: Economic integration in the Kim Dae-Jung and Roh Moo-Hyun era – Korea as the "hub of East-Asia"?

16.1 Korea as a "hub of East Asia" and the Singapore benchmark

Korea's successful co-hosting of the World Cup 2002, a "mark of modernity" (Cha, 2002), has enhanced Korea's image in the world. While Korea's economic performance after the East Asian crisis has been successful, Korea under the Kim Dae-Jung and Roh Moo-Hyun administration strived for more, trying to become a regional hub of Northeast Asia. This means nothing else than a complete transformation from a competitive industry to an attractive investment location, a center for international economic activity. "Korea as a hub of Northeast Asia" became an official government goal in mid-2002. The dictionary describes a hub as a "center of activity or interest", but besides, the idea of a hub is not very well defined in economic geography. This is partly so, because a "hub" has many dimensions. Originally, "hub and spoke" systems are used in information technology and transportation, e.g. with regards to aviation or maritime transport. Then the concept was applied to other fields, like the financial sector or the international trading system. Later, the concept became rather a symbol for being a central power in Northeast Asia, and in this fuzzy sense it became politically relevant during the Kim and Roh administration.

A hub first of all and most often means a center for transportation, which means a well-functioning airport, harbor and/or railway and street system as well as the transportation services and regulatory environment (for example, customs clearance system) necessary for a smooth transportation system. Singapore as well as Hong Kong are examples for transportation hubs in East Asia. Besides a strategic geographic location also path dependency (in the case of Singapore as well as Hong Kong the British colonial history) is an important ex-post explanatory factor. A hub can also be the center of industrial production in a region. This can be a sectoral phenomenon (for example, Germany as a center of car production in Europe or Japan and later Korea as a center of ship-building in East Asia), but can also indicate a generally strong concentration of industries in one country. A regional hub might provide financial and banking services. Again, Singapore and Hong Kong are examples for financial hubs of East Asia. Here, regulatory environment and information technology available are important factors to consider. A regional hub also can be the location of regional headquarters of multinational companies. This is one of the goals the Korean government most strongly aimed at. While the location of regional headquarters does not say itself anything about the location of production, and thereby also about the size of foreign investment and consequential benefits (like taxes paid or employment created by foreign companies), it is nevertheless an important factor for the prestige and political importance of a location. Lastly, one might imagine a hub in terms of other factors, for example tourism or agriculture. While these are various dimensions of a possible hub, there is no clear quantitative description, what means to be a hub. Additionally, several countries in a region might be competing hubs.

The next question is, then, what makes a country a hub? Again, the definition is too fuzzy to come to a clear hypothesis. However, using the idea of "Singapore's 6 G", one might approach the idea of a regional hub. Singapore defines itself as a hub due to the following characteristics, namely being:

a *gateway* to Asia
a *global partner* of business and technology
a place were *global talent* is abundant
a place for *global funds*
a place with a pro-business government
and a place with a great living environment.

In a more analytic way, one can describe these six characteristics as:

- accessibility and economic integration
- being at the forefront of business and technology, including production
- a high level of human resource availability and a flexible labour market
- a modern and healthy financial and banking sector and a high level of financial integration
- a government accommodating business and a transparent system of governance
- attractive living conditions for foreigners.

While this list is not exhaustive, it may be a good starting point to discuss the question of whether Korea might have the potential to develop to a regional hub in East Asia.

The first characteristic, accessibility, is only limited for Korea. Geographically, South Korea is isolated, which makes it less attractive as a transportation hub despite its modern harbour and airport facilities. One of the aims of the Roh administration in Korea was to change this with its proactive engagement policy to North Korea, trying to connect railroads on the East and West coast, ultimately linking them to the Transsiberian railroad and thereby creating an "iron silk road" as well as highways (the so-called Asian Highway no. 1 concept). Besides the geographical isolation, South Korea also lacks membership in a regional trading arrangement, making it less attractive as an investment location, because the domestic market is much smaller than for the closest neighbors, China and Japan.

Second, South Korea can be said to be successful on the forefront of business and technology. The impressive development of high technology in Korea, notably in the areas of information and communication technology, are an example. Especially, South Korea's economy is driven by a constantly high level of corporate investment, guaranteeing a modern and competitive capital stock. Regarding basic research, despite some improvements (for example programmes in the field of research like BK 21) Korea's research landscape in the wake of the Asian crisis still lacked internationality.

This was partly linked to the third area, namely human resources. While Korea had a strong and well-educated labour force, it was not very much internationalized. For example, CEOs of MNCs complained that international training is difficult for Korean employees lacking the appropriate language ability. The labour market was a constant additional source of problems for foreign companies in specific sectors, where the trade unions are strong. Also, labour market flexibility today is still among the lowest in OECD countries, while the comparative cost advantage of low labour cost is long past.[266]

The banking and financial sector of Korea underwent great changes in the aftermath of the financial crisis. While financial services are developed and institutional preconditions like currency regulations are liberalized, the banking sector is partly state-owned. Negotiations with foreign investors, including European banks, have been difficult and often unsuccessful. Disputes arising in the wake of the crisis regarding the Lone Star investment company took a decade to solve (Menke, 2007; Schopf, 2007; and the savings banks crisis in Korea since 2010 shows that regulatory issues are still unresolved).

The answer of the Korean government to the financial crisis can be qualified as pro-business. The rhetoric of the "four sectors reform" (private, public, labour market, financial market) has been aggressively pro-business, and reforms have indeed been more thoroughly than in all other countries affected by the crisis. However, the reforms often exhibited an ideology of government control of the markets, which is far from a real pro-business attitude for example in the government-led big deals. While government can be qualified as pro-business – given the important stress from all South Korean governments on the goal of

266 At the same time Korea had an extremely large unregulated sector of barely protected labour, making the overall labour force quite flexible. But this was not the case for larger foreign-invested as well as domestic companies. Temporary employment stood at 17 percent in 2001 and increased to 29 percent in 2006 (Grubb et al., 2007).

growth since the 1960s – problems of stability and transparency of the government remain. Political strife as well as intransparent and occasionally corrupt policies diminish the advantages from a pro-business government.

The living conditions in Korea were for a long time not considered to be very accommodative for foreigners. First, the level of English language is relatively low, compared with other competitors for the hub position like Singapore or Hong Kong. Second, the transportation system, the environmental quality, and educational facilities were often deemed inferior to those of the same competitors. Lastly, the price level is no longer a reason to live in Korea, especially in Seoul. So, the overall living conditions were not an additional reason for foreigners to settle down in Korea. The subsequent policies of Seoul mayors (in particularly Lee Myung-Bak and Oh Se-Hun) to improve the image of Seoul as a modern Asian and world city, however, bore fruit after a decade of investment and transformation,. Today, Seoul's image around the world as a modern city has dramatically improved, together with the image of Korea as not only an economic powerhouse, but also a cultural world center.

The discussion shows that Korea cannot be said to be *a priori* a successful contender for a regional hub position given its current position in regional economic geography. It should be noted that as a hub candidate, Korea has to not only be as good as its competitors, but also offer additional incentives to cover the costs of an eventual switch of companies from other places to Korea, since the hub position is linked to economies of localization (i.e. economies of scale in terms of location, for example the existing of competitors, infrastructure, labour in the same field in the same place).

16.2 The Chinese experience – becoming a hub by opening special investment zones?

Two basic strategies are possible to enhance a country's position in regard to its attractiveness as an investment location (and, ultimately, its possibility to act as a region's hub). These strategies are either the improvement of basic market functioning or the creation of special incentives for investment. Also, as in the case of Korea, both strategies can be applied. The Korean government with the "four plus one" policy (reform plus market opening) in the wake of the Asian crisis tried to improve the functioning of markets. The results of this attempt were impressive, namely a V-shaped recovery of the economy. In the area of investment, the liberalization and deregulation led to higher foreign direct investment (FDI) inflows due to improved market conditions. However, the Roh Moo-Hyun government also introduced special investment zones governed by special laws to attract foreign investment. Will the five economic zones be able to overcome the path-dependent location of the transportation, management and financial services hubs in East Asia in favor of Korea? A brief review of the development of special economic zones (SEZs) might help to answer this question.

Since the 1960s, so-called Export Processing Zones (EPZ) were established in various parts of the world with the goal to attract FDI and promote industrialization. While the Latin American experience of EPZ was mixed, in East Asian countries like South Korea and Taiwan EPZ became centres of export-driven growth. When China under Deng changed its development strategy, in July 1979, Guangdong and Fujian Provinces were granted the right to carry out economic experiments, and four SEZs were set up in Shenzhen, Zhuhai, Shantou of Guangdong Province and Xiamen of Fujian Province. All these regions were coastal, rich in labour and located close to the successful market economies of Hong Kong and Taiwan. The economic opening of these regions should promote growth and exports, but the possibility of growing economic ties with Hong Kong and Taiwan should also facilitate eventual reunification.

The most successful of these zones, Shenzhen, experienced a development divided in three phases: The first phase was the experimental phase, when the institutional preconditions for growths were created and lasted until 1990. During this time the economic framework for the SEZs as "windows to technology, management, knowledge and foreign policies" (Deng Xiaoping 1984) was established. The inflow of foreign capital, mainly from Hong Kong, was slowly accelerating since the mid-1980s, but the production processes were contrary to expectations mostly characterized by low technology intensity and based on the comparative advantage of low labour costs. Twice, in 1985 and after the events on Tiananmen Square in 1989 the SEZs were criticized by conservative communist party leaders. In the early 1990s the take-off phase of Shenzhen's development began. Foreign companies from all over the world rushed in; in 1997, 51 out of the world's top 500 enterprises have taken root in Shenzhen. The export volume of Shenzhen increased to around one seventh of China's total (USD 26.4 billion in 1998). The much-publicized trip of Deng to Shenzhen in 1992 helped to gain the trust of domestic and foreign investors. The technology intensity of production also increased and, in 1998, more than 35 percent of the production was in the high and new technology sectors. The third phase of development began with the challenge of the Asian financial crisis in 1997 and the preparation of China for entry into the WTO. It brought a major redirection of economic activities in the Shenzhen SEZ.

When first EPZ were established, they were delineated areas to provide procedural and operational ease for producers, offer tax holidays, tax reductions and the duty-free import of capital goods and raw materials for export manufacture.

This policy was designed to attract FDI, generate employment, earn foreign exchange and eventually link the less developed hinterland and facilitate technology transfer and the transfer of modern management practice. Infrastructure in EPZ was limited to industrial estate development. The Chinese SEZs additionally focused on the provision of supportive infrastructure like housing, airport, roads, ports, telecommunications, electricity and transportation. Also, the reform activities comprised a wider scope and included agriculture, commerce, the development of the financial sector including the opening of a stock exchange, tourism and the service sector and increasingly in the mid-1990s, the privatization of state-owned enterprises and housing. Thereby, the Shenzhen SEZ could escape from the fate of many EPZ, which only attracted labour intensive, low technology production processes with few possibilities for economic development of the hinterland. Since a general liberalization of the Chinese economy was not possible due to political considerations, the SEZs were a possibility to establish a role model for the reform of the rest of the economy in a closely controlled area. This indirect effect of the SEZs as models for the economy is as important as the direct effect of attraction of FDI and the transfer of technology and modern management practices.

The Shenzhen SEZ did not only become one of the centers of export, technology and economic reform in China, but also gradually could cope with the early problems like growing inequality, the fate of migrant workers and environmental degradation. However, the economic position of the Shenzhen SEZ has to be redirected: labour costs are increasing and firms migrate to cheaper locations in Guangdong province. The mushrooming of the SEZs and the introduction of open ports and special zones for technological development as well as the reforms for the rest of China make competition for FDI harder. In the future, the upgrading of production and infrastructure, especially in areas like education, become crucial for the Shenzhen SEZ.

The Shenzhen experience holds many interesting lessons for South Korea (as also for North Korea). Shenzhen became successful only in an international and national environment, where market access to the rest of the country was restricted and capital (especially flows of Chinese mainland capital via Hong Kong toward the SEZ) was abundant, but investment possibilities were scarce and an attractive domestic market was accessible (domestic sales to mainland China were equally import for the SEZ than exports). Even then, not all SEZs automatically became successful. In Korea, none of these factors are given. From a purely theoretical point of view, a SEZ might be justified, if economies of localization (economies of scale) can be reached by an SEZ, for example through a critical mass of foreigners to build schools for foreigners, allow the official use of English etc. At the same time, the conditions described above should be true. For Korea, both are questionable. To the contrary, special foreign investment zones could even lead to ghettoization, a lack of access to the Korean market and government (given the high degree of centralization), and adverse cost effects (like higher living costs and wages for a privileged labour force).

Therefore, market reforms comprising all of Korea seem to be preferable to a strategy of punctual and locally restricted foreigner zones. It could be argued that the existing hubs like Singapore and Hong Kong are themselves results of a specific institutional structure characterized by state-intervention rather than results of a market-driven and market-conform competition process among contenders for the position as a hub of East Asia. While this is true, it does not mean that new distortions might "correct" older ones in the regional economic geography. The change of the regulatory environment and a country-wide acceptance of the challenge of globalization in its economic and cultural meaning seems to be a better approach toward competitiveness for investment than new, market-distorting investment zones only loosely linked with the rest of the country. This does not preclude the possibility of the accumulation of special types of foreign (and domestic) firms of an industry, for example financial services, in one place. The decision of the South Korean government in late 2011 to decrease dramatically the size of special investment zones seems to be the recognition of the fact that this instrument has not really fulfilled the expectations with which it was introduced.

Overall, it seems to be the more promising strategy for Korea not to try an isolated marketing for an isolated Korea, but rather as part of a strong regional economy. In cooperation with other states, bilaterally, but especially multilaterally, Korea could maintain its position and even enhance its position as an interesting investment location for foreign companies. The instruments for such a strategy would rather be diplomatic efforts and domestic economic policy efforts to overcome exterior and interior opposition toward integration, instead of market-distorting special incentives. To achieve such a position of being a medium-sized, but strong link in a strong regional economy, Korea still has to go a far way. The next chapter looks at this greater picture of East Asian unity and the potential gains of South Korea in such a system.

Chapter 17: The quest for an Optimum Integration Area and the future of Korea in East Asia

17.1 Introduction

For observers of East Asia's attempts of economic integration, the last decades brought a new complexity which makes the analysis of the status of economic integration in East Asia far less straightforward. Until the early 1990s, the analysis of East Asian "*de facto*" integration compared with Europe's *de jure* integration as well as East Asia's "subregional" integration compared with Europe's regional integration has been more or less a consensus view. The reasons for this particular way of development were seen in the differences in economic development status, diverging political regimes leading to principles of strict non-interference, and that means, a much smaller scope for legally binding integration measures, as well as the historical burden of the Japanese expansion policies before 1945. With the Asian economic and financial crisis, the search for alternatives to the international financial institutions (the IMF and World Bank) like the ultimately unsuccessful idea of an Asian Monetary Fund added the interest in macroeconomic cooperation to the existing interest in the integration of markets for goods, and, to a lesser extent, services and factors of production. At the same time, the rise of China and then India as new economic powerhouses influenced the geo-economic and geo-political situation of the region, transformed the interest in economic integration (for example, from purely market-access driven integration to raw material-access driven integration) and challenged the formerly undisputed position of Japan as the first economy in the region.

Moreover, the new situation also led to a two-track approach to regional economic integration in most East Asian countries: The new pan-regional integration movement, beginning with the "ASEAN plus three (China, Japan, Korea)" summits culminated in the formation of a new institution simply called "East Asian Summit" at the summit meeting of Kuala Lumpur on December 14, 2005 (ASEAN General Secretariat, 2005). The role of this new summit meeting as the focal point for a new regional architecture and eventual economic community is ambitious. However, the size of the new integration area is problematic: the participation of India meant that not only Northeast- and Southeast Asia, but also the economically and geographically most important country of South Asia is included. The inclusion of New Zealand and Australia meant that the original idea of an "Asians only"-club was given up. And the observer status for Russia, which is interested in full membership in the new integration area, means that the danger of overstretching like in the case of APEC looms for the new integration area.

At the same time, there is a proliferation of bilateral integration through free trade agreements in the region. These are driven by the desire to gain free access to important markets, due to the rise of intra-Asian trade, by the desire to gain stable supply of raw materials, especially for rapidly growing China and its competitors on energy markets, like Japan, and, last but not least, by the fear to be left out of regional integration, a fear particularly prevailing in the Northeast Asian economies of Japan and Korea. It is not clear, if both tracks, regional and bilateral integration, will be compatible in the long run (Rajan, 2005). Since all the FTAs in the region vary in scope and size, the danger of a "spaghetti bowl effect", i.e. negative side effects due to the structure of preferential trade agreements, is great.[267] Even the participating states see it often only as a second best solution compared with comprehensive regional integration.

A comprehensive approach to economic integration in East Asia has first to tackle the problem of finding a balance of large member states and small member states, defining (at least preliminary) the borders of the new integration area, integrating the existing FTAs into its structure or find a way to abandon them, and maintaining a constructive balance between the possible dominating member economies. In this situation, the chances of regional economic integration for Korea are not yet clear. Will integration mean a greater voice for Korea, or will it mean that Korea as an economic powerhouse, but as a relatively small country compared with China, Japan and India loses by a multilateral (regional) agreement? Which institutional structures, if any, can lead to a balanced approach to integration attractive to the dominant economies as well as giving the smaller economies a stronger voice rather than forcing them on a way they would not choose otherwise? These questions will be discussed in the remainder of this chapter.

267 In February 2006, the head of the Asia Development Bank (ADB), Haruhiko Kuroda, spoke of the "Asian noodle effect" with respect to the 15 FTAs and other preferential agreements under implementation in the region, 10 close to be signed, more than 20 more under negotiations and at least 16 more proposed. Currently, a number of those close to be signed already has been concluded (see Business Time 2006: 1).

17.2 Some observations on the size of states and integration areas – is there an optimum integration area?

Regional integration is a multi-faceted affair. Among the dimensions of integration the area of integration (economic, social, political, cultural), the form of integration (*de jure* vs. *de facto*, i.e. institutionalized vs. non-institutionalized) and more specifically, the institutional design in economic integration (FTA, customs union, common market, economic and monetary union, etc.), the underlying economic rationale (positive vs. negative integration) and the size of the integration area have been widely discussed. The last point is at the interface of economic and political integration theory. Given the highly political nature even for "purely" economic integration projects, like in the beginning of European integration, the analysis of the size of an economic integration area is particularly important. And this does not only refer to the external borders of the integration area, but also to the composition of the integration area, i.e. to the size of member states and their balance.

When focusing only on trade, but not on possible macroeconomic and microeconomic policy coordination in an economic integration area, there is no reason to limit integration to a particular area. The world is then the first best integration area. The WTO is built on this principle. The more countries participate in free trade, the more the beneficial effects of trade (greater division of labour, greater specialization, more competition and consequently, more innovation) can work. However, such a solution might not be available if it comes to closer policy coordination. Even an integration area only focusing on free trade might be interested in common rules, e.g. on competition policy and state aid. In this case, the costs of policy coordination have to be juxtaposed to the gains from an enlarged integration area (or, the opportunity costs of non-integration). The resulting so-called interdependence costs have a minimum, and this is the point where theoretically the optimum size of integration can be located. In reality, such a point can not be found, since in particular the dynamic effects (and that means here, gains) of trade cannot be predicted.[268] Even more, there is not only one dimension, but policy coordination can include many fields, e.g. microeconomic policies influencing

268 Neoclassical economic theory circumvents this problem by attaching an artificial "rate of innovation" (or technical progress, or productivity increases) to a mathematically determined growth function; this, however, is only possible by ignoring the nature of evolution, which is not predictable, allowing only for pattern predictions ("more competition will lead to greater competitive pressure to innovate and ultimately, thereby, to more innovation"), but not for exactly measurable data.

the structure of factor markets and markets for goods and services or macroeconomic coordination in the fields of currency, monetary and fiscal policy. In this case, there is a tendency for coordination costs to rise, i.e. for the theoretical optimum integration area to shrink.

The theory of optimum currency areas (OCAs) postulates that a combination of measurable criteria (relating to asymmetric shocks, product diversification and intra-industry trade and market structures on factor markets) determines the optimum size of an integration area.[269] Given the difficulty of measuring and comparing some of the criteria (e.g. various regulations on labour markets), this claim seems to be doubtful. More doubtful it is to speak of an optimum integration area similar to an OCA. The interdependence of political and economic factors and the importance of evolutionary effects of integration in economies (e.g. higher innovation rate through increased competition) and in politics (e.g. growing mutual understanding through increased interaction) cannot be adequately predicted, let alone be measured. Therefore, it is rather correct to speak of advantageous forms of integration, rather than optimal forms of integration. For sure, there might be some forms which can clearly be ruled out as suboptimal; but this does not mean that the determination of the optimum size of integration is equally possible.

Additionally, integration might be understood as the joint production of a public good called international economic order.[270] In the case, the international public good is not produced in a satisfying quantity, there might be room for a regional production of the good, and this seems to be the case in the last one and a half decades. Maull (2006) sees the pressures of globalization and inadequate policy responses, in particular by the United States, as the reason for a mixture of an unbalanced dispersion of power in international relations, with an erosion of state authority and political legitimacy leading to a fragile international order. In this situation, the regional production of international order can be a second-best solution; it needs mechanisms of burden sharing and the sharing of potential benefits; usually, it is related to regional hegemonic powers.

If regional international order, for example in the form of rules for economic exchanges and their enforcement, is produced by a club, the questions of club size and club fees have to be answered (Sandler/Tschirhart, 1997). If the club is too small, the beneficial effects of trade or other exchange, e.g. on factor markets,

269 More precisely, the existence of asymmetric macroeconomic shocks precludes a currency area to be optimal in the absence of other adjustment mechanisms like flexible factor markets, free migration and interregional re-distribution. For an introduction see Baldwin/Wyplosz (2004).

270 A public good is characterized by non-excludability and non-rivalry in consumption (marginal costs of zero), leading to underproduction without international coordination or domination (hegemony). Impure public goods, where the conditions apply only partly, are called club goods.

might not be significant. If it is too large, then the coordination costs might be too big. At the same time, it is important to see that the production costs of the public good (or club good) "international economic order" are not given (as sometimes assumed in model-building) as exogenous, but they are dependent on the kind of integration chosen, the nature (size, rules) of the club and the competition by other clubs. In other words, institutional competition works. Countries compare the costs of maintaining international order or setting up a new regional organization with the costs and benefits of these efforts in other regions; as well institutional innovation (new forms of institutional regimes) as institutional imitations (of successful role models) are possible.

Due to its long history and accumulated experience with various forms of economic integration, the European integration area often was a role model to be followed and sometimes also a deterring model not to be followed by other integration areas. While the comparison with other areas serves an important benchmarking function, the preconditions for a particular type of integration should not be forgotten. A pure copy of a type developed elsewhere seems to be scarcely possible. This becomes clear, for example, in the discussion of a possible monetary integration in East Asia, where an Asian Currency Unit as a first step seems to make sense, like in the European case in the 1970s, but where the preconditions are completely different from those prevailing in Europe after the end of the Bretton Woods system (Wilson 2006). Institutional learning is possible, given enough flexibility and adjustment is built into the new integration area.

Another consequence of the multi-faceted nature of economic integration is the lack of a single peak in economic integration. Not one model beats all other models. This also is an important lesson sometimes forgotten, when increasing integration (from the FTA to the common market and the economic and monetary union) is seen as a value *per se*, not as instrumental for achieving particular goals. While the establishment of a pure competition order (i.e. freedom of competition, to be achieved through negative integration) indeed can be seen as a value *per se*, it is different with policy coordination. Having greater policy coordination has a number of potentially desirable features (many of them being non-economic, like increased exchanges among politicians leading to increased mutual understanding), but also a number of potential costs (mostly economic, like the possibility of substituting market processes by bargained, "fair", i.e. politically acceptable, results enforced by politics).

With regard to the internal balance of the club members, various mechanisms can be established to ensure the functioning of the club at moderate costs. The foremost solution is the limitation of club membership to a relatively small number of states with a relatively high degree of similarity in their national interests. This has been to a large degree the single most important success factor behind

European integration; and the gradual shift from a small, homogeneous, to a large, heterogeneous union is the single most important factor in explaining a certain Europe fatigue, as exemplified by the rejection of a European constitution in 2005, as well as the problems the Euro-zone currently faces in coordinating monetary and fiscal policy. In the 1950s, the first integration attempts were made among six states (France, Germany, Italy, Benelux) which were relatively similar in economic development (with the exception, until today, of the Mezzogiorno, Italy's South). This guaranteed a similarity of interests in many respects. With the enlargement process of the European Union to now 27 states there was growing heterogeneity and consequently, the old decision making mechanisms worked less and less well and new had to be found (Ahrens 2006).

However, such a solution might not be available to states. In East Asia, the Southeast Asian region experienced some commonalities in economic development, like the common experience of the role of Japanese capital and Chinese trading networks in the region. However, the status of development soon was far apart between Singapore, a group of more successful Southeast Asian states like Thailand and Malaysia, and the less successful states. Also, enlargement by the poor CVLM states (Cambodia, Vietnam, Laos and Myanmar) added to regional heterogeneity. Even more pronounced, there was a large heterogeneity in Northeast Asia, where Japan, China and Korea were all sharply distinct. Adding a political perspective, the heterogeneity in East Asia even becomes more clear, with a number of sharply diverging political systems co-existing, compared with the (now Pan-European) model of democratic market economy and welfare state in Europe.

When heterogeneity is growing, the need to balance divergent interests is also growing. The most secure way to prevent any form of predatory behaviour of strong over small partners in an integration area is the requirement of unanimity (in other words, a veto right) in decision making. Unfortunately, this also is the strongest limitation possible to economic integration, since it leads to opportunistic and strategic behaviour.[271] Nevertheless, some form of consensual decision-making might be stable and bring integration areas forward better than arrangements based upon majority decision making. It is important, though, that rather than an overall unanimity clause like the non-interference clause of the ASEAN, there is the possibility of opting out for new policies or particular policies only.[272] This creates a community of "multiple speed", where some economies integrate faster than others as in the case of the ASEAN Free Trade Area, which

---

271 The "policy of the empty chair", when France did boycott European decision-making, is a prime example.

272 Yamagake (2005) discusses the principle of non-interference of ASEAN and its possible impact on regional community building, especially with relation to a democratization of the region.

is originally only established by some core members. Also, it can result in a multitude of overlapping, single-issue communities, all with a different membership. This solution, however, is only different from the current situation of the creation of a "spaghetti bowl" of FTAs, if there are basic principles to be adhered to, like free trade as an ultimate goal of diverging communities moving toward the goal.

A more supranational form of regional integration might be able to substitute strict unanimity with some form of majority voting. To prevent the dominance of particular economies, e.g. large or small ones, forms of qualified majority voting can be introduced. For example, for a decision to take place, a majority of states of a community plus a majority of inhabitants and maybe other requirements, e.g. a majority of GDP for economic decisions (preventing involuntary redistribution from smaller rich, to larger or more populous poor areas) might be required. While this form of decision making deviates from the democratic principle of "one man, one vote", it is nevertheless a second-best solution to balance heterogeneous interest in the integration area.

In East Asia, the lack of a commitment to regional integration and the current preference for "bilateral agreements first" can to a large part be explained by a lack of consensus on the decision making mechanisms of a new East Asian community. In the next part, this will be more analyzed, and possible ways to overcome this problem are discussed.

17.3 Toward comprehensive East Asian regionalism? Some reflections on the issues of size and composition of an East Asian community

The geo-economic and geo-political structure of East Asia has been described elsewhere, but particularly in this section, the question of size and composition of the integration area will be discussed.[273] Naturally, such a discussion is not independent from the realm of integration, a possible new East Asian integration area. Given the current inclination of East Asian nations, the declarations of the various "ASEAN plus three" summit meetings and the current status of East Asian economies, the most probably realm of integration will be as follows:[274] First, the creation of a region-wide free trade area within a long transition period of maybe ten to twenty years. Second, the introduction of technical facilities for

273 For an introduction into the geo-economic and geo-political situation in East Asia see Seliger (2002a).

274 For a comprehensive review of the ASEAN plus three process see the contributions in Seliger/Schönfisch (2004).

this goal, including some form of dispute settlement mechanism, has to be implemented. Third, additional measures to foster policy cooperation without mandatory features might follow. Finally, measures for additional policy coordination in the field of currency cooperation, i.e. the extension of the current swap facilities to prevent possible currency crises in the region, are likely.[275] Also, the set-up of a special regional funding system as an embryonic system of regional redistribution is possible, either in the form of a cooperation of the new area with the Asian Development Bank (ADB), or in the form of a separate fund, maybe also sub-regionally as a Northeast Asian Development Bank (Seliger 2010).

Given such a scope of integration, what can be said about the size of integration? An initial consideration could be to look at the existing integration areas in the region, especially Asia-Pacific Economic Cooperation (APEC) as the only pan-regional (and even inter-regional) integration process. Given that there has been a certain amount of time, money and trust already spent to make APEC run, it might seem more likely than any new body to succeed in integration efforts. However, the size of APEC is an important warning for the dangers of overstretching the integration areas. The first round of APEC included the United States plus East Asia with a few additional states. The focus was clearly trade oriented, and, even more, narrowly defined to overcome obstacles of GATT negotiations. Then, the goal was shifted, in particular with the Bogor declaration of 1994, to free trade between members, for developed member states until 2010, for developing member states until 2020. The following decision of so-called Individual Action Plans for liberalization was severely altered by the effects of the Asian crisis and afterwards APEC lost its attractiveness as an integration area (Ahn, 1999). While the goal of free trade was never renounced, APEC lost its function to advance multilateral trade negotiations, e.g. in the defensive way Japan and South Korea acted in agricultural negotiations. At the same time, regional extension made consensual decision-making more difficult. The inclusion of Latin American economies as well as of Russia means that economies from North and South America, East Asia, Australasia and Russia (as a distinctly European power with a huge, but economically much less important Asian annex) were APEC members. In this situation APEC remains an important body to rally support for multilateral trade liberalization and to allow informal contacts, e.g. between Taiwan and the Chinese mainland, but it lost its driving force and focus. Therefore, a comprehensive economic community cannot be built along the APEC lines, and APEC has to find a new approach, as the summit of Kuala Lumpur did.

---

275 Since the Asian crisis and the so-called Miyazawa initiative, attempts to establish an alternative regional financial architecture (Asian Monetary System or Asian Monetary Fund) have been discussed. A review of this discussion is not possible here; see, however, Beeson (2003).

A second consideration, then, concerns the large states. Among the biggest obstacles to integration in East Asia has been the historical role of Japan as aggressive expansionary power, thinly veiled under the plan for the "Greater East Asia Co-Prosperity Sphere." While large-scale development aid and a moderate foreign policy could overcome some of the historical antagonism, there are still highly symbolic contentious issues between Japan and its neighbors. At the same time, the Japanese model of economic development underwent a grave crisis in the last two decades, making the formerly admired Japanese model less convincing. This does not mean that Japan automatically lost its role as strong economic force in the region and is substituted by China, the new rising power (Mulgan, 2005). On the contrary, the transformation of Japan to a more "ordinary regional power" (Inoguchi/Bacon, 2005) means that Japan and the region for the first time have the chance to overcome the former fear of an again-dominant Japan.

China is definitely the new rising power in East Asia, but it is far from being a hegemonic power. While smaller countries like South Korea saw China throughout the 1990s mainly as an insatiable export market and an outsourcing opportunity for expensive labour, the Chinese fear factor shifted this outlook dramatically in the last years. China is seen as a rising nationalist force, which at the same time attracts its neighbors, but also repels them (Ahn, 2004). Triggered by China's raw material thirst as well as by its more aggressive FTA policy in recent years, this might be understandable. The answer, however, to retreat from East Asian integration and to pursue mainly bilateral free trade projects, is rather short-sighted. A comprehensive East Asian community, including Japan and China, would neutralize their alleged hegemonic aspirations and their real economic power and force them to find allies among the smaller states in the region without neglecting the large partner economy at the same time.

An inclusion of India, another rising economy in the region, would help to overcome a possible dichotomy between China and its potential allies as well as Japan and its potential allies in the East Asian community. However, this would come at a cost since India's economic orientation is far less eastbound. India would not only bring in a South Asian orientation, including an attraction of South Asian economies to join the new integration area for benefiting from integration with its large neighbour, but by that also would bring in countries with a very different economic development experience. The possible costs of such an inclusion might well be higher then the possible benefits, e.g. of being a third large state mediating between Japan, China and other regional economies. The less clear the rules for membership and the scope of membership is, the actual costs would be higher. For a pure regional FTA, the obstacles would be much less than for a deeper integration approach.

A similar consideration can be made for the possible inclusion of New Zealand and Australia. While their inclusion in a regional FTA seems to be less problematic, a more comprehensive community might have the problem that the political culture of these states differs widely from that of the East Asian states proper, leading to potential disputes, and that their adherence would bring in the whole Oceanian region, though this would be a minor problem from the economic point of view. While the racist undertones of the "Caucus without Caucasians" – model proposed by Prime Minister Mohamad Mahathir of Malaysia in the 1990s were rather damaging to his project, the concentration on an area of greater similarity, which excludes Australia and New Zealand, can indeed be justified. Also, Russia, which has been an observer at the summit of Kuala Lumpur in December 2005, but pressed for full membership, is a questionable partner. While undeniable an East Asian power, Russia's main economic and population concentration as well as interest lays in the European part of the country. The Asian part, Siberia and the Russian Far East, currently shifts from the regional development under central planning, with a heavy emphasis on its development regardless of costs, to a more market-driven regional development. The most likely outcome will be a Russian Far East returning to the old function of a resource colony for the European mainland. An exclusion of the possible partners discussed above might be objected on the grounds that the economies in question are usually large and richer than average (in the case of Australia and New Zealand) or potentially powerful (India and Russia). However, a smaller East Asian community would have the advantage of bringing together more like-minded nations, thereby reducing the transaction costs of economic integration. Given the still abundant number of problems within this smaller community, this approach appears to be more realistic.

What is, then, the situation of the middle powers and the small powers in regional community building? A certain form of closer cooperation in informal alliances, like the CVLM group and core ASEAN (Singapore, Thailand, Philippines, Malaysia, Indonesia) might be helpful. In European integration, the Benelux group of small nations exerted an extraordinary influence, not the least due to their policy coordination. Korea, however, does not fit into such a group. However, it fits into a possible Northeast Asian sub-grouping, being a potential mediator between the large neighbors. In this situation, the deterioration of political relations to both neighbors experienced in particular under the Roh Moo-Hyun government is alarming. Overall, the small states could be well protected from predatory behaviour of the large neighbors by unanimity clauses or qualified majority voting.

A possible way to a comprehensive East Asian community could begin with a number of communities of different speed, then. The core of these communities would be a region-wide, WTO-compatible free trade pact. This free trade pact would maybe not include all sectors, but it would refrain from particular exceptions of single countries. It would be fostered by a dispute settlement mechanism for trade conflicts. Additional, a second layer of integration could be achieved in communities with varying size. For example, the Northeast Asian group could cooperate over pressing energy security questions and include a political dialogue to solve outstanding issues in politics. A group of least development countries (Cambodia, Laos, Myanmar) could be receiver of particular community-wide forms of economic aid for transformation. The ASEAN could co-exist with the new structure as the established Southeast Asian policy forum.

17.4 The role of Korea in East Asian economic integration and the goal of Korean unification

Korea as a large state among larger ones is in an uncomfortable geo-political situation in Northeast Asia. It cannot play the role of a regional hegemonic power, though the idea of being the balancer of Northeast Asia discussed above pretended this role to be feasible. Under the former administration of Kim Dae-Jung, there was some hope that South Korea could play the role of a catalyst of economic integration (Seliger, 2002e). Later, the attempt to become the "hub of East Asia" through the attraction of companies' regional headquarters, transportation facilities and R&D facilities as well as financial services was not only unrealistic, but also showed a remarkable lack of the will to coordinate policies with the neighbouring countries (Seliger, 2004a). The idea of a regional balancer developed later, when the deterioration of relations to the neighbors led to nationalistic responses. While Korea could indeed play a role as mediator, the chosen word "balancer" indicates the desire to play off the two neighbors against each other – and neither of them will be particularly pleased with this perspective.

Good relations to the neighbors are not only an aim in itself, but are especially important for the implementation of South Korea's first geo-political goal, namely national unification. Until recently, the role of the Democratic People's Republic of Korea (henceforth North Korea) in East Asian economic integration has been seen only as one of the obstacles to closer cooperation in Northeast Asia. The cautious opening of North Korea, forced upon the hermit state by the loss of major economic partners since 1989, the economic catastrophe and famines in the mid-1990s, leads to the question, if East Asian integration can be helpful in enhancing the North Korean transformation process. Economic integration in that sense has three aspects: there is a geographical aspect, a functional aspect and an institutional aspect.

Geographically, North Korea can act as a land bridge between South Korea and Japan on one side and Russia and the European countries on the other side. Therefore, the plan to revive railway links between North and South Korea, found great interest in the last years. The 'iron silk road' via the Trans-Siberian railroad to Europe could greatly reduce transportation costs for South Korean industry and allow North Korea to profit from transit. However, until now the euphoria over the 'iron silk road' seems to be highly premature, due to uncertainty about the actual willingness of North Korea to open its railroads for South Korean and Japanese goods, and also due to the uncertain possibilities on the Russian side of the border to transport large amounts of goods. However, if one day the railroad is realized, it will aid to modernize the transportation system in North Korea and also link the region closer with the Russian Far East, until now a neglected region in Northeast Asian economic cooperation. A similar importance could take the project of a Russian gas-pipeline leading through North Korea to South Korea and Japan, allowing North Korea large earnings from transit rights, opening a new, attractive market for Russian gas and reducing the Japanese and Korean dependence on expensive liquefied gas. Again, North Korea would have to agree and stick with an agreement to make this possibility come true.

Functionally, economic integration in the form of bilateral or multilateral agreements is the precondition for increased trade and investment. North Korea can act as a 'prolonged workbench' for companies from the region, i.e. it can specialize according to its comparative advantage of low labour cost. The implementation of the Gaesong Industrial Complex is a first step in such a direction. Thereby, North Korea can earn urgently needed foreign currency and slowly upgrade its production facilities and management qualifications. However, there is also another important function, namely the possibility for North Korea to adapt its economic system to a politically accepted role model like China. While South Korea and Japan are economically the most developed states of the region, ideologically they are difficult to imagine as role models for North Korea's economic transformation under the current political regime. China, with its apparent reconciliation of successful market reforms and the maintenance of a suppressive political regime, has more appeal to North Korea. While China as a role model is not necessary linked to East Asian integration, an integration process has two additional benefits: First, it creates more ample opportunity and necessity for opening, simply due to more frequent meetings with less media attention. Second, it allows the rapprochement toward South Korea and Japan and the reform of the economy in a politically more accepted framework. If contacts are carried out in a regional framework, less ideological confrontation is probable, since the contacts are less prominent and more routine business.

Last, but not least, there remains the question which institutional framework is best for achieving the aforementioned goals of economic integration. Here, it is most realistic to discuss the existing (and nascent) integration projects, especially APEC, ASEAN Plus Three (China, Japan and Korea), and the membership in international organizations like the ADB, the WTO and the IMF. Integration in the framework of APEC first would have the advantage of the relative loose institutional level of integration. However, for North Korea, the presence and intellectual leadership of the USA in the APEC process would especially pose a problem in accepting APEC membership. Also the liberalization goals, laid down in the Bogor declaration (1994) and the subsequent Osaka Action Agenda (1995) and Manila Action Plan (1996) are an obstacle, at least to North Korean full membership.

More successful could be the concentration of efforts of the nascent East Asian community, to include the North Korea problem in its agenda and eventually, to create an "ASEAN plus four." For the possible role of the East Asian community for North Korea, the fact that no agenda is yet fixed works as an advantage, since it reduces the requirements for participation or observer status to a minimum of political will. China as an important player in ASEAN plus three may help to make the more problematic membership of Japan and South Korea, the arch-enemies, more acceptable. The membership is similar to the ASEAN regional forum, where North Korea takes part, but the focus is more on economic questions, which from North Korea's perspective under any scenario of political development is preferable.

In a scenario of no political change, with the current leadership remaining in power for an indeterminable time, regional integration can be the first step for a cautious opening and offers possibility for more multilaterally coordinated aid. Also, gradually, a modernization process of industry can begin, relying on various sources of foreign investment. In any scenario of political change, where either by incremental change or by collapse of leadership the economic system changes, regional integration can be helpful economically, but also in resolving the rising geopolitical questions by a possible Korean unification. Economically, foreign competitors instead of only South Korean investment can increase the degree of competition in North Korea, thereby transforming the old monopolistic structure, and also in South Korea. The macro- and microeconomic advantages of any type of foreign direct investment are well-known yet often forgotten or neglected in the case of national unification due to pressure from domestic companies eager to expand their oligopolistic power to the unified area.

For the new East Asian community based on ASEAN plus three, an inclusion of the North Korean problem can become the cornerstone of a "second pillar" besides free trade, the proof that also political cooperation is feasible. While without the US no sustainable solution to the nuclear crisis is thinkable, the East Asian community could prepare a possible solution, make it palatable to both the US and North Korea, and, finally, help in implementing it. As a community effort, it would be less of an affront to the US, and as an approach including the pivotal players South Korea and China as well as Japan on the sidelines, but with the great possible promise of potential reparations, North Korea would feel much more obliged to follow such a solution approach than in dealing bilaterally with these countries. The role of China is of great importance in any solution of the North Korean issue (Ong, 2006). Basically, China has no interest in loosing North Korea as a buffer state against South Korean capitalism and US military forces as well as a card to be played off against the US in relation to the Taiwan problem and against South Korea with regards to any possible conflict, e.g. trade disputes. In such a situation, South Korea's interest is straightforward: It has to forge an integration area, where the possible benefits of integration loom larger than the benefits of a perpetual division of Korea.

The last possibility for greater economic integration is the participation of North Korea in multilateral organizations, like the ADB, WTO or IMF. Membership would offer many advantages, especially concerning North Korea's macroeconomic unstable situation. Principally, the case of the former socialist countries joining the IMF long before any transformation process shows the compatibility of a political socialist system with these organizations. However, besides the political problems of the nuclear crisis the unresolved debt problems, the information requirements and the conditionality of all possible aid make the application for the ADB seem premature. Changes required would be much too drastic for the current political regime, namely forcing it to abandon their protective shield against change, the reclusion. From the discussion above it becomes clear that the nascent East Asian community (ASEAN plus three, resp. plus four) is the most appropriate framework for trying to extend East Asian economic integration to North Korea, offering the flexibility of agenda and including the appropriate participants.

17.5 Conclusion

East Asian economic integration is currently in a difficult stage. The proliferation of bilateral FTAs will prove to be an obstacle to the attempts to create a "new economic integration strategy: Moving beyond the FTA" (Fukagawa, 2005). The forerunners of bilateral trade agreements, like Singapore and Thailand, always contend that their approach of bilateralism will lead to a final, greater free trade area, but it might well be that the result is a jungle of FTAs too thick to cut through; or, in other words, that their efforts are region-divergent (Dent, 2006). The ASEAN plus three process, resulting in the attempt in Kuala Lumpur in December 2005 to form a new East Asian community, offers a preferable alternative to bilateralism. In such a situation, South Korea has to find its own place in the nascent regional geo-economic and geo-political structure.

Until now, South Korea did not overcome its position in the region based upon a strong but not always stable alliance with the United States and an indifferent position between its neighbors. Mostly, the lacking will from the side of Japan to clear its historical role is cited as the main stumbling block to greater regional efforts in Northeast Asia. It is always difficult to draw historical parallels. Often, Germany and Japan are compared with the allegation that Japan represents the unrepentant, unreformed state compared with Germany. While there might be some truth in the comparison as far as national symbolism is concerned, though Japan frequently did clearly express its regret over the past and paid billions to make good on it, those invoking the historical parallel often forget one thing: European integration did not begin after the relation of Germany and its neighbors were mended. Rather, courageous political leaders on both sides began to embark on a way of integration, when it was still inconceivable to most observers and to the population at large. It can only be hoped that such courageous politicians can also be found in Northeast Asia. Then, overcoming the shadows of the past, economic integration benefits all states in the region. The voice of bigger states in the region gets fostered by the support of smaller and medium powers and vice versa. Certainly, this is true for all states in the region. But, given its unique geo-political situation, the words apply nowhere more true than for Korea.

Chapter 18: After the dust settled …

12 years after the onset of the Asian crisis, South Korea is a vibrant economy that has withstood the international financial crisis in a remarkable manner, exercising international leadership in the field of green growth and rising to the status of a large and respected middle power on an equal footing with Japan, for instance. Though economic debates and fears of the past still resound, as protests against the KORUS FTA in 2011 have shown, Korea underwent major change. This change can be understood best by applying lessons learned from the transformation theory.

The experience of centrally planned economies' transformation holds important lessons for a more general analysis of institutional change. While the transformation of former centrally planned economies in Central and Eastern Europe (CEE) and the transformation of the East Asian "tiger states" after the East Asian crisis of 1997 and 1998 are completely different in terms of their causes and the responses to the crises, there are still some similarities: in both cases, there had been quite a few critics of the former economic model, but the timing and scope of the crisis was completely surprising. And in both cases the states affected tried to solve the crisis with the help of institutions imitated from other states, under the guidance of international organizations. Transformation in CEE created a lot of "economic systems laboratories" in a scientific field, which is perennially plagued with the problem of every social science that there are no possibilities for laboratory experiments. One of the most important lessons after 25 years of transformation is the lack of theoretical foundations for transformation: there was no theory of transformation and the existing mainstream theory (neoclassical economics) had few things to say about transformation. Theoretically, the lack of institutional factors of explanation led to the change from the theoretical monism of mainstream economics to the flourishing of more heterodox explanations.[276] In transformation policy, the expectations of simple and swift institutional renewal and subsequent economic recovery after transformation were disappointed (see Seliger, 2002f).

Three main fields were identified as especially relevant to the understanding of the problems in transformation economies: the relationship between formal and informal institutions; implications of this relationship for institutional design and efficiency; the role of the cultural context of institutional systems (embeddedness) and institutional competition; and its impact on the evolution of economic systems as explanatory factors for outcomes on the market for institutions (Seliger, 2012). The case studies of monetary policy in South Korea after the Asian crisis, of foreign direct investment (FDI) policy and of external economic policies, indeed confirm

276 Voigt (1996) speaks of methodological eclecticism as the 'toolkit' of the constitutional economist.

that these three fields are also central to the understanding of transformation in the wake of the financial and economic crisis of 1997 and 1998. In this sense, they contribute not only to the understanding of the crisis in South Korea, but also to a more general theory of economic transformation. In particular, there are three lessons.

First, markets for institutions are shaped by the interplay of formal and informal institutions, both of which have to be taken into account in their analysis. Every economic system is characterized by formal and informal institutions and their interplay. Formal and informal institutions can be distinguished by their enforcement mechanism (the state monopoly of coercive power, i.e. centralized, for formal institutions, private enforcement, by internalisation, i.e. decentralized, for informal institutions). The functioning of formal institutions is only understandable by their interdependence with informal institutions. However, since informal institutions are observed and quantified only with great difficulty, they are often neglected in the discussion of economic systems or only applied to explain otherwise unexplainable residuals. In transformation theory, they were only lately re-introduced, after the models entirely neglecting institutions or only focusing on formal institutions have failed to explain various transformation paradoxes. Informal institutions are not static, but change occurs in a piecemeal, long-term fashion. This is a possible explanation for the fact that the same formal institutions render different results in different economies: they interact with different informal institutions, and their efficiency is dependent on this interaction. The case study of the changes of monetary policy in South Korea after the Asian crisis shows that formal institutions indeed were changed drastically (from the former, Ministry of Finance – dominated and growth-oriented institutional regime to a framework based on central bank independence and relying on monetary policy on inflation targeting, including the necessary preconditions like transparency and accountability rules). Informal institutions, however, did not change so rashly and this inevitably created contradictions. These show in the continuing attempts of the Ministry of Finance and the Economy (MOFE) after 1998 to influence or prejudice monetary policy decisions. Among the informal institutions important to study, particularly in the case of the Bank of Korea (BOK), the informal networks and hierarchies of decision-makers are important. While conflicts in monetary policy can also be analyzed with interest group and public choice approaches, the outcomes shaped by informal institutions are escaping these theories; in this way the analysis of the interplay of formal and informal institutions makes an important contribution to our understanding of institutional regimes.[277]

277 Among other things, the idea of efficient contracts for central bankers, like outlined for example in Gärtner (2003), will not work in the same fashion in countries like South Korea; this will also be true for many developing countries with informal institutions deviating from those prevailing in most OECD economies.

Second, informal institutions are based on the perception and expectations people have about the functioning of the economic system and its enforcement mechanisms. The functioning of both formal and informal institutions requires that market actors have stable expectations of them. For formal institutions to be legitimate, the enforcement mechanism by state action requires that market actors expect a sufficient degree of enforcement taking place. The functioning of informal institutions requires that they are sufficiently internalized by the market actors, for instance through education or experience. When external as well as internal institutions result in behaviors and outcomes anticipated by all economic actors, an expectation-equilibrium is reached, and the economic system can be said to be stable. Since market actors and external observers such as economists do not have complete information, they build hypotheses about the functioning of the system, which are important for their goal setting and choice of instruments. For example, in monetary policy the time inconsistency problem gained considerable interest.

The hypotheses about the economy again are shaped by the cognitive schemata of actors operating in an uncertain environment. If they are permanently frustrated, new hypotheses are formed. However, this does not necessarily translate immediately into changed behavior. As long as the enforcement mechanisms for institutions work, even the frustration of hypotheses might temporarily be accepted, since a deviation of behavior can still effectively be sanctioned. But then, even small additional changes in perception might create the critical mass for a massive shift in behavior by the actors: transformation of the economic system occurs. The analysis of transformation processes therefore must begin with an analysis of the relevant market for formal institutions. This market is shaped by national political formal institutions, by their interaction in international institutional competition and by their interaction with informal institutions. An expectation-equilibrium is the situation where all in all the expectations of actors about the functioning of institutions are matched. These expectations again are dependent on the cognitive models the actors developed about the institutions. Economic theory until now mostly neglected the importance of these models. They are formed by actors according to their own perceptions, interacting with the perception of other actors. The expectation-equilibrium is not the same like a normative, theoretical welfare optimum. Stable expectations exist also in dictatorships and in economies achieving only weak economic results. Only, if the results of economic activity deviate constantly from the anticipations of actors, a crisis of the economy, for example macroeconomic disequilibria, can translate into a crisis of the economic model that actors have. The term "model" is here not used as a Weberian "ideal type", but as the model that actors formed their economy with. The crisis of the model leads to a transformation process, which again has two characteristics. The first is that the political actors initiate formal institutional change. As important as the initiated and intended institutional change are the changes unintended by the state actors, the side effects of transformation.[278] Unintended consequences, for example, occur through the interaction of changed formal institutions with old, unchanged informal institutions. A deeper understanding of the formal and particularly informal institutions of an economy can only be acquired through the understanding of the cultural basis of these institutions.

In the case of South Korea, expectations of international investors as well as of the public were permanently frustrated by cases of economic mismanagement (as in the spectacular bankruptcy cases of Hanbo and Kia) in the prehistory of the crisis. This was also true for the failed expectations for other East Asian economies, put (rightly or wrongly) in the same category of "tiger states". State collusion with large business and state intervention into the economy underwent a transformation process in the crisis of 1997 and 1998, though due to the unintended consequences, the expectation of international actors to establish a market economy closer to that of its Western role models often did not come true. Monetary policy was part of the transformation process. To study the effectiveness of change of the formal institution BOK among other things, self-perception as well as the public's perception of the BOK is important. Having been a "gatekeeper of growth" (Maxfield 1997) for decades, a function deeply affected by the colonial and post-colonial experience of Korea, the new BOK on numerous occasions continued to follow this old leitmotif rather than following the one established by the new BOK law. As the case of the BOK shows, the study of the cultural background of institutional regimes offers insights into the informal institutions of an economic system and the stability of an economic system in terms of expectations of economic actors. In South Korea, the post-crisis expectation-equilibrium includes a changed role of the central bank, though this should not be confounded by economic analysts, as it is often done, with the complete substitution of the "East Asian development state" with a model "Western market economy", allowing the safe and unequivocal applicability of theoretical models developed for the latter.

Analyzing the underlying ideas of the functioning of the market economy can also help to explain the shifts in the stance toward FDI. Old perceptions of the specific institutional features of the Korean economy were shattered, and this opened the chance for a new view on international economic cooperation, including a complete change of attitude toward FDI from reluctance to enthusiasm as well as the opening of formerly protected areas, such as the field of cultural policy. And

278 The analysis of unintended consequences of man's action, of the results of human interaction, but not human design is for Hayek the most important goal of social science; see Hayek (1979: 41).

this change of perception is equally an important factor in explaining new international integration approaches driven less by historic grievances and more by economic benefits.

Third, formal institutions are subject to international institutional competition (the interaction of the market for politics and the markets for goods, services and factors). Metaphorically speaking, formal institutions are formed on a country's "market for institutions". This is a metaphor for the interaction of the market for politics and the markets for goods and services of a country. The market for politics consists at the supply side of political entrepreneurs and the bureaucracy, offering various policies and packages of publicly produced goods. The demand side consists of consumers, taxpayers, workers and investors, who decide among the various offers using their democratic voice. Interest groups are part of both the supply and the demand side of politics, since they take part in policy making by offering asymmetric information to the former while they are bundling their members' demand for politics and fueling the latter. The exit-option, including import of goods as an exit of national goods markets, or capital flight, links the market for politics with the markets for goods and services. Institutional alternatives in other countries or alternatives forwarded by opposition parties, which are perceived to be more advantageous, will be preferred. Capital or persons can exit an economy (e.g. by capital flight or migration) and can voice their protest, for example in demonstrations or through the voting process. The intensity of institutional competition is dependent on the international regimes, for example for trade and flows of factors of production, labour and capital.

The very core issue of monetary policy in South Korea after the crisis was the imitation of a formal institutional regime successful elsewhere, namely that of an independent, but accountable central bank using an inflation targeting regime. External pressure by the IMF was pivotal to introduce such a system.[279] But also in monetary policy decisions afterwards, considerations of the position of Korea's monetary policy in institutional competition were important in explaining outcomes of monetary policy, e.g. considerations of effects of interventions by the MOFE on investor confidence. So, the concept of institutional competition proves to be instrumental in understanding change of formal institutions in 1997 and 1998 and at the same time is important in understanding continuous external constraints put on monetary policy afterwards (see an elaboration on such constraints in Seliger, 2002g). Similarly, in external economic policies it could be seen how external pressure, through market-opening and subsequent locational

279 One aspect of this pressure was, however, that is was welcome by more reform-minded politicians and economists as a means to overcome domestic bureaucratic and political opposition to a redesign of the BOK and as a way to "borrow" credibility from a system successful abroad.

competition as well as institutional changes elsewhere, changed Korea from assuming a more inward-looking to a more outward-looking stance, including the pursuit of bilateral FTAs, comprehensive integration and locational policies.

The epoch-making changes in CEE as well as the similarly unsettling changes in East Asia after 1997 could be called a blessing in disguise for the profession of economists. It helped to clarify the role of institutions, culture and the external constraints in the process of the change of economic systems, and, particularly, economic transformation. By doing so, not a completely new theory of transformation was created. Basically, the "prescriptions" of the Washington consensus are still a quite good description of the tasks in transforming centrally-planned economies into market economies. And basically, explanations of the rise of East Asian states with strong authoritarian features with the help of export-led growth and frequent state interventions are still true. However, the new, institutional approach can enlighten the difficulties and failures of transformation merely based on a theoretical model which does not explicitly model institutions and their change.

This more general theory of transformation is, after all, only a subspecies of a more general (institutional) theory of economic systems and the economy. As already Ludwig von Mises pointed out: "It is a poor makeshift to call any age an age of transition. In the living world there is always change. Every age is an age of transition." (Mises 1963: 860). Still, given the importance in terms of politics, welfare and stability of understanding economic transformation processes, it is justified to view transformation economics and, in particular, the institutional and more general theory of transformation as a subfield of economics, and a very important one at that. This field offers the opportunity to re-integrate institutional approaches largely outside the mainstream into the centre of the economic discussion. It is not a theory restricted to one or two historical episodes in economics, like the transformation of centrally-planned economies to market economies. Rather, it is a useful theory to understand economic change in the sense of Mises cited above everywhere in the world, but particularly in those large-scale, state-led and rapid processes of change we call transformation.

The identification of external and internal institutions, the cultural background of transformation countries, the underlying cognitive schemata of economic actors in these countries, and the external constraints are certainly not a simple task. They require country-specific knowledge and call for an integration of economics with area studies approaches. This is another important result of the more general theory of transformation. Ultimately, however, such effort can be rewarded by an analysis without the superficial certainty of "optimal" outcomes of mathematical models, but leading to a much deeper understanding of the transformation process and its direction, thereby leading to a more realistic and finally more successful analyses of real-world transformation processes. If this book can contribute to achieving integration for the field of Korean studies, its purpose is fulfilled.

References

Adamovich, Ivan (2001), "Die Wachstumsdiktatur: ein seltenes institutionelles Arrangement", *List-Forum für Wirtschafts- und Finanzpolitik*, Vol. 27, no. 2, pp. 139-157.

Adler, Nancy J., Jill de Villafranca (1983), "Epistemological Foundations of a Symposium Process: A Framework for Understanding Culturally Diverse Organizations", *International Studies of Management and Organization*, Vol. 12, no. 4, pp. 7-22.

Ahn, Byung-Joon (2004), "The rise of China and the future of East Asian integration", *Asia Pacific Review*, Vol. 11, no. 2, pp. 18-35.

Ahn, Hyungdo (1999), "APEC After 10 years: Is APEC Sustainable?" *KIEP Working Paper*, no. 99-08, Seoul: Korea Institute for International Economic Policy.

Ahn, Hyungdo et al. (1999), "Assessment of Korea's Individual Action Plans of APEC", *KIEP Working Paper*, no. 99-28, Seoul: Korea Institute for International Economic Policy.

Ahn, Seo-Hwan (1999), "Evaluation of Korea's investment environment after the Asian economic crisis", *MARC briefing note*, Geneva: Modern Asia Research Centre.

Ahn, Yonson (2005), "Nationalism and the mobilisation of history in East Asia: the "War of History" on Koguryo/ Gaogouli", *Internationale Schulbuchforschung*, Vol. 27, no. 1, pp. 15-29.

Ahrens, Joachim, Renate Ohr, Götz Zeddies (2006), "Enhanced cooperation in an enlarged EU", *Center for Globalization and Europeanization of the Economy (CeGE) Discussion Paper*, no. 53, Göttingen: Georg-August-Universität Göttingen.

Aleksandrowicz, D. (1998), "Kulturelle Kosten der Transformation", *Arbeitsberichte des Frankfurter Instituts für Transformationsstudien*, no. 3.

Alesina, A., L.H. Summers (1993), "Central Bank Independence and Macroeconomic Performance: Some Comparative Evidence", *Journal of Money, Credit and Banking*, Vol. 25, no. 2, pp. 151-162.

Alesina, A., V.U. Grilli (1991), "The European Central Bank: Reshaping Monetary Policy in Europe", *CEPR Discussion Paper Series*, no. 563, London: Centre for Economic Policy Research.

Allen, George C. (1958), *Japan's Economic Recovery*, Oxford: Oxford University Press.

Anand, Jaideep, Andrew Delios (1997), "Location Specificity and the Transferability of Downstream Assets to Foreign Subsidiaries", *Journal of International Business Studies*, Vol. 28, no. 3, pp. 579-603.

Anderson, K. – R. Blackurst (eds.) (1993), *Regional Integration and the Global Trading System*, New York: St. Martin's Press.

Angresano, J. (1996), *Comparative Economics,* 2nd ed., Upper Saddle River: Prentice Hall.

Anyadikes-Danes, M.K. (1995), Comment on "Measuring the Independence of Central Banks and its Effect on Policy Outcomes" by Cukierman, Webb, Neyapti, *The World Bank Economic Review*, Vol. 9, no. 2.

Aritake, Toshio (2002), "Japan, Korea Sign Investment Agreement As First Step to Free Trade Agreement", *International Trade Reporter*, Vol. 19, no. 13.

Arndt, H. (1979), *Irrwegen der Politischen Ökonomie*, München: C.H. Beck Verlag.

Artis, M. (2002), "The Performance of the European Central Bank", *International Review of Applied Economics*, Vol. 16, no. 1, pp. 19-29.

ASEAN General Secretariat (2005), *Kuala Lumpur Declaration on the East Asia Summit on 14 December 2005*, Kuala Lumpur, Internet file: http://www.aseansec.org/18098.htm (retrieved May 10th, 2005).

Asian Wall Street Journal (4 November 1998), "Why Indonesia Never Got a Debt Deal", p. 1.

Assmann, Jan (1997), Das kulturelle Gedächtnis. Schrift, Erinnerung und politische Identität in frühen Hochkulturen, München: C.H. Beck.

Baang, Y.M., June-Dong Kim (1996), "Foreign Direct Investment Policy of Korea", *Korea Institute for International Economic Policy*, The Korean Economy: Current Status and Policy Directions, Seoul: MOFE, pp. 66-82.

Bade, R. – M. Parkin (1985), "Central Banks Law and Monetary Policy", *Manuscript*, Canada: University of Western Ontario.

Baecker, D. (1998), Poker im Osten: Probleme der Transformationsgesellschaft, Berlin: Merve.

Balabanis, George, Adamantios Diamantopoulos, Rene Dentiste Mueller, T.C. Melewar (2001), "The Impact of Nationalism, Patriotism and Internationalism on Consumer Ethnocentric Tendencies", *Journal of International Business Studies*, Vol. 32, no. 1, pp. 157-175.

Baldwin, R. (1995), "A Domino Theory of Regionalism", in: R. Baldwin. – P. Haaparanta – J. Kiander (eds.), *Expanding European Regionalism: The EU's New Members*, Cambridge: Cambridge University Press.

Baldwin, Richard – Charles Wyplosz (2004), *The Economics of European Integration*, New York: McGraw Hill.

Bank of Korea (ed.) (2000), *The Bank of Korea: A History of Fifty Years*, Seoul: Bank of Korea.

Bank of Korea (ed.) (2001), Miguk Jonjun gwa Hanguk Eunhaeng, ottoke dareunga? (The US Fed and the BOK, how are they different?), Seoul: Bank of Korea.

Barfield, C. (April 2002), "Preferential Trade Arrangements, Asia, and the World Trading System", *Japan Economic Currents*, no. 19, pp. 5-7.

Bates, R.H., C. Johnson, I.S. Lustick (1997), "Symposium: Controversy in the Discipline: Area Studies in Comparative Politics", *PS: Political Science & Politics*, Vol. 30, no. 2, pp. 166-179.

Baughn, C. Christopher, Attila Yaprak (1996), "Economic Nationalism: Conceptual and Empirical Development", *Journal of Political Psychology*, Vol. 17, no. 4, pp. 759-778.

Beasley, W. (1987), *Japanese imperialism 1894-1945*, Oxford: Clarendon Press.

Beeson, Mark (2003), "East Asia, the international financial institutions and regional regulatory reform: A review of the issues", *Journal of the Asia Pacific Economy*, Vol. 8, no. 3, pp. 305-326.

Benda, H. (1967), "The Japanese interregnum in Southeast Asia", in: G. Goodman (ed.), *Imperial Japan and Asia*, New York: Columbia University Press, pp. 65-79.

Berger, H., J.D. Haan (1999), "A state within the state? An event study of the Bundesbank (1948-1973)", *Scottish Journal of Political Economy*, Vol. 46, no. 1, pp. 17-39.

Berger, H. (1997), "The Bundesbank's path to independence: evidence from the 1950s", *Public Choice*, Vol. 93, no. 3, pp. 427-453.

Bernard, M. (1996), "States, social forces, and regions in historical time: toward a critical political economy of Eastern Asia", *Third World Quarterly*, Vol. 17, no. 4, pp. 649-665.

Berry, C. (2003), "What's big about the big film? 'De-Westernizing' the blockbuster in Korea and China", in: J. Stringer (ed.), *Movie blockbusters*, London: Routledge, pp. 217-229.

Bhagwati, Jagdish (2005), *In Defence of Globalization*, New York: Oxford University Press.

Bibow, J. (2002), "The Monetary Policies of the European Central Bank and the Euro's (Mal-) Performance: a stability-oriented assessment", *International Review of Applied Economics*, Vol. 16, no. 1, pp. 31-50.

Bitterli, Urs (1992). *Alte Welt – neue Welt*, München: Deutscher Taschenbuchverlag.

Blinder, Alan S. (1998), *Central Banking in Theory and Practice*, Cambridge (Mass.): MIT Press.

Boettke, P.J. (1999), "Why Culture Matters: Economics, Politicas and the Imprint of History", *New York University Working Paper*.

Bohnet, A. (1989), "Konvergenz der Systeme?" in: Bundeszentrale für politische Bildung (ed.), *Grundfragen der Ökonomie*, Vol. 277, pp. 51-83.

Boisot, M. (1995), Information Space: A Framework for Learning in Organizations, Institutions and Culture, London: Routledge.

Borrero, A.M. (2001), "On the long and short of central bank independence, policy coordination, and economic performance", *IMF working paper*, no. 01/19, Washington, D.C.: International Monetary Fund.

Botzenhardt, P. (2001), Konzepte zur Messung der Unabhängigkiet von Zentralbanken, Marburg: Tectum.

Boulding, K.E. (1968), "The Theory of Viability", in: B.M. Russett, *Economic Theories of International Politics*, pp. 323-340.

Boyer, William W. (2000), "The United States, Taiwan and China: Any Lessons for South Korea?" *International Area Review*, Vol. 3, no. 1, pp. 3-18.

Braudel, F. (1958), "Die lange Dauer (La Longe Durée)", in: Gräubig, K.-T. Schieder (ed.), *Theorieprobleme der Geschichtswissenschaft*, Darmstadt 1977, pp. 164-204.

Bruner, Jerome S. – Jacqueline J. Goodnow – George A. Austin (1956), *A study of thinking*, New York: Wiley.

Buchheim, C. (2001), "Die Unabhängigkeit der Bundesbank: Folge eines amerikanischen Oktrois? " *Vierteljahreshefte für Zeitgeschichte*, Vol. 49, no. 1, pp. 1-30.

Burki, S.J. – G.E. Perry (1998), Beyond the Washington Consensus: institutions matter, Washington D.C.

Burnell, Peter (1986), *Economic Nationalism in the Third World*, Brighton: Westview Pr.

Business Time (9 February 2006), "Asia risks spaghetti bowl trade deal mess", *ADB*, pp. 1.

Busse, Matthias, Franziska Jerosch (2007), "Reform of the EU Sugar Market", *Intereconomics*, Vol. 41, no. 2, pp. 104-107.

Card, James (23 December 2005), *A chronicle of Korea-Japan 'friendship'*, Asia Times, Internet file: http://www.atimes.com/atimes/Korea/GL23Dg02.html (retrieved 1 November 2011).

Cargill, T.F. (1995), "The statistical association between central bank independence and inflation", *Banca Nazionale del Lavoro Quarterly Review*, Vol. 48, no. 193, pp. 159-172.

Cargill, Thomas F. (2001), "Central Bank Independence in Korea", *The Journal of the Korean Economy*, Vol. 2, no. 1 (spring), pp. 1-33.

Castellano, Marc (1999), "Post crisis Japan-Korea economic relations: the ups and downs of trade and foreign direct investment", *JEI report*, no. 13A, pp. 1-10.

Castley, Robert J.Q. (1996a), "The role of Japan in Korea's acquisition of technology", *Asia Pacific Business Review*, Vol. 3, no. 1, pp. 29-53.

Castley, Robert J.Q. (1996b), "The role of Japanese foreign investment in South Korea's manufacturing sector", *Development Policy Review*, Vol. 14, no. 1, pp. 69-88.

Centre for European Policy Studies – Korean Institute for International Economic Policy (2007), *A Qualitative Analysis of a Potential Free Trade Agreement between the European Union and South Korea*, Internet file: http://trade.ec.europa.eu/doclib/docs/2007/december/tradoc_136964.pdf (retrieved 7 December 2007).

Cha, Victor (2002), *The World Cup and Sports Diplomacy*, Comparative Connections, second half 2002, Washington, D.C., internet file: http://csis.org/files/media/csis/pubs/0202qjapan_korea.pdf (retrieved 1 November 2011).

Chang, C.S. (1998), "The Confucian Capitalism: Impact of Culture and the Management System on Economic Growth in South Korea", *Journal of Third World Studies*, Vol. 15, no. 2, pp. 53-66.

Chang, Chan-Sup (1994), The Korean Management System – Cultural, Political, Economic Foundations, Westport (CT): Quorum Books.

Cheong, I. (1999a), "Korea's FTA Policy Consistent with APEC Goal", *KIEP Working Paper*, no. 99-04, Seoul: Korea Institute for International Economic Policy.

Cheong, I. (1999b), "Economic Integration in Northeast Asia: Searching for a Feasible Approach", *KIEP Working Paper*, no. 99-25, Seoul: Korea Institute for International Economic Policy.

Cheong, I. (2000), "A Korea-Japan FTA: Economic effects and policy implications", *Global Economic Review*, Vol. 29, no. 3, pp. 55-68.

Cheong, I. (June 2002), *A Korea-Japan FTA: Is Korea Losing?* KIEP Working Paper, Internet file: http://www.gtap.agecon.purdue.edu/resources/download/1142.pdf (retrieved 13 March 2004).

Cheow, E.T.C. (2002), "Towards an East Asian Model of Regional Cooperation", *Internationale Politik und Gesellschaft*, no. 4, pp. 143-158.

Cho, H.J. (1988), "Die Autonomie der koreanischen Zentralbank", *Kyongsang-nonch'ong/ Han-dok yongsang hakhoe*, Vol. 6, pp. 46-69.

Cho, L.J. (1994), "Culture, Institutions, and Economic Development in East Asia", in: L.J. Cho – H.H. Kim (eds.), *Korea's Political Economy*, Boulder: Westview, pp. 3-41.

Cho, L.J. – Yoon-Hyung Kim (1998), *Korea's choices in emerging global competition and cooperation*, Seoul: Korea Development Institute.

Cho, S.J., J. Kang (1999), "The impact of monetary policy on bank lending behavior", *Economic papers/ the Bank of Korea*, Vol. 2, no. 1, pp. 1-19.

Cho, Yoon-Jung (7 April 2000), "Ban on Japanese toons ends soon, but Korean kids already hooked", *Korea Herald*, pp. 11-12.

Choi, G. (1999), The Korean Experience with Financial Crisis: A Chronology, Financial Research Paper 99-05, Seoul: Korea Institute of Finance.

Chopra, A., K. Kang, M. Karasalu, H. Liang, H. Ma, A. Richards (2001), "From Crisis to Recovery in Korea: Strategy, Achievements and Lessons", *IMF Working Paper*, no. 01/154, Washington, D.C.: International Monetary Fund.

Chopra, Ajai D., Kenneth Kang, Meral Karasulu, Hong Liang, Henry Ma, Anthony Richards (2002), "From Crisis to Recovery in Korea: Strategy, Achievements, and Lessons", in D.T. Coe – S. Kim, *Korean Crisis and Recovery*, Seoul: International Monetary Fund – Korea Institute for International Economic Policy, pp. 13-104.

Chosun Ilbo (18 November 1997), "Editorial: The Government's Role In A Financial Crisis", *Chosun Ilbo*, Digital Chosun, English edition.

Chosun Ilbo (25 February 1999), "Central Bank Head Criticizes Gov't Interference", *Chosun Ilbo*, Digital Chosun, English edition.

Chosun Ilbo (6 May 1999), "BOK To Maintain Interest Rate At Current Levels", *Chosun Ilbo*, Digital Chosun, English edition.

Chosun Ilbo (1 November 1999), "Korean Economic Issues In 2000: Economic Desk", *Chosun Ilbo*, Digital Chosun, English edition.

Chosun Ilbo (7 February 2000), "Gov't Bodies Quarrel Over Interest Rate Policy", *Chosun Ilbo*, Digital Chosun, English edition.

Chosun Ilbo (7 April 2000), "Gov't Stalls on BOK Policy Committee Appointments", *Chosun Ilbo*, Digital Chosun, English edition.

Chosun Ilbo (11 April 2000), "Nominees for Top BOK Committee Announced", *Chosun Ilbo*, Digital Chosun, English edition.

Chosun Ilbo (28 March 2001), "BOK Defies State Intervention", *Chosun Ilbo*, Digital Chosun, English edition.

Chosun Ilbo (16 July 2001), "President Calls for Measures to Boost Economy", *Chosun Ilbo*, Digital Chosun, English edition.

Chosun Ilbo (8 August 2001), "BOK to Decide on Rate Cut Thursday", *Chosun Ilbo*, Digital Chosun, English edition.

Chosun Ilbo (24 September 2001), "BOK Head Expresses Anger over Comments on Money Rate", *Chosun Ilbo*, Digital Chosun, English edition.

Chosun Ilbo (29 October 2001), "Steps Required to Avoid Adverse Effects of Low Interest Rates", *Chosun Ilbo*, Digital Chosun, English edition.

Chosun Ilbo (7 November 2001), "Seoul to Boost Loans, Stocks", *Chosun Ilbo*, Digital Chosun, English edition.

Chosun Ilbo (23 November 2001), "BOK to Buy W1 Trillion Worth State Bonds", *Chosun Ilbo*, Digital Chosun, English edition.

Claessens, Stijn, Daniel Oks, Rossana Polastri (1998), "Capital Flows to Central and Eastern Europe and the Former Soviet Union", *World Bank Discussion Paper*, no. 11/4/98, Washington, D.C.: World Bank.

Copenhagen Economics, J.F. Francois (March 2007), *Economic Impact of a Potential Free Trade Agreement (FTA) Between the European Union and South Korea*, Short study by Copenhagen Economics & Prof. J. F. Francois, Internet file: http://trade.ec.europa.eu/doclib/docs/2007/may/tradoc_134707.pdf (retrieved 7 December 2007).

Couplet, X. – D. Heuchenne (1998), *Religions et Développement*, Paris: Economica.

Crafts, N. (1999), "East Asian Growth Before and After the Crisis", *IMF Staff Papers*, Vol. 46, no. 2, pp. 139-166.

Crowley, J. (1966), Japan's quest for autonomy: national security and foreign policy 1930-1938, Princeton: Princeton University Press.

Csaba, L. (1997), "Economic Transformation: State of Art and Some Theoretical Reflections", *Frankfurt Institute for Transformation Studies Discussion Papers*, no. 7/97, Frankfurt/ Oder.

Cukierman, A., S.B. Webb, B. Neyapti (1992), "Measuring the independence of central banks and its effect on policy outcomes", *The World Bank Economic Review*, Vol. 6, no. 3, pp. 353-398.

Cumings, Bruce (1998), *Boundary Displacement: Area Studies and International Studies during and after the Cold War*, Bulletin of Concerned Asian Scholars, Internet file: http://www.mtholyoke.edu/acad/intrel/cumings2.htm.

De Ceuster, Koen (2001), "The Nation Exorcised: The Historiography of Collaboration in South Korea", *Korean Studies*, Center for Korean Studies, University of Hawaii, Vol. 25, no. 2, pp. 207-242.

De Jonquires, Guy (16 October 2001), "Bilateralism and Regionalism", *Financial Times*.

De Mente, Boyé Lafayette (2004), NTC's Dictionary of Korea's Business and Cultural Code Words, Boston: McGraw Hill.

De Soto, H. (11 September 1993), "The Missing Ingredient: The Future Surveyed", *The Economist*, pp. 8-12.

Dehay, E. (1995), "La justification ordo-liberal de l'independence des banques centrales", *Revue française d'économie*, Vol. 10, no. 1, pp. 27-53.

Demsetz, Harold (1969), "Information and Efficiency: Another Viewpoint", Journal of Law and Economics 12 (April 1969), pp. 1-22.

Dent, Christopher M. (2006), "The New Economic Bilateralism in Southeast Asia: Region-Convergent or Region-Divergent?" *International Relations of the Asia Pacific*, Vol. 6, no. 1, pp. 81-111.

Dewatripont, M., G. Roland (March 1992), "The virtues of gradualism and legitimacy in the transition to a market economy", *The Economic Journal*, Vol. 102, pp. 291-300.

Dhanji, F. (1991), "Transformation Programs: Content and Sequencing", *American Economic Review*, Vol. 81, no. 2, pp. 323-328.

Doner, R.F. (1993), "Japanese Foreign Investment and the Creation of a Pacific Asian Region", in: J.A. Frankel – M. Kahler (eds.), *Regionalism and Rivalry: Japan and the United States in Pacific Asia*, Chicago.

Dong-A Ilbo (27 March 2001), "KDI forecasts 4% economic growth this year", *Dong-A Ilbo*, Digital edition.

Dowling, Malcolm, Chia Tien Cheang (2000), "Shifting comparative advantage in Asia: new tests for the 'flying geese' model", *Journal of Asian economics*, Vol. 11, no. 4, pp. 443-463.

Dunning, John H. (1993), *Multinational Enterprises and the Global Economy*, Wokingham: Addison-Wesley.

Dunning, John H. (2002), *Global Capitalism, FDI and competitiveness*, Cheltenham: Edward Elgar.

Durham, William H. (1992), "Applications of Evolutionary Culture Theory", *Annual Review of Anthropology*, Vol. 21, pp. 331-355.

Dvorsky, S. (2000), "Measuring central bank independence in selected transition countries", *Focus on transition*, no. 2, pp. 77-95.

Eatwell, J. – M. Milgate – P. Norman (1987), *New Palgrave's Dictionary of Economics*, London: Palgrave Macmillan.

Eckert, Carter – Ki-Baik Lee – Young Lew – Michael Robinson – Edward W. Wagner (1991), *Korea Old and New: A History*, Cambridge (Mass.): Harvard University Press.

Eckert, Carter J., Ki-baek Lee, Young Ick Lew, Michael Robinson, Edward W. Wagner (2002), *Korea Old and New, A History*, new ed., Seoul: Ilchokaka Publishers (for Korea Institute, Harvard University).

Eggertson, T. (1990), *Economic Behavior and Institutions*, Cambridge: Cambridge University Press.

Eijffinger, S.C.W., E. Schaling (1995), "Central bank independence: criteria and indices", in: H.H. Francke (ed.), *Konzepte und Erfahrungen der Geldpolitik*, Berlin: Duncker&Humblot, pp. 185-218.

Eijffinger, S.C.W., J. De Haan (1996), "The political economy of central bank independence", *Special Papers in International Economics*, no. 19, Princeton (N.J.): Princeton University.

Eijffinger, S.C.W., L.H. Hoogduin (1998), "The ultimate determinants of central bank independence", in: S.C.W Eijffinger (ed.), *Positive political economy: theory and evidence*, Cambridge: Cambridge University Press, pp. 47-74.

Eramilli, M.K., Chatrati P. Rao (July 1993), "Service Firms' International Entry-Mode Choice: A Modified Transaction-Cost Analysis Approach", *Journal of Marketing*, Vol. 57, pp. 19-38.

Eucken, W. (1952), *Grundsaetze der Wirtschaftspolitik*, Tuebingen/Berne: UTB, Stuttgart, p. 184.

European Commission (2006a), *Global Europe: Competing in the World*, Internet file: http://trade.ec.europa.eu/doclib/html/130376.htm (retrieved 5 December 2007).

European Commission (2006b), Commission Staff Working document, Annex to the Communication from the Commission to the Council, the European Parliament, the European Economic and Social Committee and the Committee of the Regions, Global Europe: Competing in the World, SEC 1230, Internet file: http://trade.ec.europa.eu/doclib/docs/2006/october/tradoc_130370.pdf (retrieved 5 December 2007).

European Commission (2011), *The EU-South Korea Free Trade Agreement (FTA)*, Internet file: http://ec.europa.eu/trade/creating-opportunities/bilateral-relations/countries/korea/ (retrieved 1 November 2011).

Falk, M., N. Funke (1993), "Zur Sequenz von Reformschritten: Erste Erfahrungen aus dem Transformationsprozeß in Mittel- und Osteuropa", *Die Weltwirtschaft*, no. 2, pp. 186-206.

Feffer, John (2004), *Korean Food, Korean Identity: The Impact of Globalization on Korean Agriculture*, Freeman Spogli Institute for International Studies, Stanford University, Internet file: http://iisdb.stanford.edu/pubs/20815/Globalization_and_Korean_Agriculture_John_Feffer.pdf (retrieved 25 March 2007).

Feigenbaum, Harvey B. (2002), *The Effects of New Technologies on Cultural Protectionism*, Occasional Paper Series, GW Center for the Study of Globalization, http://www.gwu.edu/~gwcsg (retrieved 15 September 2005).

Feldmann, H. (1995), Eine institutionalistische Revolution? Zur dogmenhistorischen Bedeutung der modernen Institutionenökonomik, Berlin: Duncker & Humblot.

Feldstein, Martin (March-April 1998), "Refocusing the IMF", *Foreign Affairs*, Vol. 77, pp. 20-33.

Fern, Sean (2005), "Tokdo or Takeshima? The International Law of Territorial Acquistion in the Japan-Korea Island Dispute", *Stanford Journal of East Asian Affairs*, Vol. 5, no. 1 (winter), pp. 78-89.

Forder, J. (1996), "On the assessment and implementation of 'institutional' remedies", *Oxford Economic Papers*, Vol. 48, no. 1, pp. 39-51.

Forder, J. (1999), "Central bank independence: Reassessing the measurements", *Journal of Economic Issues*, Vol. 33, no. 1, pp. 23-40.

Forder, J. (2002), "Interests and 'Independence': the European Central Bank and the theory of bureaucracy", *International Review of Applied Economics*, Vol. 16, no. 1, pp. 51-69.

Forsberg, Aaron (2000), *America and the Japanese Miracle,* Chapel Hill, NC: University of North Carolina Press.

Fraas, Claudia (2005), *Schlüssel-Konzepte als Zugang zum kollektiven Gedächtnis, Ein diskurs- und frameanalytisch basierter Ansatz*, Beitrag auf dem Kongress der Internationalen Vereinigung für Germanistik (IVG), August 2006, Paris, Internet file: http://www.tu-chemnitz.de/phil/medkom/mk/fraas/schlues selkonzepte.pdf (retrieved 25 March 2007).

Frankel, J.A. (1997), *Regional Trading Blocs in the World Economic System*, Washington, D.C.: Institute for International Economics.

Fratianni, M., J.v. Hagen, C. Waller (1997), "Central banking as a political principal-agent problem", *Economic inquiry*, Vol. 35, no. 2, pp. 378-393.

Freund, Caroline – Simeon Djankov (2000), *Which firms do foreigners buy? Evidence from the Republic of Korea*, Washington, D.C.: World Bank.

Fuhrt, Volker (2005), "Der Schulbuchdialog zwischen Japan und Südkorea – Entstehung, Zwischenergebnisse und Perspektiven", *Internationale Schulbuchforschung*, Vol. 27, no. 1, pp. 45-58.

Fujiki, H. (1996), "Central bank independence indexes in economic analysis: a reappraisal", *Monetary and Economic Studies*, Vol. 14, no. 2, pp. 79-101.

Fukagawa, Yukiko (2000), *Japan-Korea FTA as a New Initiative in East Asia: Beyond Bitterness*, Glocom Platform Position Paper, Internet file: http://www.glocom.org/opinions/essays/200005_fukagawa_jp_kr_fta (retrieved 13 March 2005).

Fukagawa, Yukiko (2005), "East Asia's new economic integration strategy: Moving beyond the FTA", *Asia Pacific Review*, Vol. 12, no. 2, pp. 10-29.

Fukasaku, Kiichiro, David Martineau (1998), "Monetary Co-operation and Integration in East Asia", in: Fukasaku, Kiichiro – Kimura, Fukunari – Urata, Shujiro (eds.), *Asia & Europe, Beyond Competing Regionalism*, Paris: OECD, pp. 134-159.

Gagné, Ellen D. (1985), *The cognitive psychology of school learning*, Boston: Little & Brown.

Galbraith, J.K. (1968), *Die moderne Industriegesellschaft*, München/ Zürich: München Knaur.

Gardner, H.S. (1997), *Comparative Economic Systems*, 2nd ed., Fort Worth: South-Western College Pub.

Gärtner, Manfred (2003), "Monetary policy and central bank behaviour", in: Rowley, Charles K. – Friedrich Schneider (eds.), *The Encyclopedia of Public Choice – Volume 1*, Boston (Mass): Kluwer Academic, pp. 159-172.

Gerken, L. (ed.) (1995), *Competition among Institutions*, London: Palgrave.

Gern, J.P. (1995), "La Problematique de la Transition", in: Idem (ed.), *Economies en transition*, Luisant, pp. 19-32.

Geue, H. (1997), Evolutionäre Institutionenökonomik: Ein Beitrag aus der Sicht der österreichischen Schule, Stuttgart: Lucius & Lucius.

Goydke, Tim (1999), "Die Korea-Krise als Chance? Eine empirische Untersuchung zum Verhalten deutscher Unternehmen nach der Krise in Korea", *Duisburger Papiere zur Ostasienwirtschaft*, no. 52, Duisburg: FIP.

Green, M.J. – P.M. Cronin (eds.) (1999), *The U.S.-Japan Alliance: Past, Present and Future*, Washington, D.C.: Brookings Institution Press.

Green, M.J. (2001), Japan's Reluctant Realism: Foreign Policy Challenges in an Era of Uncertain Power, New York: Palgrave.

Gregory, P.R. – R.C. Stuart (1998), *Russian and Soviet economic Performance and Structure*, 6th ed., Boston: Addison Wesley.

Grilli, V.U., D. Masciandaro, G. Tabellini (1991), "Political and Monetary Institutions and Public Financial Policies in the Industrial Countries", *Economic Policy*, Vol. 13, pp. 341-392.

Gros, D. – A. Steinherr (1995), Winds of Change: Economic Transition in Central and Eastern Europe, New York: Longman Pub Group.

Grubb, David, Jae-Kap Lee, Peter Tergeist (2007), "Addressing Labour Market Duality in Korea", *OECD Social, Employment and Migration Working Papers*, no. 61, Paris: OECD.

Haan, J.d., W. Kooi (1997), "What really matters: conservativeness or independence?" *Banca Nazionale del Lavoro Quarterly Review*, Vol. 50, no. 200, pp. 22-38.

Haas, P. (1992), "Knowledge, Power and International Policy Coordination", *International Organization*, Vol. 46, no. 1 (winter), pp. 1-35.

Haggard, S. (1990), Pathways from the Periphery: The Politics of Growth in the Newly Industrializing Countries, Ithaca: Cornell University Press.

Haggard, S. (2000), *The Political Economy of the Asian Financial Crisis*, Washington, D.C.: Institute for International Economics.

Halbwachs, Maurice (1925), *Les cadres sociaux de la mémoire,* Paris: Félix Alcan.

Hampden-Turner, Charles – Alfons Trompenaars (1993), *The Seven Cultures of Capitalism*, New York: Currency Doubleday.

Hanaki, N. (2000), "Effects of policies and institutions on economic volatility and growth: A literature review", *Working Paper*, Washington, D.C.: Columbia University.

Hayek, F.A. (1944/1994), *The Road to Serfdom*, Chicago: University of Chicago Press, pp.41-45.

Hayek, F.A. (1952), *The Sensory Order,* Chicago: The University of Chicago Press.

Hayek, F.A. (1969), "Die Ergebnisse menschlichen Handelns, aber nicht menschlichen Entwurfs", *Freiburger Studien*, Tübingen: Mohr, pp. 97-107.

Hayek, F.A. (1980), *The Counter-Revolution of Science: Studies on the Abuse of Reason* (1952), 2nd ed., Indianapolis: Liberty Fund.

Hayek, F.A. (1979), "Choice in Currency: A Way to Stop Inflation", in: D.C. Colander (ed.), *Solutions to Inflation*, New York: Cambridge University Press, pp. 93-103.

Hayo, Bernd, Stefan Voigt (2005), *Inflation, Central Bank Independence and the Legal System*, ICER Working Paper Series 2, Torino: ICER, Internet file: http://www.icer.it/docs/wp2005/ICERwp2-05.pdf (retrieved 20 March 2007).

Hays Gries, Peter (2005), "The Koguryo Controversy, National Identity, and Sino-Korean Relations Today", *East Asia*, Vol. 22, no. 4 (winter), pp. 3-17.

Heilperin, Michael A. (1960), *Studies in Economic Nationalism*, Genf: Librairie E. Droz.

Henderson, G. (1969), *Korea: The Politics of the Vortex*, Cambridge: Harvard University Press.

Hein, Laura (1996), "Free-Floating Anxieties on the Pacific: Japan and the West Revisited", *Diplomatic History*, Vol. 20, no. 3, pp. 411-437.

Herche, Joel (1992), "A Note on the Predictive Validity of the CETSCALE", *Journal of the Academy of Marketing Science*, Vol. 20, no. 3, pp. 261-264.

Herche, Joel (1994), "Ethnocentric Tendencies, Marketing Strategy and Import Purchase Behavior", *International Marketing Review*, Vol. 11, no. 3, pp. 4-16.

Herrmann-Pillath, C. (1991), "Der Vergleich von Wirtschafts- und Gesellschaftssystemen: Wissenschaftsphilosophische und methodologische Betrachtungen zur Zukunft eines ordnungstheoretischen Forschungsprogramms", *ORDO*, Vol. 42, pp. 15-67.

Herrmann-Pillath, C. (1994), "China's transition to the market: a paradox of transformation and its institutionalist solution", in: Hans-Jürgen Wagener (ed.), *The political economy of transformation*, Heidelberg: Physica-Verl., pp. 209-241.

Herrmann-Pillath, C. (1998a), "Wirtschaftspolitische Steuerung versus institutionelle Selbstorganisation politisch-ökonomischer Systeme: Die Transformation post-sozialistischer Volkswirtschaften", in: Schweitzer, Frank, *Evolution und Selbstorganisation in der Ökonomie, Selbstorganisation, Jahrbuch für Komplexität in den Natur-, Sozial- und Geisteswissenschaften*, Vol. 9, pp. 333-360.

Herrmann-Pillath, C. (preprint 1998b), "Staat und Transformation – Theoretische Reflektionen über einige offene Fragen der Forschung", *Working Paper*, no. 54, *Faculty for Economics*, Witten: University Witten/ Herdecke. (Herrmann-Pillath, C. (1999), "Staat und Transformation – Theoretische Reflektionen über einige offene Fragen der Forschung", in *Höhmann, H.H., Spontaner oder gestalteter Prozeß? Die Rolle des Staates in der Wirtschaftstransformation osteuropäischer Länder*, Baden-Baden: Nomos, pp. 371-390.)

Herrmann-Pillath, C. (1999a), "Was ist und wie betreibt man wirtschaftskulturelle Transformationsforschung?" *Arbeitspapier*, no. 40, Witten: Fakultät für Wirtschaftswissenschaft der Universität Witten/ Herdecke.

Herrmann-Pillath, C. (1999b), "Eine Krise der Wirtschaft als Krise der Kultur: Der "asiatische Kapitalismus" und seine Beobachtung", *Duisburger Arbeitspapiere zur Ostasienwirtschaft*, No. 49/1999, Dusiburg.

Hetzel, R.L. (1990), "Central banks' independence in historical perspective: a review essay", *Journal of monetary economics*, Vol. 25, no. 1, pp. 165-176.

Hewstone, Miles, Colleen *Ward* (1985), "Ethnocentrism and Causal Attribution in Southeast Asia", *Journal of Personality and Social Psychology*, Vol. 48, pp. 614-623.

Higgot, R. (1998), "The Pacific and beyond: APEC, ASEM and regional economic management", in: Thompson, G. (ed.), *Economic Dynamism in the Asia-Pacific*, London/ New York: Routledge, pp. 335-355.

Higgott, Richard (1998), "The international political economy of regionalism", in: Coleman, William D. – Geoffrey R.D. Underhill, *Regionalism and global economic integration*, London: Routledge, pp. 42-80.

Hiley, Mark (1999), "The dynamics of changing comparative advantage in the Asia-Pacific", *Journal of the Asia Pacific economy*, Vol. 4, no. 3, pp. 446-467.

Hilton, Isabel (8 February 2007), *Surfing the dragon*, Eurozine, Internet file: http://www.eurozine.com/articles/2007-02-08-hilton-en.html (retrieved 25 March 2007).

Hirschmann, A.O. (1970), Exit, Voice, and Loyalty – Responses to Decline in Forms, Organizations, and States, Cambridge: Cambridge University Press.

Hodgetts, R.M. – F. Luthans (1997), *International Management*, 3rd ed., New York: McGraw-Hill.

Hofstede, Gerd (1991), *Cultures and Organizations*, London: McGraw Hill.

Hong, Sun-Hee (11 September 1999), "Popular Japanese Culture Makes Big Strides Into Korea", *Korea Times*, p. 1.

Hong, Yoo-Soo, "Technology-Related FDI Climate in Korea", *Working Paper*, no. 98-15, Seoul: KIEP.

Höpken, Wolfgang, Michael Lackner, Steffi Richter (without year), Selbstbestimmung, Selbstbehauptung, Fremdwahrnehmung: Neufundierung von Identitäten und Geschichtsrevision in Ostasien seit den achtziger Jahren des 20. Jahrhunderts (Projektantrag bei der Volkswagenstiftung), Internet file: http://www.uni-leipzig.de/~oarev/download/oarev_voll.pdf(retrieved 25 March 2007).

Horne, J. (1995), "The Economics of Transition and the Transition of Economics", *Macquarie Economics Research Papers*, no. 7/ 95, Sydney: Wiley.

Horwitz, Steven (2000), *From The Sensory Order to the Liberal Order: Hayek's Non-rationalist Liberalism*, Review of Austrian Economics, Vol. 13, pp. 23–40, Internet file: http://english.yna.co.kr/Engnews/20040426/301900000020040426100028EP.html (retrieved 15 September 2005).

Huer, J. (1989), Marching orders: the role of the military in South Korea's 'economic miracle', 1961-1971, New York: Greenwood Press.

Huh, C.G. (8 May 2001), "The fleeting dream of central bank's goal of price stability", *Korea Herald*, p. 8.

Hundt, David, Roland Bleiker (2007), "Reconciling Colonial Memories in Korea and Japan", *Asian Perspective*, Vol. 31, no. 1, pp. 61-91.

Huntington, Samuel P. (1996), *The Clash of Civilizations and the Remaking of World Order*, New York: Simon & Schuster.

Huntington, Samuel P. (2001), "Japan's role in global politics", *International Relations of the Asia-Pacific*, Vol. 1, pp. 131-142.

Hutter, M. (1994), "Fünf Jahre Systemtransformation: Evolutionstheoretische Beobachtungen und Folgerungen", *Discussion Paper*, Faculty for Economics 05/94, Witten: University Witten/ Herdecke.

Im Yoon-Sang (2002), "The Economic Consequences of a Free Trade Agreement with Major Countries", *Bank of Korea Working Paper* (in Korean).

IMF (2000), *Republic of Korea: Economic and Policy Developments*, December 1999, Washington, D.C.: International Monetary Fund.

International Crisis Group (1 February 2006), "North Korea and China – Comrades Forever?" *Asia Report*, no. 112, Brussels: International Crisis Group.

Inoguchi, Takashi, Paul Bacon (2006), "Japan's emerging role as a 'global ordinary power'", *International Relations of the Asia-Pacific*, Vol. 6, no. 1, pp. 1-21.

Irwin, Douglas A. (2002), *Free Trade Under Fire*, Princeton, N.J.: Princeton University Press.

Ishihara, Shintaro, Akio Morita (1989), *The Japan that can say no*, translated on: http://www.totse.com/en/politics/the_world_beyond_the_usa/japan.html (retrieved 25 March 2007).

Iwabuchi, Koichi (2002), Recentering Globalisation: Popular Culture and Japanese Transnationalism, Durham: Duke University Press.

Jaeger, Friedrich – Jörn Rüsen (2001), "Erinnerungskultur", in: Karl-Rudolf Korte – Werner Weidenfeld, *Deutschland TrendBuch*: *Fakten und Orientierungen*, Wiesbaden: Leske und Budrich, pp. 397-428.

James C. Schopf (2007), "The Lone Star Scandal: Was it Corruption?" *Korea Yearbook*, Vol. 1, pp. 83-111.

Japan Korea Joint Study Group (2003), *Japan-Korea Free Trade Agreement Joint Study Group Report*, Internet file: http://www.mofa.go.jp/region/asia-paci/korea/fta/report0310.pdf (retrieved 1 November 2011).

Jens, U. (1993), "Schocktherapie oder Gradualismus? Zur Transformations einer Zentralverwaltungswirtschaft", *Wirtschaftsdienst*, Vol. 73, no. 3, pp. 158-164.

Jha, Prem Shankar (2002), *The Perilous Road to the Market*, London: Pluto Press.

Johnson, C. (1982), *MITI and the Japanese Miracle, 1925-1975*, Stanford: Stanford University Press.

Johnson, C., E.B. Keehn (1994), "A Disaster in the Making: Rational Choice and Asian Studies", *The National Interest*, no. 36 (summer), pp. 14-22.

Johnson, C. (1995), *Japan: Who Governs?* New York: Norton.

Johnson, Harry G. (ed.) (1968), *Economic Nationalism in Old and New States*, London: Allen & Unwin.

Jomo, K.S. (1998), Tigers in trouble: financial governance, liberalization and the crises in East Asia, London: ZED.

Jones, F.C. (1974), *Japan's New Order in East Asia*, 1937-1945, London.

Jwa, Sung-Hee (1995), "Korea's Recent Capital Flows: Trends, Determinants, and Evaluation", *KDI Working Paper*, no. 9502, Seoul: KDI.

Jwa, Sung-Hee, Inkyo Kim (1997), "Globalization and Domestic Adjustments in Korea", *KDI Working Paper*, no. 9702, Seoul: KDI.

Kang, J.U. (2002), "European FDI in Korea – an empirical analysis", *Master Thesis*, HUFS Graduate School of International Area Studies: unpublished.

Kang, S., Y. Wang, D.R. Yoon (2002), "Hanging Together: Exchange Rate Dynamics between Japan and Korea", *KIEP Working Paper*, no. 02-06, Seoul: Korea Institute for International Economic Policy.

KDI (August 2001), *Major Indicators of the Korean Economy*, Seoul: Korea Development Institute.

Khan, Mohsin S. (2003), *Current Issues in the Design and Conduct of Monetary Policy*, IMF Working Paper WP/03/56, Washington (D.C.): International Monetary Fund, Internet file: http://www.imf.org/external/pubs/ft/wp/2003/wp0356.pdf (retrieved 20 March 2007).

Kim, J.D. (25 August 1999), "Despite progress, foreign investment still faces numerous legal obstacles", *Korea Herald*, p. 8.

Kim, Mi-Hui (19 February 2002), "China, not Japan, the biggest threat to Korea's top export products: survey", *Korea Herald*, p. 10.

Kim, Wan-Soon (2000a), "Foreign direct investment in Korea: the role of the ombudsman", in: ADB/ OECD, *Sustainable recovery in Asia: mobilising resources for development*, Paris: OECD, pp. 159-171.

Kim, Yang-Hoi (2002), "Plan to step up FDI in Korea through FTA between Korea and Japan", *Korean Institute for International Economic Policy Working Paper* (in Korean).

Kim, B.K. (1965), "Central Banking Experiment in a developing economy", *The Korean Studies Series*, Vol. 12, Seoul: The Korean Research Center.

Kim, B.W. – P.S. Kim (1997), Korean Public Administration, Managing the Uneven Development, Seoul: Hollym.

Kim, Byung Hyun (2001), "An interindustry analysis of production between Korea and Japan (through foreign trade)", *Korean Economic Review*, Vol. 17, no. 2, pp. 207-234.

Kim, Eun-Mee (2004), "Market Competition and Cultural Tensions Between Hollywood and the Korean Film Industry", *The International Journal on Media Management*, Vol. 6, no. 3&4, pp. 207-216.

Kim, H.K. (1999), "Foreign Direct Investment in Korean Economy", *Korea Observer*, Vol. 30, no. 3 (autumn), pp. 385-396.

Kim, Hyun Kyu (2004), "Reflections on the Problems of Colonial Modernity and 'Collaboration' in Modern Korean History", *Journal of International and Area Studies*, Vol. 11, no. 3 (winter), pp. 95-111.

Kim, Il-Hwan (1987), "Direct foreign investment in Korea", *Monthly Review/ Korea Exchange Bank*, Vol. 21, no. 10, pp. 3-13.

Kim, Pyung-Hee (20 September 2000), "Korean business culture for foreign investors", *Korea Herald*, p. 11.

Kim, Seung-Hwan (2002), "Anti-Americanism in Korea", *The Washington Quarterly*, Vol. 26, no. 1, pp. 109-122.

Kim, Taeho (2005), "Sino-ROK Relations at a Crossroads: Looming Tensions amid Growing Interdependence", *The Korean Journal of Defense Analysis*, Vol. 17, no. 1 (spring), pp. 129-149.

Kim, Tae-Jong (30 June 2005), *KOREA: Culture-related laws set for major reforms*, The Korea Times, Internet file: http://www.asiamedia.ucla.edu/article-eastasia.asp?parentid=26305 (retrieved 15 September 2005).

Kim, Tae-Jun, Ryou, Jai-Won, Wang, Yunjong (2001), "Regional Arrangements to Borrow: A Scheme for Preventing Future Asian Liquidity Crises", *Policy Analysis, no.* 00-01, Seoul: Korea Institute for International Economic Policy.

Kim, W. Chan, Peter Hwang (1992), "Global Strategy and Multinationals' Entry Mode Choice", *Journal of International Business Studies*, Vol. 23, no. 1, pp. 29-54.

Kim, H.E. (1999), *Crisis vs. Role of Central Bank*, Essay 99-04, Seoul: Center for Free Enterprise, Internet file: http://www.cfe.org/english/major/essay_9904.htm (retrieved 26 March 2004).

Kirzner, Israel M. (1960), *The Economic Point of View*, Princeton et al.

Kissmer, F., H. Wagner (1999), "Central bank independence and macroeconomic performance: a survey of the evidence", in: N. Healey – Z. Wisniewski (eds.), *Central banking in transition economies*, Torun: Torun Business School, pp. 283-330.

Kiwit, D., Voigt, S., Black Markets (1995), "Mafiosi and the Prospect for Economic Development in Russia – Analyzing the Interplay of External and Internal Institutions", *Diskussionsbeitraege*, magazine no. 05-97, Jena: Max Planck Institute for Economics.

Kloten, N. (1989), "Zur Transformation von Wirtschaftsordnungen", *ORDO*, Band 40, pp. 99-127.

Knight, Frank H. (1921), *Risk, Uncertainty, and Profit*, Boston: Houghton Mifflin Company.

Koch, L.T. (1996), Evolutorische Wirtschaftspolitik, Tübingen.

Kogut, Bruce, Harbir Singh (1988), "The Effect of National Culture on the Choice of Entry Mode", *Journal of International Business Studies*, Vol. 19, pp. 411-432.

Koh, Woosong (1993), "Foreign capital as a catalyst for state capacity in Korea", *Korea observer*, Vol. 24, no. 1, pp. 49-70.

Köllner, P. (1997), "Konfuzianismus und Wirtschaftsentwicklung in Korea: Eine integrative Übersicht über die Literatur, " in: Korea 1997, Hamburg: IfA, pp. 215-248.

Köllner, P. (1998), Südkoreas technologische Abhängigkeit von Japan: Entstehung, Verlauf und Gegenstrategien, Hamburg: Institut für Asienkunde.

Kolodko, G.W. (1999), "Transition to a market economy and sustainable growth. Implications for the post-Washington consensus", *Communist and Post-Communist Studies*, Vol. 32, pp. 233-261.

Koo, Hagen (2001), *Korean Workers: The Culture and Politics of Class Formation*, Ithaca (N.Y.): Cornell University Press.

Korea Herald (7 May 1999), "Stocks skyrocket past 800", *Korea Herald*, p. 1.

Korea Herald (19 April 2000), "Can media mogul Rupert Murdoch succeed in entering Korean market", *Korea Herald*, p. 10.

Korea Herald (8 September 2000), "BOK leaves rate unchanged despite concerns on inflation", *Korea Herald*, p. 1.

Korea Herald (23 April 2001), "Local sale prices of LGE products three times higher than export prices", *Korea Herald*, p. 8.

Korea Herald (28 April 2001), "Foreign wholesalers said discriminated", *Korea Herald*, p. 13.

Korea Herald (18 August 2001), "Central bank chief urges banks to cut lending rates", *Korea Herald*, p. 14.

Korea Herald (5 September 2001), "Rate cut again on agenda this month", *Korea Herald*, p. 10.

Korea Herald (9 October 2001), "BOK expected to cut short-term rate Thursday", *Korea Herald*, p. 10.

Korea Herald (12 November 2001), "Gov't says maturing corporate bonds no cause for concern", *Korea Herald*, p. 11.

Korea Herald (27 November 2001), "Politics shaping debate on budget policy", *Korea Herald*, p. 14.

Korea Herald (29 November 2001), "Central bank head stresses importance of reasonable economic policies", *Korea Herald*, p. 14.

Korea Herald (5 December 2001), "IMF calls for expansionary fiscal policy", *Korea Herald*, p. 9.

Korea Herald (11 December 2001), "Economy seen to grow 3% in 4th quarter", *Korea Herald*, p. 1.

Korea Herald (14 December 2001), "Yen's move closely watched: Jin", *Korea Herald*, p. 1.

Korea Herald (15 December 2001), "Finance minister expresses concern over weaker yen", *Korea Herald*, p. 14.

Korea Herald (17 December 2001a), "Seoul leaving FX rates to market unless yen's depreciation dives", *Korea Herald*, p. 1.

Korea Herald (17 December 2001b), "Top official sees economy bottoming out in 1st quarter", *Korea Herald*, p. 11.

Korea Herald (19 December 2001), "BOK head vows to keep financial market from turning speculative", *Korea Herald*, p. 11.

Korea Herald (9 November 2002), "Japan hesitates on free trade with China, but eager to promote talks with Korea: expert", *Korea Herald*, p. 13.

Korea Herald (9 June 2003), "N.K., history still fault line", *Korea Herald*, p. 3.

Korea Institute for Industrial Economics and Trade (1999), "Sectoral Effects of a Korea-Japan FTA and Policy Response", *KIET Policy Discussion Paper*, Seoul: Korea Institute for Industrial Economics and Trade.

Korea Institute for Industrial Economics and Trade (2001), *A Study on Free Trade Agreement and Investment Agreement as a new External Economic Policy Instrument*, Seoul: Korea Institute for Industrial Economics and Trade.

Korea International Trade Association (2003), *Korea and the World, Key Indicators*, Seoul: KITA.

Korea National Tourist Organization (2005), *Hallyu*, Internet file: http://www.knto.or.kr/eng/hallyu/hallyuintro.html (retrieved 15 September 2005).

Korea Net (27 February 2005), Two-thirds of Asian visitors influenced by 'Hallyu.'

Korea Times (17 November 1998), "Kim Unveils Initiative to Solve Asian Crisis", *Korea Times*, p. 1.

Korea Times (23 February 1999), "Asians Want to Work With Foreigners to Weather Crisis: PERC", *Korea Times*, p. 12.

Korea Times (16 March 1999), "Disputes Erupt Over Leaked AmCham Report", *Korea Times*, p. 9.

Korea Times (1 May 1999), "Foreign Capital Inducement Policy Loses Moment – as Local Currency Recovers", *Korea Times*, p. 9.

Korea Times (3 May 1999), "Interest Rate Policy in Dispute Again", *Korea Times*, p. 1.

Korea Times (12 May 1999), "Chaebol Call for Interest Rate Cut to 5 Pct Range", *Korea Times*, p. 1.

Koreacontent News Team (ed.) (13 August 2005), *S. Korea`s film exports up nearly 30 percent in 1st half*, Internet file, www.koreacontent.org (retrieved 15 September 2005).

Korean Institute for International Economic Policy (2001), *The Economic Effects of and Policy Directions for a Korea-Japan FTA*, Seoul: Korean Institute for International Economic Policy.

Korean Overseas Information Service (2005), *Dokdo: The Korean Position*, Press Release April 25, 2007, Seoul: KOIS.

Kornai, J. (1990), *The Road to a Free Economy*, New York: W W Norton & Co Inc.

Kozul-Wright, R., P. Rayment (1996), "Closing the Institutional Hiatus in Economies in Transition: Beyond the "State versus Market" Debate", in: M. Knell (ed.), *Economics of transition: Structural adjustments and growth prospects in Eastern Europe*, Cheltenham: Edward Elgar Publishing Ltd, pp. 210-240.

Kraus, W. (1994), "Westliche Wertvorstellungen und fernöstliches Denken", in: *Orientierungen zur Wirtschafts- und Gesellschaftspolitik*, no. 62 (4/1993), pp. 48-54.

Krause, Lawrence (2003), "Can Korea become a Hub?" *The Korea Economic Institute Joint U.S.-Korea Academic Studies*, Vol. 13, pp. 29-37.

Krugman, P. (1994), *The Myth of Asia's Miracle, Foreign Affairs*, Vol. 73, no. 6, pp. 62-78.

Küchler, C.G. (1996), "Wettbewerbsfähigkeit von Standorten – Zur Kontroverse um einen Begriff, " *Schweizer Monatshefte*, Vol. 75/76, no. 12/1, pp. 32-35.

Kwan, Cai Hee (1998), "The Theory of Optimum Currency Areas and the Possibility of Forming a Yen Bloc in Asia", *Journal of Asian Economics*, Vol. 9, no. 4, pp. 555-580.

Kydland, Finn E., Mark A. Wynne (2002), "Alternative Monetary Constitutions and the Quest for Price Stability", *Federal Reserve Bank of Dallas Economic and Financial Policy Review*, Vol. 1, no. 1, Internet file: www.dallasfedreview.org/articles/v01_a01.html (retrieved 15 March 2007).

Lachman, R., A. Nedd, B. Hinings (1994), "Analyzing Cross-National Management and Organizations: A Theoretical Framework", *Management Science*, Vol. 49, no. 1, pp. 40-55.

Lankes, H. P., Nicholas Stern (1997), "Capital Flows to Eastern Europe and the Former Soviet Union", *EBRD Working Papers*, no. 27, London: EBRD.

Lasserre, P. – H. Schütte (1995), *Strategies for Asia Pacific*, London: Macmillan.

Lavigne, M. (1995), The Economics of Transition: From Socialist Economy to Market Economy, New York: Palgrave.

Lawrence, R.Z. (1991/ 1995), "Emerging Regional Arrangements: Building Blocks or Stumbling Blocks?" in: J.A. Frieden – D.A. Lake (eds.), *International Political Economy*, 3rd ed., New York: St Martin, pp.407- 415.

Lebra, J. (1975), Japan's Greater East Asia Co-Prosperity Sphere in World War Two: selected readings and documents, Kuala Lumpur: Oxford University Press.

Lee, Hee-Ok (26 October 2004), "Current Activities of China's Northeast Project and Participant organizations", presented at the conference, *The Northeast Project: Its True Nature and Falsehood*, Koguryo Research Foundation, conference proceedings, pp. 64-72.

Lee, B.S. (1991a), "Der Handlungsspielraum der Bank of Korea", *Kyongsang-nonch'ong/ Han-dok kyongsang hakhoe*, Vol. 9, pp. 1-20.

Lee, B.S. (1991b), Die Probleme der Staatsfinanzierung durch die Notenbank unter Berücksichtigung ihres Handlungsspielraums in Korea, Köln: Müller Botermann Verlag.

Lee, Chung H. (2002), "The State and Institutions in East Asian Economic Development: The Past and the Future", *The Journal of the Korean Economy*, Vol. 3, no. 1, pp. 1-17.

Lee, Dong-Hoo (21-23 June 2002), "Media Discourages on the Other: Japanese History Textbook Controversies in Korea", Third Annual Convention, Marymount Manhattan College, Proceedings, Media Ecology Association, Vol. 3, Internet file: http://www.media-ecology.org/publications/proceedings/v3/Lee03.pdf (retrieved 25 March 2007).

Lee, Doowon (2003), "Economic Developments of Korea and China: Focusing on Role of FDI", *Journal of Economic Research*, Vol. 8, pp. 71-102.

Lee, E.J. (1996), "Problematik der "Konfuzianismus"-Lehre", in: Afrikanisch-Asiatische Studentenförderung, *Ökonomische Ethik, Die sozioökonomische Wirklichkeit in Afrika und Asien zwischen Theorie und Praxis*, Frankfurt/ Main: AASF, pp. 1-18.

Lee, E.J. (1997), Eine ostasiatische Kritik an Max Webers Rationalisierungskonzept (und der damit verbundenen Modernisierungsstrategie), Frankfurt/ Main: Lang.

Lee, Ho-Chul, Mary Patricia McNulty (2003), "Korea's Economic Crisis and Cultural Transition towards Individualism", *ESRI discussion paper*, no. 71, Tokyo: Economic and Social Research Institute.

Lee, J.Y. (2000), *Monetary and Financial Policies in Korea After the Crisis* (revised version: January 7, 2000), Seoul: Korea Institute of Finance.

Lee, Jong Won (2003a), "Korea and the World Economy – Economic Development Experience of Korea and Its Future Policy Agenda", *The Journal of the Korean Economy*, Vol. 4, no. 1, pp. 117-143.

Lee, K.T., I. Cheong (2001), "Is APEC moving toward the Bogor Goal?" *KIEP Working Paper 01-03*, Seoul: Korea Institute for International Economic Policy.

Lee, K.Y. (2000), From Third World to First: The Singapore Story 1965-2000, New York: HarperCollins.

Lee, Kyong-Hee (25 March 2002), "What Koizumi left unsaid", *Korea Herald*, p. 6.

Lee, Kyoung-Ryoung (1991), "Foreign direct investment in Korea", *Monthly Review/ Korea Exchange Bank*, Vol. 25, no. 1, pp. 3-10.

Lee, Won-Bok, Hyun-Soo Shin (2000), "Competitive and supplementary manufacturing relationship of Korea, China, Japan", *KIET Industrial Economic Review*, Vol. 7, no. 5, pp. 5-15.

Leipold, H. (1992), Privatisierungskonzepte im Systemwandel, Arbeitsberichte zum Systemwandel, no. 16, Marburg.

Leonard, Andrew (14 March 2007), "The history war in Northeast Asia", *Salon*, Internet file: http://www.salon.com/tech/htww/2007/03/14/history_wars/index.html (retrieved 25 March 2007).

Lichtenstein, P.M. (1996), "A New-Institutionalist Story about the Transformation of Former Socialist Economies: A Recounting and an Assessment", *Journal of Economic Issues*, Vol. 30, no. 1, pp. 243-265.

Lim, L. (1996), "Southeast Asian business systems: The dynamics of diversity", in: W. Dobson – A.E. Safarian (eds.), *East Asian capitalism: Diversity and dynamism*, Toronto, pp. 91-117.

Lim, L., P. Gosling (1997), "Economic Growth, Liberalization and the Chinese in Southeast Asia", in: D. Chirot – A. Reid, *Insiders and Outsiders: Chinese and Jews in the Modern Transformation of Southeast Asia and Eastern Europe*, Seattle.

Lim, Sam-Jin (2006), "Die Wiederbelebung des japanischen Militarismus und der Frieden in Nordostasien", *DJF-Quarterly*, no. 2, pp. 9-14, Internet file: http://www.djf-ev.de/quarterly/2006-02/05_wiederbelebung%20jap%20militarismus.pdf (retrieved 25 March 2007).

Lim, W. (2000), The Origin and Evolution of the Korean Economic System, Policy Study 2000-03, Seoul: Korea Development Institute.

Lindsey, B. – A. Lukas (1998), *Revisiting the "Revisionists": The Rise and Fall of the Japanese Economic Model*, Cato Institute Trade Policy Analysis, no. 3/1998, Washington, D.C.

Lipton, D., J.D. Sachs (1990), "Creating a Market Economy in Eastern Europe: The Case of Poland", *Brookings Papers on Economic Activity*, no. 1, pp. 75-133.

Lipton, D. – J.D. Sachs (1992), "Prospects for Russia's Economic Reforms", *Brookings Papers on Economic Activity*, no. 2, pp. 213-284.

Mahathir, Dato' Seri (2002), *Look East Policy – The Challenges for Japan in a Globalized World* (speech by H.E. Dato' Seri Dr. Mahathir bin Mohamad, Prime Minister of Malaysia, at the Seminar for the 20th Anniversary of the Look East Policy in Japan), http://www.mofa.go.jp/region/asia-paci/malaysia/pmv0212/speech.html (retrieved 25 March 2007).

Mahbuhani, K. (1998), Can Asians Think? *The National Interest*, Singapore.

Mahbubani, K. (2001), Can Asians think? Understanding the Divide between East and West, Hanover (NH): Steerforth.

Maier, P., J.d. Haan (2000), "How independent is the Bundesbank really? A survey", in: J.d. Haan (ed.), *The history of the Bundesbank: lessons for the European Central Bank*, London: Routledge, pp. 6-42.

Mangano, G. (1998), "Measuring central bank independence: a tale of subjectivity and of its consequences", *Oxford economic papers*, Vol. 50, no. 3, pp. 468-492.

Mankiw, G. (1995), "The Growth of Nations", *Brookings Papers on Economic Activity*, Vol. 1, pp. 275-326.

Marcel, Jean-Claude, Laurent Mucchielli (1999), "Un fondement du lien social: la mémoire collective selon Maurice Halbwachs", *Technologies. Idéologies. Pratiques. Revue d'anthropologie des connaissances*, Vol. 13, no. 2, pp. 63-88.

Marshall, Roger, Indriyo Gitosudarmo (1995), "Variation in the Characteristics of Opinion Leaders Across Cultural Borders", *Journal of International Consumer Marketing*, Vol. 8, no. 1, pp. 5-21.

Martin, Bradley K. (2004), *Under the loving care of the fatherly leader*, New York: St. Martin's Press.

Marvasti, Akbar – E. Ray Canterbery (2005), "Cultural and Other Barriers to Motion Pictures Trade", *Economic Inquiry*, Vol. 43, no. 1, pp. 39-54.

Maull, Hanns W. (2006), "The precarious state of international order: Assessment and policy implications", *Asia Pacific Review*, Vol. 13, no. 1, pp. 68-77.

Maxfield, S. (1994), "Financial incentives and central bank authority in industrializing nations", *World politics*, Vol. 46, no. 4, pp. 556-588.

Maxfield, S. (1997), Gatekeepers of growth: the international political economy of central banking in developing countries, Princeton, N.J.: Princeton University Press.

McCoy, A. (ed.) (1980), *Southeast Asia under Japanese occupation*, New Haven: Yale University Press.

McKibbin, W.J. – J.W. Lee – I. Cheong (2002), "A Dynamic Analysis of a Korea-Japan Free Trade Area: Simulations with the G-cubed Asia-Pacific Model", *KIEP Working Paper 02-09*, Seoul: Korea Institute for International Economic Policy.

Menke, M. – Dirk Schiereck (2007), "Private Equity Investments in the Banking Industry – The case of Lone Star and Korea Exchange Bank", *Banks and Bank Systems*, Vol. 2, no. 2, pp. 22-34.

Meyer, Klaus E. (1996), "Direct Investment in East Asia and in Eastern Europe: A Comparative Analysis", *CIS Middle Europe Centre Discussion paper*, no. 34, London: London Business School.

Meyer, Klaus E. (1998), "Multinational Enterprises and the Emergence of Markets and Networks in Transition Economies", *CEES Working Paper*, no. 12, Copenhagen: CEES.

Miller, G.P. (1998), "An interest-group theory of central bank independence", *The journal of legal studies*, Vol. 27, no. 2, pp. 433-453.

Miller, G.P. (November 2002), "Three Myths about Central Banks", *Economic Commentary, Federal Reserve Bank of Cleveland*, Internet file: http://www.clevelandfed.org/research/commentary/2002/1101.pdf (retrieved 20 March 2007).

Milner, H.V. (1997), "The Political Economy of International Policy Coordination", in: M.U. Fratianni – D. Salvatore – J. v.d. Hagen (eds.), *Macroeconomic Policy in Open Economies, Handbook of Comparative Economic Policy*, Vol. 6, Hemel Hempstead: Harverster Wheatsheaf, pp. 177- 218.

Mimiko, N.O. (1997), "The 'Capitalist Developmental State' and the Invalidation of Neo-Classicism in Korea's Economic Development Process", *Korea Observer*, Vol. 28, no. 2, pp. 241-267.

Ministry of Finance and the Economy (1998), *DJnomics*, Seoul: MOFE.

Mises, L. (1926), "Kritik der Interventionismus", in: Ludwid Erhard Foundation (ed.), *Grundtexte zur sozialen Marktwirtschaft*, Stuttgart/New York 1981, pp. 213-225

Mises, L.v. (1963), Human Action, 3rd ed., San Francisco.

Mobius, M.J. (April 1966), "The Japan-Korea Normalization Process and Korean Anti-Americanism", *Asian Survey*, Vol. 6, no. 4, pp. 241-248.

Mok, Sakong (2003), "The Effect of Korea – Japan's Bilateral Investment Treaty and Its Implications", in: *KIET Industrial Economic Review*, Vol. 8, no. 1, pp. 31-44.

Moon, Woosik, Rhee, Yeongseop, Yoon, Deok Ryong (2000), "Asian Monetary Cooperation: A search for Regional Monetary Stability in the Post Euro and the Post Asian Crisis Era", *The Bank of Korea Economic Papers*, Vol. 3, no. 1, pp. 159-193.

Moore, Thomas G., Yang, Dixia (1999), "China, APEC and Economic Regionalism in the Asia-Pacific", *Journal of East Asian Affairs*, pp. 361-411.

Mueller, D.C. (1989), *Public Choice II*, Cambridge (Mass.): Harvard University Press.

Müller-Armack, Alfred (1952), Stil und Ordnung der sozialen Marktwirtschaft, Köln: Institut für Wirtschaftspolitik.

Mulgan, Aurelia George (2005), "Why Japan still matters", *Asia Pacific Review*, Vol. 12, no. 2, pp. 104-121.

Müller, R. (1996), "Die Finanzmittelallokation ausländischer Banken in Südkorea", in: B. Fischer – B. Reszat (eds.), *Internationale Integration der Devisen-, Finanz- und Kapitalmärkte*, Baden-Baden: Nomos, pp. 145-184.

Mummert, U. (1995), "Informelle Institutionen und ökonomische Analyse", in: B. Priddat – G. Wegner, (ed.), *Institutionelle und Evolutionäre Ökonomie*; Marburg: Metropolis, pp.79-111.

Mummert, U. – M.E. Streit (1996), "Grundprobleme der Systemtransformation aus institutionenökonomischer Perspektive", *Discussion Paper 09/96 aus dem Max-Planck-Institut zur Erforschung von Wirtschaftssystemen*, Jena: Max-Planck-Institut zur Erforschung von Wirtschaftssystemen.

Mummert, U. (1998), "Informal Institutions and Institutional Policy – Shedding Light on the Myth of Institutional Conflict", *Discussion paper 02/99 aus dem Max-Planck-Institut zur Erforschung von Wirtschaftssystemen*, Jena: Max-Planck-Institut zur Erforschung von Wirtschaftssystemen.

Myers, Robert J. (November 1998), *The Faltering Economic Reforms of South Korea*, JPRI Working Paper No. 51, Japan Policy Research Institute at the University of San Francisco Center for the Pacific Rim, Internet file: http://www.jpri.org/publications/workingpapers/wp51.html (retrieved 1 November 2011).

Nakajima, T. (2002), "An Analysis of the Economic Effects of Japan-Korea FTA: Sectoral Aspects" *The Journal of Econometric Study of Northeast Asia,* Vol.4, no.1, Economic Research Institute of Northeast Asia.

Nam, Sang-yirl (2000), "Competition and Complementarity in Northeast Asian Trade: Korea's Perspective", *KIEP Working Paper 200-02*, Seoul: Korea Institute for International Economic Policy.

Neiss, H. (1999), Economic Restructuring and Reform, Conference Proceedings, KDI International Conference on Economic Crisis and Restructuring in Korea, Seoul: KDI.

Neisser, Ulric (1976), Cognition and Reality: Principles and Implications of Cognitive Psychology, San Francisco: W.H.Freeman & Co Ltd.

Nelson, Laura C. (2000), Measured Excess: Status, Gender, and Consumer Nationalism in South Korea, New York: Columbia University Press.

Nelson, R.R. – S.G. Winter (1982), *An Evolutionary Theory of Economic Change*, Cambridge (Mass.).

Neumann, M.J.M. (1996), "Problems in measuring central-bank independence", *Discussion paper: Sonderforschungsbereich 303 'Information und die Koordination Wirtschaftlicher Aktivitäten'*, Bonn: Rheinische Friedrich-Wilhelms-Universität.

New York Times (28 June 2005), "Roll over, Godzilla: Korea rules", *New York Times Internet Edition*, Internet file: www.nytimes.com (retrieved 28 June 2005).

Nora, Pierre (1990), *Zwischen Geschichte und Gedächtnis*, Berlin: Wagenbach.

Nora, Pierre (1997), *Les Lieux de Mémoire*, Paris: Gallimard (3 Bde).

Norberg, Johan (2003), *In Defense of Global Capitalism*, Washington, D.C.: Cato Institute.

North, D.C. (1990), *Institutions, Institutional Change and Economic Performance*, Cambridge: Cambridge University Press.

North, D.C. (1996), *Economics and Cognitive Science*, Internet file: http://www.econ.iastate.edu/tesfatsi/North.EconCognition.pdf, (retrieved 25 March 2007).

Oda, Shigeru (January 1967), "The Normalization of Relations between Japan and the Republic of Korea", *The American Journal of International Law,* Vol. 61, no. 1, pp. 35-56.

OECD (1995), Regionalism and its Place in the Multilateral Trading System, Paris: OECD.

Oh, J. (March 1999), "Inflation Targeting, Monetary Transmission Mechanism and Policy Rules in Korea", *Bank of Korea Review*, Vol. 2, no. 1.

Oh, Sungji (without year), *Korean Cinema and Hollywood*, http://www.cinekorea.com/forum/paper02.html (retrieved 15 September 2005).

Okimoto, Daniel I. (1989), Between MITI and the Market: Japanese Industrial Policy for High Technology, Stanford, CA: Stanford University Press.

Olson, M. (1965), *The Logic of Collective Action*, Cambridge (Mass): Harvard University Press.

Olson, M. (1982), The Rise and Decline of Nations: Economic Growth, Stagflation, and Social Rigidities, New Haven CT: Yale University Press.

Ong, Russell (2006), “China, US and the North Korean issue”, *Asia Pacific Review*, Vol. 13, no. 1, pp. 118-135.

Onishi Norimitsu (2005), *South Korea adds culture to its export power*, International Herald Tribune Internet Edition, http://www.iht.com/articles/2005/06/28/news/korea.php (retrieved 29 June 2005).

Onkvisit, S. – J.J. Shaw (1997), *International Marketing – Analysis and Strategy*, 3rd ed., Upper Saddle River.

ORC Korea (2001), Gukne Shinchul Oekukkiope daehan gukmineuishik yoronchosa kyolgwa bokoseo, Seoul: ORC.

Ozawa, Terutoma (2005), Institutions, Industrial Upgrading, and Economic Performance in Japan – The ‘Flying-Geese Paradigm of Catch-up Growth, Northampton, Massachusetts: Edward Elgar Publishing.

Padmanabhan, P., Kang Rae Cho (1996), “Ownership Strategy for a Foreign Affiliate: An Empirical Investigation of Japanese Firms”, *Management International Review*, Vol. 36, no. 1, pp. 45-65.

Pai, Hyung-il, Timothy R. Tangherlini (1999), “Introduction: Nationalism and the Construction of Korean Identity”, *Nationalism and the Construction of Korean Identity,* Korea Research Monograph, no. 26, Berkeley (CA): Institute of East Asian Studies, University of California, pp. 1-12.

Park, H.C. (1986), *Development and state autonomy: South Korea 1961-1979*, Bloomington, Ind.: Indiana University Press.

Park, W.S. (10 September 2001), “Shocks of current ultra low interest rates on Korean economy”, *Korea Herald*, p. 9 and 13.

Park, Yoon-Shik (2003), “FDI into Korea: The Past as Prologue”, Korea Economic Institute, *Raising the Bar, Korea as a Global Economic Player*, Washington, D.C.: KEIA, pp. 221-238.

Park, Young-Ho, Mi Kyung Yun (1999), “The role of foreign investment in Korean privatization”, *Taeoe-kyongje-chongch’aek-yonku kaegan*, Vol. 3, no. 2, pp. 29-70.

Pascha, W., T. Goydke (2000), “Zehn Jahre APEC”, *Wirtschaftswissenschaftliches Studium*, Vol. 29, no. 11, pp. 616-621

Pascha, W. (1997), “Nachholende wirtschaftliche Entwicklung in Japan und Südkorea: die Rolle der Industriepolitik”, *List-Forum für Wirtschafts- und Finanzpolitik*, Vol. 23, no. 2, pp. 192-213.

Pascha, W. (2002), “Wirtschaftspolitische Reformen in Japan – Kultur als Hemmschuh?” *Duisburger Arbeitspapiere Ostasienwissenschaften*, no.44.

Pascha, W. (2004), “Economic Integration in East Asia and Europe: a comparison”, *Duisburger Arbeitspapiere zur Ostasienwissenschaft*, no. 68, Duisburg: FIP.

Peattie, M. (1988), “The Japanese colonial empire 1895-1945”, in: P. Duus (ed.), *The Cambridge history of Japan, vol. 6: the twentieth century*, Cambridge: Cambridge University Press, pp. 217-270.

Pelikan, Pavel – Gerard Wegner (2003), *The Evolutionary Analysis of Economic Policy*, Cheltenham: Edward Elgar.

Polanyi, M. (1966), *The tacit dimension*, London: Routledge.

Polterovich, V. (1999), “Towards a New Theory of Reform”, *Russian Economy: The Month in Review*, no. 7, p. 4.

Prestowitz, C. (1993), Trading Places: How We Are Giving Our Future to Japan and How to Reclaim It, New York: Basic Books.

Prosi, G. (1998), “Globalisierung als Beschränkung der Handlungsmöglichkeiten nationalstaatlicher Politik”, Comment on: F.W. Scharpf, in K.E. Schenk et al. (eds), *Globalisierung, Systemwettbewerb und nationalstaatliche Politik, Jahrbuch für Neue Politische Ökonomie*, Vol. 17, Tübingen, pp. 75-83.

Pye, L.W. (ed.) (1975), *Political Science and Area Studies: Rivals or Partners?* Bloomington: Indiana University Press, pp. 3-22.

Raiser, Michael (2001), “Informal Institutions, Social Capital and Transition: reflections on a neglected dimension”, in: Cornia, G.A. – V. Popov (ed.), *Transition and Institutions: The experience of gradual and late reformers*, a study prepared for the World Institute for Development Economics Research of the United Nations University (UNU/ WIDER), Oxford: Oxford University Press, pp. 218-239.

Rajan, Ramkishen S. (2005), “Trade liberalization and the new regionalism in the Asia-Pacific: taking stock of recent events”, *International Relations of the Asia-Pacific*, Vol. 5, no. 2, pp. 217-233.

Rauscher, Anton (ed.) (2006), Nationale und kulturelle Identität im Zeitalter der Globalisierung, Berlin: Duncker & Humblot.

Rawwas, Mohammed Y.A. – K.N. Rajendra – Gerhard A. Wuehrer (1996), “The Influence of Worldmindedness and Nationalism on Consumer Evaluation of Domestic and Foreign Products”, *International Marketing Review*, Vol. 13, no. 2, pp. 20-39.

Reed, Stephen K. (2007), *Cognition – Theory and Applications*, Seventh Edition, Belmont (CA): Thomson Wadsworth.

Riker, W.H., D.L. Weimer (1995), “The political economy of transformation: liberalization and property rights”, in: J.S. Banks – E.A. Hanushek (eds.), *Modern Political Economy: Old Topics, New Directions*, New York, pp. 80-107.

Rogoff, K. (1985), “The optimal degree of commitment to an intermediate monetary target”, *Quarterly Journal of Economics*, Vol. 100, no. 4, pp. 1169-1190.

Ronen, S., O. Shenkar (1985), "Clustering Countries on Attitudinal Dimensions: A Review and Synthesis", *Academy of Management Journal*, September, pp. 435-454.

Rosenbaum, E.F. (1999), "Culture, Cognitive Models and the Performance of Institutions in Transformation Countries", in: Höhmann, H.H. (ed.), *Spontaner oder gestalteter Prozeß? Die Rolle des Staates in der Wirtschaftstransformation osteuropäischer Länder*, Baden-Baden: Nomos, pp. 78-96.

Rozman, G. (2002), "China's changing images of Japan 1989-2001: the struggle to balance partnership and rivalry", *International Relations of the Asia-Pacific*, Vol. 2, pp. 95-129.

Ruffini, Pierre-Bruno (1999), "Foreign direct investment in banking: a theoretical perspective and the specific case of Korea", in: S.G. Lee (ed.), *The global integration of Europe and East Asia: studies of international trade and investment*, Cheltenham: Elgar, pp. 240-261.

Rüsen, Jörn (1992), "Geschichtskultur als Forschungsproblem", in: Klaus Fröhlich (ed.), *Geschichtskultur* (Jahrbuch für Geschichtsdidaktik, Bd. 3), pp. 39-50.

Rüsen, Jörn (1994), "Was ist Geschichtskultur? Überlegungen zu einer neuen Art, über Geschichte nachzudenken", in: Klaus Füßmann – Heinrich Theodor Grütter – Jörn Rüsen (eds.), *Historische Faszination. Geschichtskultur heute*, Köln: Böhlau, pp. 3-26.

Saaler, Sven (2005), "Politik, Erinnerung und Geschichtsbewusstsein in Japan", *Internationale Schulbuchforschung*, Vol. 27, no. 1, pp. 31-44

Sakong, Il – Wang, Yunjong – Montes, Manuel F. (1999), *The Asian Crisis and Its Regional Implications for Financial Cooperation in Northeast Asia*, A Study on the Economic Integration in Northeast Asia, Seoul: Asia-Pacific Institute, pp. 23-46.

Sakong, Il (1993), *Korea in the World Economy*, Washington, D.C.: Institute for International Economics.

Samuels, R.J., M. Weiner (1992), "The Political Culture of Foreign Area and International Studies", *Essays in Honor of Lucian W. Pye*, Washington.

Sandler, Todd, John Tschirhart (1997), "Club Theory: Thirty Years Later", *Public Choice*, Vol. 93, no. 3-4, pp. 335-355.

Sasse, W. (1988), "Korea als Kulturbrücke zwischen China und Japan", in: R. Machetzki – M. Pohl (eds.), *Korea*, Stuttgart.

Schmölders, G. (1984), "Historische Schule", in: O. Issing (ed.), *Geschichte der Nationalökonomie*, München, pp. 107-119.

Schulders, G. (1998), "Die Besonderheiten der asiatischen Transformationsprozesse", *Frankfurt Institute for Transformation Studies Discussion Papers*, no. 14, Frankfurt/ Oder.

Schumpeter, J.A. (1942), *Capitalism, Socialism, and Democracy*, New York.

Schumpeter, J.A. (1954), "Gustav von Schmoller und die Probleme von heute", in: ders. (ed.), *Dogmenhistorische und biographische Aufsätze*, Tübingen, pp. 148-199.

Seliger, B. (1998), "Integration of the Baltic States in the European Union – Considerations in the light of the theory of institutional competition", *Communist Economies and Economic transformation*, Vol. 10, no. 1, pp. 95-109.

Seliger, B. (1999a), "Ubi certamen, ibi corona", Ordnungspolitische Optionen der Europäischen Union zwischen Erweiterung und Vertiefung, Frankfurt/ Main. Lang.

Seliger, B. (1999b), "Socio-cultural change, institutions and transition theory: some lessons from German unification", *Zeitschrift der Koreanisch-Deutschen Gesellschaft für Sozialwissenschaften*, Vol. 9, no. 2, pp. 325-351.

Seliger, B. (1999c), "Djnomics – Ordnungspolitische Entwicklungen in der Republik Korea seit der Asienkrise", *Occasional Paper*, no. 7, Seoul: Konrad Adenauer Stiftung.

Seliger, B. (1999d), "Big Deals – Wettbewerbspolitik als Antwort auf die Krise in Südkorea", *Wirtschaft und Wettbewerb*, Vol. 49, no. 6, pp. 574-581.

Seliger, B. (1999e), "Südkorea: Konzentration und Kooperation als Krisenursachen", *Orientierungen zur Wirtschafts- und Gesellschaftspolitik*, no. 79, pp. 62-66.

Seliger, Bernhard (1999f), *The Double Integration: Siberia as part of Russia and Siberia as part of North East Asia*, Paper presented at the International Conference, Relations between Korean and Siberia, Korean-Siberian Economic Association, Seoul, November 27, 1999, Proceedings, pp. 51-76.

Seliger, B. (2000a), "Public Choice, Institutional Competition and the Eastern Extension of the European Union", in: J.W. Owsinski – Z. Nahorski (eds.), *Models and Analyses of the National Change and International Integration Process*, London, pp. 79-114.

Seliger, B. (2000b), "Die Lage nach den Wahlen in Südkorea", in: Konrad-Adenauer-Stiftung, *KAS Auslandsinformationen*, Vol. 16, no. 6, pp. 58-73.

Seliger, B. (2000c), "Institutional Competition and Transformation: Innovation, Imitation and Transfer Strategies in the former GDR and Central and Eastern European States", *Paper presented at the Symposium in Commemoration of the 10th Anniversary of the Establishment of the Korean-German Association for Social Sciences*, Retrospect of Relationship between Korea and Germany, Seoul 10.6.2000, Conference Proceedings, pp. 13-49.

Seliger, Bernhard (2000d), "Politische Ökonomie der Systemtransformation – Stand der Forschung, ungelöste Probleme und eine Fallstudie zu Südkorea", *Wittener Diskussionspapiere*, no. 68, Witten.

Seliger, B. (2000e), "Die Interdependenz von Wirtschaftsordnung und politischer Ordnung – das Beispiel der Asienkrise (The interdependence of economic and political order – the example of the Asian crisis)", in: E. Keynes (ed.), *Willensbildungsprozesse und Demokratie*, Frankfurt/ Main 2000, pp. 209-226.

Seliger, B. (2001a), "Südkorea und die wirtschaftliche Integration Ostasiens – wirtschaftliche und politische Herausforderungen", in: Patrick Köllner (ed.), *Korea Jahrbuch 2001*, Hamburg: Institut für Asienkunde, pp. 141-157.

Seliger, B. (2001b), "The Varieties of Asia-Sclerosis", *Korea Herald*, 2 November, p. 6.

Seliger, B. (2001c), "The Second Advent of Eurosclerosis? The Problematic Future of the European Union", *Korean Journal of EU Studies*, Vol. 6, no. 1, pp. 151-192.

Seliger, B. (2001d), "Trade Relations between Korea and the EU: Current issues and a political economy perspective", *Journal of Korea Trade*, Vol. 5, no. 1, pp. 1-21.

Seliger, B. (2002a), "Institutional Competition and External Constraints of Transformation", *Journal of International and Area Studies*, Vol. 9, no. 1, pp. 103-122.

Seliger, B. (2002b), *Towards a hub of East Asia? Korea as a trade partner and investment location for the European Union*, Paper presented at the conference: "The Cooperation between Korea and Europe – Trade, Investment, Logistics, and e-Trade", Korea Trade Research Association, Korea International Trade Association, Seoul, October 25, 2002, Conference proceedings, pp. 95-110.

Seliger, B. (2002c), "Central Bank Independence and Monetary Policy after the Asian Crisis – the Case of South Korea", *Wittener Diskussionspapiere*, no. 104, Witten: Fakultät für Wirtschaftswissenschaften, Universität Witten/ Herdecke.

Seliger, B. (2002d), "Juche", in: Christensen, K. – D. Levinson (eds.), *Encyclopedia of Modern Asia*, New York: Scribners.

Seliger, B. (2002e), "Korea's Role in East Asian Regional Cooperation and Integration", in: Korea Economic Institute of America (ed.), *Korea's Economy 2002*, Washington, D.C.: KEIA, pp. 59-67.

Seliger, B. (2002f), "Towards a more general theory of transformation", *Eastern European Economics*, Vol. 40, no. 1, pp. 36-62.

Seliger, B. (2002g), "Zentralbankunabhängigkeit und Geldpolitik in Südkorea", in: Patrick Köllner (ed.), *Korea Jahrbuch 2002*, Hamburg: Institut für Asienkunde, pp. 95-118.

Seliger, Bernhard (2002h), "Economic Integration in Northeast Asia: Preconditions and Possible Trajectories", *Global Economic Review*, Vol. 31, no. 4, pp. 17-38.

Seliger, B. (2003), "The Economics of Higher Education and the Role of Competition for Universities – A Consideration of the Korean Case", *Journal of Asia-Pacific Affairs*, Vol. 5, no. 1, pp. 43-68.

Seliger, B. (2004a), "Südkorea als wirtschaftliche Drehscheibe Ostasiens? Kritische Anmerkungen zu einem aktuellen Konzept (South Korea as the hub of East Asia? Critical remarks on an actual concept)", in: Patrick Köllner (ed.), *Korea 2004 – Politik, Wirtschaft, Gesellschaft*, Hamburg: Institut für Asienkunde, pp. 67-89.

Seliger, B. (2004b), "Area Studies and Social Science – from uneasy coexistence to integration?" *Korean Review of International Area Studies*, Vol. 3, pp. 3-43.

Seliger, B. (2004c), "Ordnungspolitik, kultureller Wandel und ausländische Direktinvestitionen in Südkorea nach 1997", in: Werner Pascha – Cornelia Storz (eds), *Wirkung und Wandel von Institutionen – Das Beispiel Ostasiens* (Schriften zur Ordnungsfragen der Wirtschaft Vol. 77), Stuttgart: Lucius& Lucius, pp. 229-260.

Seliger, B. (2005a), "Ordnungspolitik, kultureller Wandel und ausländische Direktinvestitionen in Südkorea nach 1997", in: Werner Pascha – Cornelia Storz (eds.), *Wirkung und Wandel von Institutionen – Das Beispiel Ostasiens (*Schriften zur Ordnungsfragen der Wirtschaft Band 77), Stuttgart: Lucius& Lucius, pp. 229-260.

Seliger, Bernhard (2005b), "A Free Trade Area between Japan and Korea – Economic Prospects and Cultural Problems", *Journal of Pacific Asia*, Vol. 12, pp. 93-129.

Seliger, B. (2007), "Economic Transformation after 15 years – a reassessment", in: Bernhard Seliger – Mica Jovanovic – Dalgon Lee – Yeon-Chean Oh – Sung-Jo Park (eds.), *System Transformation in Comparative Perspective*, Berlin: LIT Verlag, pp. 45-79.

Seliger, B. (2010), "Creating a Good Bank for North Korea (and a bad bank within) – Creative Capacity-Building as a Domain for Asian-European Cooperation", in: Bernhard Seliger, Myungkyu Park, Sung-Jo Park, "Europe – North Korea, Between Humanitarism and Business?" *Global Cultural and Economic Research*, no. 6, Berlin: LIT, pp. 225-245.

Seliger, Bernhard (2012), "Opening of cultural markets of South Korea between economic nationalism and international pressure", in: John A. Lent – Lorna Fitzsimmons (eds), Asian Popular Culture in Transition, London: Routledge.

Seliger, B. – Karl-Peter Schönfisch (2004), *ASEAN plus Three (China, Japan, Korea) and the future of East Asian economic integration*, Seoul: Hanns Seidel Stiftung Seoul Office.

Seliger, B. – Alec Gordon (1999), *Regionalization in Northeast Asia and Western Europe*, Paper presented at the International Conference in Commemoration of the 10th Anniversary of the Establishment of the Korean Society of Contemporary European Studies, "For the New Millenium – The Relations between Asia and Europe: the 3rd Seoul ASEM in 2000", Seoul.

Seliger, B. – Carsten Herrmann-Pillath (2000), "Wettbewerb auf Gütermärkten, politischer Wettbewerb und Systemwettbewerb", *Das Wirtschaftsstudium (WiSu)*, Vol. 29, no.8-9, pp. 1148-1155.

Selmayr, M. (1999), "Wie unabhängig ist die europäische Zentralbank? Eine Analyse anhand der ersten geldpolitischen Entscheidungen der EZB", in: M. Beise (ed.), *Europa als Union des Rechts: eine notwendige Zwischenbilanz im Prozess der Vertiefung und Erweiterung*, Köln: Bachem.

Seong, Somi (1996), "Competition and Cooperation among Asian Countries and the Future Prospect of Korean Industrial Policy", *KDI Working Paper*, no. 9601, Seoul: KDI.

Sergi, B.S. (2000), "A new index of independence of 12 European national central banks: the 1980s and early 1990s", *Journal of transnational management development*, Vol. 5, no. 2, pp. 41-57.

Seybold, Dietrich (2005), Geschichtskultur und Konflikt. Historisch-politische Kontroversen in Gesellschaften der Gegenwart, Bern: Peter Lang.

Shim, Sun-ah (2005), "Japanese Pop Culture, Once Banned, Makes Soft Landing in S. Korea", *Yonhap News*.

Shimp, Terence A. (1984), "Consumer Ethnocentrism – The Concept and a Preliminary Empirical Test", *Advances in Consumer Research*, Vol. 11, pp. 285-290.

Shimp, Terence A., Subash Sharma (1987), "Consumer Ethnocentrism: Construction and Validation of the CETSCALE", *Journal of Marketing Research*, Vol. 24, no. 3, pp. 280-289.

Shimp, Terence A., Subash Sharma, Jeongshin Shin (1995), "Consumer Ethnocentrism: A Test of Antecedents and Moderators", *Journal of the Academy of Marketing Science*, Vol. 23, no. 1, pp. 26-37.

Shin, Mincheol (2001), "The Animosity Model of Foreign Product Purchase Revisited: Does It Work in Korea?" *Journal of Empirical Generalisations in Marketing Science*, Vol.6, pp.1-14.

Shleifer, A. (1997), "Government in Transition", *European Economic Review*, Vol. 41, pp. 385-410.

Siegmund, U. (1997), "Warum Privatisierung? Eine Dogmengeschichte der Privatisierungstheorien", *Kiel working paper*, no. 785, Kiel: Des Instituts für Weltwirtschaft.

Sim, J.W. (14 October 2000), "Policy dilemma: growth or price stability", *Korea Herald*, p. 15.

Sinn, G. – H.W. Sinn (1994), *The Economic Unification of Germany*, Cambridge (Mass.).

Smith, H. (1995), "Industry Policy in East Asia", *Asian-Pacific Economic Literature*, Vol. 9, no. 1, pp. 17-39.

Smith, W. (1996), "Management in Malaysia", in: M. Warner (eds.), *International Encyclopedia of Business and Management*, London, pp. 2951-2961.

Smithin, J. (1994), *Controversies in Monetary Economics*, Aldershot: Edward Elgar.

Soh, C. Sarah (2001), *Japan's Responsibility Toward Comfort Women Survivors*, JPRI Working Paper No. 77, Encinitas (CA): Japan Policy Research Institute, Internet file: http://www.jpri.org/publications/workingpapers/wp77.html (retrieved 25 March 2007).

Sohn, C.H. (ed.) (2001a), *Economic Effects of a Korea-Japan FTA and Policy Implications*, Seoul: Korea Institute for International Economic Policy (in Korean).

Sohn, C.H. (12-13 June 2001b), *Korea's FTA Developments: Experiences and Perspectives with Chile, Japan, and the U.S.*, Paper presented at the PECC Trade Policy Forum, "Regional Trading Arrangements: Stocktake and Next Steps", Bangkok.

Sohn, Yong Taik – Kwang, Jae Kim (1998), *Fact and Fallacies about Korea*, KEDI CR 98/1, Seoul: Korea Educational Development Institute.

Solveen, R. (1997), *Der Einfluß der Unabhängigkeit auf die Politik der Zentralbank*, Kieler Studien 288, Tübingen: J.C.B. Mohr (Paul Siebeck).

Song, H.Y. (19 July 1998), "Presidential Economics: Taepyongro", *Chosun Ilbo*, Digital Chosun.

Starbatty, J. (1996), "Anmerkungen zur Interdependenz politischer und wirtschaftlicher Ordnungen im Transformationsprozeß", *ORDO*, Band 47, pp. 33-50.

Steinberg, D.I. (11 September 1999), "On Ritual Retribution", *Korea Times*, p. 6.

Stephan, J. (1998), "Faktoren wirtschaftlicher Erholung in Transformationsländern – eine Wachstumskomponentenanalyse", *Wirtschaft im Wandel*, no. 13, pp. 10-16.

Stern, J.J. – J.H. Kim – D.H. Perkins – J.H. Yoo (1995), *Industrialization and the State: The Korean Heavy and Chemical Industry Drive*, Cambridge (Mass.): Harvard Institute for International Development.

Stiglitz, Joseph E. (2002), *Globalization and its Discontent*, New York: WW Norton.

Straubhaar, T. (1994), "Das Konzept "internationale Wettbewerbsfähigkeit einer Volkswirtschaft" auf dem analytischen Prüfstand: Grundsätzliche Bemerkungen zu einem vielfach (miß-) verwendeten Begriff", in: H. Albach (ed.), *Globale Soziale Marktwirtschaft*, Wiesbaden.

Streissler, E. (1980), "Kritik des neoklassischen Gleichgewichtsansatzes als Rechtfertigung marktwirtschaftlicher Ordnungen, " in: E. Streissler – C. Watrin (ed.), *Zur Theorie marktwirtschaftlicher Ordnungen*, Tübingen, pp. 38-69.

Streit, M.E., M. Wohlgemuth (1997), "The Market Economy and the State. Hayekian and ordoliberal conceptions,“ *Discussion paper 06-97*, Jena: des Max-Planck-Instituts zur Erfoschung von Wirtschaftssystemen.

Sturm, J.E., J.D. Haan (2001), "Inflation in developing countries: does central bank independence matter? New evidence based on a new data set", *Working Paper*, University of Groningen.

Sumner, William Graham (1906), Folkways: The Sociological Importance of Usages, Manners, Customs, Mores, and Morals, New York: Ginn&Co.

Suzuki, Shogo (March 2007), "The importance of 'Othering' in China's national identity: Sino-Japanese relations as a stage of identity conflicts", *The Pacific Review*, Vol. 20, no. 1, pp. 23–47.

Tajfel, Henri, Turner, John C. (1986), "The social identity theory of intergroup behaviour", in: Stephen Worchel – William G. Austin (eds.), *Psychology of intergroup relations*, Chicago (IL): Nelson-Hall, pp. 7-24.

Tanaka, Yuki (2002), Japan's Comfort Women: Sexual Slavery and Prostitution During World War II and the US Occupation, London: Routledge.

Tessler, M. – A. Banda – J. Nachtwey (1999), "Introduction", in: Idem (eds), *Area Studies and Social Science: Strategies for Understanding Middle East Politics*, Bloomington: Indiana University Press, pp. 7-21.

The Economist (7 March 1998), "East Asian Economies: Tigers Adrift", *The Economist.*

The Economist (16 August 2001), "To spend or not to spend?" *The Economist.*

Thieme, H.J. (ed.) (1993), Privatisierungsstrategien im Systemvergleich, Berlin.

Thies, Cameron G. (2004), "Individuals, Institutions and Inflation: Conceptual Complexity, Central Bank Independence and the Asian Crisis", *International Studies Quarterly*, Vol. 48, no. 3, pp. 579-602.

Tokunaga, S. (ed.) (1992), Japanese Foreign Investment and Asian Economic Interdependence, Tokyo.

Tu, Wei-Ming (1996), Confucian Traditions in East Asian Modernity: Moral Education and Economic Culture in Japan and the Four Mini-Dragons, Cambridge (Mass.): Harvard University Press.

Usunier, Jean-Claude – Pervez Ghauri (1996), *International Business Negotiations*, Amsterdam: Pergamon Press.

Usunier, Jean-Claude (2003), "Cultural Aspects of International Business Negotiations", *International Business Negotiations*, pp. 93-118.

Valdés, Benigno (2003), "An Application of Convergence Theory to Japan's Post-WWII Economic 'Miracle'", *Journal of Economic Education*, Vol. 34, no. 1, pp. 61-81.

VANK (without year), *Story of VANK*, Internet file: http://www.prkorea.com/english/etc/about1.htm (retrieved 25 March 2007).

Visco, I. (1999), "Structural Reform in Korea after the 1997 economic crisis: the agenda and the implementation", *Conference Proceedings: KDI International Conference on Economic Crisis and Restructuring in Korea*, Seoul: KDI.

Vlachoutsicos, Charalambos (1999), "Internal Barriers in Transition of Enterprises from Central Plan to Market", *Davidson Institute Working Paper Series*, no. 277, Michigan: WDI.

Voigt, S. (1996), "Pure eclecticism: the tool kit of the constitutional economist", *Constitutional political economy*, Vol. 7, no. 3, pp. 177-196.

Wagner, H. (1999), "Central Bank Independence and the Lessons for Transition Economies from Developed and Developing Countries", *Comparative Economic Studies*, Vol. 41, no. 4 (winter), pp. 1-22.

Wang, Y., H. Zhang (1998), "Adjustment reforms in Korea since the financial crisis: December 1997-June 1998", *KIEP policy paper 98-02*, Seoul: Korea Institute for International Economic Policy.

Webber, Ross A. (1969), *Culture and Management*, Illinois: Richard D. Irwin.

Web-Japan (7 December 1998), *Breaking the ice: South Korea Lifts Ban on Japanese Culture*, Internet file: http://web-japan.org/trends98/honbun/ntj981207.html (retrieved 15 September 2005).

Weder, B. (1998), "Any Lessons from East Asia? A review of the literature on the East Asian Miracle", *WWZ Discussion Paper*, no. 9806, Basel.

Weinert, R. (1999), "Ideologie, Autonomie und institutionelle Aura: zur politischen Soziologie von Zentralbanken", *Kölner Zeitschrift für Soziologie und Sozialpsychologie*, Vol. 51, no. 2, pp. 339-363.

Wentzel, Dirk (1999), "Die Rolle der Medien bei der Transformation von Wirtschaftsordnungen", in: *H.H. Höhmann* (eds.), *Spontaner oder gestalteter Prozeß? Die Rolle des Staates in der Wirtschaftstransformation osteuropäischer Länder*, Baden-Baden: Nomos, pp. 95-115.

Williams, R. (1958), *Culture and Society*, London: Penguin.

Williams, R. (1981), *Culture*, Fontana New Sociology Series, Glasgow: Collins.

Williamson, J. (1990), "What Washington means by policy reform", in: Ders. (eds.), *Latin American adjustment: how much has happened?* Washington, D.C.: Institute for International Economics.

Williamson, J. (1996), "Lowest common denominator or neoliberal manifesto? The polemics of the Washington consensus", in: R.M. Auty (ed.), *Challenging the orthodoxies*, Basingstoke, pp. 13-22.

Williamson, J. (1997), "The Washington consensus revisited", in: L. Emmerij (ed.), *Economic and development in the XXIst century*, Washington D.C.: Inter-American Development Bank.

Wilson, Peter (2006), "Prospects for Asian Exchange Rate Cooperation: Why an ERM Solution Might be the Most Palatable", *Journal of the Asia Pacific Economy*, Vol. 11, no. 1, pp. 1-34.

Wilson, Robert A. (2005), "Collective memory, group minds, and the extended mind thesis", *Cognitive Processing*, Vol. 6, no. 4, pp. 1612-4782.

Windhoff, B. (1971), Darstellung und Kritik der Konvergenztheorie. Gibt es eine Annäherung der sozialistischen und kapitalistischen Wirtschaftssysteme?, Bern/Frankfurt a.M..

Wischermann, Clemens (ed.) (1996), Die Legitimität der Erinnerung und die Geschichtswissenschaft, Stuttgart: Steiner.

Witt, U. (1995), "Evolutorische Ökonomik – Umrisse eines neuen Forschungsprogramms", in: B.P. Priddat – E.K. Seifert (eds.), *Neuorientierungen in der ökonomischen Theorie*, Marburg, pp. 153-179.

Wohlgemuth, M. (1995a), "Institutional competition: notes on an unfinished agenda", *Journal des economistes et des etudes humaines*, Vol. 6, no. 2, pp. 277-299.

Wohlgemuth, M. (1995b), "Economic and political competition in neoclassical and evolutionary perspective", *Constitutional Political Economy*, Vol. 6, no. 1, pp. 71-95.

Wolf, Marin (2005), *Why Globalization Works*, New Haven: Yale University Press.

Woo-Cumings, Meredith (July 2003), *South Korean Anti-Americanism*, JPRI Working Paper No. 93, Encinitas (CA): Japan Policy Research Institute, Internet file: http://www.jpri.org/publications/workingpapers/wp93.html (retrieved 25 March 2007).

Wood Masalski, Kathleen (2001), *Examining the Japanese History Textbooks Controversies*, Japan Digest, Internet file: http://www.indiana.edu/~japan/Digests/textbook.html (retrieved January 10, 2007).

Wood, B. (1968), "Area Studies", *International Encyclopedia of the Social Sciences*, Vol. 1, New York, pp. 401-407.

Woolcock, Stephen (2007), *European Union policy towards Free Trade Agreements*, ECIPE Working paper, no. 3, Internet file: http://www.ecipe.org/european-union-policy-towards-free-trade-agreements/PDF (retrieved 1 December 2007).

World Bank (1993), The East Asian Miracle, Economic Growth and Public Policy, New York: Oxford University Press.

World Bank (1996), "From Plan to Market", *World Development Report*, Oxford.

Yamakage, Susumu (2005), "The construction of an East Asian order and the limitations of the ASEAN model", *Asia Pacific Review*, Vol. 12, no. 2, pp. 1-9.

Yamashita, S. (ed.) (1991), Transfer or Japanese Technology and Management to the ASEAN Countries, Tokyo: University of Tokyo Press.

Yamazawa, I. (1998), "Economic integration in the Asia-Pacific region", in: Thompson, G. (ed.), *Economic Dynamism in the Asia-Pacific*, London/New York, pp. 163-184.

Yamazawa, Ippei (2001), "Assessing a Korea Japan Free Trade Agreement", *The Developing Economies*, Vol. 39, no. 1, pp. 3-48.

Yang, Gi-Hwan (12 September 2004), *Screen Quota System to Ensure Cultural Diversity*, Speech on the seminar, "Why UNESCO Should Adopt a Convention on Cultural Diversity", Paris: The International Liaison Committee of Coalitions for Cultural Diversity.

Yang, Junsok (2000), "Regulatory Reform in Korea: At Crossroads?" in: Ministry of Foreign Affairs and Trade – Korea Institute for International Economic Policy (ed.), *Korea in the OECD Perspective: Shaping up for Globalization*, Seoul: Korea Institute for International Economic Policy, pp. 145-168.

Yoon, Hwy-tak (2004), "China's Northeast Project: Defensive or Offensive Strategy?" *East Asian Review*, Vol. 16, no. 4 (winter), pp.99-121.

Yoshimi, Yoshiaki (2001), Comfort Women: Sexual Slavery in the Japanese Military During World War II, New York: Columbia University Press.

Yu, Y.J. (2 October 2000), "Influence of foreign capital on domestic market surging rapidly", *Korea Herald*, p. 11.

Emerging Markets Studies

Edited by Joachim Ahrens, Alexander Ebner, Herman W. Hoen, Bernhard Seliger and Ralph Michael Wrobel

The Peter Lang series *Emerging Markets Studies* includes works which address opportunities, problems, and challenges of socio-economic development and reform in so-called emerging markets. These comprise middle-income developing and transition economies which are relevant for the world economy due to a large market potential, a favorable or improving investment climate, or due to the availability of important natural resources. Emerging markets have realized or show the potential to generate sustained socio-economic development and growth processes over time.

The volumes in this series seek to address three key questions: What are the determinants of successful socio-economic development, What are appropriate reform strategies to overcome impediments to catching-up processes, and How do politico-institutional factors affect the performance of an emerging economy?

The scope of the series is comparative, institutionalist, and international. The overall focus of all titles is to enhance the understanding of socio-economic catching-up processes and their institutional foundations from a political-economy perspective. Due to the complexity of development processes and policy reform, various methodological tools and academic approaches may prove to be appropriate. Hence the series includes contributions from various disciplines such as economics, political science, or sociology.

Vol. 1 Dominik F. Schlossstein: Institutional Change in Upstream Innovation Governance. The Case of Korea. 2010.

Vol. 2 Manuel Stark: The Emergence of Developmental States from a New Institutionalist Perspective. A Comparative Analysis of East Asia and Central Asia. 2012.

Vol. 3 Bernhard Seliger: The Shrimp that Became a Tiger. Transformation Theory and Korea's Rise After the Asian Crisis. 2013.

www.peterlang.de